PSYCHOLOGY AND MENTAL RETARDATION

Psychology and Mental Retardation

Perspectives in Change

Seymour B. Sarason

5341 Industrial Oaks Blvd.
Austin, Texas 78735

Library of Congress Cataloging in Publication Data

Sarason, Seymour Bernard, 1919–
    Psychology and mental retardation.

    Bibliography: p.
    Includes index.
    1. Psychology—Addresses, essays, lectures.
2. Mental retardation—Addresses, essays, lectures.
I. Title.
BF149.S316   1985   362.3   85-603
ISBN 0-936104-46-5

5341 Industrial Oaks Blvd.
Austin, Texas 78735

10 9 8 7 6 5 4 3 2 1   85 86 87 88 89

To

Henry Schaefer-Simmern

and

Burton Blatt

Contents

Preface

I am grateful to Dr. Michael Begab for inviting me to select and comment on some of my writings in the field of mental retardation. For a number of years Dr. Burton Blatt, a dear friend and colleague, had been urging me to do such a book and I have reason to believe that he also urged Dr. Begab to invite me to prepare such a volume. If for a time I resisted the idea, it was largely because of two beliefs. The first is that you have to convince yourself that reprinting what you have written (in my case, over 40 years) will serve the field well—that what you have said is still worth saying. That is not an easy decision because it can be so heavily influenced by self-serving overevaluation. I am quite sensitive on this point, but what was decisive was another manifestation of self-satisfaction: I knew I would enjoy reviewing my 40 years in the field: the me of today scanning and analyzing the mes of yesterdays. And it was fun, up to a point. That brings me to the second belief: A volume of selected writings should be more than just a collection but should attempt to satisfy the reader's curiosity (assuming my reaction to such volumes is representative) about the personal-intellectual-historical context from which each piece emerged, and about the commonalities (if any) that you think course through seemingly disparate writings. This second belief was particularly pertinent in my case because I have written in several fields: mental retardation, clinical psychology, community psychology, and education. In my mind, however, I have always been absorbed by a few ideas that shaped whatever I wrote, regardless of field. So, if I were to be consistent with that belief, the book would not just be a collection but would also contain a fair amount of new writing. That is why I said that preparing this book was fun, up to a point. Writing is a form of self-imposed torture because you have to think and then fit thoughts into ordered language which, one hopes and prays, is also clear. As I write these words, I am aware of another motivation that propelled me to prepare this book: It is a way of saying thank you to that crazy quilt of people and events that account for my career beginning in the field of mental retardation, a field I never left. The dedication of this book says thanks to two people whose friendship has meant so much to me. And I also wish to thank Grace Petro for typing the manuscript and, of course, Yale's Institution for Social and Policy Studies, where I am so comfortably and graciously housed.

CHAPTER 1

Plan of the Book

When you reflect upon and write about your development in a field, you are, willy nilly, selective, and must make judgments about what you think is important—what seems to have passed the test of time. That, of course, is a very risky business, subject as it is to the self-serving traps of personal motivation and of your own inevitably partial view of the complex field with which you are identified. One fact was ultimately decisive in my undertaking the task: I have lived through decades during which the field of mental retardation has undergone dramatic changes. Unfortunately, too many people in the field (as in many other fields) are ahistorical, viewing history as a museum of relics to be visited occasionally, if at all, the assumption being that the past is discontinuous with the present. In the case of the field of mental retardation, this stance is especially frequent because of the obvious ways in which the field has changed as reflected, for example, in judicial decisions, legislation, funding, and professional and societal attitudes. If that stance is frequent and understandable, it is nevertheless misleading to the extent that it diverts our attention from what has not changed and why. One feature of the changes in the field of mental retardation should have been warning enough that a good deal of the past was extant. I refer to the fact that the most important source of change has been court decisions, or, more correctly, court battles in which the plaintiffs were usually parents (and their organizations) and the defendants were professionals heading some type of institution. Far from evolving peacefully or just plain slowly over many years, these changes erupted volcano-like, with ever-widening effects. The fact is that these changes were strenuously resisted by institutions that reflected dominant societal attitudes and policies, a resistance that did not evaporate (or become transformed into its opposite) once the legal and legislative basis for the resistance was undermined. For example, when in 1954 the Supreme Court declared school segregation to be unconstitutional, many people breathed a sigh of relief at the prospect that, in the foreseeable future, segregation would be at an end. It did not work out that way for a variety of reasons, among which is the slowness with which longstanding attitudes change. Similarly, legislation and court decisions that accorded mentally retarded individuals (and their families) rights and opportunities were cause for satisfaction, but they provided no basis for the belief that society was willingly and enthusiastically unfurling the welcome mat to heretofore uninvited guests. In no way do I wish to undervalue the significance of the changes that have occurred. But neither do I wish to be seen as a cynic or spoilsport when I point out how far we have yet to travel. Because there has been victory in battles does not mean the war has been won.

In reviewing what I have written over the past four decades I saw a pattern that simplified decisions about the structure and contents of this book. Chronologically speaking, this pattern begins with studies of individuals, moves on to a concern with families, and then focuses on issues of educational and public policy—with much overlap. No less obvious than that pattern are three problems that powered whatever I wrote: the way we understand and lessen the discrepancies between what a person is or does and what he or she can learn to be; factors that prevent most people from viewing and responding to mentally retarded individuals as persons, not empty organisms; and the inevitable role of culture and social history in determining how any subgroup in the society occupies a particular niche. Given my interest in these problems, my emphasis on the dynamics of and obstacles to individual, family, institutional, and social change should occasion no surprise. At the core are a belief and an obligation. The belief is that people's capacity to underestimate the potentials of the human animal is disturbingly great and that this has been the case throughout history. The obligation is that our imagination and courage should err on the side of overestimation rather than underestimation. To me, the most stirring events in the history of mental retardation have been those at the center of which was an individual willing to run the risk of overestimating another person's capacity to learn and change.

Chapter 2 of this book reprints (in part) and discusses in detail my early studies on *individuals*. It is far clearer to me today than it was 40 years ago that I was essentially demonstrating how similar mentally retarded persons are to "us"—that they, like us, think about and yearn for loved ones; that they react with bewilderment, dejection, and despair to enforced separation; and that many of them are capable of responding sensitively and appropriately to sustained interpersonal relationships. They dream and fantasize; they are no less and no more sexual than anyone else. In those studies I accorded them the status of *persons* and *personhood*, emphasizing our similarities as thinking and feeling people and trying to counter the dominant view that they are incomplete, damaged, semi-empty vessels who are obviously human but equally obviously devoid of the "inner life" *we* know so well. This is such an important point that I decided to reprint a large part of the chapter on individual psychotherapy from *Psychological Problems in Mental Deficiency* (1949). I learned more about mentally retarded people as persons and about the effects of prolonged institutionalization from my psychotherapeutic relationship with Lottie than from all books I had read or the conventional wisdom I had heard. It is strange that in the intervening years, no case report was comparably detailed until Dr. Gaston Blom, a psychiatrist, psychoanalyst, and educator, wrote up his enthralling and fascinating psychotherapeutic relationship with Heather, a case of Down's syndrome (1979–1980). I am grateful to Dr. Blom for allowing me again to reprint part of his account, which relates one of the stirring moments I alluded to earlier. The final part of Chapter 2 describes three cases where my diagnostic acumen left much to be desired. Call them failures or errors, they are enormously revealing of how much we do not understand either about brain-behavior relationships or about individual differences among parents in commitment, imagination, and courage in regard to their seriously retarded infants. These three cases and their startling development demonstrate the core of the way I think—first, that people have always vastly underestimated the potentials of the human animal and second, that we have an obligation to use our imagination and courage in the service of overestimation. Why, I ask, is there not a single, serious, comprehensive, longitudinal study of retarded infants? Among the thousands of researchers in child development not one has seen fit to do such a study. As is often the case, what does not get studied turns out to be more fateful than what is studied.

Chapter 3 deals with two questions: What is the relationship between problem-solving behavior in naturally occurring and contrived or standardized testing situations? Second, why has this question received practically no attention in theory and research, although evidence suggests that the relationship is far from high? From my earliest days at the Southbury Training School, I was literally compelled to recognize that the quality and level of problem solving in test situations were frequently discrepant with what individuals were able to do in natural settings in which they perceived a problem as meaningful and challenging. I wrote about this in one of my earliest papers, but my "evidence" was anecdotal and of the single-case variety. The fact is that living *in* the training school and interacting with and observing the residents in *every* type of situation made it impossible for me not to note that the level of problem solving in the testing situation was often well below that outside of it. These observations were (and still are) obviously relevant to the nature-nurture controversy, which revolves around the significance of test scores. If, in fact, my observations were valid, they had to be explained both by the advocates of nature and those of nurture. But, as the residents of Southbury would say, "nobody paid me any mind." Any doubts that I was raising an important and unexplored issue were dissolved when I read Ginzberg and Bray's (1953) *The Uneducated*, an analysis of the army performance of low test scoring recruits. Chapter 3 summarizes their findings and my attempt to raise again the problem of the relationship between problem solving in the test and the naturally occurring situation.

When I came to Yale, I struck up a friendship and collaboration with Dr. Thomas Gladwin, an anthropologist. As a group, anthropologists are refreshingly relatively free of the tendency to conceptualize human behavior independently of cultural context, knowing as they do how amazingly different people in different cultural contexts can be. In their studies of so-called "primitive" societies they do not rivet on one situation but instead attempt to see the individual within the cultural context that distinguishes his or her society. Through my reading of the anthropologic literature and my relationship with Tom, I saw that the "Southbury Problem" was not limited to Southbury. These so-called primitive minds were able to solve problems in their natural setting that would never have been predicted from their performance on any of "our" tests. The clincher was Gladwin's (1970) *East Is a Big Bird*, a book which relates how natives in the South Pacific could travel in their little boats over the trackless ocean and get to where they wanted to go. Chapter 3 discusses the significance of this book, which, incidentally, was recognized as a classic as soon as it was published. As Tom emphasized, the level of abstraction that these natives demonstrated in their navigation is not even hinted at in their test performance. One of the major reasons Tom did the study (he knew their language and apprenticed himself to their navigators) was his interest in the relationship between poverty and problem solving *in our society*.

Finally, Chapter 3 expresses my indebtedness to a man, his ideas, and his "products." The man is Henry Schaefer-Simmern, a political refugee from Nazi Germany, an art theorist and educator who demonstrated with Southbury residents what can be achieved when an individual becomes engrossed in an activity that is quintessentially problem solving in nature. I use the word "engrossed" to emphasize the significance of observing problem solving in a situation that is satisfying, stimulating, and challenging to the individual—a situation that the individual voluntarily

selects. Henry Schaefer-Simmern was the most important intellectual influence on me in my adult years. He not only opened my eyes to the es-
thetics of art but, no less important, to the nature and development of
artistic activity. For Schaefer-Simmern, artistic ability is *not* a special talent; rather, it is a human attribute too often stunted by the imposition of
arbitrary criteria of what is good or bad art, of what is right or wrong. I
learned from him what *gestalt* really means. If it seems strange that a
book devoted to mental retardation contains material on navigational
systems and artistic activity, I hope that, after reading this chapter, their
relevance will become clear. As I said earlier, selections from my writings
were based on the criterion that they focus on issues that, despite all the
changes that have taken place in the field of mental retardation, have
not—but should—receive far more attention than they have gotten to
date. Chapter 3 may well be the best example of consistency with that
criterion.

     Chapter 4 basically has one theme: The unit of study should be the
family, not the individual. By focusing on the individual we ignore the fact
that from the moment of birth (indeed, even before) the family affects and
is affected by the newborn, retarded or not. From the standpoint of understanding the infant and child, that focus is essential. From the standpoint of preventing (in secondary and tertiary ways) problems and human suffering, the focus on the individual is wasteful and unjustified.
The concept of "patient" is singular; it refers to *an* individual who has
symptoms. This approach makes it too easy to ignore the fact that "out
there" in external reality family members are constantly interacting—
psychologically, there are no boundaries among them. This section provides clinical examples of what happens when we are unaware that our
self-created tunnel vision is drastically narrowing the scope of diagnosis
and help. From my earliest years in the field I knew that one of the most
unfortunate consequences of this tunnel vision was reflected in how the
diagnosis of mental retardation was communicated to the family. Providing information is not always synonymous with being helpful. Far more
often than not, the family was told the name of the condition and some of
its developmental implications, and was given some expression of sympathy. It was not that the communicator was insensitive to what the news
might mean to the family. On the contrary, the communicator was frequently acutely and agonizingly aware that the family would forever be
affected by the news. However, because the communicator did not know
how to deal with the family *qua* family, he or she retreated, in collusion
with the family, to talking exclusively about the afflicted infant or child. If
that was frequently the case, one could not be indifferent to those instances where the communicator was in fact insensitive to the implications of the diagnosis for the family. In both types of instances the glaring
omissions and deficiencies of professional training (especially in medical
training) were egregious and, I would contend, more harmful than help-

ful. The early editions of *Psychological Problems in Mental Deficiency* contained a chapter on how to think about and conduct the communication of the diagnosis. With the passage of years and the increasing public recognition of the problems confronting families with a retarded youngster, I assumed—why, I do not know—that the communication of the diagnosis had improved. I have been told by colleagues in the field that it was a mistake to have omitted that chapter in later editions. They were, unfortunately, right. So, in this chapter I have reprinted it. As is so frequently the case, the literary artist depicts reality far better than anyone else, and in connection with the theme of this chapter, Joseph Heller's 1975 novel *Something Happened* is a case in point. In the Sarason and Doris (1979) book *Educational Handicap, Public Policy, and Social History* I discussed that novel, excerpts of which are contained in Chapter 4. I confess to skepticism about how long it will take for the professional community to unlearn its exclusive focus on the individual and to learn how to conceptualize the problem in terms of the family, thus dramatically expanding the help it can render and diluting the adverse consequences that are so frequently experienced by the family.

Chapter 5 interconnects three topics: the infancy-childhood period, cultural factors, and history. In one way or another, these three topics have always been implicated in the cyclical nature-nurture controversies. A major theme in this chapter is that the longitudinal study of mentally retarded infants and children is remarkable for its absence. And by longitudinal, I mean repeated and comprehensive observations and evaluations of the familial and cultural contexts into which these individuals are born and reared. By longitudinal I do not mean collecting test scores, although I do not have any objection to test scores if they are but one facet in a more comprehensive assortment of data. In my years at Southbury, I found myself asking: How was this or that child reared? What was the pattern of stimulation? What worked for or against acquiring competencies? There were studies which, varying in rigor and comprehensiveness, suggested that the child-rearing context could not be ignored, although the field managed to do just that. The first time I discussed this problem was in *Psychological Problems in Mental Deficiency* (Sarason, 1949). After I left Southbury I tried to get funding to research the hypothesis contained in that chapter, but with no success. I sought funding from the National Institute of Mental Health shortly after it came into existence, and that was a time when the neuroses, psychoses, and psychotherapy were the objects of public concern. It was not until two decades later that interest in impoverished environments and cultural deprivation came to the fore, although even then the longitudinal approach was well in the background. However, I was fortunate in the fifties in being able to collaborate with anthropologist Dr. Thomas Gladwin in a survey of research which was published in the monograph *Psychological and Cultural Problems in Mental Subnormality: A Review of Research* (Sarason and Gladwin, 1958). Precisely because of his anthropologic orientation, our collaboration focused primarily on the longitudinal approach in the cultural context. One chapter from that monograph is reprinted here. Few things that I have done in the field of mental retardation were more satisfying to me than the opportunity via that collaboration to bring attention to the longitudinal approach in the context of the cultural settings. Given my interest in the history of the individual, it should not be surprising that I became absorbed in seeing individual history in the sweep of social history. My collaboration with John Doris, a psychologist and historian, insured that my interest in individual history would not stay within parochial limits. This is best illustrated in the brief summary chapter in our 1979 book, which is reprinted here (Sarason and Davis, 1979). That chapter summarizes our approach not only to social history but also to the developmental transactional processes between child and family. Chapter 5 ends with the most personal paper I have ever written: "Jewishness, Blackishness, and the Nature-Nurture Controversy" (Sarason, 1973). Using my own life as text, I endeavor to demonstrate not only why history, culture, and individual development within a particular family should never be ignored, but also why they must be seen in relation to each other.

Chapter 6 deals with a question that will be familiar to most readers: Why is it that almost all human services settings constantly struggle to get additional resources and see themselves, and are seen by others, as falling very short of their intended goals? It took me years to recognize that in the creation of these settings there was an assumption that was as wrong as it was understandable. I call it "the myth of unlimited resources." I came to see this myth for what it is largely because of three experiences I had in the field of mental retardation. The first experience was at the Southbury Training School, where I joined the staff shortly after it opened and remained for four years. When I left, it was already apparent that the hopes for and glories of Southbury were fading. The second experience was my participation in the planning and creation of the New Haven Regional Center and in the subsequent affiliation of the Center with the Yale Psycho-Educational Clinic. The third experience was the planning and creation of the Central Connecticut Regional Center and, again, its relationship to our clinic. These were exhilarating, intellectually stimulating, and yet ultimately disillusioning experiences for reasons that are explained in this chapter. Why I have chosen to reprint two consecutive chapters from *The Creation of Settings and the Future Societies* is also explained (Sarason, 1972). The first of these chapters is titled "The Myth of Unlimited Resources" and the second "Resources and Values." These two chapters discuss issues that in my opinion have gone relatively unrecognized in public policy about and funding for the area of human services.

We must never forget that like all concepts, the concept of mental retardation is literally an invention and always bears the stamp not only of the inventor but of his or her society. So, when we talk about mental retardation, we are talking about the society in which that concept was invented and changed over time. For whom does the bell of mental retardation toll? It tolls for all of us. The book ends with an epilogue centering on the theme of the implications of the "invention" of the concept of mental retardation.

CHAPTER 2

The Individual

Personality Studies

I have never read a biography or autobiography of someone who came to adulthood in the 1930s that did not contain many pages explaining how World War II transformed his or her world. World War I was no tea party— in terms of killing off the intellectual cream of western Europe, it was a carnage—but it was not a global war in the way World War II was, and it did not impact as massively on as many people in the United States. Our country entered World War I towards its close; in contrast, we were in World War II for several years. If anything guaranteed that our entry into the war would bring in its wake legislation affecting everyone, it was the simple fact that for some time after December 7, 1941, it was by no means clear that victory was a realistic possibility. France had been conquered, Britain seemed to be tottering, Hitler was deep into Russia, Japan was chalking up victory after victory in the Far East, and we were far from ready to be of real help.

Metaphorically speaking, Pearl Harbor signaled the end of the Great Depression and the beginning of its opposite: a manpower shortage.

Women, old people, and handicapped people were brought into the work force. I remember reading a newspaper article that described the aircraft industry's need for small people (e.g., midgets) who could work inside the nose cones of airplanes. The needs of a wartime society required that everyone who wanted to and could contribute to the war effort would be encouraged to do so, prewar rules, regulations, and traditions to the contrary notwithstanding. "Anyone" included individuals to whom the label "mental defective" had been given. Those were the days when mental deficiency referred to three levels of performance: idiot, imbecile, and moron. The term "mental retardation" (not a frequent or a consistently defined one) tended to refer to those whose test scores were below the normal range (sometimes markedly so) not because of a damaged or malfunctioning brain but for other reasons, e.g., psychologic, social, or educational. In those days, there was no outcry about the demeaning connotations of labels like "feebleminded," "idiot," "imbecile," or "moron." A "mongolian" was called a mongolian and not "someone with Down's syndrome." What argument there was had nothing to do with language but a lot to do with the hereditary-environment dichotomy. More specifically, the question some people asked was: How many individuals, in and out of institutions, had scores in the mentally defective range that might be explained in terms of development in social-cultural milieus foreign to the milieus of those upon whom the psychologic tests had been standardized? How many individuals became and remained "defective" because they were institutionalized at an early age and, therefore, had little or no intellectual stimulation? In western society, at least, it seems that each generation plays out its own version of the nature-nurture controversy. That was no less true of the thirties than of the decades before and since. I venture the hypothesis that the frequency and passion levels of the nature-nurture controversy are greater in the United States than elsewhere because we are a nation of immigrants towards each group or wave of which we have attributed intellectual and social peculiarities. Indeed, throughout our history we have tended to view immigrant groups as intellectually and socially inferior. Swedes, Germans, Poles, Italians, Jews, Chinese, and other immigrant groups were judged to be intellectually inferior to whomever were "native" Americans at the time. It is as if each group was seen as a threat to the society's standards and viability, at least by a number of influential (professional, social, or political) people who sought action that would preserve the quality of the nation's intellectual stock. Such actions, and the attitudes they reflected, were countered by others less ready to make judgments about intellectual inferiority. No one needs to be told that we are (and continue to be) a nation of immigrants, but we do have to be reminded that whatever pride we take in that characteristic should not obscure the pejorative attitudes immigrant groups encountered and the basic intellectual inferiorities attributed to them.

If this legacy of immigration insured that the country would be concerned with intellectual inferiority and its explanations, it did not mean that those who appeared to be intellectually inferior would be seen as persons. By "seen as persons," I refer to the substance and consequences of a stance and process by which we try to fathom in others those thoughts, feelings, and tendencies which we know characterize ourselves. This stance allows us to say about ourselves that we are *persons*, that the forces that shape us are the forces that shape everyone else, and that these forces have to be invoked regardless of whether we are trying to explain similarities or differences, superiority or inferiority. The fact is that those whom the society labeled as mentally defective were, for all practical purposes, not seen as persons but as organisms lacking a crucial ingredient; there was so much emphasis on what was lacking as to rob them of personhood. I have often put this point in this way: If your neighbor's child, who has an IQ of 180, takes your cat and chokes it to death, you would not say that the child did it *because* he or she has an IQ of 180. If that same child had an IQ of 60, the chances are very high that the low IQ would be invoked as a causal or etiologic agent, i.e., we would "blame" the low IQ. And by blaming the IQ—assuming in the process that we have "explained" the person's behavior—we do not have to wrestle with the question: Why is such behavior so rare among people with identical IQs? Why did this individual and not the others act in this way? As soon as we ask these questions, we are viewing the individual as a person with a distinctive, indeed unique, personal, interpersonal, familial history that gave substance, organization, and direction to that individual's covert and overt behavior. That is to say, whatever conceptions we think we understand about the individuality of ourselves, and those like us, we also invoke in the effort to understand why *this* person did what he or she did. This may sound logical, rational, or simply fair, but the fact is that only in recent years has the retarded individual been studied and reacted to as a person like ourselves, i.e., as someone who seeks social intercourse, possesses a private life, experiences emotions and sexual urges, and confronts and attempts to deal with the problems engendered by interactions with the milieu.

Only recently has the retarded individual been accorded educational and legal rights that the rest of us never had to "win" or even think about. It was, so to speak, part of our birthright. But we should never confuse according people rights with viewing them as people whose lives, no less than ours, were shaped by certain internal and external forces that bear the stamp of a particular society.

How far we have come from the pre-World War II years, and how far we still have to go, can be illustrated and discussed on the basis of the first three papers I published after taking my first professional job in 1942 at the Southbury Training School in Connecticut. I had just completed three years of graduate training at Clark University, where my doctoral thesis advisor was Saul Rosenzweig. Rosensweig had been a student of Henry Murray at Harvard and also had been a member of that unusual group of psychologists Murray had brought together at the Harvard Psychological Clinic. From that group, under Murray's intellectual leadership, emerged *Explorations in Personality*, one of the most influential publications in American psychology in this century (Murray, 1938). What was so important about Murray's project was the diverse perspectives and techniques that were brought to bear on the study of *individual* lives. In contrast to what was then mainstream psychology, Murray sought to develop a comprehensive conception schema and to utilize psychologic "tests" that together would broaden and deepen our understanding of the internal "needs" and external "presses" that interact, affect, and alter our lives. The "tests" were far from conventional both in format and modes of interpretation, geared as they were to discerning the conscious and unconscious meanings of the individual's verbalizations to stimulus materials that facilitated the role of fantasy and the mechanism of projection. They were not (for the most part) tests in the sense that the Stanford-Binet, personality inventories, and attitude questionnaires of the time were tests. One of the new tests was developed by Murray himself and it was called the Thematic Apperception Test (TAT). I daresay there is no psychologist alive today who needs to be told what the TAT is. But in the mid-thirties it was a new and strange test, consisting of a set of pictures to each of which the individual made up a story. These stories, Murray demonstrated, revealed a good deal about the person. The TAT made it easy for an individual to indulge in "fantasy play," putting into words the springs of motivation and the perception of the social terrain. Interviews and projective tests: Those were the major ways in which Murray and his co-workers pioneered in the study of the person. So, more than four decades later, Nevitt Sanford, a student of Murray and later the intellectual leader of a Murray-like study of the authoritarian personality, said:

> The authors of *The Authoritarian Personality* were taught and inspired by Henry Murray. Accordingly, in their studies a group of investigators used a variety of techniques to increase understanding of personality—what Murray called "that vast and intricate architecture." These authors would say today that almost everything they learned about authoritarianism in personality they learned from interviews and projective tests. (Sanford, 1982, p. 903)

It was foreordained that when I got to Southbury I would start to study the applicability of projective tests for the understanding of mentally retarded individuals. And that is the point: Why was there any question in my mind about whether these individuals had an "inner life" in the way I had, whether the basic themes of their fantasies and dreams would overlap with mine, whether their separation from home and loved ones would leave wounds as it would (and did) for me?

The following excerpts are from three publications: The first two excerpts are from studies of the use of the TAT with institutionalized girls and boys, respectively. The third excerpt is from a study comparing the content of TAT stories to that of dreams in institutionalized girls.

The Use of the Thematic Apperception Test with Mentally Deficient Children

I. A Study of High Grade Girls [1]

The purpose of this study was, first, to determine if one could administer the Thematic Apperception Test to a mentally deficient population; second, whether the data so secured give a revealing picture of the more or less unconscious motivational life of the subjects; and third, the possible clinical uses of this test.

Nature of the Test　The test is made up of the original set of pictures which have been described in an article by Morgan . . . and in Murray's *Explorations in Personality*. . . . In this projective technique the subject is shown a series of pictures and is asked to make up a story about each of them. The subject is told, "You can tell me what is happening in the picture, what did happen, and how it will end. You can tell me how the people in the pictures feel, what they are saying, and what they are thinking." These directions are modified and repeated until the subject comprehends what is expected of him. If the stories told are not clear or unambiguous, the examiner may ask such questions as: "What led up to it? How will it end? Tell me more about it?" All leading questions are avoided. Everything said by the subject is taken down verbatim.

In the telling of such stories, it has been found, one tends to be, consciously or unconsciously, autobiographical. That is, the story teller identifies himself with one of the characters in the narrative and the wishes, fears, desires, etc., manifested by the latter are the same as those of the subject. The basic mechanisms at work in such a situation are those of identification, and of projection: attributing motives to others which are possessed by one's self. By carefully examining each story told and determining the character with whom the identification has taken place, one can formulate the thema which best epitomizes the relationships expressed. For example the following is a story given by one of the subjects in the present study:

> The girl is asking what she should do—Mother gives a suggestion—girl is mad cause she don't like it—Mother says if she don't like it she can think of something herself—girl thinks of something and Mother doesn't like it—they get mad at each other.

The writer, after studying and analyzing this one story, decided that the identification had been with the young girl, and that the thema is one of rebellion—in this case against the mother. Another story from which the same thema is extracted is the following:

> Mother wants girl here—tries to give her vitamins—gives her juice—the girl says I don't want to take it—like stubborn children do—mother says take it—kid says no—child won't come—mother says you'll be sorry if you don't take juice for breakfast—vitamins are good for you—girl says I don't care—like I do sometimes—I can say it's me.

Each story is analyzed in the above fashion. A tabulation is then made of the frequency of appearance of each thema and if found at least twice it is considered as a facet of that subject's personality. In practice, the major themas which emerge from an individual's projections appear several times and those found only twice are considered minor and used in a supplementary fashion. No hard and fast rules can be rigidly maintained, however. The writer has had the experience of basing an analysis largely on a thema derived from one story and finding himself essentially correct when a check was made with the psychiatric case history. In such a case the story was told with such heightened feeling and vividness of detail that the thema expressed was felt to be a basic one . . . Never having administered this test to a mentally deficient population, and no reference to such an attempt having been found in the literature, the writer did not know what difficulties might arise. It is obvious from the nature of the test that some creative imagination must be present if stories and not mere descriptions are to be given. A fair amount of concentration is also necessary in order to give a fairly well organized narrative. From the stories to be presented later it will be seen that these girls possessed enough imagination and concentration to make plausible and fairly coherent stories. In many cases they were slow to comprehend directions and sometimes the first picture of the series had to be done by the examiner as an illustration. There was a tendency for stories to be descriptions—this being typical of the "concrete" attitude characteristic of the mentally deficient as opposed to the "abstract" attitude found in the normal subject. There was also a tendency for the stories to lack a certain consistency and coherency. On the whole, however, the administration of this test to this group of girls and the analysis of their stories presented no special problems which an experienced worker with this technique could not adequately meet.

Results   Before analysing the stories of any one subject, it is advisable to discuss some of the themas which most frequently appeared with this group of girls. The two themas which occurred with almost equal frequency were concerned with feelings of aggression and with a desire for affection. A thema of aggression was said to be present when the character with whom the identification had taken place acted in a pugnacious, destructive, illegal or harmful manner. The following are examples:

> Man on right is in prison—the other came to see him—he told him he knows a good way to escape from prison—they got out—one of the cops saw them—he rang all bells—called all cops—one man escaped—cops shot the one on the right down—the other escaped.

> He looks mad—as if he's going to fight or kill somebody—he is in great anger—I don't know how it will turn out when he gets through—he may have had words or a fight with someone—he doesn't want to take all the blame for what happened—he has quite a bit of anger in him.

A thema of desire for affection was said to be present in a story when the central character gave, received, or yearned for love and affection. Illustrations of such a thema are seen in these stories:

> The one on the left looks like he needs food, home, clothes—lots of vitamins—needs help—a job—must get Doctor care—maybe the other man brought him to see if he can help him—he is telling Doctor what other needs and says he himself will pay for it—maybe he has a friend who can take care of him.

> Devoted to one another—it is New York—fellow and a girl met—afterwards fell in love—he says to girl I love you and I always did ever since I seen you—girl says I love you too—let's get married—poor boy says no—his number called in army—after I come back we'll be married—she says four years is a long time to wait for you—maybe you'll be shot and I won't have you—don't worry about me—pray and keep chin up—we have to win this war—I'm going to win this war—kisses her goodbye—he sailed away—don't forget to write me.

It may seem paradoxical that these two seemingly antithetical thema should be found in such frequency, but logical analysis will reveal that one is a function of the other. It is not unusual in working with children to find that the aggression displayed by many of them stems from a situation in which affection was desired and given, but none obtained in return. The child, for example, who is suddenly displaced by a younger sibling feels such a lack of affection keenly and the aggression displayed by him toward the sibling and parents is a means of revenge, on the one hand, and an assertion of a desire to remain in the superior position, on the other. Aggression is used here as a retribution for something not received. Thus the mentally deficient child, made to feel different from others, unable to compete on equal terms for the attention and affection of others, unconsciously grasps aggressive means as a way of breaking through a maze of frustrations.

Two other thema which appear frequently, and which are related to those of aggression and affection, are concerned with rebellion against the parents (usually the mother), and with feelings of guilt. It is a problem of classification whether rebellion against the parents should be subsumed under aggression, since there is so much overlapping between the two. Certainly rebellion against the parents must be termed aggressive. The child, who is made to feel different from his siblings, rejected by his parents, separated from the home in many cases against his wishes, undoubtedly develops hostile feelings toward his parents in addition to the hostility which we know to be attendant on the normal course of development. Rebellion, however, was separated for classificatory purposes from aggression because the former wherever found was specific and unmistakable while the latter was more general and not as personalized. We have already seen examples of stories from which a thema of rebellion emerges. One from which a thema of guilt can be extracted is the following:

> A girl who didn't seem to care much—she was running around—has nothing to herself—if she did care she would have more than a bed and chair and she would have more clothes—she's sorry now cause she learned her lesson from it now—now she knows what a burden is to her—she has nothing left.

Another such thema is seen in another story by this same girl:

> Man on right did something—man on left is explaining to him so he wouldn't get into difficulty—but it's too late—he didn't care—if he had listened it wouldn't have happened—he didn't seem to care.

The thema of guilt was quite prominent with several of the girls. Generally it was found as a consequence of aggressive action and was expressed either in terms of the central character having committed a wrong or by a poignant admission of remorse. It would appear from these two thema that the difficulty in the community adjustment of high grade girls is not so much a lack of knowledge of what is right and wrong as it is faulty and impulsive judgment. These girls do know what society considers right and wrong, but they are incapable of seeing the relationship between a set of abstract moral rules and their own behavior in a given situation. The importance of the abstract attitude cannot be overemphasized.

The last thema which will be discussed concerns itself with feelings of loneliness—that is, the character with whom the identification has taken place is pictured as alone, and bereft of friends and home. Examples of this thema are the following:

> Little boy has no home—lost—a runaway—he is hungry—maybe he has no people—just a little boy—strolling off somewhere—taking a long walk—looking at scenery—maybe he has no home—maybe looking for a dog—maybe his father is lost.

Little girl is sad—people gone away—looking out of window won-
dering whether they'll be back—if she was bigger she could go—
she is staying with aunt who is mean to her—keeps looking and
looking—cries—aunt calls her—you better come Jane—supper—I
don't want supper—I want mother—aunt says it will only be for
a few weeks—no—she thinks—I'll go with my mother—packs
clothes and runs away—is with mother and is very happy.

When one stops to consider the development of the institutionalized
child, such feelings of loneliness are to be expected. In several cases this
thema was outstanding and accompanied by much anxiety.

The Use of the Thematic Apperception Test
With Mentally Deficient Children

II. A Study of High Grade Boys [2]

The present paper is concerned with a similar study of a group of twelve
mentally deficient high grade boys. The average chronological age was 22
years 4 months with a range of 15 to 36 years. The average intelligence
quotient was 63 with a range from 45 to 76. A comparison between the
subjects in this and the previous study reveals their similarity in chronological age and mental level.

In addition to the variables noted above, the two groups of defectives come from similar socio-economic backgrounds where neglect, pri-
vation, and lack of a stable family atmosphere are marked. With two such
similar groups, therefore, one would not expect the results of the present
study to differ in any fundamental way from those of the previous one,
and this expectation is largely borne out. One finds again that aggression,
rejection, ambivalence towards the parents, guilt, and fear of loneliness
are the prevalent themas. The mother remains the key character: the individual from whom love and security are sought, and whose rejection of
the child brings forth from it aggression and destructive reactions. However, when one compares the stories of the girls with those of the boys a
difference begins to emerge which analysis reveals to be one of degree
and not of kind. That is, the stories given by the boys in response to the
pictures, while similar in content to those of the girls, are not told with as
much heightened feeling or emotional fervor. Stated in another way one
could say that the boys, as a group, do not feel or do not express their
more or less unconscious attitudes in as direct or obvious a manner as
the girls. With the boys aggression is less specifically directed and more
generalized, affection is not as eagerly sought, feelings of guilt less severe,
and fear of loneliness not as poignant. This finding assumes significance
when seen in terms of the present environment of these children. The

discussion that follows must be considered as only one possible explanation of the difference noted above, and of the related fact that at the
Southbury Training School girls present many and more difficult problems than boys.

At the Southbury Training School the high grade children are placed
either in the boys' or girls' village. The dwelling unit is the cottage each of
which houses approximately 25–30 children. On the boys' side each cottage is supervised by a cottage matron and master. Each cottage has its
own kitchen and cook. On the girls' side the physical arrangements are
the same but instead of a cottage mother and father one has a cottage
matron who is assisted by attendants. It is clear from such an arrangement that a home-like atmosphere is more likely to be approximated in
the boys' than in the girls' village. This difference in home-like atmosphere is, for example, reflected in the following subtle fashion: the number of times that a cottage matron and master on the boys' side is called
"Mom" and "Pop" is far greater than the frequency with which a cottage
matron is called "Mom" on the girls' side. Another manifestation of this
difference can be seen in the greater amount of group activity among the
boys. Largely under the supervision of their cottage father the boys have
such organized groups as Boy Scouts, athletic teams, and a night school
class. The girls have none of these. An attempt has been made to start a
4-H club with the girls but sufficient bickering and apathy have already
been shown to make a favorable prognosis doubtful.

In the light of such a tentative explanation it becomes understandable why boys would not show aggression, feelings of rejection, and fear
of loneliness as strongly as the girls. When one remembers that the majority of these children come from poorly supervised homes in the lowest
socio-economic brackets where neglect and poverty are the rule and not
the exception, one begins to see how emotionally satisfying and stabiliz-
ing can be a home-like atmosphere such as exists in the boys' village at
Southbury.

One other explanation which can be advanced to explain the difference between the strength of the boys' and girls' stories is based on the
assumption that in the test situation girls will more easily transfer to a
man than will boys. One would expect, therefore, that the girls of the previous study would be more ready "to talk" and unburden themselves in
response to the thematic pictures than the boys. To some extent this explanation probably plays a part in the differences noted between the two
groups but since no systematic investigation has been reported of the differential effects of this factor, the weight that can be attached to it in this
study is indeterminate.

Clinical Uses   In the placement of a mental defective in the community
a constant fear of authorities concerns the possibility of sexual irregu-
larities. One has only to read random samples of case histories from any

state institution for mental defectives to realize the solid foundation for such a fear. It was of interest, therefore, to the writer to investigate the uses of the Thematic Apperception Test with two boys who were thought to possess certain of the more obvious homosexual characteristics: high pitched, mild voice, feminine mannerisms, and a female-like gait. The case history of one of these boys makes only slight mention of possible homosexuality and no mention at all is to be had in the history of the other. The following are some of the stories told by one of these boys:

> She's trying to hold the baby but the baby is trying to get away from her. She's trying to rock it to sleep—the baby is laughing at her— baby is having more fun than the lady is.

> She is in love with this man—it looks like he isn't very much in love with her—he thinks she went off with another man and she is try- ing to kid him along that she didn't—it looks like he's going to kill the man she went out with.

> He's trying to put a man to sleep—looks like he's trying to make this man do something in his will power—kill a girl or something.

> Man is accused of something—he's climbing up a pole—someone is chasing him—he did something wrong—he did something dirty with a girl or something—her husband is after this guy.

> He's trying to get hold of girl and kill her—she's trying to get away— he's going to choke her—she's scared—she done something wrong to his son.

The other themes which emerge from these and other stories are con- cerned, first, with aggressive or destructive tendencies toward women, and second, with feelings of sexual guilt—themes which psychosexual theory and clinical observation have shown to be characteristic of the ho- mosexual personality. Women are here characteristically depicted as un- desirable and immoral people "having done something wrong," and from several of the stories feelings of sexual guilt can be demonstrated. Al- though the attitudes expressed in these stories are different from those of the other boys, the writer felt that the strength of this boy's aptitude had not been sufficiently exposed. In order to probe more deeply, the follow- ing was said to the boy:

> It has happened sometimes that after showing all these pic- tures to the other fellows some of them have said that they didn't tell me everything that came into their minds because they thought I might not like what they were thinking about and that I would hold it against them. Of course, this isn't so because I told you to tell me whatever came into your mind and that you should keep nothing back. Therefore, I'm going to show you the pictures again

and if you see one where you didn't tell me everything, you go right ahead and tell me everything now.

Following these additional directions the boy elaborated on three pictures in all of which, interestingly enough, the characters seemed scantily dressed. These were his remarks—told with much display of revulsion and indignation:

> It isn't fit to look at—a boy shouldn't look at it—she hasn't much on her body.

> An older person should look at this picture—not boys—gives bad thoughts and habits.

> That ain't fit to look at either—whoever made these pictures must be crazy—they should have more sense than to put these pictures in.

It becomes clearer from these statements how strongly this twenty-year-old boy feels towards any display of sexuality, and it is not delving into the mystical realms of theory to maintain that this boy's conscious attitudes might well be a reaction-formation against his homosexual tendencies. It is of interest to note that when other boys in this study were asked to go over the pictures a second time, one did not find their elaborations tinged with the revulsion which was noted above even though they were responding to the same picture. One of these boys, of the same age as the case that has just been discussed, responded with a shamefaced and embarrassed smile, "This girl has no decency. She doesn't care what she did or where she went. The $1.00 and $1.25 kind. I've seen enough of them."

When the stories of the second boy with homosexual characteristics were analyzed, one finds again the feelings of sexual guilt and aggressive tendencies towards women. When the pictures were shown to him a second time this boy elaborated on only one picture as follows:

> This gives a person funny ideas—perhaps a boy never saw a woman naked—perhaps a boy would feel as if he were married and could get children—perhaps he never had experience with a lady.

When the test was completed the boy was sent back to his job assignment. A half hour later the writer was met by the same boy who said he had some problems on his mind and promptly proceeded to tell of a large number of homosexual experiences he had had and was having. He told his adventures with an evident mixture of revulsion and pleasure. It should be borne in mind that the writer tried at all times to say nothing during the administration of the test which would inaugurate such a train of associations in the boy. The homosexual experiences he related seem rather to have been awakened by his own responses to the thematic pictures. This illustrates in a concrete way how the attitudes revealed in the stories are intimately related in the minds of subjects, whether on a conscious or unconscious level, to basic tendencies in the personality.

Dreams and Thematic Apperception Test Stories[3]

Case 1

Sabina is a 22-year-old girl with an IQ of 55. At the time of her initial admission to an institution the case history stated that this girl was a "poor risk to leave in the community because of the combination of her defectiveness, abnormal interest in boys, and a poor home environment." The girl's home was considered so poor that she was placed with a foster family. When the home conditions had improved, Sabina was returned but "she was very unruly, stubborn, and the entire family resented her presence." The psychological summary reads: "a high grade girl who is emotionally unstable and who is easily flustered and frustrated when confronted with a new task. These characteristics result in impulsiveness which lowers her accuracy. She is highly suggestible. This combination of facts makes Sabina a poor bet for an essentially successful placement."

The themes which were found with most frequency in the thematic stories were ambivalence toward the mother, insecurity, fear of separation from loved ones, and guilt connected with a fear of retribution. The following sample story is in part illustrative of the rebellion toward the mother:

> It's as if she's trying to get rid of the baby—she doesn't look like a good mother—her hair is not neat—she should have neater hair for a mother—if she was neat she'd bring the child up right—if authorities saw her treating the child like that they would take it away from her and put it in a school like this and bring it up right.

In several other stories a more positive attitude toward the mother is indicated, but in general the hostility seems stronger. Two stories are given below which indicate the girl's insecurity—seen most clearly in anxiety about the lack of food:

> It's as if he wandered away from home—he has no place to go—he looks at the house over the bridge as if he thinks he'll go in there and stay—he looks kind of cold standing there—by going in there he'll find food and stay alive.

> This might be a sailor whose ship went down—he was the only one saved from the ship—he has no way of getting food—he is hungry—it looks as if he'll fall down any minute cause he hasn't had food for such a long time.

It should be noted that insecurity and anxiety were also manifested in other stories in which some fear as to mental status was indicated. Stories in which either the themes of fear of separation or guilt are revealed follow:

Maybe it's her mother or grandmother—she don't look well—she is pale—the girl brings her water—she tells her to sit down—the girl looks like a very young lady—the grandmother explains what to do in the house—the girl looks interested and listens to her—she goes and does what grandmother says—she comes back every once in a while to see if the grandmother is all right cause if she died she'll lose one of her best friends—then she'd have to go somewhere where they wouldn't treat her as well—they would have stricter rules.

He looks strong and husky—somebody down on the ground—he is trying to get him down from the pole—it's as if he's afraid to come down and take his punishment because it would be a severe one.

She has her back to the boy—it is his mother—she is not pleased with him—she doesn't want to listen to what he says—he done something wrong—she looks worried as if he's going to be put away in prison—she has no one to support her after he is put away.

It should be pointed out that the fear of separation from loved ones comes out very strongly in her stories. In the final analysis of this girl's thematic test it was felt that there was a causal relationship between the ambivalence toward the parents and the fear of separation from them. The following are dreams of this girl:

1. I was in institution X—I dreamt of my father—I was praying for my father—my mother came and pulled my hair—I screamed—she said I'm pulling your hair because father don't need prayers—I do.
2. My brother was in the army—he came home on a furlough—my aunt wrote in for me—I went home for the first time—I was glad to be home.
3. I went out with Mrs. Jones—we sang in Father Smith's church—I came back to the school.
4. I saw snakes on the floor—I got so frightened that I woke up to see if the snakes were looking at me.
5. We went to institution A—Mr. Roselle (superintendent of Southbury) said he was going to leave me there cause my people wanted me there—I yelled in my sleep: please leave me in Southbury.
6. I had a fight with Mary S.—it took some of the staff to keep me from hurting her—I don't like her so well.
7. My mother was walking on the street—the boys and girls said there was my mother—I was afraid to look at her cause I knew she was dead—she hollered, "Sabina, Sabina, come to me, I'm your mother—don't be scared because the devil will never hurt you."

The major theme which can be abstracted from these dreams is concerned with fear, anxiety, and ambivalence toward the mother. On the one hand, the mother maltreats the child and is a source of fear and guilt and, on the other hand, the mother is asking in what seems a pleading fashion for the child to be reunited with her. The separation theme comes out strongly in dream 5 when she begs not to be left in an institution; it is of interest to note that the blame for the contemplated separation is laid to "my people." This projection of blame seems to corroborate the conclusion that this girl's ambivalence is in some way connected with her separation from home. In general, the main themes found in her stories are found with equal strength in her dreams.

Case 2

Helen is a 19-year-old girl who is the youngest child in a family of six. Her parents are foreign born who have taken on few American customs. The mother has been inadequate in supervising and disciplining her children. Helen was brought to the attention of the police after having had numerous experiences with boys who picked her up. The type of sexual activity in which she participated was described as "perversions." Helen's stay in the institution has been marked by many temper tantrums in which her excellent knowledge of abusive terms comes to the fore. She is stubborn and recalcitrant with those who supervise her and it has been necessary to change her job very frequently.

On the Wechsler-Bellevue Full-Scale this girl obtained a quotient of 72.

The main theme found in this girl's stories was rebellion toward authority in general and the mother in particular. Connected with this theme were those of rejection, aggression, and guilt—the guilt coming out in stories in which people "have learned their lesson." Sample stories in which these themas are brought out follow:

> The mother is carrying the baby from something like an accident— she's carrying the baby so it won't get into danger—it was an accident or something—the mother didn't seem to care at first or the accident wouldn't have happened—now it's too late—she care for him now—it wouldn't have happened if she cared.

> The girl is trying to explain something to the mother—the mother is sick and the girl is trying to talk to the mother nicely but it doesn't seem to work out—the expression shows the mother doesn't care much about it—the girl is trying to be polite and reason—but the mother doesn't seem to care.

> The boy is supposed to take violin lessons—he doesn't care about it—he's sort of sleeping—he doesn't care to take violin lessons by the expression on his face—he didn't care to take lessons in the first place—he didn't listen to his elders—if he did he would take lessons.

The boy doesn't want to listen to his mother—he did wrong—his mother told him to be good—he didn't care—she told him not to bother her any more—she doesn't seem to care for him—if he listened to his mother nothing would have happened—he'll learn his lesson what his mother told him but it is too late.

From these stories, it seems clear that feelings of rejection are a basic factor in her personality organization and that as a result one finds her reacting by placing blame both inward onto herself and outward onto the family. Moralization appeared frequently in the stories as an expression of her own guilt feelings. Her dreams follow:

1. I dream of going out someday—my brother is in the service and I dream will I ever see him again.
2. I dreamt how I had a fight with a girl—we had an argument—we made up—and we were good friends after that.
3. Someone asked me to change my faith or be killed—I said I would rather die—I died in the dream.
4. I dreamt I was home—I went to a party—it ended late—my mother asked me to come home early—I told my friends that—they said: "The fun is just beginning"—I said I had to—one of the boys took me home—I was home in time.
5. I dreamt I ran away—I went home—I banged on the door—my father said he was coming to the door—but he never came—I waited—but I got tired—I went back to face my punishment.
6. I went home on Christmas—everything seemed different—I told them I was put away for training—they said I should have another chance.
7. I dreamt I walked out on a job—I felt awfully sorry—people told me how it would have been better if I didn't walk out.
8. I dreamt I would find a boy who liked me—I would have a nice home and children of my own.

The mixed feelings toward the home are again demonstrated. In several of the dreams one finds not only the strong desire to be home but also the deep feeling of rejection from the home this girl harbors. In dream 6 the parents forgivingly grant the girl "another chance" but in dream 5 the girl is not allowed admittance into her own home. In dream 4 the conflict between the rules of the mother and the desires of the girl is in evidence. In addition to dream 4 where there is an undercurrent of rebellion, dreams 3 and 7 are also illustrative of this girl's aggressive recalcitrance. The feelings of guilt, which seem connected with her negativistic attitude toward authority, are seen in dream 5 where she ran away but ultimately "went back to face my punishment," and in dream 7 in which "she felt awfully sorry" for walking out on a job—a usual occurrence in her institutional experience. It is clear that the projective material in the thematic stories and the dreams are largely concerned with similar personality factors.

Case 3

Rose is a 38-year-old woman who has been in institutions for mental de-fectives since 1915. She comes from a most disreputable family, in which the girl's father "traded the patient's mother for an alarm clock to his brother." Rose is a chronic runaway during which times she has had sex-ual intercourse with any and all men—a propensity which necessitated sterilization. Her IQ on the Stanford-Binet (1916) was 63. She has long had the reputation for possessing a fertile imagination of which intensive song and poem writing are only two examples. She has felt neglected be-cause her family has shown so little interest in her, and her disappoint-ment about this went so far as to deny at times that she knew anything about her people—maintaining that she had been found wrapped in a blanket beside a river.

Four main themes emerged from this girl's stories. The first had to do with ambivalent feelings toward the parents—especially the mother. In several stories the mother is described as being neglectful of the child and too authoritative, and in others the mother is seen as a benevolent, affectionate woman who becomes distraught at any misfortune which befalls her children. The following are two stories which illustrate the ambivalence:

> The mother shouldn't hold the baby that way—you are supposed to hold them more gently—she's a funny-acting woman—they ought to take the baby away because she don't know how to take care of it—(patient then demonstrated how gently one must handle a baby)—maybe she was married and had a child—her husband deserted her—she went a little wacky—I guess—she doesn't wear no shoes—suppose she thinks she's a Spanish dancer who doesn't need shoes.

> This little girl is sad—her people have gone away—she's looking out of the window—wondering whether they'll be back—if she was bigger she could go—she is staying with an aunt who is mean to her—she keeps looking and looking—she cries—her aunt calls her—you better come, Jane, it is supper—I don't want supper—I want my mother—her aunt says it will only be a few weeks—no, said the girl—I'll go with my mother— she packs her clothes and runs away—she is with her mother and is very happy.

The second theme which occurred frequently was concerned with a de-sire for money and recognition. In these stories the central character is usually one who from a humble and lowly position in life is able to rise to one of power and greatness. The following story is illustrative:

> This was a long time ago—his name is Bobby—his father said to him, I want you to be a musician like I was—the father bought him

a violin—he told Bobby to practice and he'll be famous like Tchai-kowsky—he got despondent one day—he put the violin down and said: Dad, there will never be any hope—I'll never be a violin player—Father said that practice makes perfect—he had to practice when he was younger—Bobby thought maybe you're right—he picks it up and starts to play—after all they bring him to New York in a con-cert—in front of Tchaikowsky—he said he was swell—he signed a contract—he became famous—Bobby now is the most famous vio-lin player in the world.

The two other themes which were considered of major importance were concerned with love and marriage, and with religious faith. Several sto-ries are concerned with "a married couple who were very happy" or with a man and woman who are "devoted to one another and fell in love." There is a tendency in these stories for the woman to be left alone be-cause the husband is sick or else "sailing away after kissing her goodbye." The theme of religious devotion, one which emerged frequently and was told with a note of fervor in her voice, is shown in the following story:

This is a hump back boy—he got it from infantile paralysis—his mother asks the doctor if his back will be all right—I don't think so, said the doctor—the only one who will make him better is to take him to Canada to the Saint's shrine—she went upstairs and prayed—before that he was laying on the couch discouraged—I'll never be better he thought—after he went to Canada he got bet-ter—now he got a job—making pretty good money—I had infantile paralysis.

There is no record of this girl's ever having infantile paralysis. It is also of interest to note how the desire for money crops out in this story as it does in many of the others. The dreams which this girl related are given below:

1. I was walking—I saw this house—it was a strange house—somebody was with me—they said go in—I said no—later I went in—I saw the snake wrapped around the pole—I got scared—I yelled and woke up.
2. I could see my father and mother—they said to me: you better be good—Pa, I said, I'm always good—they gave me a big crucifix—it shined pretty—I said to my mother: I always wanted one and never could get it.
3. I was walking on top of the water—then I went underneath it—as if there was an opening—I saw a mermaid—I said: what is this place called—this is wonderland—if you come with me I'll show you beau-tiful things—I walked with her—we came to a door—a golden door—I touched it—then beautiful things like diamonds and crystals came through it.
4. I dreamt I had St. Theresa's book—I put the book under my pillow—I

came out of the house—I saw my mother—she said where is St. Theresa's book—I said I didn't know—she said don't lie to me—she got awful mad at me—I tried to run away from her—she had hold of me—I couldn't go—I started crying—we came to a manhole—she said—you find me St. Theresa's book or I'll push you in—she pushed me in.

5. I dreamt I'm getting murdered—these men they shoot—I get it in the back—I can feel their hands around my neck—they are looking at me—I get scared—I can hear a lot of shooting.

6. Miss C took me to her home—her mother was there and my mother— she took me upstairs and showed me to her room—it was all in blue— a pretty blue—I said what a wonderful home—she said yes—I don't have to work for money anymore because I'm a millionaire—I came down stairs—I smelled something cooking—yelled upstairs: what are you cooking—chicken, she said—it don't smell like chicken—I went to the table—picked up the casserole—there were all kinds of ice cream—I ate and ate and ate.

7. I dreamt I was dying—I could see myself going—you can see the angels and the Lord—I saw the Lord right in front of me—it was so like real—I tried to wake up but couldn't—my heart beat faster—I heard voices saying—poor girl, she's dying.

8. I went out of here (Southbury), I was singing my songs in front of a microphone—I said to Al Jolson: do you think I'll go over big—sure, he said—I said: I've been practising and practising—I want to be a good singer and dancer—then I was on the stage—I had a beautiful gown on—I was tap dancing—in Hollywood—what a beautiful gown I had on.

When one remembers that the main themes which were elicited from this girl's stories were ambivalence to the parents (especially the mother), desire for recognition and greatness, love and affection, and religiousness, the significance of Rose's dreams becomes apparent. Again one finds (dreams 2 and 4) parents as being, on the one hand, protecting and kindly, on the other, harsh and condemning. The hostility of the mother towards the girl bears out the analysis of the thematic stories as to mixed feelings toward this parent. The guilt and anxiety which are found in the dreams, however, are not as strongly in evidence·in her stories. The desire for greatness, money, and recognition, which appeared so strongly in her stories, comes out with equal force in dreams 3, 6, and 8. The religiousness which was so obvious in her story likewise appears in dreams 2, 4, and 7. The theme of love and affection, the least clear of the major themes, is also only vaguely presented in the dreams.

The similarity between dreams and thematic stories illustrated in the three cases presented is also found when one analyzes the data obtained from the remaining subjects. Not in every case were all the major themas in the thematic found in the dreams, but in no case were data from any one subject at complete variance. The validity of thematic interpretations is felt to be demonstrated. The results of this study also show how easily obtained, projective data such as dreams can be used to corroborate a thematic analysis; another means is thus placed at one's disposal of reducing the errors introduced by the interpreter's biases.

What was I trying to prove in these earliest papers? Perhaps a better question is, what was being emphasized? I have no doubt that the emphasis was on the test and its applicability to mentally retarded individuals. Of course I was making the point, albeit very indirectly, that these individuals had "personality" in the same way that so-called normal people have a personality. But the main emphasis was on a way to get at certain aspects of personality in a population primarily seen and reacted to in terms of intellectual deficits. By inference, I was being critical of this emphasis and suggesting that the scales be more balanced. What I did not say in print but felt very strongly about was wrapped in the question: When will the field wake up to the fact that mentally retarded individuals are *persons*? When will that fact enter into our relationships and sense of obligations to them? When will we accord them the rights that go with being persons? Although these early studies had no discernible impact on the field, they certainly forced me, as I shall now show, to change certain of my attitudes.

From the day it opened, Southbury literally became an international showcase in terms of its architecture, facilities, and educational philosophy. Its cottages reflected a serious effort to make living there as homelike as possible. Nestled in a valley of rural Connecticut, Southbury looked like the campus of a small college. Southbury departed from traditional institutional architecture in obvious and esthetically pleasing ways. Its educational philosophy was no less innovative in that it aimed to give reality to the "revolving door" metaphor: Individuals could come in, have their needs assessed, have an appropriate program formulated, and, in the foreseeable future, would return to home and community. This policy was deliberately called a "revolving door" one to underline the intent to keep Southbury from becoming a custodial institution. It was not to be a medical institution; it was to be an educational one. When I came to Southbury, I truly marveled at its beauty and unrivaled facilities (both for employees as well as for the retarded residents). *Wasn't that retarded individual fortunate who could benefit from the opportunities Southbury provided?* If I, along with every other staff member, thought the residents were fortunate, the residents certainly thought otherwise. They did not want to be in Southbury; they wanted to be "outside," and running away was not rare. How more ungrateful (and stupid!) could anyone be? That is putting it somewhat strongly, but it does convey the mammoth gulf between their and our perception of what was good for them. *It was in the course of doing the TAT and dream studies—listening to and pondering the significance of the stories and dreams and relating those significances to the developmental-familial-social histories of each individual—that it began to dawn on me how little we understood those we sought to help.* From our perspective we did not see persons who had been separated from family and community, who yearned to be reunited with those most familiar to them, who felt unwanted and rejected by friends and family and grossly misunderstood by institutional personnel. What *we* saw were intellectually limited individuals, most of whom came from impoverished, unstable, and disabling homes in which the parents could not or would not meet the needs of their children, frequently abused and neglected them, and neither felt nor were able to manifest appropriate parental love. Given this stance, it never could occur to us that when you wrench an individual from the people and settings that are integral and indissoluble components of his or her sense of identity— even though the people and setting may violate your sense of what is good and bad, right and wrong—you cannot expect that individual to say "Thank you!" and to genuflect before your benevolence. You expect that only if you do not regard these individuals as persons capable of feeling loss, loneliness, remorse, and every emotion that has ever been described. As soon as you accord to another individual a sense of personal identity—that sense of I-ness and Me-ness—forged by the same forces in the same type of setting with similar types of people (e.g., family members), you have given the individual the status of a person and you have established kinship. You and that person may be wildly and dramatically different, you may have very different kinds of personality. Your histories may seem to be at polar opposites, but you have in common personhood, i.e., you both possess a sense of personal identity, know that you both have grown up in and belong to networks of kin and friends, attach this sense to circumscribed geographical areas, and are capable of experiencing the range of human feeling and emotions. If this concept of personhood seems fuzzy, muddled, and gooey, the following assertions may be clarifying:

1. The Nazis could lead people to the gas chambers because they did not regard their victims as persons. Instead, their victims were viewed as subhuman, inhuman, or antihuman.
2. Those who enslaved blacks did not view them as persons. First they had to view them as a kind of "object" and then they could justify enslaving them, buying them, or selling them.
3. When the early settlers began the process of forcing Indians to leave where they had long lived, it was because the Indians were not seen as

persons who had rootedness, a sense of personal and tribal identity, and embeddedness in a religious world view. Whatever the Indians were, they were not persons in the sense that the settlers regarded themselves as persons.

These are extreme instances of what can happen when people are denied the status of personhood, but they illustrate the fact that such a denial permits, indeed frequently justifies, treating people as if they were incapable of longings, attachments, intimacy, fantasy, mourning, striving, etc.

Why I came to Southbury predisposed to regard the residents as persons would require an unnecessary autobiographical excursion. Suffice it to say, my radical political ideology and experience as a Jew (in what was a far less tolerant world than today) predisposed me to identify with the residents, to try to see the world from their standpoint. To say more would add nothing to the fact that the very existence of Southbury implied that its residents had an incapacity for personhood: It was isolated in the middle of rural nowhere, with the state as court-appointed guardian; involuntary commitment was the rule rather than the exception; and the residents were regarded as and called "children," regardless of age and appearance.

In no way am I calling into question the sincerity or humanness of those who created and maintained Southbury. They did create a setting that was qualitatively different and better than that which existed elsewhere; they wanted to and did attempt to provide the residents with more stimulation and opportunity. But their desire to be more humane rested on the explicit assumption that those they sought to help lacked the capacity for personhood: *They were like clay to be molded into this or that form, and to do this did not require one to know the ingredients of which the clay was compounded.* And that is the point: For all practical purposes the internal psychologic states of the residents were at best ignored and at worst interpreted as the hallmark of their intellectual deficits. The TAT studies demonstrated that many of the residents had a keen sense of personhood: who they were, to whom they were related, the need to love and be loved, the fear of loss and separation, and a sense of territoriality (where home was and what it was like).

But why this emphasis on personhood? Have not attitudes and practices changed since the early forties when the TAT studies were published? Are not the conclusions drawn from these studies "old hat"? Am I suggesting that there has been a great deal of change but far less of progress? I have no doubt that today more people think of and respond to mentally retarded individuals as persons than ever before. As we shall see in later chapters, there are many reasons for this change, remarkable both for its direction and speed. But one reason needs to be noted here because it casts the change in a very interesting light. That reason is the parents' movement, which emboldened increasing numbers of parents to keep their retarded children at home in their "natural community" and

to resist advice and attitudes that ignored what so many parents knew—
that their children, however handicapped, were embedded in a network
of reciprocal relationships no less important to their existence than the
air they breathed. To many parents, their children were not "objects" but
persons who *experienced* their milieu; they were not empty vessels who
could or should be placed here or moved there. Parents knew that however different the style or organization of experience might be from those
of "normal" individuals, the content, quality, and duration of experience
were influenced by the same internal and external factors we conceptualize in order to understand *any* person's behavior. In my experience, the
greatest progress toward regarding retarded individuals as persons has
been among parents, for whom the change has been far greater than for
any other group associated with the field of mental retardation. Put in
another way (leaving parents aside), I am not impressed by the amount of
change that has occurred either in relating to or in studying retarded individuals as persons. It is true, of course, that as a society we have accorded these individuals rights and opportunities they never had before,
and that this is a cause for gratification. But let us not assume that in
according them rights we are also according them the status of personhood. To accord the status of personhood requires that we see and act on
the similarities between ourselves and others, all differences to the contrary notwithstanding. "To see and act on the similarities"—by these criteria, not many people know how to accord personhood to retarded individuals. To elaborate on this point, I turn next to an activity that followed
and was very much influenced by those initial TAT studies. That activity
was individual psychotherapy, an activity that, whatever else it may be,
involves people in a mutually meaningful relationship in which one person seeks to be helpful to another person.

Individual Psychotherapy

It is one thing to interact with people for the purpose of "studying" them
(e.g., as in the TAT and dream studies); it is quite another thing to interact
for the purposes of understanding and helping them. The former is a
"one way street" interaction in which it is clear that the other person has
something you need or want to know for which you pledge little or nothing in return. The latter is based on an agreement that feelings and attitudes will be verbalized and discussed for the purpose of a mutual understanding that is the vehicle by which one of the parties seeks to be
helpful and the other gains the sense of being helped. What is distinctive
(not unique) about psychotherapy is that it rests on the implicit but bed-
rock assumption that the two interacting individuals share a number of

common characteristics. They may be very different kinds of people, but each acts as if his or her similarities will permit mutual understanding and give to both an increased appreciation of their similarities. The therapist accords to the other person his or her own status: personhood. When we say that one of the characteristics of an effective psychotherapist is the ability to identify with the other person, we mean (among other things) that there is sufficient similarity between the two to enable the therapist to put himself or herself into "the client's world" with the consequence that that world becomes comprehensible. "If I saw the world (or any part of it) the way the client sees it, I would have similar thoughts and feelings and I would act in similar ways"—this stance is not possible unless the therapist assumes the existence of certain similarities in personhood.

One feature of the psychotherapeutic relationship is as obvious as it is important: The client experiences "psychologic pain," e.g., anxiety, sadness, inferiority, guilt, shame, or some combination of these. And the client wants to feel otherwise. I did not have to spend many hours at Southbury to conclude that many of its residents were "hurting" psychologically. And it did not take more hours to discern that the sources and manifestations of the hurting were explained by the staff in the most superficial ways—when they were explained at all. I have to emphasize that as a group the staff was in those days as motivated, caring, and solicitous as one could wish. But it was a caring that saw almost every manifestation of hurting as a result of being a child, of intellectual defects, or of both. Rarely was so much explained by so little. No one consciously or deliberately denied the residents the status of personhood. They just could not imagine that these residents had an "inner life" the way they did, i.e., an inner world of fantasy, longing, guilt, shame, memories, etc. And when I say "imagine," I refer to that process by which you try to enter another person's world. Nobody tried to enter the world of the Southbury residents. How (or why) can you enter a world you assume either hardly exists or the substance and organization of which are not explainable (or worth explaining) by "our" psychology?

Let me say a few words about the institutional, professional, and social-historical context in which our (Esther Sarason and I) efforts have to be viewed. In those days the practice of psychotherapy was considered a medical-psychiatric activity. Psychologists did testing and research, social workers visited homes and wrote up case histories, and psychiatrists did psychotherapy at the same time that they "led" the mental health team. From the standpoint of the medical profession these arrangements were rooted in law as well as in tradition and professional preparation. There was nothing resembling a challenge to this delineation of roles. But there were always a few psychologists who considered these arrangements more a manifestation of professional imperialism than of demonstrable validity or of rational argument. More important, these role boundaries were obstacles to the development of new psycho-therapeutic approaches to diverse groups in the society. Professions change far more in response to outside challenges and societal changes than they do in response to the dynamics of their internal structure, traditions, and membership characteristics. So, for example, if you want to understand why the field of mental retardation remained relatively unchanged in its basic outlook, practices, and accomplishments until recent decades, your understanding will be grievously incomplete unless you take into account the degree to which the field was dominated (in terms of policy and power) by the medical profession. I do not say this in the spirit of criticism but rather as a way of emphasizing that the definition and approach to any social problem are in part a function of the professional group to which the larger society has given a leading role. That professional group both reflects and affects the social perspective. Again, Southbury is a case in point. When it came time to appoint a superintendent for this new and innovative institution, the Board of Trustees recommended to the governor Mr. Ernest Roselle, an educator who had been the chief consultant to the Board during the years Southbury was being planned and built. When the medical association got wind of this, it exerted its considerable influence to abort the recommendation and to make sure that a physician would be appointed. It was quite a donnybrook in which everyone agreed on one point: To appoint a nonphysician was a dramatic departure from tradition. The recommendation was close to rejection when the Board made it clear to the governor that they would have no choice but to resign *en masse* if their nominee was turned down. Mr. Roselle was appointed. The medical fraternity was absolutely correct in predicting that Southbury would be different from other institutions for the mentally retarded if the superintendent was not a physician. That is precisely what the Board intended, and for a number of years Southbury was regarded, nationally and internationally, as an *educationally* distinctive institution. And this reputation undoubtedly made it easier for others to depart from a tradition that had become stultifying.

As the chief psychologist at Southbury I was directly responsible to Mr. Roselle, who rarely, if ever, told me what to do. The medical director, Dr. Herman Yannet, was a research-oriented pediatrician who did not take kindly to psychiatrists and who was completely supportive of what I was doing. There were no psychiatrists at Southbury. For all practical purposes, there were no restrictions on what I could do, innovative or not, as long as it raised no moral or ethical issues. In short, it was a very atypical setting that stimulated and supported new approaches. Indeed, at that time Southbury was unique among institutions. As a result, when we decided to "try out" psychotherapy with some of the residents, we simply went ahead and tried it out. Below is reprinted a large fraction of a chapter on psychotherapy that appeared in *Psychological Problems in Mental Deficiency* (Sarason, 1949), a book that I began to write as soon as I left Southbury to go to Yale. I have included the beginning segment of that chapter, containing a literature review, for three reasons. The first is to convey the degree to which mentally retarded individuals were responded to as individuals incapable of reflecting upon their experience, communicating thoughts and feelings in the process of forming a relationship explicitly geared to altering behavior, and communicating attitudes toward self and others. The second reason, related to the first, is that this way of viewing mentally retarded individuals was so strong, so "obviously valid," that any evidence to the contrary was ignored. The third reason, and from my standpoint the most important, is that I do not think that the situation *today* is dramatically different from that of those far-off decades. But more about that later.

Psychotherapy[4]

It is generally assumed that the mentally defective individual is unable to benefit from a psychotherapeutic relationship. The paucity of studies in this area is witness to this assumption. The inability of such an individual to control or delay emotional expression, to see and to accept socially appropriate substitute activities in the face of frustrations and restrictions, to view objectively the behavior of others, to adjust or to want to adjust to the needs of others, to realize the sources and consequences of his behavior—these have been considered the liabilities of the defective individual which make it difficult for him to comprehend and to adjust to the purposes of the psychotherapeutic interview. When one considers that language is almost the sole means of communication between therapist and patient and that the defective individual has inordinate difficulty in using and comprehending verbal generalizations, it is not surprising that the usual psychotherapeutic interview has been viewed as unfeasible with such individuals. For an individual to be aware that he "has a problem" implies that he has verbalized to himself or others his reaction to certain experiences and relationships; he sees or judges himself in terms of other people's behavior or standards. Without verbalization of the problem he is unable to take steps to solve it. This is implied in Allen's statement (1942), "The therapeutic process occurs as a unique growth experience, *created* by one person who accepts the responsibility of offering it. This basic structure characterizes each potentially therapeutic setting irrespective of methods or techniques employed or of whether it is a child or adult who seeks assistance" (italics mine). It has generally been felt that the defective individual's inability to see or verbalize (and to become aware of) the interpersonal nature of his problems makes him unable to seek help (to create the therapeutic relationship) or to understand the purposes of an individual offering it.

It should be clearly stated that the above conclusions about the un-

TABLE 1. Recommended environmental changes as related to intellectual level in 292 clinic referrals

	Defective	Borderline	Dull normal	Average	Superior
Number in group	29	48	94	102	19
To remain in present placement	24%	48%	43%	44%	26%
Foster home recommended	7%	21%	39%	42%	63%
Institution recommended	66%	18%	4%	4%	0%
Other change recommended	3%	12%	14%	10%	11%

feasibility of psychotherapeutic interviews with defective children have been based more on deductions from theoretical considerations than on systematic research findings. Many practical considerations have prevented research in this area. The tremendous demand for psychotherapeutic help, the scarcity of trained personnel, and the amount of time which such efforts entail have forced clinicians to give what little time they have to those cases which promise the most results in the shortest period of time.

The disposition of the defective individual referred to a clinic can be seen from Rogers' survey (1937) of treatment measures used with 292 children. The data in Table 1 show that institutionalization is by far the most frequent recommendation made in the case of defective individuals. Gaudet and Gaudet (1940) in a survey of 1040 cases diagnosed as mentally defective in twelve mental hygiene clinics in New Jersey, also found that institutionalization was the most frequent recommendation. Rogers' statement that theoretical considerations suggest that the defective individual is "scarcely receptive to (psychotherapeutic) treatment" reflects the attitude of other clinicians (Harrower-Erickson, 1940; Healy and Bronner, 1939; Hutton, 1945; Lurie, Levy, and Rosenthal, 1944; Witmer, 1946). In their follow-up study of 400 cases treated at the Judge Baker Guidance Center, Healy and Bronner (1939, p. 22) stated that "very rarely have we accepted for treatment any case that was graded as feeble-minded." They found that the lower the I.Q. the greater the probability of a later unfavorable adjustment. That caution must be exercised in the interpretation of these findings is evident from the following statement by them (Healy and Bronner, 1939, p. 34):

> But we insist that there are many reasons for caution in inter-
> pretation. In particular no inference can be drawn that there is a
> direct causal relationship between the quality of the career and the
> I.Q. For example, in trying to determine why there was such a large
> proportion of unfavorable careers in the I.Q. 70–79 group we found
> other factors largely involved. In three cases the family and general
> social situation of the individual was so bad that it could not be
> modified; three others suffered from severe biological handicaps as
> well as from poor family circumstances; two had early established
> such prevailing patterns of delinquent behavior that they could not
> be broken; one was an abnormal personality; and the only individ-
> ual with an I.Q. as low as 70 was so defective and had such a sense
> of inferiority and insecurity that he was not capable of responding
> to clinical treatment.

> On the other hand, in five cases of the same intelligence level
> the reasons for favorable careers were equally clear. Four of them
> came from families who were co-operative with us and fairly ade-
> quate in understanding—which was not true for any single one of
> those showing unfavorable careers. In one instance, after consider-
> able attempt at treatment by the clinic much devoted work was
> done on the case by a probation officer.

Although each child in the study was seen for at least one interview, the range being from one to over a hundred, it is not possible to deter-mine the number of times each of the children with I.Q.'s between 70 and 79 was seen. In the case of those who made favorable adjustments it would have been interesting to know the number of times each child was seen in an individual interview and the degree of therapeutic gain ef-fected thereby. It may have been that these cases had relatively few inter-views and that improvement in adjustments was effected through work with the parents. Since the exceptional case can be extremely instructive, it is unfortunate that the case with whom a probation officer did "much devoted work" was not elaborated upon. It is not clear from Healy and Bronner's discussion whether none, some, or all of the cases with I.Q.'s between 70 and 79 were mentally defective. They do state that two of these cases "were considered to be morons." Since all cases had an I.Q. of at least 70, it is not clear how the two cases were distinguished from non-morons of similar I.Q. It may be that there were only two cases in the series who were considered mentally defective, but in the absence of ex-plicit criteria this point cannot be clarified.

It should be stated here that one of the chief difficulties in evalu-ating the feasibility of psychotherapy with mental defectives is that the criteria for the diagnosis of cases so labeled either are not stated or are restricted to an intelligence test score. In other instances, the use of test-score classifications beclouds rather than clarifies the problem. For example, Cooley (1945–46) compared psychotherapeutic results with a group of dull and of bright children referred to a child guidance clinic. The bright group was comprised of 25 children with I.Q.'s above 115. The dull group consisted of 16 children with I.Q.'s between 76 and 84 and 9 with I.Q.'s between 61 and 74. Cases were matched for sex, age, and economic status. A question that immediately arises about the "dull" group concerns its homogeneity. With the use of inclusive criteria of mental deficiency, how many of these cases would have been diagnosed as mentally defective? Is the use of the label *dull* an indication that *all* these cases did not meet the inclusive criteria for mental deficiency? If these cases had been seen in other clinics, how many would have been diagnosed as defective, and of these how many would have been given psychotherapy?—a speculation intended to emphasize the disparity in criteria and practices employed by various clinicians and agencies. The data necessary for answering these questions are not given.

The importance of these questions may be seen from Cooley's finding that there is no particular relationship between test-score level and adjustment at the close of psychotherapeutic treatment, a result similar to that obtained by Glassman (1945) and Wegman (1943). "Over half of the children of inferior intelligence had from one to ten hours of therapy, while only four of the bright children had so few interviews with a psychiatrist. Only five of the children of low intellectual level had more than twenty hours of therapy, in contrast to thirteen, or over half, of the superior children. Since the outcome of therapy appeared to be equally successful with the dull group, it would appear that the children of inferior intelligence required no more and in many cases less expenditure of time in treatment than the superior children" (Cooley, 1945–46). Although Cooley's results indicate that "dull" children are amenable to and benefit from psychotherapeutic interviews, the fact that only the I.Q. of the cases was reported sheds merely suggestive light on the feasibility of such procedures with mentally defective individuals.

Although in his study of psychotherapy with "fifty-five 'bad' boys" Hartwell (1940) states that cases with mental defect were not selected for treatment, he does include one such case in his reports. This boy, who was classified as feeble-minded in the moron range, was referred to the clinic because of the appearance of psychotic-like symptoms: increased tendency to stay by himself and active daydreaming "which causes him suddenly to laugh aloud."

In psychiatric interviews Melvin responded differently from most children with his mental equipment. He reached the rapport of personality contact very quickly. Because of his responses he has been encouraged to maintain this relation and has been seen regularly during the past two years. He has given during that time and in that rapport much interesting material to think about. In his slow, plodding way he has thought with me about many problems that most children with an intelligence quotient of 73 could not recognize as existing.

Melvin has never been questioned deeply about his mental problems or urged to tell about them. He wants to do so, and at each visit he has new questions to ask and he asks the old ones over again, saying he has forgotten. But he has not forgotten. He likes to hear again such encouragement as someone whom he can trust may give him.

"Is there ever any boys who can't learn like me who maybe get so they can learn fast? Does an engineer on a train have to be smart? Are you sure you know I can make my living when I grow big? I wish I was big now, only I'm afraid I can't make my living. How did my brothers learn to be smart? What makes folks like my brothers better than me? Does it hurt you to die? Can anyone always be good if they try to?" On every occasion I have seen him, he has talked about and wished he were older and could earn his own living. Over and over again he says he does not want other folks to have to give him money. He never has failed to thank me at the close of the interview for talking to him.

Melvin and I have thought about many practical things that might help him with his problems. (At one time we decided that it might help to make his home more pleasant if I were to see his brothers. Possibly this helped with the situation somewhat. The brothers willingly came. They proved to be intelligent boys who were anxious to help Melvin in any way they could. They had been noticing his increased unhappiness and were concerned about it.) We thought about Melvin's unusual ability to find his way in strange places. He can be trusted to go from one part of the city to another, even though he has never been there before, as well as the average boy of his age or better.

When I first knew Melvin, he was just entering a somewhat premature puberty. At that time he was disgusted and worried about some experiences he had had with another boy, who had attempted to teach him sex habits. Recently he has been more concerned about these old happenings and about his own developing sex emotions. He says: "One reason I want to come and see you is that you will tell me more about these dirty things." He badly needs someone to think both with him and for him concerning his sex problems. At his last interview he told me that he could not refrain from hunting for news dispatches about sex attacks and sex murders. He would find them and persist until his grandmother would read them to him. He says that the ones that tell about crazy men who perpetrate these attacks made him feel "awful funny and bad."

He says: "They make me feel like if maybe I would do such things some time, but then I won't. I'd be afraid. Anyway, it's wrong." Melvin has never masturbated.

He has always talked about suicide. At first it was simply because of an interest he had in it. More lately he has been thinking about suicide. He says: "I might do it if I were not a coward, but I won't. It would hurt me, and I'm afraid."

One interesting thing about this boy is the fact that he is always happier and less worried and upset for a time after he talks with me. He is always anxious to come for an interview. He is very careless about his dress (though he is painstaking about most things) except when he is coming to the clinic, when he will dress himself with great care.

Results: His parents feel that his interviews do him so much temporary good that they are of great help, both to them and to the boy. He seems less discouraged and a little more extroverted for a short time after them. He seems to do a little better in his school work. (He is working in an ungraded class and making but little progress, though he always tries hard). I have tried to encourage Melvin in every way I could without doing so in a way that would make him unhappy later. He considers me a very good friend and thinks I understand how he feels. While this latter belief, I fear, is not true to any great extent, it is one that may be encouraged without later doing him harm.

The family believes that to some extent the boy's personality traits have been changed for the better. This is very doubtful. However, two definite things have been accomplished: one is that the boy has been made happier, and the other is that I have established myself in his and the family's confidence to the extent that if he becomes an institutional case, as he probably will soon, I may be of help to them in adjusting to the situation.

During the year following my first interviews with Melvin the boy was for several months in a foster-home on a large farm. Here he did well, but finally became dissatisfied and is now at home again. He sees either Dr. Bronner or me occasionally. He desires these interviews. He still has remarkable insight into his mental life for a boy who is presenting many definite psychotic symptoms. Perhaps if he can continue to have a little psychiatric bolstering up from time to time he may live always outside of an institution. But I feel that he will always be of potential danger to others as well as to himself.

Hartwell's doubts about the boy's future adjustment should not obscure the fact that he considered the boy to have benefited from treatment. It would seem that this case at least allows one to ask the question whether other defective boys with nonpsychotic-like symptoms would have benefited even more from individual psychotherapy. It should be noted that aside from an I.Q. of 72 the data on which the diagnosis of mental deficiency was made are not given.

> He was eleven years old when first seen. His health has always been good, his physical development somewhat above the age average. The change in the appearance of the boy may be judged from the notes in regard to this taken from his first and last physical examinations. The first describes him as "an active, healthy, good-looking youngster"; the last, "a dull, coarse, irregular-featured boy." The psychological examinations which have been made at intervals of about a year show a remarkable consistency in all respects. His intelligence quotient as first determined was 73, at the second test given him 72, and at the last two 73. This is particularly interesting because of the fact that the boy, in his appearance and somewhat in his responses, seemed to be gradually deteriorating. His school-work had always been below that of his mental age.

It is not clear from this account whether the boy's inadequacies represent the effects of developmental arrest due to presumed constitutional factors or are related to a not too well-understood psychological process.

Chidester and Menninger (1936) reported a case of a supposedly mentally defective boy with whom psychoanalytic therapy was attempted. Because this study contains far more data on background and therapeutic technique than other reports, it is presented in some detail.

> Henry was the first of four children. Birth was normal. Artificial feeding was begun in the sixth month. He walked and talked at a normal age and was said to have been trained in toilet habits early. He was subject to frequent colds until his third year at which time his tonsils and adenoids were removed.
>
> At the time that Henry's parents were married his father was a university student and was unable to provide a home for his wife, who remained with her parents until several years after the child was born. When the patient was about four years old the mother went to her husband and they established a home of their own, but were persuaded to leave Henry with his grandparents. They had three more children, but Henry was never a part of that household. He continued to live with his grandparents and alone he occupied the room that he had formerly shared with his brother.
>
> A cousin was born into the household of the grandparents when Henry was in his fourth year and from birth was Henry's rival for the family attention.
>
> The grandparents first suspected that the patient was retarded when he repeatedly failed in school. During his first year in school,

the grandparents made an extended trip, leaving him with his parents. While they were gone he did poor school work. A nurse reported his poor vision (16 percent) but his parents neglected to do anything about it. The child became increasingly unhappy and when his grandparents returned they found him acutely ill with appendicitis. Against his father's will they removed him to a hospital for an operation.

Afterward the grandparents took the boy away with them, had his eyes fitted with glasses and started him in another school. He failed several times and passed twice on condition. He made excellent grades in reading and spelling, but his arithmetical comprehension was nil and his writing was poor. After five years he was promoted to the third grade because of his ability to read. It was evident that he was wholly unable to compete with boys of his age even in their play. Therefore, he was placed in the Southard School at the age of eleven years.

Entrance examination revealed little organic pathology except for poor motor coordination and defective vision corrected with glasses. Our neurologist who later examined the child was of the opinion that he had acalculia due to definite organic lesion such as has been described by Gerstmann, Singer and Low. He scored an I.Q. of 62 (Stanford-Binet) and his emotional development gauged by his general interests, was equally retarded.

He was a small boy who constantly hung his head as though abashed. His deep voice contrasted strangely with his immature appearance and he was exceedingly awkward. His face seldom lost its pleasant expression and he seemed unmoved by the struggles that went on around him. He appeared to like everyone at the school, but demonstrated no affection for them nor any desire for affection from them. Instead of loving people he seemed to attach his fondness to inanimate objects, and spent most of his time collecting indiscriminately such things as empty cereal boxes, tin cans, milk bottle stoppers, discarded auto tags, and other debris. Those he put in his room and carefully guarded them, and when any such possession was lost or discarded in the process of house cleaning, it was nothing less than a tragedy to Henry, who burst into tears as though a relative had died.

He was tremendously selfish. He freely partook of the candy and toys of the other children, but his own he enjoyed in solitude. Though he demanded many gifts he was never grateful for them. In conversation he eagerly asked for information, but volunteered none and when asked the simplest questions was disinclined to give any information. His conversation was often so incoherent as to be unintelligible, and he was exasperatingly slow in all aspects of his behavior like a long drama in slow-motion pictures.

During the first year at the Southard School he studied first grade arithmetic but was able neither to understand number facts nor to retain them from rote memory. His writing remained scarcely legible, but he read rather well and enjoyed the newspapers especially.

Because the boy had no appreciation of his problems it "was necessary to devote a period to wooing Henry's affection and confidence. The therapist saw him for an hour each day, during which time games were played and small gifts made to him. After this preparatory period the patient was instructed to lie down on a couch and to express freely any ideas that came to him. The psychologist sat a little distance from the head of the couch and out of the patient's sight." Many difficulties were encountered by this orthodox psychoanalytic procedure.

There was little evidence of spontaneity, he exhibited no initiative in play, work or study; in general there appeared no eagerness to learn, he was not especially alert to his immediate surroundings and often could not evaluate what he did see. He produced no memories antedating his coming to the school. Instead of being pliable, his whole personality manifested a quality of inelasticity, a fact that was very discouraging to the therapists. And most of all his appreciation for reality seemed feeble as manifested by (1) his tendency to daydream excessively, (2) his lack of knowledge about and judgment concerning the objects of his most immediate environment and (3) his frank delusions. His thought processes seemed exceedingly retarded so that his speech was monotonous, slow, and halting. He often required as much as fifteen minutes to complete one sentence.

These liabilities made it necessary for the therapist to present interpretations to the boy in a direct fashion.

During the first few months much resistance was expressed in the form of sullenness, tardiness, silence, or constant questioning on the part of the patient. By Christmas the child was consciously resentful of having to come for treatment and at last he asked to be excused from it. He announced that he did not like the psychologist, and when questioned he gave as his reason the fact that she talked to the other children at the school. This admission of jealousy was an opening wedge for a strong relationship and hence, further treatment, for it was explained to him that someone else must have abandoned him for another child. Immediately he admitted that his mother had given him to his grandmother and he felt that the love she once bestowed on him was withdrawn and reinvested in his younger sister. Thus the boy was helped to see that the hostility that he expressed toward the psychologist was that which he felt toward his mother. After realizing this the child of his own accord decided to continue treatment, and was much more cooperative.

He expressed great disdain for his father and for his father's profession and demanded to be called by the name of his grandparents rather than that of his father. At first he refused to speak of his mother and siblings, and when questioned about them, professed to have forgotten their names and ages although he had visited them but a few months before.

One day the psychologist came with a new permanent wave, and the boy refused to have anything to do with her. He said that her hair was too kinky and it reminded him of Negroes. When asked who else had kinky hair, he replied that his siblings had such hair. After much persuasion he showed their pictures to the therapist. They did appear to be Negroid and were much darker than others in the pictures. Henry made numerous remarks to the effect that these children were not smart, not pretty, and not good children.

About this time he began to fantasy that he would like to have a child and be its mother and nurse it. He would want only the one child, he said, unless he got married, and then he might have three more. This was his idea of what his mother had done. That is, he believed himself to be illegitimate. . . .

During the second period he began to relate his dreams and through their interpretations he began to be aware of his hostility toward his father and his desire to replace the latter in his relations with his mother. It was also by means of his dreams that he realized his tremendous hostility toward his cousin and his jealousy of the attention which his grandmother gave the boy. Following his awareness of hostility, he, once mild and passive, became very sadistic, kicking and beating the smaller boys with a ruler which he carried concealed in his trousers. At the same time he talked to the psychologist of the unfair treatment he had received from his cousin. She was able to correlate his behavior with the children at the school with his feelings of anger for his cousin and to interpret his sadism as meant for the cousin. Following this interpretation his sadism receded.

As his confidence in the psychologist developed he began to confess his excessive night prowling. He said that he frequently woke in the night and went through the house and yard naked, touching his penis compulsively to the back of his teacher's chair and going to the barn loft where he covered his feet and genitals with dirt. On other nights he tried to peep at the women and girls and stole their clothing, especially shoes, hose and pajamas. Sometimes he slept in these articles and fantasied that one of the women was in bed with him. The climax of these erotic fantasies was that

they would expose themselves to each other and defecate and uri-
nate together. How extraordinary it is to get such information and
fantasies from retarded children need scarcely be mentioned!

He bought a gaudy ring, wore red nail polish, carried a com-
pact and demanded feminine lingerie. He reported fantasies of having babies and dreams of having intercourse with men. After seeing
the moving picture "State Fair" he identified himself with the beautiful trapeze artist and wished "that I could have some nice looking
man like that fall in love with me." The realization that he wanted to
be a woman and could not be one depressed him for days. He envied women their breasts and frequently expressed a desire to in-
jure those of the psychologist so that men might cease to pay attention to her and turn to him.

In the beginning period of the second year of treatment the boy's
interest in anal matters, masturbatory activity, and sexual fantasies became more and more marked. "During this period of anal indulgence, he
was making excellent grades in his number work and for the first time he
had been able to report quite a few perfect lessons in arithmetic. In general his school work seemed to have improved rapidly." When he returned to school after a month at home during the midwinter holidays,
he displayed extremely aggressive behavior.

Upon his return to the school two aspects of his behavior were
prominent, his insistence on the monopoly of the bathroom and his
sadism toward a smaller boy whom he kicked till the child was
bruised from his hip to his ankle. But his conversation during the
treatment period concerned only his tremendous envy and jealousy of the younger and brighter cousin, his old rival. When his
mistreatment of the poor child was interpreted to him as his desire
to hurt his cousin he told one of a number of delusions which he
held, namely, that he believed that when a boy left the school and
later a new boy entered, the new boy was the old one disguised. The
boy whom he kicked he had believed for many months to be the
cousin in disguise who had come to spy upon him.

As a punishment for some of his aggression, he was denied the
privilege of reading the newspapers for a time. Immediately he became sullen and less cooperative. In reporting this matter to the
psychologist, he added, "And I was as mad as a hungry bear." At this
same time he confessed that he had begun eating garbage and food
that had been given to a dog. Writing he had equated to the excre-
tion and smearing of feces, and reading what someone else wrote
seemed to be a mode of incorporating this valuable substance—a
sublimation. And when this sublimation was denied him, he regressed to a more primitive stage, that of eating refuse or unclean
matter.

He had become much more insistent on monopolizing the bath. He said he spent much time trying to expel large quantities of feces and would stand and gaze at his excrement for considerable periods. He said he liked to see what large quantity he could get which was the exact expression he used in speaking of his collections of useless objects. He began to go to the bathroom as soon as it was vacated by others in order to ascertain the quantity of their excrement so as to compare it with his. Once after viewing that left by a girl he remarked disdainfully, "That was much smaller than mine." Thus it was possible to see that both his hoarding and his toilet interests were attempts to compensate for his fear of sexual inferiority. He was able to see that he was annoying everyone but said he wished to annoy the psychologist for having continued to see other children and that he wished to annoy his teachers for hurrying him with his number work in which he had become exasperatingly slow and exceedingly inaccurate. When asked what he objected to being hurried in doing, he said, "I don't want to be hurried about my bowel movements." He was told that arithmetic as well as some other things at which he insisted on taking his time were symbolic of the toilet activity. Again he began to do good school work. . . .

At times he regressed in his arithmetic and in his bathroom habits. At such times he was often resistant to his treatment but it always turned out that he has been unable to stand seeing the teachers giving any quantity of attention to the other children and purposely failed in his arithmetic to provoke the teacher to nag and give him attention. Then he stayed in the bathroom so long so that he would be punished, and thus absolve his guilt. With this interpretation both forms of misconduct decreased, and he began to show definite progress.

One day the psychologist had an opportunity to watch Henry with his arithmetic. His teacher assigned the lesson, then those of the other children one by one. Then she returned to Henry who had not written a thing, but who on hearing her approach, scratched his head, knitted his brows, bit his pencil and looked fixedly at his problems. The teacher began, "Why, Henry, haven't you written a thing?" Henry shifted his position, scratched his head, leaned closer to the paper and made as though to write. The teacher then went to the next pupil. When she returned again Henry had made a few marks and spent most of the time erasing them. He was no farther along than before. This time the teacher was a bit more severe. She stood by him watching him and told him to get to work. Henry went through all the appearances of profound cerebration, but produced nothing, offered no explanation, asked no help. Finally as the teacher became very insistent he slowly marked down some answers which were remarkably inaccurate. One was reminded of a mother who has set an infant on the toilet seat and insisted that he defecate. The child grunts and grimaces and gives all the appearances of making strenuous effort to defecate, when in reality he is trying hard not to.

During the third year of treatment there was a marked improvement in his attitude and relations with other children, an improvement which disappeared as soon as he went home for a vacation. He returned in bad humor and was very indifferent to treatment.

In order to overcome his resistance, he was charged 10 cents a day for his treatment after March, 1935, and the school offered to pay him 10 cents for various small jobs. That is, the psychologist unwittingly charged the child his total earnings, his entire childish fortune. He refused any work whereby he could earn the dime and became very resistant and day after day he seemed to regress in the type of material he brought, in his school work, and in his general attitude. An eating disturbance appeared and although he was given five meals a day he steadily lost weight. In June 1935 when he was again given psychometric tests, he scored an I.Q. of 75 on the Stanford-Binet and much worse on the performance tests. In this regressed condition he went home for the summer. When he returned this fall he still scored very low on the tests and he seemed less able to adjust to situations around him. The psychologist felt that either there was an organic deterioration or more likely there was insufficient gratification to permit progress. It occurred to her that since she took as payment all the money he made, he was deprived of all the pleasure of the money he earned and hence the endless paying and working must seem futile to him. Therefore, she began returning to him a dime of his earnings each week, and praised him for his efforts. Very soon his interests improved and his psychomotor retardation lessened. He began to bring new aspects of his conflicts and seemed able to accept and assimilate interpretations. On tests given in his improved condition he scored a mental age of 13 years 2 months, and an I.Q. of about 90 on the Stanford-Binet, and a mental age of 15 years on the Porteus Maze tests. The performance tests were solved correctly but still a little slower than normal.

For the first time he was aware that some situations appeared real and some unreal to him, and discovered that his participation in a situation, particularly if he were able to make decisions, enhanced its reality value for him. He began to see himself in relation to his environment and made definite efforts to be like others and to accept reality.

Results from the Binet which was administered periodically during the four years of treatment follow:

September	1931	I.Q. 62
September	1932	I.Q. 65
February	1933	I.Q. 73
May	1933	I.Q. 77
October	1933	I.Q. 80
April	1934	I.Q. 87
September	1934	I.Q. 88
March	1935	I.Q. 90
June	1935	I.Q. 75
September	1935	I.Q. 77

One of the questions that might be asked about the case reported by Chidester and Menninger concerns the validity of the original diagnosis of mental deficiency. This question may be raised because two of the criteria of mental deficiency are that it is a condition that is likely to obtain at maturity and is essentially incurable. The problem may be posed as follows: Although before treatment this boy was socially incompetent for his age, very retarded intellectually, and showed indications of a brain lesion, was there evidence for believing that the condition was curable? If there was such evidence before treatment, the diagnosis of mental deficiency could be questioned. Although Chidester and Menninger stated that "the patient presented numerous symptoms indicative of a severe long standing emotional disturbance," they did not state whether they considered the disturbance the sole cause or effect of the boy's intellectual deficiency. The fact that they termed their study an experiment suggests that they entertained doubts about the curability of the case. In effect, their therapeutic efforts served as a test for their original diagnosis. More important, perhaps, than the question of the validity of the original diagnosis is the speculation about the number of times that similar cases (low I.Q., social incompetence, positive neurological signs) referred to clinics have been diagnosed as mentally defective without any therapeutic test of the diagnosis. Although clinicians are aware that the learning process may be seriously affected by emotional factors, the fact that a given case has a low I.Q. in addition to positive neurological signs (which are sometimes given undue weight) usually disposes the clinician to deemphasize etiological factors of a psychological nature and to emphasize the organic factors. Had Chidester and Menninger considered their case as one of mental deficiency due to some organic factors (the exogenous type of defective) in which psychotherapeutic procedures were not indicated, their diagnosis would not have been questioned by most clinicians.

The therapeutic problems posed by the above case and the way in which they were handled deserve discussion. Since this boy had no appreciation of his illness and was not set to communicate his feelings and thoughts to other people, the necessity of a "wooing" period is clear. The therapist had to behave in a manner which would make the boy want to see her and which would engender and reinforce his dependence on her. This relationship had to be of a nature which would make responsiveness to the therapist more satisfying than avoidance. By utilizing her power of "reward," she was in a position to make the child inhibit certain kinds of responses while increasing the frequency of expression of others. The preparatory period, in effect, served to make the child begin to be aware of and to respond to external rather than internal stimuli, the beginning of reality testing. The technique of direct interpretation may be said to have served a similar function in that such statements put into words the boy's relation to and attitude toward others. For example, when Henry decided to discontinue treatment because the therapist was talking to other children in the school, the direct interpretation offered served to make him think of, to become more aware of, his feelings toward the therapist (another external figure) as well as to reevaluate his feelings toward the therapist (another external figure). His decision to continue treatment indicates that he was aware of external as well as internal factors. It should be realized, of course, that the therapeutic value of a direct interpretation depends on how and when it is offered, the degree of generality with which it is verbalized, and the number of times it is made. Many times it is extremely difficult to determine from published studies the degree to which acceptance of a direct interpretation is a function of the patient's understanding the problem the way the therapist does. In any event, direct interpretation as employed by Chidester and Menninger seems to have had results. Another feature of this case that bears discussion is the fact that the boy was treated in an institutional setting in which he was sympathetically but consistently handled, his activities observed and controlled, and the family situation in which his difficulties arose absent. It is reasonable to assume that the fact that this boy was in a strange setting made it easier for him to respond to the therapist's friendly overtures. In effect, the therapist had no competitors for his affection and confidence. It goes without saying that an institutional setting which does not provide parental substitutes or some kind of consistent and satisfying interpersonal relationship will more often than not have a retarding rather than an accelerating effect on intellectual-social growth.

It will be obvious to the reader that the improvement shown in the above case took place over a long period of time (four years) and was the result of painstaking efforts. It might be argued that the amount of time spent on this one case could have been employed in the treatment of many children with lesser difficulties and more favorable prognoses. While this practical objection may be true, it cannot be denied that this case is of great value in that it challenges the validity of some prevalent diagnostic practices and underlines the necessity for research in an area which has been neglected for too long. Since mental deficiency is considered an incurable condition which responds in only a limited way to various types of educational and vocational training, it is surprising that psychotherapy as a test of the validity of the diagnosis of mental deficiency has received scant clinical and research attention. . . .

There are few published data on the use of and benefits from individual psychotherapy with institutionalized defectives. This is not surprising when one considers that the institutionalized defective has usually been viewed as either a medical-custodial or a narrowly conceived educational-vocational problem. The lack of attention which the institutionalized defective has received from psychologists and psychiatrists can be seen from Humphreys' survey (1935) of the publications of the American Association on Mental Deficiency. The survey, done in 1935, covered 59 years of the Association's publications. Humphreys (1938) "found that of the six hundred and eighty-one papers studied according to content, nearly 19% could be classified under 'Psychology and Psychiatry' but the percentage of papers dealing with analytical studies of the emotional life of the individual defective amounted to only 1.5% of the total papers of the Proceedings. The statistical and psychiatric trend survey of the paper showed that no matter what the exact percentages may be, or what psychiatric activities may be included under the general term of custodianship, very little well integrated psychiatric work has been done in the American State Schools. However, a recognition of increasing interest in psychiatry in relation to the study of mental deficiency, was clearly shown." This increased interest, however, has not been reflected in the area of psychotherapy with these cases, although the need for such work has been emphasized by Humphreys (1942).

Thorne's report (1948) of the results of systematic psychotherapy with institutionalized defectives is one of the few in this area. In setting up the psychotherapeutic program the usual institutional manner of handling problem children was changed. "Under previous administrations disciplinary problems at the schools had been handled by repressive methods involving rather strict punishment including occasional corporal punishment for serious offenses. The old plan of training was oriented toward the general objective of making each child into a compliant institutional inmate who was supposed to submerge individuality in becoming a cog in an impersonal organization." The basic objectives of the psychotherapeutic program involved "(a) accepting the mental defective as being a worthy individual in spite of his defects, (b) permitting expression and clarification of emotional reactions, (c) patiently teaching him methods for resisting frustration and achieving emotional control, (d) outlining standards for acceptable conduct within the ability of each individual child, (e) building up self-confidence and respect by providing experiences of success, and (f) training the child to seek help intelligently through counseling when faced with unsurmountable problems."

The psychotherapeutic methods employed by Thorne were suggestion, persuasion, advice, and reassurance. Nondirective methods were also found effective at certain times:

> In our experience, the nondirective methods developed by Rogers are very effective in certain stages of treatment when the objective is to assist the child to express and clarify his feelings and emotions. When dealing with the child who is emotionally upset, it is desirable to listen quietly to the initial outburst of feeling, reflecting and clarifying feelings nondirectively. If the child quiets down within a reasonable period of time, counseling goes to a discussion of what can be done to solve the difficulties. If the child is so disturbed as to be completely unapproachable, he is placed in isolation until the emotional storm has subsided and he is willing and able to discuss the situation reasonably.

. . . The causes for referral for psychotherapy were insubordination, fighting and quarreling, elopements, severe temper tantrums, stealing, and sex problems. In evaluating the results of psychotherapy the following factors were considered: conduct record, number of breaches of discipline, school and work records, and clinical judgments. With these criteria, 45 cases were considered improved, 16 unchanged, and 7 worse.

The difficulty which the clinician encounters in setting up a psychotherapeutic program can be seen from the following statement by Thorne: "The most difficult obstacle to the accomplishments of this program is to convince all concerned that it can be done. At the beginning of the program the older employees made dire predictions and stated that nobody could handle these cases without strict and repressive punishments. Corporate punishment died a hard death. . . . Perhaps more difficult is to convince employees that they largely make their own problems through failure to use psychological methods of studying and handling the children under their care." The significance of Thorne's conclusion that psychotherapy with defectives is both possible and profitable and that an extensive research program should be undertaken to exploit its possibility has not been recognized by many institutional administrators.

The following two cases treated by the writer are presented in some detail in order to emphasize the role of psychotherapy with institutionalized defectives and to illustrate some technical problems that arise.

The Case of Lottie

Lottie was born in 1922. She was committed together with her mother and brothers to the State Institution for Defectives in 1929. Lottie was committed "because of neglect at home and low mental rating. Before admission she was living with her parents and younger brother on the Town Farm. The mother is reported to have left school at 15 years of age. She had reached the fifth grade and was profane, quarrelsome, fault-finding, and totally incapable of caring for her family. She could not cook, take care of a house and the children were filthy." The father was described as a drunkard who was completely irresponsible. The following is an excerpt from an institutional report written several months after admission:

> Lottie is an able-bodied, attractive-looking, seven-year-old child with a mental age of four years, six months, and an intelligence quotient of 74. Her mother is also a patient in this institution. She is very tidy, careful of her clothing and very clean in her personal habits. She is most attentive to her teeth and nails. Mrs. B. reports that in her opinion she is nearer normal than any other child in the institution. She talks a good deal and usually in a quiet, sensible way. She mixes well with the other children, and is a leader in all her games. Her manner is polite, and her table manners excellent. She knows how to use her head. She shows fair judgment and reasoning powers. Insofar as a child of her age is able, she can make herself very useful. Often in the evening she will report incidents of the day, happenings at school and sometimes her remarks are very shrewd, and cute. One evening while her group was being undressed for bed, an announcement was made that the superintendent was making rounds with visitors. Mrs. B. was downstairs in the clothes room, and for a few minutes there was much excitement and confusion in an endeavor to get things straightened out, clothing readjusted, etc. After everything was put in order she said: "Oh Mrs. B. I was so scared that everything wouldn't be all right until I saw you coming. Everything went off fine, didn't it?" On another occasion she was kept in quarantine for a few days. When released she wouldn't allow other children to come close to her, "for fear they might get it too." This child has undoubtedly promising possibilities.

The following was written one year after admission:

> This little girl of eight years is very attractive in appearance and plays like a normal child. She plays quite well with the group of children her own age, occasionally shows a very naughty disposition. If unable to run things as she wishes, she will sulk and has lately been biting her hands when angry. She did this the other day because another child refused to come into the building and get her a drink of water. When questioned concerning her behavior, she said that she bit herself because she had seen other children do the same.

It was also noted in the history at this time that the older girls in the institution were inclined to make a pet of Lottie and that there was a tendency for her to be spoiled. The following is typical of later institutional reports:

(School report for 1936) Lottie has very little ability for academic work. She is impertinent and makes disturbances in class. She talks loudly, gets angry instantly, and it is difficult to make explanation to her at times as she sees things her own way. Conduct is unsatisfactory, very moody, doesn't accomplish much, has shown a slight improvement in personality the last few months. In leader work, she gets excited easily. When criticized she becomes sulky, cries and carries on, mean and nasty to her classmates, quarrels with them often, striking them, disobedient, sassy and troublesome, bad tempered, boisterous, swears frequently.

(1938) Lottie has been moody this year. One day she is interested in her work and the next day she is ready to give up. She grumbles and complains constantly, is very silly and boisterous, seeking attention from older girls by becoming sulky and disagreeable, quarrelsome, carries stories and tries to start trouble. Her work hasn't been good as it has been in other years.

In 1940 Lottie was transferred to a new institution for defectives. Again one finds in institutional notes mention of surliness, insolence, and bravado. A more rounded picture of this girl is given in the following excerpt from a report written by a schoolteacher toward whom Lottie had always seemed unusually well disposed:

When Lottie was admitted here in 1940, she appeared to be a very unhappy, discouraged, contrary girl. She was extremely untidy and discouraged about her appearance, feeling that it was useless to bother as she felt herself very homely and queer-looking and that no amount of fussing would change her looks. She also felt that no one cared about her appearance, happiness, or future. In fact, she felt that her only future was here in the institution and that she was even too "dumb" to get a decent job here. She was inclined to be sulky and when spoken to would act very rudely in order to hide her embarrassment. She would very deliberately break rules to prove her braveness. She would repel any overture of friendliness for fear that you were being sorry for her. She would be insolent to anyone being kind to her so that no one could feel she was currying favor.

She was very fond of her brother (who together with the mother had also been transferred), but beyond a very superficial interest, he paid no attention to her. She took little if any part in athletic activities and yet at heart is rather a tomboy. She visited her mother in the T.B. unit whenever possible but worried after every visit. One of her major fears is being left alone without friends or family.

The following are the intelligence quotients reported from different examinations: in 1928 an I.Q. of 59, in 1929 an I.Q. of 74, in 1939 an I.Q. of

45, in 1942 an I.Q. of 48, and in 1944 an I.Q. of 51. Lottie had always been diagnosed as a familiar (garden-variety or endogenous) defective.

The decision in September 1945, to attempt psychotherapeutic interviews with Lottie stemmed from her refusal to take some psychological tests. The psychologist had come to her classroom to take her to his office, but when the teacher asked her to accompany him she refused to do so. She sat in her seat muttering to herself and indicating with facial expressions that she did not want to go. After some prodding by the teacher, which had no effect on Lottie, the psychologist said somewhat angrily that if she did not want to take the tests she did not have to and he left the classroom. Later in the day the psychologist sent for Lottie to come to his office. When she came in, it was obvious that she had been crying a great deal. However, she was very sullen and unresponsive and answered routine questions in a barely audible tone, never once looking at the psychologist. Shortly after the administration of a test was begun, tears came to her eyes. She tried to keep them back but soon she was crying very hard. The psychologist let her cry for several minutes, after which he asked her if she would tell him why she felt as unhappy as she did. Lottie, who kept her head down on her chest, merely shook her head. The psychologist then asked her if she would accompany him to the school canteen where they could get some ice cream. Lottie, her face still out of sight, did not answer and when the psychologist came over to her and took her hand she very meekly accompanied him. During the walk to the canteen she kept her face buried in her chest but held the psychologist's hand very firmly. In the canteen she was very ill at ease and said that she did not want anything but when ice cream was placed before her, she began to eat it in a very self-conscious manner. When the psychologist jokingly asked her why she always had her face down on her chest (making the eating of the ice cream quite a feat), she said, "My face is nothing to look at." When the psychologist said that he disagreed with her, she obviously appreciated the comment. In answer to a question about whether her brother had written to her from the Army, Lottie shook her head and when the psychologist expressed surprise she said, "I'm disappointed and not disappointed at Tom for not writing me—he did that before." During the walk back from the canteen the psychologist said that he felt badly about the fact that Lottie was so unhappy and he would like very much to help her, if Lottie thought he could help her. Would she like to come to see him regularly and talk things over? Lottie nodded and the psychologist went on as follows:

> It's probably going to be hard for you to talk about some of the things that bother you but unless you do tell me what's on your mind I won't be able to be of much help to you. I've got to know how you feel, why you do and did certain things, and what you think will make you happy. I want to tell you now that when we talk things

over I may not always agree with what you have said or done. Because I don't agree with you doesn't mean that I don't like you. Just as I always want you to feel that you can talk to me about anything, I want to feel that I can tell you what I think. I don't want you to keep anything back because you think I'm "Staff" and I might tell others what you tell me. Whatever you tell me stays with me—that's something between you and me and it will be no one else's business. I expect, of course, that whatever we talk over you will also keep to yourself. Unless we trust each other we are not going to get very far. Again I want to say that if I tell you that I think you've done something wrong, I'm telling it to you not because I don't like you or I want to make you feel bad but because I want to help you. Sometimes I'll probably be wrong in what I say but I want to feel that I can tell you what I think. If you feel that you will not be able to talk to me about what bothers you, then I wish you would tell me now. If you decide that you want to come to see me regularly, I'll set aside some time three days a week when we'll get together. That time will be for you and no one else. Another thing, any time you decide you don't want to see me any more all you have to do is say so. Don't feel that if you decide not to come I'll be angry and hold it against you. Regardless of whether you come or not I'll always be ready to help you in any way that I can.

When asked if she wanted to assent to the "agreement," Lottie nodded. Appointments were made for stated times on three days of the week.

One of the most difficult obstacles in establishing a "give-and-take" relationship with this girl was her fear and unwillingness to verbalize feelings and attitudes. During the initial interviews she would sit with her head either down on her chest or turned to the side—anything in order not to look at the psychologist. When he came into the office she would say hello in a friendly manner, but as soon as she sat down in the chair the "avoidance" behavior would begin and she would be unable to talk. If the psychologist said nothing, long periods of silence would ensue during which Lottie might occasionally look furtively at the psychologist, giggling embarrassedly when he registered mock surprise at her attempt. During the first seven interviews this girl could not initiate a conversation and it was necessary for the examiner to adopt a very direct approach. The first "problem" attacked was why she could not look the psychologist (and other people) in the face. Her replies to these inquiries were, "If you were like me, you couldn't look people in the face either." She would not and could not elaborate on this reply. When the psychologist said that the reason he thought she behaved this way was that she felt she was not pretty and that people would not like her, she remained silent for some time and finally nodded her head in agreement. When the opinion was expressed that she was a rather attractive girl and that there were people who had said that they liked her a great deal, Lottie became very embarrassed and although she denied the validity of the statements she obviously was pleased by them. She would react similarly when the psychologist said that he liked her.

Sometimes she would mutter something that was inaudible but when she was asked what she had said she would shake her head or say that she had said nothing. On one of these occasions the psychologist thought that Lottie had said, "I'll always be unhappy. You can help it but it will never happen to me." Questioning did not result in any reply. When this occurred the psychologist would remind her of the original agreement between them about talking and would indicate his disappointment and displeasure at her failure to adhere to it, statements which sometimes resulted in a sort of hostile silence. When this occurred during the seventh interview, the psychologist said that he could not be of help to her until she felt that she could talk to him. Lottie sat in silence for the rest of the allotted interview time and when the psychologist indicated that the time was up she walked out of the office in an aggressive fashion banging the door after her. When she came in the next time, she appeared like a penitent child. After a period of silence she said, "Why didn't you look at me at breakfast? (Lottie helped as a waitress in the dining room for the breakfast and supper meals. During the day she worked in the sewing room.) You looked at the floor but you did not look at me. You wanted to show me how bad it is not to look at a person." At the end of the interview Lottie, for the first time, looked directly at the psychologist when she said goodbye. She appeared somewhat flustered and self-conscious because she knew she was doing something she never had done before.

There were many opportunities for discussion of Lottie's fear and avoidance of people. When Christmas time came, she reported that she had refused to participate in the school pageant. "I refused to be in the pageant. I don't like people staring at me. That's why I stand with my head down in the dining room. I'm shy." At another time the psychologist was conducting some visitors around the institution and when they entered the unit in which Lottie was working, she turned her head away and never once looked at the psychologist or the visitors. When this problem was discussed with her Lottie would usually react in a somewhat sullen and hostile fashion, saying that it didn't matter how she acted, that she would always be in an institution, and that she just didn't want people looking at her. It was invariably pointed out to her that her avoidance of contact with people was due to the unrealistic attitudes toward herself and that the effect of her behavior was to give people the wrong impression of her. "You're afraid that people will think you are not pretty and that you are not smart. So you are afraid to look at them and talk to them because then you would be giving them a chance to see that you are neither pretty nor smart. But by acting that way people will really think that you are not smart—which is the one thing you don't want them to think." In answer to this Lottie once remarked, "The next time you bring visitors around, I'm going to dig a hole and hide till they go away." Another time she said, "I may look dumb but I'm not."

When it was pointed out to her that her fear of meeting people would make it difficult for her when she left the institution, Lottie's feeling of hostility and futility were blatantly expressed. She would laugh sarcastically at the ideas that someone thought she "would ever get out of here. It may happen to somebody else but it will never happen to me. What difference does it make how you act if you never get out of here?" This girl's conviction that she would never leave the institution ("They'll carry me out in a box") was so deep-seated that encouragement and reassurance by the psychologist had no effect. Lottie's attitude was, of course, completely understandable. She had been told innumerable times that "some day" she would be sent out of the institution. She had seen other children leave it and could never understand why she had been ignored. She had never been given a concrete indication that plans were being made for her to be placed in the community. With this background of institutional promises it is understandable why it was less painful for her to believe that she would never be placed than to entertain a hope which was inevitably followed by disappointment. From this attitude of futility it was only one step to the formula: "If they won't do anything for me, why should I do anything for them? If you're bad you don't go out and if you're good you don't go out." This created a most difficult therapeutic problem. As long as Lottie believed that she would never leave the institution the therapist was powerless to influence her behavior. If she could not believe that the psychologist's reassurance about placement had any likelihood of occurrence, then there was no reason for her to want to follow his suggestions and advice.

The manner in which this problem might be handled was largely determined by the nature of the relationship between Lottie and the psychologist. There were many indications of her attachment and fondness for him. For example, on several occasions when disapproval or disappiontment was expressed at her behavior (sullenness, angry spells, difficulty with supervisors, refusal to talk, etc.), Lottie would say, "You really don't like me. You like to criticize me." Sometimes this would be said in a worried tone of voice and at other times in a manner as if to say, "You see, you really don't like me the way you said. You never meant it. I can't believe you." On several occasions after interviews in which Lottie either petulantly refused to talk or expressed pride in having acted aggressively toward her supervisors, or had announced her unwillingness or inability to change her behavior, the therapist received a note from her asking forgiveness and hoping that he would want to see her again.[5]

One day Lottie came to the office wearing glasses, something which the therapist had never seen her wear before. He expressed surprise at the glasses and inquired about how she found out that she was in need of them. To his surprise Lottie replied that she had had the glasses for a long time.

Psychologist: How come you are wearing them today?

Lottie: The cottage matron said I was supposed to wear them and that I couldn't go out today until I put them on.

Psychologist: Why haven't you worn them before?

Lottie: (At this point her head went down to her chest, a movement which the psychologist had learned to recognize as an indication that she did not want to answer the question.)

Psychologist: (After several minutes silence.) The reason I asked that question, Lottie, is that I was puzzled about why you haven't worn glasses before today. Now I'm puzzled about why you don't want to answer the question. You remember our agreement about talking. It may be hard for you to answer the question and so I'll give you as much time as you need to answer it. Until you show me that you will stick to the agreement, there's nothing I can do or say.

Lottie: (After approximately ten minutes of silence.) Because the girls called me four eyes.

Psychologist: When the girls call you four eyes, it reminded you of what you think of yourself, that you are not pretty. (Nods her head in agreement.) But I still don't understand why it was so hard for you to answer the question. Why couldn't you tell it to me?

Lottie: (Another ten minutes of silence.) Because you wear glasses.

Psychologist: (Somewhat recovered from his surprise.) You thought that I would be hurt the way you were by what the girls said.

Lottie: Yes.

The girl's fondness for the therapist was also revealed by cottage and work reports which indicated that she talked inordinately about how much she liked him, kept tabs on all his activities, and became impatient when the time for the interview approached. It was also indicated that she was very proud of the fact that she had regular appointments with the psychologist (and could make others if she felt it necessary) and was not above flaunting the relationship as a sign of distinction to other girls. As might be expected, in the interviews Lottie could express her fondness only in the most indirect manner. It was the therapist's impression that as Lottie's fondness for him increased, the fear of being rejected and unliked by him also increased, making it more likely that she would "find" in his statements and mannerisms evidence for her fear. It also seemed to the therapist that much of Lottie's aggressive and petulant behavior in the interviews was a way of testing his feelings toward her.

Whenever he felt that these attitudes toward self and therapist were behind her behavior, he would reiterate his fondness for her and emphasize that because he disagreed with or criticized her should not be taken as an indication of dislike.

Lottie's growing fondness for the therapist and her dependence on him as a source of satisfaction were utilized by him as a means of shaking her conviction that she would never be given an opportunity to return "to the outside." During an interview in which she cried and repeated her belief that she would always be in the institution, the psychologist forcefully replied: "If you really believe that, then it means that I haven't been of help to you. I have told you time and time again that you will be given a chance to go out, but I suppose you think that I just tell it to you to make you feel good. What I haven't been able to make you understand is that if I thought you would never go out, I wouldn't waste my time seeing you. There are other boys and girls whom I could see who would be willing to try to change their behavior so they could do a good job when they go out. You deserve to go out but there is a lot you have to learn first. But since you don't believe you're ever going out, you're not willing to try to change yourself. I feel very badly that you feel it's all hopeless because it means I've failed to help you. I haven't been able to make you see that you will go out if you will only make an effort to act differently in some ways. I'm sorry that I've failed because I like you and I wanted to help you. If I didn't like you and I thought I couldn't help you, I never would have started to see you. Since you can't believe what I say about going out, I suppose you ought to stop coming to see me because I don't see how I can help you. Unless you believe what I say and really try to change some of your actions, I suppose we ought to call it quits. What do you think. It's your decision." Lottie remained silent for several minutes and then said that she believed what the psychologist said about going out and she wanted to continue seeing him. After this statement from Lottie the psychologist stated what proved to be the chief theme of all subsequent interviews: that he would help her in every way to help herself.

In the subsequent months there was a marked change in Lottie's behavior. Her work supervisors and cottage matrons noted that her angry spells and sullenness had noticeably decreased in frequency and that her relationship with other girls was also more smooth. In the interviews she was more spontaneous and frequently reported in proud manner her own awareness of a change: "I don't mutter anymore. I try to look at people when they talk to me. It's hard but I keep my temper." During a period when the psychologist was ill, he received the following note from Lottie:

Dear Dr:
        I was very sorry to hear that you wher sick in bed but I hope you get butter soon.

I am still keep my head that some day I will get what I wish for. I am try to be a good girl for you wild you are sick in bed. So please don't think I am be a bad girl girl wild you are sick.

Please stay in bed wild you are sick. And I can wait for you to get butter so don't think of me wild you are sick in bed. I will close. I hope that you get butter.

From your friend
Lottie

The following is a report of Lottie's continuation-schoolteacher:

She is very much improved in several ways. She is no longer insolent in the dining room. She is courteous and agreeable and her reserved manner is friendly now rather than repellent. She is trying very hard to obey laws pleasantly and quietly without the undercurrent of muttering that usually accompanied her objections. She feels that she is not hopeless and can really learn something and so she has doubled her endeavor. Her progress in Continuation school has been good. Her greatest progress has been made recently.

She will read aloud now in the presence of strangers where before she would read only if I would take her alone. She is still afraid of new situations but she will attempt to solve rather than ignore them. Arithmetic is very difficult for her but for the first time in her life she is really attempting to do it.

The following is from a report of the supervisor of the employees' dining room in which Lottie worked:

Five months ago her attitude was so indifferent, one can hardly believe today's girl is the one who then went into a rage at the slightest upset. To suggest a divergence from routine brought an outbreak of words in such an awful voice there seemed no way to calm her. Then followed such melancholy I pondered much on how to break it. With these came many jealous spells which could scarcely be broken. At that time she would only handle six or seven people at mealtime.

Now rarely, very rarely, does Lottie have a suggestion of nerves. It is weeks since an unpleasant vocal outbreak. There is no evidence of jealousy, much greater goodwill for the girls, and an ever readiness to fulfill any request of mine. Daily she serves thirteen people for lunch. When an emergency arises, let it be hard work, an errand, or an employee party, Lottie will exclaim, "Let me do it. I can do it."

Although there was a noticeable change in Lottie's institutional adjustment, on more than one occasion her relation with the psychologist resulted in return of her sullenness and aggressiveness. In one interview (seventh month) Lottie was obviously, for some undetermined reason, feeling very aggressive. She avoided looking at the psychologist, gazed indifferently out of the office windows, and responded to questions about her actions in a tart and hostile manner. After several minutes of silence during which she seemed the picture of feigned disinterest, the therapist said: "I wish I knew why you feel the way you do and why you are acting this way toward me. Since you feel the way you do, maybe you would rather cut things short today and leave." To this she replied testily: "If you want me to leave, I'll leave. Goodbye." She banged the door after her. The next day the psychologist received a call from her supervisor, who reported that Lottie was upsetting the unit, was refusing to do as she was told, and was as negativistic as she had been months before. When Lottie came in for her interview on the following day, she was obviously somewhat depressed. When the psychologist said to her, "You felt pretty angry toward me the last time, didn't you?" Lottie readily agreed. She was silent for a while, then said, "Why are they always saying that they're going to tell you what I do? They're always saying, 'I'll tell Dr. Sarason about that. I'll tell Dr. Sarason.'" Lottie's imitation was, to say the least, caustic.

> Psychologist: When these people say that, it gets you pretty angry. When that happened a couple of days ago, you let it out on me. I sort of have the feeling that underneath it all you're angry at me too because I tell you when I think you're wrong.
> Lottie: (With feigned annoyance.) They tell me these things as if I'm your daughter and you're my father.
> Psychologist: Can it be, Lottie, that the reason you acted up yesterday was because after you left last time you felt I didn't like you?
> Lottie: I know you don't like me because of the way I act. I can't help it.
> Psychologist: (Sighing.) Maybe I'm expecting too much.
> Lottie: (A little scared.) I can change if I want to.
> Psychologist: It would make you and me happier if you did.

During the eighth month of interviews the psychologist informed Lottie that plans were being made to secure her a placement and that it might be a good idea for them to discuss some of the problems that she might encounter. The possibility that she would be leaving the institution in the next few months produced mixed reactions in Lottie. On the one hand she felt elated, and on the other she was apprehensive about how she would make out. The psychologist told her in a direct fashion that her chief difficulties would be (1) feeling of unlikability, (2) fear of rejection, (3) fear of new people and situations, (4) and inability to communicate feeling to other people. "You've lived in an institution for most of your life. You're going to see new people and places. You're going to be asked to do things that you may not have done before. At first you're going to be frightened at the newness of being outside. You're going to be lonesome. You may even cry at the beginning. But you must remember and always be sure to remind yourself that when you feel frightened and lonesome and unsure of yourself that it is perfectly natural for you to feel that way. If I were in your place, I would feel that way too. At the beginning everything is going to be new to you but that will wear off. After awhile you're going to wonder why you were ever scared." The attitudes which placement engendered in Lottie may be gleaned from an excerpt of an interview in which she was not "in a talking mood."

Psychologist:	I'm wondering what you're going to do when the woman you work for asks you questions.
Lottie:	I won't answer her.
Psychologist:	For example, what if she asks you about your mother?
Lottie:	I'll say I haven't any.
Psychologist:	You think that's a good answer?
Lottie:	That's what they used to tell me. When I lived with my grandmother they told me that. Wouldn't it be good for the woman I work with if she didn't have to talk to me?
Psychologist:	You still think that no one could like you and that people will think you are not smart.
Lottie:	Other girls are smarter than me. They can talk to people. It's hard.
Psychologist:	I don't think I agree with you. You're just as smart as the other girls and you can do the things they do. But the important thing is not what I think but that you think the way you do about yourself. That's why it's so hard for you to talk to people. You're afraid they won't like you and that they will think you are not smart. That's why it was so hard for you to talk to me at first. But you got over that with me and you have to get over that with other people.
Lottie:	It's hard. You don't believe me. (Is silent for several moments and then says with difficulty). I've been locked up for so long that it's hard for me.
Psychologist:	But it's not hard as it used to be.
Lottie:	No. But it's still hard. But I'm trying.

The following excerpt is from an interview which took place the day after the psychologist had visited Lottie's work unit in the course of showing a visitor around the institution. The visitor had spoken to Lottie about her work and she had responded with no sign of discomfiture—in marked contrast to her reactions to a similar situation several months ago.

Psychologist: How do you think you acted yesterday?

Lottie: All right. I wasn't afraid. I didn't want you to think I was scared.

Psychologist: I certainly did not think you were scared. You really showed me that you can talk to people. Don't you think that it will be easier for you on the outside when you meet people?

Lottie: That's different.

Psychologist: Why?

Lottie: Maybe she'll be all right for a few days and then she won't like me any more.

Psychologist: You worry a great deal about that?

Lottie: Yes. I hope we'll understand each other.

In the last month of interviews the psychologist presented to Lottie in a direct fashion the kinds of problems she would encounter on placement, her probable initial reactions, and the manner in which they might be handled. A realistic picture of what to expect was always accompanied by reassurance and support.

Lottie's placement was viewed with some misgivings. Although there was little doubt that her handling of interpersonal relationships had improved, it was recognized that this change took place in a restricted environment in which she was the recipient of special handling. The fact that she was going "outside" to a world in which she would be a stranger meant that she would encounter situations which could only arouse anxiety. She had grown up in a restricted geographical and psychological atmosphere. She was being put into a situation which would be taxing to an individual of higher capabilities and more varied experience. Against these considerations were the following opinions: (1) She was as prepared to go out as she would ever be, (2) prolonged institutionalization would make placement in the future more hazardous, (3) even if she failed on this placement she would benefit from having had direct contact with another world, an experience which would make the probability of success of future placements greater. It should be noted at this point that the psychologist had told Lottie on many occasions that if she had to be brought back to the institution, it would not be considered that she had failed.

Lottie was placed in the home of a middle-class family. There were several children in the home, the youngest being a newborn. The following is from an early report of the social worker:

Employer said that patient was very slow, was sluggish in walking and in all her actions, did not have a way with children. Employer thought she might make trainable material but her work was not of good quality. Employer has been tied up with the baby in the morning and so had to let patient go ahead on her own but she showed no initiative. Employer says she is a rather sweet girl but very shy, tended to be a little nervous and did not seem to let down and mix well in the family group. The worker interviewed Lottie, who said she liked the home but naturally found it strange. She said she was lonesome the first few days and cried a little. Is trying hard to work satisfactorily. She did not seem to know what to do with herself during her free time.

Two observations recur in later reports: not knowing what to do with her leisure time and being frightened and unable to "unbend and relax." Homesickness and lonesomeness were also frequently noted. "The worker took Lottie out with some other girls on placements and the worker noted that Lottie in comparison to some of the others was quiet and had not learned to unbend." Because the employer could not give Lottie individual attention and expected her to be able to carry on by herself, the placement was considered by the employer and worker as unsatisfactory. Another placement was secured, this time on the farm of an elderly woman and her daughter. The social worker reported as follows:

> Lottie took the change in placement as a personal defeat. Her first employer reiterated that if someone could spend a great deal of time with Lottie she had great possibilities. The workers explained to the new employer that Lottie was not too well trained but the worker thought that she was quite trainable but would need quite a bit of patience. The employer did not like this too well. There was great confusion in the home when Lottie got there and when the worker left Lottie was crying a great deal.

The placement did not work out very well and Lottie was returned to the Training School. The social worker's concluding note stated that she "did not feel that Lottie was entirely to blame for her failure in the last home as the worker is not yet sure just what type of woman the employer was."

In evaluating Lottie's adjustment to placement the following should be borne in mind: (1) From the time that Lottie left the institution she was under the supervision of the Social Service Department which at that time was located quite a distance from the institution; (2) although the psychologist had acquainted the social worker with his experiences with Lottie, the worker's knowledge of Lottie was secondhand; (3) because of the pressure of her case load the worker was able to visit Lottie only on the average of once a week; (4) people who take institutional children to work in their homes generally expect to receive rather than give service. These factors indicate that Lottie was placed in environments wherein she did not receive the reassurances she needed in the consistent way in which she needed it if feelings of insecurity, inadequacy, and rejection were to be avoided.

The crippling effects of prolonged institutionalization upon Lottie are best revealed by the following incidents. In her second placement Lottie was given a room on the second floor, the employer and her mother sleeping on the ground floor. Each morning the employer would find Lottie asleep on the living room couch on the first floor. When questioned by the employer, Lottie said that she was afraid to sleep upstairs by herself. Despite the employer's disapproval, Lottie always came downstairs to sleep on the couch after the others had gone to bed. When several weeks later the psychologist was discussing this with her, Lottie said, "*Of course I was afraid. All my life I've slept in dormitories with a lot of other girls. I can't sleep alone.*" In her notes the social worker several times referred to Lottie's complete amazement at traffic lights, large trucks, juke boxes, etc. On one occasion when the worker took her out for the day, Lottie was so overwhelmed by these sights and asked so many questions that she herself said to the worker, "You're going to be tired of answering all my questions." It may be assumed that aside from the visit of the social worker Lottie did not feel free to ask a fraction of the questions which came to her mind.

The primary purpose of presenting the case of Lottie is to demonstrate the feasibility of psychotherapy with a defective child in an institutional setting. At the end of ten months of interviews this girl's periods of sullenness and depression had noticeably decreased, she was more spontaneous, she did not avoid new people and situations with as much apprehension, her efficiency at work had improved, and she did not feel as personally isolated as previously. That this girl "failed" in her placement cannot be used to evaluate the effects of the psychotherapy. The placement notes indicate that procedures which were successful in other cases were not adequate for Lottie's needs. That Lottie needed special handling seemed to be due more to the effects of prolonged institutionalization than to an intellectual deficiency per se.

In a preceding paragraph Lottie was referred to as a mentally defective child. The reader may be interested in some of the writer's feelings toward and opinions about Lottie. Never once during the interviews was he ever aware that Lottie was defective. That she was very immature was painfully evident. In fact, he never regarded her in terms of her chronological age. He felt toward her and undoubtedly acted toward her like a big brother—a fact which did not prevent Lottie from regarding him as father. It is the writer's opinion that his being unaware of Lottie's defectiveness was due not only to the fact that he responded to her as one would to a younger child, but also to the fact that he considered her intellectual, social, and personal inadequacies not as being due either to a deficiency which existed at or shortly after birth, or was of constitutional origin or of a nature which precluded normal development. Many times he was surprised at the degree of insight which Lottie had about her own behavior. Although she had difficulty in communicating feeling, it was not because she did not know how to express feeling or thought but because she did not want or was afraid to verbalize it. When she did express herself it was always coherent and to the point. She had no difficulty in understanding the generalizations of others and in formulating her own on the basis of her own experience. Her conception of time and space, as is to be expected from one institutionalized for such a long period, was unrealistic. She knew only certain kinds of people in certain kinds of roles and her fantasies about the "outside" were undoubtedly bizarre. Her absolute fund of knowledge was pitifully small. What she could not comprehend seemed to be due to lack of experience rather than of capacity. What constantly surprised the writer was not what she did not know or could not do but what she did know and how quickly she grasped the nature of problems with which she was faced. His attitude toward Lottie might be formulated as follows: "If I experienced what she did, I'd be what she is today." He did not feel that Lottie's inadequacies were the result of an initial lack of the potentiality for normal growth. The validity of this opinion may be questioned, although, as was pointed out in Chapter 6, the data necessary for its proof or disproof are not available and the question will be decided only by future research. From the standpoint of the therapeutic relation, however, it may be said that the fact that the psychologist felt the way he did about the girl was reflected in his actions toward her, actions which made it easier for her to respond and adjust to the realities of her environment.

The Case of Stephen

Stephen was born in 1929 at the State Farm for Women where his mother had been committed. His mother, who had an I.Q. of 45, was noted for her promiscuity. The paternity of four of her six children was never clear. When she became pregnant with Stephen, the putative father is supposed to have made arrangements to marry her but they never materialized and he left the state before Stephen was born. It is not clear from the history how long Stephen remained at the State Farm, but it appears that at a very early age he was transferred to a Catholic orphanage where he remained until his commitment to the State Training School for defectives.

There were few developmental data in the case history. At birth Stephen was noted as having a microcephalic head, but later examinations did not mention anything unusual about the size or shape of his head. He walked at eighteen months. On only rare occasions did he ever have an outside visitor. The following is taken from the admission report:

Stephen has threatened to damage the oil burner at the orphanage by throwing matches at it. He threatens the sisters in the institution in general. He lies and disappears from the grounds. He also steals other children's belongings and sells them for a few cents. Since Stephen is considered an extremely troublesome and dangerous child, the sisters have asked to make arrangements for his commitment as soon as possible. Although only 13 years old, he is large for his age.

He has no control of social situations, shouts in classroom at school, leaves the room and wanders about. He is untrustworthy, lazy, sloppy, friendly, heedless and indifferent. His reading ability is good but in other respects he has not made academic progress.

He loves to work (in the orphanage) in the kitchen and he enjoys doing this because he knows that after he has helped bake pies he will get two of them which he shares with other boys at the orphanage. He enjoys everyone being well fed because he himself likes to eat. He shares what he takes from the kitchen with others. He cares for the younger children at the orphanage, entertains them quite well and reads stories to them. He is a leader and loves to get up amateur shows. The little ones respect him very much. He plays the piano by ear fairly well and as he plays the piano the little children follow him in song. He loves to play games with the children.

Stephen was admitted to the training school in 1943. The initial diagnosis was garden-variety deficiency. On psychological tests he received an I.Q. of 63 (1937 Binet), a Kohs Block Design score at the 11-year level, and academic achievement scores between the third- and fourth-grade levels. His institutional program consisted of half a day in a vocational assignment and the remainder in the academic school. Two years later he was given a full day's work assignment (bakery) and went to the continuation school one evening a week.

The possibility of attempting psychotherapeutic interviews with Stephen was raised in 1945 by his schoolteacher. She had noted that he was moody and unhappy; he complained of his dissatisfaction with his cottage placement and did not seem to get along too well with the other boys. It was the teacher's impression that "if his feelings could be straightened," he could function more efficiently and at a higher level. It was suggested to her that she sound out Stephen about wanting to talk to the psychologist. If he indicated that he wanted to come, the teacher was to tell him that she would try to arrange for an interview. The aim of this procedure was to make Stephen feel that he was seeking out the psychologist, and not vice versa. Stephen expressed a strong desire to see the psychologist and an interview was arranged. An incident which occurred two years earlier during the initial psychological examination probably played a role in Stephen's eagerness to come. During this initial examination the psychologist was called away from the testing room for several minutes. In this interval Stephen had gone through the therapist's desk and taken a stop watch. When the psychologist returned, the examination was resumed and it was not until later in the day that the watch was missed. Stephen was not questioned directly, but his cottage father was asked to look through his things. The watch was found, irreparably damaged, among his clothes. In accordance with institutional rules he was put in isolation for several days. On his release the psychologist called him down to his office. When he entered the office it was obvious that he considered the worst punishment was yet to come. When the psychologist said that he was more worried about Stephen than about the watch, the boy was visibly surprised. The fact that the psychologist hoped that Stephen would always feel free to come and talk to him when things bothered him and that he would always be ready to help him in any way that he could had a profound effect on the boy. Stephen left the office feeling he had gained a friend.

In the first psychotherapeutic interview it was clear that this boy would have no difficulty in communicating his problems. He was ill at ease for several minutes, shifted uneasily in his chair, and tended to avoid looking at the psychologist.

> Psychologist: Mrs. K. was telling me that you wanted to talk to me about some things that were on your mind.
> Stephen: Yes. Where should I start? I don't know where to begin. There's a lot.
> Psychologist: Start wherever you want. I know it's hard to begin.
> Stephen: I'll tell you about myself.

Stephen then began to recount the story of his life. He talked so fast that it was very difficult to distinguish one sentence from another. He went into such minute detail and went from one event to another so that it was extremely difficult to follow him. Every now and then he would pause for a moment, ask a question, usually answer it himself, and then go on with his stories. This silence was as much due to bewilderment at the mass of detail as it was to technique. The following are some of the things that the boy related:

1. He came to the orphanage when he was two years old.
2. He was always stealing things. "I was sneaky. I did slicky things. I did things behind the nuns' back. Now I know that if I keep busy I don't get itchy fingers. I used to steal money from the poor box. Once I took the money and bought a pair of shoes. I used to steal a lot of food too."
3. He was not sure about his relationship to his mother, present stepfather, and siblings. "My mother used to visit me when she'd come. She stopped because her legs bothered her. She limps on one foot." At another time he said, "I don't know who my father was. My mother has pictures of my father in the coffin. She married again. I got a sister and there's Tom and Richard but I don't know if they are my brothers. I thought they were but I don't know." He also described his stepfather, who was a drunkard and fought constantly with his mother. "I'm

ashamed to tell you these things but maybe you heard worse cases. Is he my real father? Is she my mother? I don't know if he's my stepfather. Sometimes he doesn't come home at all. I don't want a stepfather like that. I once saw him try to stab my mother. I was in the struggle. I got the knife away."

When the psychologist agreed that Stephen had many problems and that it might be a good idea to talk more about them, the boy said he would like very much to come again. Appointments at stated hours three times a week were scheduled.

In the second inteview Stephen began to talk as fast as before and it was difficult to follow him. The psychologist said that it was difficult to follow him and wondered if he always spoke that way. (The psychologist knew that it was not his usual manner of talking.) Stephen replied, "I don't always speak that way. But I'm nervous."

> Psychologist: Why do you feel nervous now?
> Stephen: Because I'm embarrassed because what I tell you. I think maybe you would change toward me. I never told anybody these things before.

Stephen was reassured about the psychologist's attitude toward him and the confidential nature of the interviews was explained. He then began to speak about his mother but referred to her now by her full name; for a moment the psychologist did not know to whom he was referring.

> Psychologist: Who is A____ H____? Is that your mother?
> Stephen: That's it, I don't know. She don't act like my mother.
> Psychologist: Is it that you don't want to believe it is your mother?
> Stephen: Yes. She doesn't act right. She drinks. She yells and fights. She told me I should get training here so I can get a job and give her money. But I said to myself that I'm not. I'll get a job with people and have a good time.

Shortly after this discussion Stephen said that he had a question he would like to ask. He overhead his cottage parents say that "he had his brain tested and he's a lowgrade. There's something wrong with his brain."[6]

> Stephen: Is there something wrong with my brain? I don't think so. The boys make fun of me because I'm in a low-grade cottage but I don't care.
> Psychologist: We certainly do not feel that there is anything wrong with your brain. We feel that you are going to get a lot from your training here and that you will do a good job when you get out.

Stephen then returned to the discussion of his mother. His earliest memory was of "this woman" coming to see him. "She came with a little baby and a strange man." Then she stopped coming and he did not see her again for a long time. The other children in the orphanage used to taunt him because he had no mother and no one came to see him. "Then she started coming again. I was ashamed when she came and I wouldn't go to her until she called me." Stephen used to visit her home but he never had a good time there.[7] There were always fights and his mother was always telling him to take money from the pockets of his drunken stepfather.

Stephen:	(Thoughtfully.) I don't know. I'm like them.
Psychologist:	How do you mean?
Stephen:	I used to see them (mother and siblings) take money and my mother would give them some but not to me. So I took. I would get nervous, but when I didn't get punished I'd do it again.

The next several interviews were largely used by Stephen for discussing the nature of his relations with the other children in his mother's home and his ambivalent feelings toward his mother. The more he talked about his mother the more his hostility toward her overshadowed his feeling that a son ought to love his mother. "She didn't act like a mother. If she did she would have tried to get me out of the orphanage. Sometimes when she came she would tell me to get some flower plants for her. I would tell her I couldn't but she would say I could if I wanted to. She used to tell me to steal things."

Following an interview in which his stealing had been discussed, Stephen came in the next time and spontaneously began talking about the reasons he took things.

Stephen:	I figured it out and now I know why I took things. I would want something and there was no way of getting it so I stole it. I wouldn't get caught so I would do it. Like when I took your watch. I opened the drawer to get a pencil and I saw the watch. It was in me—temptation—I·said I needed a watch. I was going to bury it in the ground in a box till they forgot about it.
Psychologist:	When else have you taken things?
Stephen:	I never took things when the Allens (cottage mother and father) were on duty. I was afraid he'd swing at me.
Psychologist:	What do you mean?
Stephen:	He's older and stronger. He could smack you and hurt you. I was afraid.

Psychologist: Who else are you afraid of?

Stephen: I'm afraid of Tony H. (a boy who worked in the bakery with him). He's always fighting and I'm afraid of him.

Psychologist: You feel that Tony is stronger than you are? (Stephen was approximately six feet tall and Tony was about five feet six.)

Stephen: (Hesitatingly.) He's got big muscles and he's good at fighting. I'm afraid of him. He's the champ boxer in the whole village. Mr. K. never says anything wrong about Tony. He's always saying how he'll make a good boxer out of him.

Psychologist: You're afraid of Tony the way you are of Mr. K. and Mr. A.

Stephen: Yes. I'm afraid they'll swing at me.

Psychologist: How long have you been afraid of people this way?

Stephen: I wasn't afraid before I came to the Training School. When I first came in the cottage I saw husky people and I never saw a cottage master before. At the orphanage the nuns took care of you but here there is a man and you've got to do as he says or else you get it. (Reluctantly.) When the nuns came after me at the orphanage I'd sometimes hit them.

For the next several months the interviews were concerned largely with Stephen's hostility toward Tony and his fear of acting aggressively toward him. Tony, who was known to be the bully type of boy, tyrannized Stephen, took advantage of him, and on several occasions made him take the blame for incidents with which Stephen had nothing to do.

Stephen: I don't want to be a sucker or a stooge. Once you're that way you always are. It's like when you're hypnotized and you do what they tell you. Even with little guys I get afraid when they say something nasty to me.

Psychologist: You want to hit back at Tony. You want to fight him and get even. You feel you shouldn't be afraid but you are. You feel that unless you fight back you'll never have a good opinion of yourself.

Stephen: That's right. But I think I'll smack them someday. Then they'll be afraid of me. I'll get even sometime.

Psychologist: You feel that once you fight back you won't be afraid any more.

Stephen: Yes. I know I should fight.

In all of these discussions the psychologist, by restatement and clarification of Stephen's own statements, attempted to reinforce his belief that he could and should fight back. In view of his position in the institution the psychologist could not tell the boy in a direct manner that he should fight back. Telling him this probably would have increased his feeling of shame without increasing the strength of his determination to fight back. Direct expression of the psychologist's feelings would have posed the problem for this boy before he himself was ready to act.

The strength of Stephen's conflict about the expression of aggression may be seen from the following dreams which he related on request of the psychologist.

Dream 1. Tony and Joe Abbot were fighting. I butted in and Joe and I pounced on Tony and beat him up.
(What comes to your mind when you think of that dream?)
It shows it could be done. It says the same thing we were talking about.

Dream 2. This was about Mr. K. A notice came in that nobody should be hit. Mr. Mc. came in and kicked him out. The boys were very happy because I told in the office about Mr. K. They were told they could smoke in the cottage.
(What comes to mind when you think of that dream?)
Someday it might come true when something will really happen. It shows I don't like Mr. K. I dreamed it because I don't like him.

Dream 3. I got kicked out of the bakery because Tony bossed me around. I walked out. They locked me up. When they needed help the boss baker came with his keys and let me out. He said he was sorry. At first I thought they would send me to the farm as punishment. But they gave me ice cream and pie and I worked with the boss baker. Next day there was ice cream missing. They blamed it on me. But I knew that Tony took it. I told the boss baker that Tony admitted it. He went to the farm. The bakery was clean. Mr. K. said he would take me to his home.
(What comes to mind when you think of that dream?)
I felt bad because they sent me to the lock-up. Tony thought he was big but they found out he wasn't. I wished that dream comes true. That's what I always say.
(What do you think these dreams show?)
It shows that I had something in my head that something would be done about Tony. You want to fight back but you're scared and then you have a good dream. But when you wake up it's the same and you wonder what's the use of living.

As time went on there were concrete indications that Stephen was expressing aggression to other boys in a direct manner. He came in one day and proudly reported a fight he had with a boy in his cottage. The boy tried to interfere with Stephen's playing of horseshoes and tried to take them away from him. Stephen resisted, hit the other boy, and pushed him to the ground.

> Stephen: I'm glad I stood up for my own rights. I'm not going to be a sucker any more. I was surprised when I got the horseshoe away from him. I thought he was stronger than me. I'm going to be different. You'll be hearing good things about me.
>
> Psychologist: You feel that maybe you've been wrong and how weak you thought you were. You're stronger than you thought and you're not going to let the fellows bulldoze you.
>
> Stephen: That's right. The other day some of the boys kidded me. I'm not afraid. I feel it coming. I'm going to swing one of these days.

One month after this discussion (in the fourth month of interviews) Stephen walked into the office with a wide grin on his face and the psychologist knew that "the" fight with Tony had taken place. He was very proud of himself and enjoyed relating how Tony was surprised when Stephen fought back after having been taunted by him.

> Stephen: I wanted to hit him more. They stopped me. I didn't want to stop.
>
> Psychologist: It didn't turn out the way you were afraid it would.
>
> Stephen: No. The strangest thing has happened. Tony has respect for me now. I can see where I've been wrong. When I was a kid I was afraid. When I wanted something I'd steal it quick without thinking. I'd be afraid of hitting somebody. I'd say let him hit me first.

For the next several interviews Stephen relived his triumphant fight. Tony was now playing up to Stephen and the latter now wanted to fight the former in the boxing matches. Stephen kept saying, "I used to be afraid but I've learned not to be. Gee, I've changed."

In the subsequent months Stephen returned again in the interviews to his feelings toward his mother, stepfather, and siblings. The two problems which concerned him most were (1) why he was sent to the orphanage and (2) the conflict between how he felt and how he thought he ought to feel toward his mother. In regard to the first problem, Stephen once said, "I thought my mother put me away because she wanted more children. (Pause.) I thought maybe it was because she had no money. (Pause.) Then I thought that maybe she took me to a doctor who said there was something wrong with my brain." Stephen's attitude toward his mother was sharpened at this time by her renewed interest in him. She sent him letters and food and would visit him more frequently than before. Stephen's reactions to her visits were similar to those he experienced when she visited him in the orphanage. He felt embarrassed because of her slovenly appearance, could not respond to her attempts to show him how much she cared for him, and felt relieved when she left. Stephen would always relate to the psychologist how his mother would urge him "to get a lot of training here so I can get a good job and help her out." These visits usually served to recall his mother's past behavior. He would relate in great detail how she never kept her promises to him, urged him to steal from the orphanage and the stepfather, and sometimes spent what little money she had on drink. Following the recounting of these stories, Stephen would sometimes say, "I feel bad that I speak about my mother this way. It means I don't like her. But I do like her. Maybe she is different now." Aside from the fact that he wanted to believe that his mother had changed, the possibility that she might take him out of the institution heightened his feelings of ambivalence.

In the sixth month of interviews Stephen's mother requested the institution to release him in her care. This request produced mixed reactions in Stephen. Initially he was overjoyed at the prospect of leaving the institution, but this was followed by the fear that he would be unhappy in his mother's home. It was surprising and gratifying to see how realistically this boy approached the problem. The mother's request for placement was turned down, but a week's vacation at Christmas time was granted. When Stephen was told this by the psychologist, he was disappointed at first but spontaneously said that he understood why the institution might not want to send him to his mother's home permanently. When the psychologist said that a week at home might enable Stephen to resolve one way or the other his conflicting attitudes toward his home, he said, "When I go home I'll write down everything that happens so I won't forget. Then we can talk about it." He also said, "When I go home I'd like to visit the orphanage. I'll be embarrassed because of the things I did there. You understand that, don't you? It wasn't the nuns who was wrong. It was me. But I'm different now. I didn't have anyone like you to talk to at the orphanage."

When Stephen came in for the first interview following his return from the vacation, he was depressed and for the first time had difficulty in talking. He revealed that his mother's home was far more filthy and disorderly than he had imagined. Both his mother and stepfather drank heavily. His mother kept repeating her desire that Stephen get a job and make money for her. The night before Stephen was to return to the school his stepfather became so drunk and abusive that it was necessary to call a policeman to quiet him. Stephen was very firm in his conviction that he did not want to return to his mother.

While he was at home Stephen questioned his mother very carefully about his real father. He insisted that she tell him his name and whatever she knew about him. At first his mother refused to do so, but on the boy's insistence she told him the name of a family in town who had known his father. When Stephen visited this family and told them who he was, he was surprised at the warmth with which he was received. In answer to his questions they said that they had known his father and, contrary to Stephen's belief, he was not dead. They said, however, that they did not know where he was. The family apparently took a great liking to Stephen and insisted that he come and visit them several times.

The fact that his mother had lied about his father served to increase his disappointment in and hostility toward her. However, the more aware he became of his hostility and necessity of "forgetting" his mother, the more he feared her retaliation when she found out his feelings.

Psychologist:	You say you've decided that you never want to be with your mother. You can't trust her and you know that she's interested in you because maybe you will be able to make money for her some day.
Stephen:	Yes. How shall I tell her how I feel?
Psychologist:	I'm not sure I know what you mean.
Stephen:	She'll be mad.
Psychologist:	You're afraid of her?
Stephen:	Yes.
Psychologist:	What do you think she'll do?
Stephen:	I don't know. She writes me letters and I don't want to answer. But I'm afraid to stop writing. When she gives me things it makes me feel bad because she doesn't know how I feel. If she did, she might do something.
Psychologist:	I sort of have the feeling that your being afraid of your mother is like your being afraid that Tony will hurt you.
Stephen:	I thought maybe she'll get Freddie (stepfather's son) to do something.

When the psychologist said that there was nothing that his mother or anyone else could do to him now or whenever he was placed in the community, Stephen felt reassured and then revealed that he had also been afraid that because of his mother he would not be put out on placement.

Since his return from vacation Stephen had been in frequent correspondence with the family who had known his father. Much to his amazement they wrote him that they were related to Stephen's father; they knew where he was and enclosed an address to which they suggested he write. Stephen's joy knew no bounds. He kept saying, "Maybe he cares for me." Stephen wrote a letter to his father, who lived in a midwestern state. He received a letter in which his father expressed his delight at having heard from his son and promised that he would come and visit. Shortly after, the father and his wife visited Stephen. Before allowing the father to see his son, the psychologist talked with him. During the interview the father, to whom Stephen bore a remarkable resemblance, expressed his guilt at having neglected his son, cried bitterly, and promised to do whatever he could for the boy. He wanted to take Stephen home with him. In a separate interview, the father's wife revealed how distraught he had been ever since he had received Stephen's letter and said that she knew he would not be happy unless Stephen came to live with them. When Stephen's background and needs were explained to her, she expressed her complete willingness to make his transition from the institution to the community as easy as possible. Since a social service investigation had revealed that the father and his wife could provide a good home for Stephen, it was decided to place the boy with them. This was done and according to the latest available reports the placement is working out very satisfactorily.

At the time that Stephen left the institution he had had interviews with the psychologist for one year. Shortly before he left he was given a psychological examination. It will be remembered that upon admission three years before, in 1943, Stephen, who was then 14 years old, had obtained an M.A. of 8 years 8 months on the Stanford-Binet (L), an M.A. of 11 years on the Kohs Block Designs, and academic achievement scores between the third- and fourth-grade levels. In 1946 Stephen obtained an M.A. of 11 years, 4 months on the Stanford-Binet (L) with an I.Q. of 76, an M.A. of 17 years 1 month on the Arthur Point Scale with an I.Q. of 114, and academic achievement between the seventh- and eighth-grade levels. In fact Stephen's achievement scores were the highest in the school and it was necessary for his teacher to give him books from her own library in order to satisfy his needs. The strength of Stephen's desire for knowledge, the need to be correct, and the way in which they aroused attitudes which interfered with intellectual efficiency are revealed in his test performance:

> Stephen viewed the tests as an intellectual challenge and, as a result, he was somewhat tense and kept saying that he was afraid that he would not do well. He appeared to be so aware of the need to grasp all that the examiner said that he would sometimes get lost in details and would lose the larger significance of a particular question. If he thought he had failed an item, he would continue to think about it when the next item was given, thus reducing his efficiency. Several times he spontaneously requested if he could go back to a previous question. After an item which he thought he had failed, he once said, "It makes me feel bad. I'll have to read more."
>
> Stephen passed all items on the Binet at the nine-year level and failed all at the fourteen-year level. Of the ten items he failed (excluding year fourteen) five of them were memory ones, failures which seemed due to the "fear of forgetting" which the instructions

for these items engendered. That memory per se was not a factor was suggested by his performance on the Reading and Report item at the ten-year level. He read the passage in 14 seconds without an error. Although he seemed to read the passage for speed rather than comprehension, when he was asked to tell about the passage from memory he was able to do so and get credit for the item. The pattern of successes and failures in this record suggest that the obtained level and quotient are not valid reflectors of the boy's intellectual capacity. It is interesting to note that the day after the examination Stephen came to the psychologist's office with a paper on which he had written down revised answers to some of the items which he failed. He had also used a dictionary to learn some of the vocabulary words which he had been unable to define.

On the Arthur Point Scale Stephen functioned more efficiently than on the Binet. While on the Binet visual cues for determining procedure are usually not given the subject, this does not hold for this performance type of test. Stephen worked quickly and efficiently with a minimum of trial and error activity. It would seem that in the face-to-face type of test situation, as in the Binet, affective factors are more likely to interfere with his functioning than when the face-to-face aspect of responsiveness is minimized. This examination does not support a diagnosis of mental deficiency.

In evaluating the effect of psychotherapy with Stephen, the more outstanding feature seems to be that this boy was helped to change his pattern of behavior in certain kinds of situations in a way that was satisfying to him. By facing rather than avoiding certain problems, he was able to resolve conflicts which had previously reinforced unhealthy attitudes toward self and others. He was not plagued as much by feelings of guilt and worthlessness, he achieved a more realistic conception of his physical adequacy, and he received the reassurance and support necessary to minimize his long-standing feelings of rejection.

In a preceding paragraph it was stated that Stephen was not a mentally defective boy. This conclusion was based not only on evaluation of his test functioning but also on his unusual academic achievement, his realistic appraisal and handling of his problems, and the behavioral indications that he would be socially and vocationally adequate in the community. There were little, if any, data in this boy's developmental history to indicate that his intellectual retardation was due to constitutional rather than environmental factors. That Stephen was born and reared in an institution, received no consistent display of attention and affection, and experienced rejection from his mother, are grounds for assuming that his capacity for growth was stifled. There is little evidence for assuming that it was limited because of constitutional factors.

In Lottie's case a doubt was also raised about the validity of the diagnosis of mental deficiency. Questions about validity of diagnoses should not obscure the fact that Lottie and Stephen are by no means rare cases in an institutional population and, perhaps more important, that they are amenable to and benefit from psychotherapy. Even though one may disagree with the writer's evaluation of the original intellectual capacity of these two children, it should not be overlooked that psychotherapy enabled them to respond more adequately to their environment, a result which institutional routine did not achieve and, in fact, may have made more difficult. How many and what etiological types of an institutional population are amenable to and can benefit from psychotherapy cannot be answered at this time because of the absence of the necessary research. What evidence is available suggests that a fair number of cases diagnosed as mentally defective are in need of and respond favorably to psychotherapeutic procedures.

Earlier in this chapter it was stated that intensive psychotherapy has not been utilized as a test of the assumption of essential incurability. The problem is more complicated than this statement may imply. Present-day psychotherapeutic techniques are not so effective as to allow one to assume that negative results necessarily mean that the diagnosis of mental deficiency has been confirmed. In the case of the garden-variety defective there is another factor which in many cases may be a barrier to psychotherapeutic gain, namely, the fact that an acquired behavioral pattern which has been continuously reinforced through an individual's life cannot be unlearned or markedly changed. The problem may be put in the form of a question: If a child has been reared for the first ten years of his life in a Kallikak-like cultural atmosphere, is one justified in assuming that through psychotherapy (or even marked environmental change) he can become "normal"? In other words, it may be that his mode of response makes it difficult or impossible for him to acquire those attitudes and motivations which facilitate learning. It may be instructive at this point to recall Goldfarb's finding . . . that children who experienced severe and prolonged deprivation during infancy are psychotherapeutically unreachable. Freeman, Holzinger, and Mitchell's finding . . . that the intelligence level of children of defective parents was related to the length of time they remained in the family emphasizes the deleterious effect that early deprivation may have on subsequent development. It may also be recalled that in Skodak's study . . . children of defective parents were placed in foster homes before six months of age. It seems reasonable to assume that their subsequent favorable development was related to their early removal from their families.

The degree to which psychotherapy can effect a change in the behavior of the defective individual must remain a problem for future research. It may be said that for idiots, imbeciles, and some morons (especially the brain-injured type) psychotherapy is neither feasible nor indicated. With the remaining cases, particularly the garden-variety defective, research in psychotherapy is indicated for both its diagnostic and its therapeutic possibilities.

Only with the passage of decades was I able to see that our psychotherapeutic effort was powered by some conceptual illogicalities that demonstrated how much a prisoner of traditional thinking I was. Some readers will have discerned that the discussion of our results (and those of others) rested on this assumption: If an individual responds in the way that theory and practice say should characterize the psychotherapeutic relationship—however different on the surface that relationship may appear—then the individual is not mentally defective. Put in another way: The quality of response to the psychotherapeutic relationship is a test of the appropriateness of the diagnosis of mental deficiency (or mental retardation). There would be nothing inherently wrong about that assumption if three things were true: 1) the criteria for making the diagnosis of mental deficiency or mental retardation were unambiguous in language and implementation so that different diagnosticians arrive at the same conclusion; 2) the assumed relationships between the mental deficits implicit in the diagnosis and overt problem solving and interpersonal behavior were based on more than conjecture or a confusion between assumptions and fact; and 3) that an earnest research effort had been made to test the appropriateness and helpfulness of psychotherapy. Instead of saying that the conceptual basis for the diagnosis of mental deficiency contained ambiguities and untested assumptions and, therefore, was a confusing and not a clarifying variable for social action and research, I was accepting the fiction that the diagnostic label validly described relationships (or a lack of them) among factors internal and external to the individual. More specifically, the diagnostic label stood for a condition "inside" the person that made a particular kind of relationship (i.e., the psychotherapeutic) impossible. So, when our efforts indicated that such a relationship was possible, the conclusion drawn was that the diagnosis was wrong. Instead of calling into question the nature of our conception of mental retardation, that conception went unchallenged and the argument focused on whether in this or that case the diagnosis was right or wrong. That mental retardation is not a "thing" in the way that a pencil or a stone is; that as a concept mental retardation is literally an invention of the human mind; that precisely because it is such an invention the chances are high that it contains unexamined biases and invalid assumptions—these considerations were far from clear to me. But there were more serious and harmful consequences of the traditional conception of mental retardation than whether the diagnosis was right or wrong in a particular case. The first of these consequences was that the diagnosis automatically precluded trying to establish anything resembling the features of a psychotherapeutic relationship, insuring that the dynamics of the self-fulfilling prophecy would be operative. (It was in all respects identical to the way in which psychotherapy used to be viewed as inapplicable to old people, even though here, too, there were clear indications that such a sweeping generalization was unjustified. There was one big difference: Whereas one could question the validity of the diagnosis of mental retardation, one could not question whether or not an individual was "old"!) The second serious consequence of the traditional conception was the support it gave to society's views of where and how mentally retarded individuals should be placed and managed. Any view that contained the assumption that it was impossible to establish with certain "labeled" individuals a reciprocal, productive, sustained, change-producing relationship justified programs that essentially denied these individuals the status of personhood. This, of course, was not a deliberate denial but rather an instance of a typical and all too easy way in which a society justified how it manages its relationships with individuals it regards as different, be that difference one of appearance, behavior, or any other departure from what the society considers acceptable and normal.

As I look back on our psychotherapeutic work I am struck by a misplaced emphasis. Certainly we were justified in utilizing psychotherapy to learn about the technique as well as about certain individuals. And we were, of course, justified in suggesting that there was a fair number of individuals labeled as mentally retarded who were far more psychologically complicated than that diagnosis would lead one to believe. But in emphasizing the technique and our results, was I not posing the issues as professional ones? Was I not talking to specialists in the field of mental retardation? Imagine the situation in which professionals were convinced that what we had to say about mental retardation, psychotherapy, and therapeutic results was valid, and everyone was off and running to determine which, how many, and to what degree mentally retarded persons could benefit from the psychotherapeutic relationship. If at the time I wrote the chapter I had reason to believe that that is precisely what would happen, I would have been delighted, to put it mildly. Should not one take satisfaction from the knowledge that a field was undergoing a long overdue change and that people were now being helped in new ways? That satisfaction, however, should have been tempered by knowledge of three facts: The number for whom that approach was applicable was probably not overwhelming; the psychotherapeutic endeavor is one of repair and not of prevention; and as an endeavor of repair, its results are far from perfect. Put in another way, what I underemphasized was the need to examine professional and societal attitudes that made the clinical or repair endeavor necessary. To the extent that the emphasis was on repair, attention was being diverted from the features of our society that created the need for repair. And there could be no doubt that one of the major features was an attitude that essentially denied mentally retarded individuals the status of personhood, an attitude that powered the way society and its representatives responded to that heterogeneous group of people who had in common an assigned label. And in many instances society's response began to exert its influence on the day of the individual's birth.

Here, again, the notable exception was parents of mentally retarded children. Although there were differences among parents, as a group they related to their children not as empty objects but as persons sensitive to changes around them, in need of attention and love, and as deserving as any other of one's energies and respect. This is not to be maudlin or sentimental or to advocate parental love as a kind of psychologic universal solvent that either prevents or dissolves the frictions. in living. The only intention is to convey that, as a group, parents *felt for and with* their children with a depth and consistency that was quite the opposite of what these children experienced from all other people who stood in some relationship to them. Granted that parental love can be a very mixed blessing and can be a pain in the neck to the professional who operates from an "I know best" stance, and granted that love is not enough—none of this lessens the significance and power of the central core of parental love: The child is a *thinking and feeling* organism, a person. It is what that core implies that the retarded child rarely experiences from others. As soon as you regard the child as capable of thinking and feeling and, therefore, of being influenceable and changeable—even if such attribution may be in part unrealistic—you have put a distinctive stamp of interpersonal sensitivity and reciprocity on your relationship with that child.

At the beginning of this chapter, I justified reprinting a large section on psychotherapy on several grounds, one of which was that however persuasive the case material contained in the chapter, one could not conclude that today, four decades later, societal and even professional attitudes have changed markedly. And by "have changed markedly" I mean that if you were to follow a random sample of retarded individuals from the time they arise in the morning to the time they go to bed at night, you would not be impressed with the frequency with which these people would be responded to as persons, not people with a label. It could be argued, and with justification, that ours is a society in which the substance and quality of too many interactions are influenced far more by role and label than by what I have called the recognition of personhood. We go, this argument asserts, from one interaction to another without the sense that we have "touched" or been touched by those with whom we interact. One feels both lonely and alone—a complex of feeling and yearning that only the rare interaction satisfies. So, the argument concludes, why should it be surprising if mentally retarded individuals are treated in the same impersonal way most of us experience in our interpersonal interactions? The question is interesting, but in one very important aspect it misses the point and confuses the issue: People labeled mentally retarded would be better off than they are if they were treated impersonally. When we say an interaction is impersonal, we do not assert that there is a basic difference between the two people. Rather, we say that there are clear restrictions about what can or should be expressed in the interaction, however unsatisfying adherence to those restrictions might be. Peoples' typical response to individuals who have been labeled mentally retarded, on the other hand, is not only impersonal but it clearly implies that there is a basic difference between responders and respondees. It is the implication of a basic difference that takes the interaction out of the realm of what we ordinarily mean by impersonal.

From another perspective, the question is illuminating because it suggests the hypothesis that, to the extent that interactions between "normal" people in the society are increasingly impersonal, it is increasingly difficult for people to respond *impersonally but not demeaningly* to those they see as basically different from themselves. In any event, the complaint about the frequency of impersonal interactions, as well as the frequency with which mentally retarded people are denied personhood, are not only psychologic but are also sociologic problems. As such they should force us to examine more closely how concepts, practices, and professional roles affect and are affected by society: its traditions, culture, social history, and the dynamics by which social change occurs and is resisted.

We have accorded to mentally retarded people civil and educational rights they did not use to have. That is cause for satisfaction, and I am in no way undervaluing these changes when I point out that they are consequences primarily of court decisions and secondarily of legislation influenced by those decisions. These rights were not given; they needed to be fought for and secured in an adversarial context. This must be appreciated because it is too easy—too readily incorporated into a self-serving, self-congratulatory stance—to confuse the accordance of rights with the attainment of personhood. That is a confusion about which women and racial and ethnic minorities need no instruction. Yes, the civil-legal-educational rights of mentally retarded individuals have been enlarged and codified in law and institutional practice. But let us not confuse these much needed changes with any pervasive alteration in understanding mentally retarded individuals as persons. An example. A dozen years ago, Robert McClellan, an unusual premed Yale senior who was working with me, became interested in the field of mental retardation, specifically, in how diagnostic labels affected perception and action. He found out that at the local regional center an excursion to two recreational sites was planned for adult retarded people. Unbeknown to me, he showed up at the regional center to go with the group for the day. He was greeted by the group leader, who asked him his name, and was then "taken into tow," the leader assuming that McClellan was a retarded individual from the community. From the moment he gave his name until the group disbanded in the early evening, he never had to make a decision, and his feelings and opinions were never sought about anything. As he put it (paraphrased): "I was a thing, something to be shepherded from here to there, a passive, well-trained, acted-upon puppy dog with no personality. It was not as if I didn't exist but rather that there was nothing inside me that would interest anyone or needed to be taken into account. It was a way of silence. It was eerie."

Relevant here is a case report of individual psychotherapy conducted in the early seventies by Dr. Gaston Blom with a young woman with Down's syndrome. I am indebted to Dr. Blom for permission to use his report. The following excerpts are from Sarason and Doris' (1979) *Educational Handicap, Public Policy, and Social History. A Broadened Perspective on Mental Retardation:*[8]

We shall begin our discussion of community attitudes by discussing a most unusual "case" that illuminates several things: negative community attitudes; changes in a positive direction; and the significance of these attitudes for our understanding of the developmental potentialities of those people society labels as mentally retarded. If the case is unusual, it is because the writer, Dr. Gaston Blom, is a very unusual person: a psychoanalyst, professor of child psychiatry, and professor of education at Michigan State University. What is more unusual than this combination is that Dr. Blom is a most unusual human being possessed of that degree of courage that leads society to confront its accustomed ways of thinking and acting.

Let us begin where Dr. Blom begins:

On April 25th of this year, just three weeks ago Heather, age 21, and Wayne, age 25, were married in a small church ceremony. In attendance were Heather's mother and father, a friend from the tea room of the Department store where Heather worked, Wayne's boss from the restaurant where he worked, and the family minister. Wayne's mother refused to attend since she was opposed to the marriage and his father is divorced and has no contact with him.

You may immediately wonder why such an episode has any particular significance. Do not many young men and women get married at this age, sometimes against a parent's wishes? Is this then not a normal event? Of course the answer to these two questions is yes. However, when I add that Heather and Wayne are young people handicapped by fates over which they had no control nor did their parents, a story begins to evolve. It is a story which Heather and her family want me to share with others who can learn from their experiences. As her mother put it—"she has helped us and I hope will continue to help others." Heather advanced in a world that tended to oppose and question her rights to as normal a life as possible.

For two years I shared Heather's inner feelings about herself and her past and current experiences with the outside world as her therapist and friend and also tried to be helpful in dealing with many realistic issues. I had the support and confidence of her parents in these endeavors with a greater willingness on the part of Heather's mother to take risks. For me the story was a sensitive and moving venture in areas where I had little experience and limited help from theoretical conceptualization. I tried to facilitate what felt right and to oppose what seemed wrong and in that process received support, indifference, and opposition from various agencies and professionals. I also slowly became Wayne's friend of the present and I say slowly because initially his trust in me as a man and particularly as a psychiatrist was limited. The love relationship of these two young people was a convincing one and to support in realistic ways its fulfillment came naturally. So I want to share my part in this story with the hope that as professionals we can provide appropriate help and advocacy to handicapped people and their families individually and collectively—of making available patterns and conditions of everyday life which are as close as possible to the norms and patterns of the mainstream of society.

Heather, the child of professional parents, was born when her mother was thirty-nine years of age at which age the incidence of Down's syndrome (mongolism) is about 1 in 660 births. And Heather had the syndrome. In 1954, when Heather was born, the mother knew that institutionalization was the most frequent recommendation in these cases but she "couldn't go through with it." Fortunately, Heather's pediatrician favored home care, and Heather grew up as a regular member of the family.

The precipitating factor which brought Heather to Dr. Blom was a psychological evaluation when she was 18 years of age "to bring her records into conformity with state regulations and to determine eligibility for continuing participation in a work-study program."

A pediatric friend asked if I would do a psychiatric evaluation on Heather who was then almost 19 years old. Her mother had a number of concerns: (1) was she psychotic, (2) how disturbed was she, (3) what were her future adjustment possibilities, and (4) what recommendations could be given to facilitate her adaptation. The questions about psychosis and severity of emotional disturbance had arisen suddenly from a school conference a month previously where the parents were told about the results of "routine psychological testing" done twelve months previously in 1972. Twelve months is a long time to delay in sharing and communicating feelings of such an ominous nature, regardless of their reliability. Again this was evidence that the normalization principle was not being practiced—i.e., the principle being that human management professions, as Wolfensberger calls us (Wolfensberger, 1972), did not use means as normative as possible to establish or maintain behaviors and characteristics that were as culturally normative as possible. Understandably the parents were frightened and confused but had sufficient ego strength to question the psychological interpretations. Heather's mother knew she was sad and troubled but had every reason to doubt that Heather was psychotic. Previous experiences with professionals had given her good reasons to question them at times and rely on her own judgment, intuition, and values—beginning with the obstetrician. As mother wrote—"I remember seeing Heather in the bassinet in the delivery room and remarking that she looked a little mongoloid. Dr. U. thought I was a rejecting mother for this comment." In another part of a developmental questionnaire she wrote about the pregnancy—"I also worried about Down's syndrome especially since I was over 35 years. We didn't know about its relation to chromosomes at that time in 1954." However, in a letter to me mother also said positively—"M.G. was Heather's pediatrician until she died. She was a great help to me when Heather was born since she favored home care rather than institutionalization (which was common then—and which I knew I couldn't go through with)."

As for Wayne, his family physician reported that he had a traumatic birth which resulted in stunted growth and slow development. He is an only child from an unhappy marriage which resulted in divorce. Although his father is living, on his mother's advice he has told people that his father is dead. Wayne's mother has fostered his dependency on her, opposed his relationship to Heather, and has actively resisted all attempts by various people to discuss the relationship and her feelings. Wayne is judged to be mildly retarded but he does have a driver's license, driving only with his mother present.

Several things are remarkable about Dr. Blom's account. Dominating the account is Heather herself: imaginative, sensitive, verbal, engaging, persistent, and troubled. Knowing that she has Down's syndrome we are simply not prepared for Dr. Blom's description of her and her interactions with him over sixty-six sessions. If we are not prepared, it says as much about us as it does about Heather. When someone looks "odd" and that oddness is supposed to be associated with intellectual and interpersonal inadequacies, we are surprised when that person does not fit our preconceptions. Indeed, Dr. Blom is quite sensitive to the possibility that his account may be seen by some people as a distortion of the true state of affairs.

Perhaps, Dr. Blom, you are not objective enough and too emotionally involved—the implication being that you can't be both objective and emotional. But let me cite some statements from a re-vised 1976 edition of a well-known textbook on mental retardation (Robinson and Robinson, 1976). In a discussion of Down's syndrome these authors indicate that retardation is usually moderate to se-vere; IQs range from 40–54 but can vary widely; "affected persons rarely marry and their libido is said to be diminished"; "emotional disturbance in retarded persons often is more a social phenomenon than an intrapsychic problem"; consultation with parents and teach-ers should be the emphasis in psychological efforts.

In this connection, let us listen to part of a report from a pediatric geneticist to whom Dr. Blom had sent Heather and Wayne for counseling about sterilization.

My meeting with Heather and her fiancee was most informal and intimate. They were, as you know, a delightful couple. I had the impression that both were slow but probably borderline. One felt innocence but also character. On occasion there was the use of words and phrases that were not fully understood, the kind of thing a precocious child who has grown up in too adult an atmosphere might say. None of this is meant to detract. I have never seen anyone with Down's syndrome as able to cope and relate as Heather.

When I asked them why they came, Heather did most of the talking and said that they were in love and wanted to get married. She knew she had Down's syndrome and understood that her chil-dren might have it. Since she did not want her children to have the problems she had, she felt she should be sterilized. We discussed this and mentioned the roughly 50% risk that any child she bore would also have Down's syndrome. Wayne was concerned lest the projected surgery would be painful and unpleasant and offered to be sterilized himself. We discussed that. He brought up the fact that his mother was not in favor of either the match or of vasectomy. We discussed the fact that the risk was Heather's and that we did not know his risk for retarded children. I supported them in their de-sires, agreeing that they might have a problem with the added bur-den of a child. I referred Heather to Dr. D. and offered to see them again if they wished. I only heard from them again by a Christmas card from Heather (several months later).

A second remarkable feature of Dr. Blom's account concerns Heath-er's parents who obviously had been crucial in her rearing. Clearly they regarded Heather as an independent human being who had to be given every opportunity to experience normal living, and if that meant taking risks, that was a problem inherent in rearing any child. This, of course, was in marked contrast to the attitude and practices of Wayne's mother as well as of school personnel and other professionals with whom Heather had contact. Whereas Heather's parents reacted to her as a unique indi-vidual, the community reacted to her in terms of labels.

The third remarkable feature is Dr. Blom himself. Like Heather's parents, he "saw" past her looks and labels, and in a manner quite atypical of professionals he actively helped her in regard to many endeavors.

Over the course of two years I saw Heather sixty-six times, eight of them being shared with Wayne as their relationship developed. I saw the parents about ten times. There were also meetings with school staff, Association for Retarded Citizens staff, child advocates, and a number of occasions when I saw Heather in places other than my office—searching for music companies who would transcribe her tapes at a reasonable price, having lunch with her at the tea room where she worked, and visiting her at the hospital when she had a sterilization procedure.

Let me first tell you about some of the expressive aspects of the therapy even though a great deal of work was also spent on planning and choices, information about plans, and feelings about plans. As you know the best made plans also with "normal" people do not always go smoothly!

Beginning with the second interview Heather would regularly write a list of problems in a book, which became her therapy book. These were the problems she wanted to discuss as well as take off points for associated concerns and problems. If I became too pressing or when Heather became too uncomfortable, she would say "OK, well" and go back to the list.

The list in the second interview consisted of:

1. Watergate is on my mind
2. How to hold a conversation without being interrupted
3. Work at Goodwill
4. Drug addicts and police
5. Make new friends
6. Two uncles died
7. Newer generation

This list of topics got us into her conservative fundamentalist values—beliefs in the president who is head of our country and can't be wrong, police as friends and protectors, and the newer generation destroying the image of God. While I was not always in agreement with her belief system, it became clear that it served a security motive and that relativism made her uncomfortable and anxious. There was some indication over the two years that as her self-esteem improved and the anxieties about death and anger diminished, Heather seemed more flexible in her values and more accepting of wrongdoing in thoughts and actions for herself and others. At her graduation ceremony from high school a young man streaked through the audience and as she told me about it she laughed saying—"he was as naked as a jaybird." Work at Goodwill

Industries as one of her work-study assignments (study was usually the weaker part) made her uncomfortable because of all the deformed and crippled people. She was anxious, cried, felt sorry for them, but didn't want to see them. As you might have expected she eventually talked with feeling about her handicaps—her sadness, anger, blame of parents, envy of others including her sisters, and the guilt such feelings engendered. Slowly she accepted my gentle encouragement that she did not have to use big words but use her own that were very acceptable. Later on with her parents she was willing to accept not understanding situations—"I'm not that smart, but. . . ."

Heather used her problem lists for quite a while but as she felt better about herself, the problems were fewer or she would not bring her therapy book because "I didn't have many problems this week." She brought her poems and transcribed song readings with background music. She was an avid country music fan, listening to KLAK and expressing love for Johnny Cash and his family. She gave me three of his books to read and I became highly informed about his life, activities, and songs. On one occasion she actually shook his hand when he arrived at the airport for a concert he was to give. She also went to the concert with a friend of the family. On another occasion she decided to enter a country music contest and asked me to help her transcribe one of her tapes in the form prescribed by the contest. I was reluctant and tried to discourage her by indicating we both enjoyed her music but I did not think it was good enough. After my hemming and hawing, Heather finally admonished me by saying—"it doesn't do any harm to try—what if I do fail!" I agreed with her and then she said, "OK let's go right now." Whereupon I made some phone calls and we explored some music shops together and finally got the tapes transcribed using her employment money to pay for it.

Her relationship to Wayne developed only a few months after these steps were unsuccessful and quickly became one of love. Heather shared with me their love notes and their secret meetings after work every day. I never had the occasion to question its genuineness. It took several weeks before I met Wayne. One afternoon he came with Heather to a Friday afternoon session which was arranged by her. He understandably felt awkward and uneasy and asked me in an inquisitory tone why Heather was seeing a psychiatrist. I explained that Heather was not crazy but had problems that were helped by talking. He then wanted to know when treatment would end. It was not until some time later he could acknowledge jealousy about Heather's warm feelings for me and his wish to have her share with him exclusively. I recognized the legitimacy of his feelings and wishes. Wayne was at times puzzled by my acceptance.

He gradually saw me as a substitute parent for both of them and could share his concerns about his mother. It was hard for him to believe that advocates and legal assistance were available to help realize his wish to consummate his relationship in marriage. Wayne was quite frightened by the power he attributed to his mother—her custody, her threats to legally classify him as incompetent. He had anxieties about separation and independence too. He used Heather's parents somewhat as his own parents and at times thought of moving in with them if he was thrown out or just had to leave. This concerned the parents who questioned this possibility. As father put it—more bluntly and realistically, "I was worried about having one dependent upon us but having two is too much and going too far." In retrospect his firmness and definiteness at many times, while not always appreciated, were helpful in establishing the reality of what Heather and Wayne wanted. Father was somewhat a skeptic towards many of the endeavors but his love for his daughter was very real and he could allow himself to be convinced where other fathers might continue to oppose.

Many attempts were made to contact Wayne's mother through phone and letter by Heather's parents without success. One letter from her seemed to shut the door on further communication. Wayne's family physician was reluctant to become involved in counseling her. It was at this point that child advocates were involved through the offices of the local association for retarded citizens. An experienced, likeable, and sensitive young couple met Heather and Wayne through my aegis with a view toward providing a relationship, support and advice in their efforts to live independently and be married.

What are the significances of Dr. Blom's account? From one standpoint it could be argued that the major significance is that he had to write it. This is testimony not only of how unaccustomed the community is to dealing with the issues that brought Heather to Dr. Blom but also as a contrast to more frequent community attitudes and practices that work so effectively against normalization. However, from another standpoint it could be argued that the account testifies to a change in community attitudes and practices in that Heather did have a school program; there was a Dr. Blom and a pediatric geneticist, advocates and other supportive services; and no legal or civil rights barriers to the marriage.

Twenty or more years ago it would have been highly unlikely that Heather's parents and Dr. Blom could have been able "to pull it off," and let us not forget that the marriage took place despite the objections of Wayne's mother and school personnel. Put in another way, the community today tolerates and, to a lesser extent, accepts mentally retarded people in its midst more than in the recent past. That is quite a contrast to the days when institutionalization or some other form of social isolation and segregation were the community's chief modes of response.

But how justified are we in stressing the change? An Associated Press report (New Haven Register, October 8, 1976) had the following large lettered headline: "Retarded Couple Make Success of Marriage that 'Couldn't Work.'" The article described the objections the young couple encountered. They met at a workshop (Fresno, California) for handicapped people, fell in love, and wished to marry. "Workshop officials there discouraged them from marrying, as did friends and relatives. But a friend took them to get blood tests and a marriage license, and a justice of the peace performed the ceremony. Seventeen states ban marriages among retarded people, but California is not among them." The couple does have the aid and advice of a social worker who said: "Their arrangement is not something I would recommend for all mentally disabled people, but they seemed to have handled it rather well." When an article like that is in the mass media, it suggests that there has been some change in regard to community attitudes to and understanding of mental retardation, but, similarly, it indicates how far we have to go before such marriages will not be considered newsworthy.

How many parents have the personal strengths and the financial resources to help their children in the way Heather's parents did? How many Dr. Bloms are there? How many parents could afford to pay a Dr. Blom for sixty-six sessions? In our experience, the answer to all these questions is: very, very few. So, although one cannot doubt that there has been a positive change in the community's attitude toward mentally retarded people, the fact remains that the change has been in greater toleration than in acceptance. And by acceptance we mean an effort to incorporate them as individuals and not as members of a labeled group, to introduce no barrier to whatever degree of social normalization of which they are capable, to refrain from reacting to them stereotypically.

———————————————

The final part of this chapter continues discussion of the significance of according mentally retarded individuals the status of personhood, but from the standpoint of three cases where my diagnostic acumen failed me. Fortunately, parental love saved the day, so to speak—in ways hard to describe or prove. They are cases from long ago—one from my Southbury days and the other two from my early days at Yale—but I doubt that any reader will deny their import for today.

Three Diagnostic Errors

At its best, a clinical case report forces you to review and reevaluate your clinical experience because the report contains description and interpretation that either are discrepant with your experience or that seem to provide a key to clinical phenomena that have puzzled you. A single case within a series of cases may not prove anything definitive (depending on what you mean by "proof"), but it can alter a field or open a new one. Itard's (Lane, 1976) report on Victor, Freud's (1925) report on Little Hans, and Kanner's (1943) report on a small number of autistic children are examples of case reports the reverberations from which can still be felt. I have no doubt that Blom's (Blom, 1979–80; Sarason and Doris, 1979) report on Heather will have a long life because of the challenges it poses for the way most people, professional and lay, think about mental retardation.

For my purposes here, Itard's report is most relevant because he failed in his goal to rehabilitate Victor. But the interest that his report has had across two centuries stems less from the fact of failure and more from its detailed, compelling, poignant descriptions about the effort to relate to and to change another human being. Indeed, his descriptions are so clear that it is not at all difficult to identify with each of the actors in the drama. And by the time one has finished reading the account, one is more impressed with what was accomplished than with what was not accomplished. One comes away inspired by Itard's persistence and ingenuity, by a doggedness that would not admit of the possibility that the Wild Boy of Aveyron could not be fully socialized and made into whatever was a normal French youngster of the time. Itard was disappointed with what he accomplished, but today we can only marvel at how much Victor changed from what he was when he was captured in the woods. Granted that Itard fell far short of the mark, and granted that the philosophical-conceptual basis for seizing the opportunity to work with Victor was wildly optimistic in its view of human perfectibility, but the following question remains: What are the conditions within which devotion and unflagging motivation will overcome what appear to be insuperable barriers? It is that question to which the following cases are relevant. If these cases do not flatter my self-image as diagnostician, I shall forever be grateful for what I learned from these errors.

Case 1

There were certain times during the week when "children" could be admitted to the Southbury Training School. Our offices were in the administration building, situated so that we could see the cars pull up to the entrance to deposit the child and the adult (or adults). Occasionally, case material was sent to us before admission, allowing us to make some preliminary judgments about a suitable cottage placement. More often than not, the case material accompanied the child on admission, and we had to make some quick decisions about cottage placement. We took cottage placement seriously because being in a "high grade" or "middle grade" or "low grade" cottage was a difference that made a difference. We could, of course, later change a placement, but that could bring in its wake complications for child and staff.

It was an admission day. A car pulled up and from the back seat emerged a rather large man carrying cradle-like in his arms what from our windows looked like an unusually large child of three or four years of age. But we knew that it could not be a child that young because at that time children had to be at least six years of age to be admitted. We went to the front door of the building to greet the party and only then could we see that what we had thought was a young child was in fact a much older male. The accompanying material (quite sparse) indicated that he was 30 years of age and had been taken care of from birth by his mother, who had recently died. The father had died years before. Why was he being carried like a baby? He was as gnarled and contorted, as muscularly and neurologically involved, as any case of cerebral palsy I had ever seen—and Southbury had loads of such cases. His body was constantly moving; he was almost constantly drooling; whenever he attempted what seemed to be a purposeful movement, the diffuseness of his body movement became more intense and widespread; and his disfigured face had a wild, "monster-like" quality to it. I looked at this man with puzzlement because I could not understand why he had not been institutionalized earlier. What little material was in the folder that accompanied him indicated that the mother had been opposed to institutionalization. If I was puzzled about that, I was not puzzled about the cottage in which he should be placed: a large, middle-grade cottage that, in truth, had as many low- as middle-grade individuals. Basically, it was a custodial cottage, unrelated to the institution's educational program. Mr. Humphrey (that was his name) was no candidate for an educational program. Of that I was sure!

It was our practice to do a formal psychological assessment within a few days after admission in order to make a final judgment about cottage placement, suitability for programs in the academic school, work assignment, special needs and cautions, etc. In the case of Mr. Humphrey, there was no need, I decided, to do an early assessment. Indeed, I was relieved that there was no particular point to a psychologic assessment in this instance. Those days were quite busy—the opening of Southbury's doors stimulated a stream of admissions (including children from schools that closed their special classes so that their occupants could be sent to Southbury where they became legal and financial wards of the state). Three weeks later, I was walking past the cottage in which Mr. Humphrey had been placed, and Mr. Rooney, the cottage "father" (there was no "mother" in *that* cottage) came out. Mr. Rooney was one of my favorite people and we began to talk about this and that and the state of the world. I remembered that we had not done an assessment of Mr. Humphrey, and I asked Mr. Rooney how he was doing. Mr. Rooney replied: "Now *there* is a smart person. He can read and he understands everything." I was surprised and my face must have shown it because Mr. Rooney, no shrinking violet and a rather good "natural" clinician, invited me to a demonstration of Mr. Humphrey's abilities. Inside the cottage, Mr. Humphrey was lying on the seat of a wheelchair; i.e., he was lying on the seat as if it were a bed. Mr. Rooney left us for a moment and soon returned with a checkerboard in each square of which was a letter of the alphabet, i.e., the top first square had a large A, the second a B, and so forth. The checkerboard had been one of the things accompanying Mr. Humphrey to Southbury. "Now," Mr. Rooney said, "you ask him a question that requires a one-word answer, then move your finger slowly from one letter to the next and when you have reached the first letter in the answer he will let you know, and you do that for each letter in the answer." How could he let me know if he was in constant motion and if his attempts at vocalization were unintelligible and only increased the level of diffuse bodily activity? I cannot remember what question I put to him, but I do remember that when my finger reached the square containing the first letter of the answer, immediately it was obvious that that was part of the answer—his facial and bodily responses were like a pinball machine gone berserk. He did know the answer to that first question and to almost all of the subsequent ones. I was dumbfounded and I felt stupid, guilty, and quite humble.

I shall not dwell on my diagnostic mistake, which is as unforgivable as it is understandable. I should have known not to go by appearances, or by what a person cannot do, but rather by what a person can *learn* to do, i.e., by signs of potential assets rather than by exclusive reliance on deficits. I had reacted to Mr. Humphrey as if he were a thing, not a person. Instead of arousing my curiosity, challenging me to figure out how I might relate to this individual, forcing me to keep separate what I was assuming from what was factual, Mr. Humphrey's appearance short-circuited the relationship between what I ordinarily believed and practiced. To someone like me, for whom Itard was a major figure in the pantheon of gods, my response to Mr. Humphrey was, to indulge understatement, quite humbling.

Once I was able to overcome (in part at least) my feelings of stupidity, guilt, and inconsistency, I realized that there were questions far more important than my diagnostic acumen. *How did the mother manage to accomplish what she did? What kept her going? What did she recognize in the infant as sparks that could ignite the fires that power learning? What was her theory and in what relation did this stand to her practices? What could we have learned if we had the opportunity to follow and study Mrs. Humphrey in the rearing of her son?* More about the last question after the other two cases are presented.

Case 2

Not long after I left Southbury to come to Yale a friend-colleague asked me if I would evaluate his son, who was two years of age. My friend was a neuropsychiatrist who was known for two characteristics: He was top flight in his field of specialization, and he was quite unstable, if not volatile. I always found him to be strange, giving, sensitive, and internally pressured. His son had clear abnormalities at birth, and a comprehensive diagnostic workup at Yale revealed massive brain damage. My friend refused to accept the clear implication that the child was and would always be mentally retarded, requiring special management throughout life. He was so disdainful of the Yale workup that he took the boy for an independent workup to a well-known Boston center. Their conclusions confirmed the Yale findings, but they were more explicit about the severe restrictions the child's condition put on his future development. He was and would always be severely retarded. I had been told all of this by several people who were concerned not only about the father's inability to accept the findings but also about the obsessive quality with which he searched the literature for what could be done to help his son. So, when he asked me to see his son, my heart sank because I had every reason to believe that nothing I could find or recommend would be what he wanted to hear. I tried to tell him that, but to no avail. We agreed that my wife and I would visit his home the following Sunday and that I would make it my business to observe his son in the context of home and family. (There was an older child, a girl of six years of age who was both bright and pretty.) Three things immediately struck me when I first saw the boy: the speed with which he was getting around the living room on hands and knees (I knew he was not yet walking); the impression of constant movement his actions conveyed, what some people then would have called "organic drivenness"; and the size of his head, which not only was large but seemed to be as large as the rest of his body. I distinctly remember saying to myself: "If my head was as large as his, I would be unable to stand erect." We visited for a couple of hours. The boy had no speech, never seemed to be at rest, and did not respond to my attempts to gain his attention or to interact with him. His sister was the only person to whom he seemed to respond, by following her wherever she went. I saw nothing to contradict the conclusion that the boy was and would always be severely retarded. I told this to the father. If, I said, at maturity the boy had a mental age of six or seven, I would be somewhat surprised. Needless to say, the father did not hear this with enthusiasm. He was polite, thanked me, and, I think, knew that I felt very badly about having to say what I did. It was obvious that he was not about to accept my conclusions any more than he had accepted earlier ones. I never spoke to him again about his son. In fact, I hardly ever saw him. But through the collegial grapevine, I learned that he devoted a lot of time to the boy, including the administration of special medications that would stimulate development. The marriage had been a rocky one and culminated in divorce, the father continuing to maintain a close relationship with his son. From the rare times I saw him, he seemed to have become more unstable and volatile, an impression that the grapevine substantiated. He remarried, and one day a few years later, he threatened his second wife with a gun. She managed to get the police, and when he saw them arrive, he killed himself. Not everyone was surprised, but everyone was shocked. The local papers had a field day. In the course of conversation with someone who had been the father's neighbor, I asked about the son. I was told that he was progressing normally in an academic high school program and that he was headed for the state university. He went and was graduated from the university.

It was small solace to me that my diagnostic conclusions and predictions were as erroneous as those emanating from prestigious centers in New Haven and Boston. Countless times I have tried to replay my visit and observations in order to see whether I had overlooked or misinterpreted something, whether the mind-set with which I came to the visit blinded me to the child's potential. I had to conclude that I had made an error the significance of which was quite ambiguous. Was the error rooted in a faulty understanding of the developmental dynamics of brain-behavior relationships? Or was the error a function of the failure seriously to try anything—pharmacologic or psychologic—to test (i.e., challenge) the diagnosis? Were the father's efforts irrelevant to the outcome? How could we answer that question without knowing what the father did pharmacologically and psychologically? I could not conclude that his efforts were irrelevant to the outcome. As in the case of Mr. Humphrey, we lacked crucial information. Aside from the diagnoses and prognoses, the one thing we knew was that this father's obsessions led him to actions and interactions that few seriously retarded persons experience.

Case 3

Not long after I had observed the boy in Case II, a colleague called to ask if I would, for purposes of assessment, visit a retarded five-year-old boy in a residential nursery in another state. A friend of my colleague, the boy's grandfather, requested an evaluation because the nursery felt that the boy, Andrew, should be moved to another setting. I was reluctant to make the trip and told my colleague that I would prefer seeing the boy in New Haven. This, it turned out, was not possible for several reasons. The boy's parents had been divorced two or three years earlier, and the father had never visited the nursery; the mother, who lived hundreds of miles away, visited once or twice a year during her shopping expeditions to New York; and the grandfather, who footed all of the boy's bills including my fee, had never visited the boy in the nursery. The grandfather had arranged for a pediatrician in the local community to be available to Andrew. Again reluctantly, I agreed to visit.

I arranged to meet with the pediatrician before going to the nursery. He told me that Andrew had had a mild polio attack from which he had recovered; there was some nonspecific brain damage associated with a "sugar-loaf" shaped skull and with an awkward gait and other motor movements. Andrew was a nice, likable, obviously retarded child.

The nursery was a large ranch house in a residential neighborhood. I rang the bell, and the door was soon opened by a young boy who, from the pediatrician's description, had to be Andrew. He did have a markedly pointy skull and seemed both distracted and anxious. He said something that was hard for me to comprehend because his articulation was not clear, and he ran back into the house and quickly returned with the chief nurse. The nurse and I talked for a while in one corner of a large living room. Andrew was almost always in sight, not because he was asked to be but, it seemed, because he did not want to be far from the nurse. She told me that Andrew was the only ambulatory child in the nursery, all the others being bed patients. She, it turned out, was the one prodding the grandfather to move the boy to a more socially appropriate and intellectually stimulating environment. She obviously liked Andrew and would miss him terribly, but she could not justify his continued residence there. In fact, she asserted, it had become harmful to his development because there literally was no one there, aside from her, with whom he could have a relationship. After indicating that from time to time she had taken Andrew for a visit to her apartment (she was unmarried), she related an incident from several months earlier. She had to go to the local drugstore for supplies and, for the first time, took Andrew with her. She had started to go into the drugstore when she became aware that Andrew was not at her side. She looked back and there was Andrew, paralyzed by fright and unable to take a step forward or backward. Instantly she realized that Andrew had never been in a store and was fearful of what awaited there. Aside from the handful of times he had been in her apartment, Andrew had not been out of the nursery and its immediate environs. She took him by the hand, went back to the car, and returned to the nursery. That incident was crucial in leading her to contact the grandfather to convince him to consider placing Andrew elsewhere.

Prior to testing, I tried to interact with Andrew. For one thing, I had trouble making out what he said. No less interfering was his clear reluctance about interacting with me. It seemed to be a reluctance powered by anxiety, which at the time mystified me, although the thought did occur to me that Andrew did not view my visit as being in his best interests. There was something very likable and pathetic about him. As soon as I tried to administer some intelligence test items, his anxiety noticeably increased and, in the most indirect ways, he let me know that he wanted no part of what was going on. It was as if he sensed that I was somebody who could be harmful to him. He whimpered, became tearful, and once or twice got up from his chair to depart. I stopped my efforts at formal testing. I had already concluded that Andrew was markedly retarded, although I did not know how seriously. I had also concluded that, regardless of the degree of retardation, this nursery placement had become dramatically counterproductive and that he had to be placed elsewhere. Finally, and crucially, what concerned me most was the implications of the fact that Andrew had one and only one significant relationship with another human being: the nurse. Psychologically, she was his mother. That is the way he related to her and she felt about him. Theirs was *not* a nurse-child relationship. I related all of this in a report to the grandfather and urged that it was essential that the nurse accompany Andrew to the new setting and stay with him until he had made some kind of positive adjustment. The thought that Andrew would be picked up at the nursery and taken (psychologically alone) to a new setting interfered with my sleep! I received no reply from the grandfather.

A year or so later, my colleague called me up to say that the grandfather was requesting another evaluation. The nurse, my colleague related, had been persuaded by the grandfather to give up her job and to devote her time and energies to caring for Andrew. He had been placed in a kindergarten in a public school and the immediate question was: *Should he be promoted to the first grade, which the school recommended?*

I did not need to be urged to visit the nurse and Andrew. Obviously, somebody was selling somebody else a bill of goods! What fool or knave was recommending that the Andrew I had seen a year or so earlier was ready for first grade? The nurse had moved into a garden apartment development. When I steered my car into the development, I had to go at about one mile an hour because the area seemed to consist of more children than blades of grass. I parked the car very near their apartment and, as soon as I got out of the car, a young boy approached. It was Andrew, but what a different Andrew! There was that pointy skull, his motor movements were not graceful but they were far more smooth than when I had first seen him, he spoke with a clarity that amazed me, and he seemed to know and to be on very good terms with the other children. He guided me to the apartment, chit-chatting with me. However, even in those early moments, I sensed that he was very ambivalent about my visit, as if he wanted to be his usual giving self but was suspicious about what my agenda was. This became more noticeable later when I tried to test him and, again, I stopped because it seemed upsetting to him. We did enough, though, with my observations, for me to conclude that Andrew tested within the normal range. Whereas on my first visit there was a question about how seriously retarded he was, the question now in my mind was how bright he might be. If on my first visit I intuited a mother-child relationship, I did not have to resort to intuition on my second visit a year or so later. She was a mother constantly seeking ways to stimulate the boy and to help him overcome a pervasive anxiety and self-depreciatory tendency. She told me that within a year or so she would like to move south and take Andrew with her. What did I think? I, of course, said that Andrew should go where she goes. As for promotion to the first grade: of course. Two years later I received a call from the nurse. She and Andrew had moved south and they were both happy and doing well. The reason for the call was that Andrew's mother had visited a number of times in the past years, developed a real interest in the "new" Andrew, and now wanted him to come live with her. How should the nurse respond? I was explicit in recommending that she try to avoid such a change. I also wrote this to the grandfather.

I shall assume that no reader will accuse me of stating or implying that parental love, devotion, and energy are unmixed blessings and that, if these characteristics could be appropriately channeled, scads of retarded persons would become "unretarded." Nor do I wish anyone to conclude that parents possess knowledge and wisdom that professionals do not, as if parents possess a productive interpersonal sensitivity and "natural" clinical acumen that is in short supply among professionals. These are arguable issues, but they are irrelevant to the reasons why I have presented these cases. The first reason why I presented the three cases is that they raise this question: How frequent are these kinds of cases? Far more often than not, we write about our successes, not our mistakes. Also, we feel more secure in our explanations of our successes than of our failures. After all, our successes presumably confirm us as thinkers and doers; our failures clearly say that we have earned the right to be humble. The second reason is to suggest that the unusual degree of involvement and commitment demonstrated in these cases is rare among parents. Their commitment and involvement are far from typical; rather they are very atypical and, therefore, there is all the more reason to focus on them. But, it might be argued, I am confusing rare with infrequent. That is to say, the outcomes associated (i.e., not in any simple cause-and-effect way) with such parental dedication may not be as rare as I am suggesting. They certainly are not frequent, but, the argument might continue, they are less rare than published cases would indicate. Parents of these children rarely write up their experience, and for obvious reasons professionals are hardly in a position to see such cases. There is a difference between incidence and prevalence; the incidence of these kinds of cases may be greater than their prevalence in the literature suggests.

But why is such parental dedication rare or infrequent? That question brings us to the third reason for presenting these cases: Professional and societal conceptions of and attitudes toward the biologic basis of severe mental retardation and its implications for prognosis are obstacles in the way of parental activity and creativity. If in diverse ways a parent is told that his or her child has a damaged brain and that there are very definite limits to what can be expected developmentally, and if these communications are unaccompanied by any concrete suggestions about how to stimulate and manage the child in regard to eating, sleeping, playing, crying, vocalizing, locomoting, etc., it is not surprising that these parents often are fearful, feel helpless, and are uncreative. I have known scores of parents at or around the time they took their severely retarded infant or young child home from the clinic or hospital after a definitive diagnosis had been made. As one of them said, summing up beautifully what almost all such parents experience: "I came home with a child and a diagnosis. But as soon as we opened the door and entered the apartment, the question popped into and remained in my head: What do I do *now*, this minute, the next hour, tonight at bedtime? No one told me anything about those kinds of very practical questions." That brings us to the fourth reason: Brain-behavior relationships have to be conceptualized within a complicated matrix of relationships bearing the stamps of the societal attitudes and their history; the status, knowledge, and influence of the professionals involved; individual experiences among parents; and the degree of compatible matching between characteristics of the child and the capabilities, interests, and temperament of the parent. So, today we know, to a degree that Itard could not, how what went on between Itard and Victor is comprehensible only in terms of what happened and was continuing to happen in France, a society in which changes in the social order had altered theories and practices about what the human animal was and could be. That is as true for how we theorize and act today as it was in Itard's time. For example, today it is most unusual for a retarded child to be observed on his or her turf, i.e., in the context of home and family. A very elaborate rationale can be developed to support the practice of the child being seen on the professional's turf. That rationale has, among other things, an economic basis that tends to be downplayed—obviously you can see more patients by schedule in your office than if you visited them in their homes. But the practice also rests on the assumption that you can validly deduce what is going on in the home from what you are told and what you observe in the office. In fact, the available evidence suggests that acting on that assumption can create as many problems as it may ameliorate. The fact is that in the past half-century an enormous change has occurred in terms of where patients are seen, the number and variety of professionals who will see them, and the economic factors associated with these changes. We would like to believe that this change is due to advances in knowledge and technology brought about solely because they are in the best interest of patients (independent of economic considerations), the self-interest of professionals, and the societal zeitgeist. But that is never the case, however much we all collude in the myth that it is. I would maintain that the failure to observe the retarded child in the context of the home and family leads us frequently to erroneous conclusions the detection and correction of which are made difficult by current practice. Moreover, this failure has robbed us of opportunities to be more helpful than we have been.

The final reason I presented the three cases is that they mightily influenced and altered my outlook on mental retardation and our society. This reason is best conveyed in the following story. Not long after I saw the last of the three, I received a call from someone in charge of a foundation devoted to mental retardation that was now seeking to have national impact. The person wanted to meet with me to get my views on what I considered the important problems in the field—the problems that the foundation ought to address. We met twice, each time for several hours. I iterated and reiterated the following points:

1. To my knowledge, there has not been a single longitudinal study of retarded infants.
2. By longitudinal, I mean periodic visits made to the home during which systematic observations are made of the child and family members. In addition, these members are interviewed, with the overarching goal of describing and understanding family structure and dynamics as they conceivably impinge on the infant's or child's behavior and development. (It may sound immodest, but I understood and articulated the conceptual basis of family therapy long before that clinical field became fashionable. That one could understand and program for *any* child without secure knowledge of home and family made as much sense as studying the earth as if the sun did not exist.)
3. Longitudinal studies might provide us with important clues about individual differences in development and about child-environment relationships that either positively or adversely affect a child's progress. If we know anything about brain-behavior relationships, it is how risky it is to predict one from the other and that we must look to other types of interactions to better explain individual differences.
4. When will we begin to take seriously the fact that whatever the justifications for longitudinal studies, they are no less applicable to the area of mental retardation than to normal development?
5. Longitudinal studies are not easy to carry out, they are beset with diverse methodologic problems, they are conducted in a world we cannot control, and they are not panaceas for our ignorance. But, potentially, and at their best, they force us to alter our thinking and actions.

I told this person about my three diagnostic errors and how they drove me to questions that could only be studied by a longitudinal approach. I concluded by saying that the absence of these studies said far more about societal and professional attitudes than it did about their importance for a better understanding of the different conditions giving rise to mental retardation. He was not impressed. But he asked me to send him an outline of the kind of study I was recommending. I did, but never heard from him. That was in 1954. Today, the situation has not changed.

In fairness to this man, I should point out that he was (and is) not alone in his lack of enthusiasm. For a period of 10 years (beginning around 1954), I was a member of different advisory committees to the National Institute of Mental Health on funding for research grants. Those were years when longitudinal ("womb to the tomb," as we called them) studies were fashionable. Not one research proposal demonstrated an interest in mental retardation. Mental retardation has never been in the mainstream of the mental health fields, a fact not explainable in terms of the number of afflicted individuals, their impact on their families (and vice versa), the economic costs, the moral sensitivity of the society, or the challenge this field poses to theory, research, and practice.

Notes

1. From "The Use of the Thematic Apperception Test with Mentally Deficient Children" by S. B. Sarason, 1943, *American Journal of Mental Deficiency*, 47(4), pp. 414–421. Copyright 1943 by American Association on Mental Deficiency. Reprinted by permission.
2. From "The Use of the Thematic Apperception Test with Mentally Deficient Children" by S. B. Sarason, 1943, *American Journal of Mental Deficiency*, 48(2), pp. 169–173. Copyright 1943 by American Association on Mental Deficiency. Reprinted by permission.
3. From "Dreams and Thematic Apperception Test Stories" by S. B. Sarason, 1944, *Journal of Abnormal and Social Psychology*, 39(4), pp. 121–126. Copyright 1944 by American Psychological Association. Reprinted by permission.
4. Reprinted from *Psychological Problems in Mental Deficiency* (1st ed., pp. 263–311) by S. B. Sarason, 1949, which is out of print. Therefore, for the reader's convenience, here and in subsequent chapters the format for the references has been changed so that citations refer to the reference list at the end of this volume. The tables have also been renumbered.
5. The following letter was sent by Lottie after an interview in which she had reported in a flippant manner some misbehavior, resented the psychologist's expression of disapproval, and left the office without saying goodbye.
   Dear Dr.
   Just a few line to said that I'm sorry that I did not said goodbye to you. You think that I don't blieve you what you said to me, but I bleive you what you tell me.
   I no that you give up talk to me, but you think that I won't act like a lady but some day you will be glad that I act like a lady.
   I hope you have a nice time read this letter so please let me know what you think of it.
   From
   Lottie
6. When Stephen was admitted, he was placed in a cottage for imbecile boys, an unfortunate placement which was later rectified. The fact that he was not

placed with boys like himself reinforced his belief that something was wrong with his brain. As will be seen later, this belief was longstanding.

7. The data supplied by the orphanage do not indicate that Stephen was allowed to visit his mother, who lived in the same city. While such visits may have been allowed, it is probably that many of them were not sanctioned and were either substitutes for going to school or mere absences from the orphanage.

8. From *Educational Handicap, Public Policy, and Social History* (pp. 97–106) by S. B. Sarason and J. Doris, 1979, New York: Free Press. Copyright 1979 by Free Press. Reprinted by permission.

CHAPTER 3

Problem Solving in Nontesting Situations

How do you account for the fact that the behavior sampled and observed in a formal testing situation can be so different from problem-solving behavior in a nontesting situation? What has permitted us to assume that the style and level of performance in a formal testing situation predicts style and level in a nontesting situation? The issue, I must emphasize, does not involve prediction from one testing situation to another (e.g., from an intelligence test to grades or achievement tests). Indeed, there is a prior issue: Why has there been such a paucity of research on problem solving in naturally occurring situations? The answer, in brief, is that it is very hard to conduct such research. Besides, educators and psychologists needed means to make relatively quick judgments about many, many individuals. In short, society (through its representatives—educators, psychologists, and social policymakers) defined the problem in terms of the needs of a mass society, and one of those needs was for relatively quick and efficient means to get information about those who comprised that mass society (e.g., schoolchildren). This definition was not in itself unjustified during the decades of a burgeoning population, unprecedented waves of immigration, the legitimation of compulsory education, and the transformation of schools into bureaucratic organizations. But in a strictly scientific or logical sense, these factors did not excuse the absence of research on the validity of the assumption that scores on formal tests permitted prediction of problem-solving ability in nontesting situations. If that assumption has less validity than current theory and practice require, it would have enormous consequences for current practices. It would also cast the cyclical nature-nurture controversies in a new light.

The Uneducated

An article I wrote in the early forties (Sarason, 1944) very briefly raised the issue of the relationship between problem solving in formal and naturally occurring situations:

> A more recent manifestation of the limitations of the intelligence test results is the number of so-called defectives who have not only successfully adjusted to the Armed Services' program but who also have become noncommissioned officers and in some instances been cited for bravery. While it is true that there are many defectives who have been inadequate in the Armed Services, the fact still remains that the intelligence quotient is unilluminating in regards to the reasons for success or failure of defectives of similar mental level. (p. 242)

The problematic nature of that relationship was far more dramatically described by Ginzberg and Bray in their 1953 book, *The Uneducated*, an analysis of World War II soldiers who were illiterate and/or mentally retarded by a psychometric criterion. That book never received the attention it deserved, so the fourth edition of *Psychological Problems in Mental Deficiency* (Sarason, 1969) devoted a section to the implications of their descriptions and findings. That section is reprinted here:[1]

> In 1953 Ginzberg and Bray published a book entitled *The Uneducated*. This book contained a searching and illuminating analysis of men who were rejected on the ground of mental deficiency for military service in World War II. It also contained a study of a sample of men who had been accepted by the armed services but who were illiterate or semi-illiterate. The men in this sample had been through a special education training program set up by the military. We shall discuss this book not only for the data it contains but also because we feel that it can serve as a basis for raising some of the most important research problems in the area of mental retardation.
> From the beginning of selective service until the end of the war,

there were 716,000 individuals who were between 18 and 37 years of age and were rejected on the grounds of mental deficiency. Some of the problems associated with the interpretation of this figure may be seen from the following quotation:

> Relatively little research has been devoted to ascertaining the number of individuals in the population who cannot meet a minimum performance criterion as workers and citizens. Some authorities estimate that approximately one per cent of the population can perform even unskilled work only under close supervision in a protective environment. It is believed that another one per cent of the population are able to work effectively only if they have some type of special supervision. According to these estimates the percentage of persons who would not meet a minimum performance standard because of intellectual deficiency would be 2 per cent. The more than 700,000 men rejected for military service under the general heading of "mental deficiency" amounted to about 4 per cent of the men examined. On the surface this might be taken to mean that the screening standards used were somewhat tight but approximately correct. Again, however, a national average obscures the truth, for nearly 14 per cent were rejected in some states and only one-half of one per cent in others. The fact that the national rejection rate was only a little higher than the theoretical rate of true mental deficiency cannot be taken as an indication that the screening validly assessed either mental deficiency or ability to give satisfactory performance. The regional patterning of the rejections indicates that the screening assessed primarily the individual's educational background. (p. 41)

We turn to Ginzberg and Bray's study of a group of men who had been accepted by the armed services but who were illiterate or semi-illiterate. These men had been through a special education training program set up by the military, a program that became increasingly larger as the standards for acceptance into the armed forces became progressively lower. The men sent to the Special Training Units were of two kinds: those who were formally classified as illiterate and those who scored low (Group V) on the Army General Classification Test. Re the latter Ginzberg and Bray state: "These men were considered 'slow learners' but in reality were mainly those who had had only a little more education than those called illiterate." The problem of illiteracy confronting the military can be seen from the following:

> More than 400,000 illiterates served within the Armed Forces during World War II. The combined group of illiterates and poorly educated who saw active duty totaled almost 700,000. To this must be added more than 700,000 additional persons, the vast majority of

whom were rejected outright for military service because of serious educational deficiencies. In short, the findings which emerge are directly relevant for appraising a group of almost one and one-half million persons out of a total of 18 million registrants who were screened. Clearly we are dealing with a significant sector of the nation's manpower resources. (p. 77)

In setting up the Special Training Program certain specific goals were sought:

1. To teach the men to read at least at a fourth-grade level so that they would be able to comprehend bulletins, written orders and directives, and basic Army publications.
2. To give the men sufficient language skill so that they would be able to use and understand the everyday oral and written language necessary for getting along with officers and men.
3. To teach the men to do number work at a fourth-grade level, so they could understand their pay accounts and laundry bills, conduct their business in the PX, and perform in other situations requiring arithmetic skill.
4. To facilitate the adjustment of the men to military training and Army life.
5. To enable the men to understand in a general way why it was necessary for this country to fight a war against Germany, Japan, and Italy. (p. 69)

The maximum amount of time that an individual could remain in the course was 120 days. "Approximately 40 per cent of the men graduated in less than 30 days. Almost 80 per cent graduated in less than 60 days. Only a very few, less than 11,000 out of 255,000 graduates, remained in a Special Training Unit more than 90 days."

Let us make the following assumptions: (a) more than a few of those formally classified as illiterates were not intellectually retarded; (b) more than a few of the "slow learners" were diagnostic errors—their true IQ was above that indicated by Army test scores; (c) more than a few of the graduates did not reach the goals previously indicated and did not in fact pass the examination in reading and arithmetic required for graduation. Making the allowances indicated by these assumptions *we think it not unreasonable to make the further assumption that the above figures suggest that the rate of learning of more than a few men was far beyond that which one would expect from their potential as inferred from test scores.* Put in another way: the performance of more than a few was better than an evaluation of the potential or capacity had indicated. Here again one cannot avoid inquiring about the possible factors which can produce an apparent discrepancy between capacity and functioning. In order to do so it would be helpful if one described some of the background charac-

teristics of the sub-sample of 400 men whose Army records were scru-
tinized by Ginzberg and Bray:

> Our sample, it will be recalled, consisted of 400 men: 200 white
> and 200 Negro, half drawn from the deep South and half from the
> border states and the North, half inducted in the latter part of 1943,
> and the other half in the last six months of 1944.
>
> All but three of the 400 men were born in the United States.
> Since, at the time of the 1940 Census, almost three-fifths of the 1.5
> million draft-age men with less than four years of schooling lived in
> small communities or on farms, it is not surprising to discover that
> most of our group also came from rural backgrounds. Almost three-
> fourths were born in communities of under 5,000 population. More
> than one-third, however, had migrated from their birth places. When
> inducted, 56 per cent lived in communities under 5,000 population;
> a little more than a fifth were inducted from cities of more than
> 100,000.
>
> Slightly under half, 179, were 20 years of age or less when in-
> ducted; 275 were 25 or less; and just under 85 per cent of the entire
> group were 30 or less. Thirty-nine were between the ages of 31 and
> 35, and 14 between 36 and 38. The median age for the entire group
> was 21.5 years. The median age for the Negroes, however, was 2.4
> years higher than for the whites.
>
> There were no conspicuous differences between the years of
> school completed by the whites and the Negroes, but the "north-
> ern" group (Camp Atterbury, Indiana) showed a higher average than
> the "southern" (Camp Shelby, Mississippi, and Fort Benning, Geor-
> gia) group. The men inducted in 1944 also had a higher average
> number of years of schooling than the group inducted in 1943. The
> most striking fact about the educational background of the group is
> that 55 per cent had completed more than four years of schooling.
> Only 3 per cent had never attended school. Almost 5 per cent had
> more than eight grades of schooling, and more than 25 per cent had
> reached at least the seventh grade. In light of these facts, it is sur-
> prising to find that of the men for whom information was available,
> 228 were designated as illiterate, while only 69 were classified as lit-
> erate and sent to special training because of a low score on the
> Army General Classification Test.
>
> More than half of the group, 226 men, had once been farmers,
> although less than half were farmers when inducted. Just more
> than two-thirds of the whites had farming backgrounds, but less
> than half of the Negroes. Only about a third of the Northern Negroes
> but almost 80 per cent of the Southern whites had been farmers at
> some time. (p. 80)

Not only is it clear from the above that these men came from rural areas where educational resources are generally inferior, but also that many of these men either learned nothing or little from their schooling, or that whatever they did absorb during school was of no significance in their later lives and consequently was "unlearned." *That an individual can go through eight grades of school and then at the age of 20 appear to be illiterate may be explained in different ways; that the same individual at age 20 can in a very short period of time demonstrate a fair amount of educational progress increases the complexity of the problem. We feel that we do not have a basis for choosing among different explanations. We do feel, however, that it is justified to suggest that we are not dealing primarily with an educational problem in the narrow sense of the word but one of motivation and attitude both of which cannot be understood unless studied in the cultural matrix in which they arise.*

Table 2 contains information concerning the occupational status of the men at induction. Since we know that these men were either illiterate or low scorers on an intelligence test, it is not surprising that they had the kinds of jobs they did. However it is one thing to say this is expected and another thing to provide an explanation. In one sense it is perfectly correct to say that these men held the jobs they did *because* of their intellectual and educational status—these are the kinds of jobs available to them. But this brings us back to the recurring question: What are the factors determining the intellectual and educational status of these men? Again leaving this question aside—primarily because our current knowledge only permits us to suggest, as indicated earlier, what some of these factors and their interaction might be—we would like to pose another question: How does one evaluate an individual's problem-solving behavior outside of a test situation? Throughout the course of the day in the life of any individual he is presented with problems the solutions to which vary in the complexity of response they require for resolution. Not only may we commonsensically assume variation through the course of a day but also among problem-solving activities in different spheres of functioning, e.g., educational, vocational, sexual, etc. Although more often than not there is a fair degree of variation or "scatter" within an individual's own test performance, it is surprising how frequently we assume that the level of problem-solving behavior outside the test situation is fairly even. When it is remembered that our discussion concerns those men whose performance in the Special Training Units suggests a capacity beyond that indicated by their test scores and educational status, we think it justified to raise the possibility that the previous non-test problem-solving behavior of these men was in some spheres or activities better than their test scores or educational status suggests. Unfortunately, there have been no systematic investigations of this problem. It is apparent that there are extremely thorny problems involved in the observing,

TABLE 2.   Occupations at induction of men assigned to special training units (from Ginzberg and Bray)

		White		Negro	
Occupation	Total	North	South	North	South
Farmer	173	43	60	22	48
Non-farm:					
Laborer	90	22	13	29	26
Janitor, porter, busboy, etc.	36	3	4	21	8
Truck driver, chauffeur, auto mechanic, etc.	44	12	6	15	11
Factory operative	26	11	8	5	2
Coal miner	13	7	2	4	0
Craftsman	7	1	3	0	3
Other	11	1	4	4	2
Total non-farm	227	57	40	78	52
Grand total	400	100	100	100	100

sampling, and recording of non-test problem-solving behavior—aside from the problem of quantifying samples of behavior obtained in situations over which we have no control. But if problem-solving behavior in test situations cannot be assured to be representative of all problem-solving, the lack of research in this problem can no longer be excused.

In the context of the present discussion it is important to report briefly the results of the analysis, of the military records of the subsample of 400 men.

To check on the reasonableness of our evaluation of the military performance of the uneducated, the graduates of the Special Training Units were compared with a control group consisting of average soldiers whose education and mentality were sufficient to enable them to enter basic training immediately after induction into the Army. This control group was constructed by selecting the man of the same race whose serial number was next higher than that of each man in the Special Training Unit group. If the man with the next higher number had also been assigned to a Special Training Unit, the man with the nearest higher number was selected. The control sample was not representative of the Army as a whole, but permitted a comparison between men inducted from the same localities who differed primarily with respect to their level of education.

While 26 per cent of the 400 Special Training Unit men had less than four years of schooling, this was true of only one per cent of the control group. Only 2 per cent of the whites and 8 per cent of the Negroes in the Special Training Unit group, but 55 per cent of the control group had attended high school. Five per cent of the control group had attended college. Obviously, there was a significant difference in the educational background of the two groups. With respect to occupational background, the size of the communities in which they had been born, the extent to which they had migrated, and their place of residence at the time when they were inducted, however, the differences between the two groups were not substantial. . . .

In order to judge the relative over-all performance of the Special Training Unit and control groups, a summary card was prepared for each man. Care was taken that the cards would contain no hint whether the case was a Special Training Unit graduate or a control case, or whether the man was white or Negro. These cards were then shuffled and sorted into the five groups: very good, good, acceptable, not acceptable, and non-chargeable. . . .

This objective comparison showed that just under a quarter of the men of the control group were very good, a third were good, another third were acceptable. Only 7 per cent of this group were not acceptable, and 3 per cent were non-chargeable. Only 9 per cent of the men of the Special Training Unit group were very good, but slightly under a third were good, and almost half were acceptable. Twelve per cent were not acceptable, and 3 per cent were non-chargeable.

This comparison demonstrates conclusively that, granted our criteria, the control group contained many more very good soldiers than the Special Training Unit graduates. One of our criteria, however, was rank, and it is to be expected that those with more pre-service education would more often qualify for higher non-commissioned-officer assignments. It was, in any case, not expected that the Special Training Unit graduates would include a great many outstanding soldiers. The question was rather whether any appreciable number would perform adequately and represent a clear gain to the Army. This question is answered unequivocally. Eighty-five per cent of the graduates performed acceptably or better as compared to 90 per cent of the control group. Clearly, at a time when the Armed Forces needed men badly, they were able with a small investment to turn many illiterates and poorly educated men into acceptable soldiers. (pp. 31–32)

It should be noted that Ginzberg and Bray were quite aware of the many problems involved in utilizing and categorizing military records. Even if one were to assume that the "true" picture of the records of the men from the Special Training Units was not as favorable as Ginzberg and Bray describe, it would still be reasonable to conclude that the problem-solving behavior of many of the men was better than objective educational and test data indicated. It would repay the reader to study the 22 case records which Ginzberg and Bray present in one of the chapters in the book. In more than a few of these cases the discrepancy between problem-solving behavior in and outside the test situation is marked.

We have previously noted that the rate of learning of many of the men of the Special Training Units was surprising. Unfortunately we do not have the data or observations with which to evaluate such a conclusion. However, the following partial description of the Training Unit has some important implications for future research on this problem.

> A "cadre" or staff of enlisted personnel form the basis for all instruction in the Special Training Unit. Each man has been selected for the position on the basis of his academic background as well as being a capable military instructor. With but few exceptions, all of the instructors are college graduates, many of them possess Master's degrees and a few holding various Doctor's degrees. Formerly they were connected with civilian school systems, ranging from the elementary through the college level. The unit is staffed by 26 officers qualified both academically and militarily.

> Experience has shown that men of the calibre that are received in the Special Training Unit learn more and faster if they are allowed to absorb the training given with the same group of men for the entire period they are here. For that reason, men are assigned to barracks and remain there until they leave. One classroom is set up on each of the two floors of the building and provided with tables, chairs, blackboards, and other instructional aids pertaining to the type of work being covered. For a short period of time after entrance into the barracks, some men are prone to exhibit shyness due to the fact that they have never associated closely with other men.

> Gradually the spirit of teamwork and cooperation are developed and within a few days the men have made an adjustment sufficient to enhance learning. Since changing from one group to another would tend to prolong the period of adjustment, that method is not employed. The military instructor, a Corporal or Sergeant, lives in the barracks with the men, eats with them and works with them and it is rare that he fails to gain the complete confidence of his men almost immediately. The instructor's job lasts 24 hours per day. During the off duty hours much of his time is taken up writing letters for the trainees or giving them advice on their personal problems. Also he will devote considerable time to additional instruction for men who are learning slower than others. (p. 81)

The implications of this excerpt might be put in a series of questions: What significance did these men attach to being sent to the Training Unit? Did they view the education they were now receiving differently than when they had previously been in school? What were the kinds and strengths of motivations engendered in these men by this experience? To what extent was their progress due to the fact that instruction was specifically geared to their needs? Were the attitudes of the instructors to the men different from those of the teachers they had in their previous school experiences? Was there a change of attitude on the part of these men toward education as a result of experiences after leaving school?

In a real sense part of the previous discussion has begged a question which, while central to any analysis of the problem of subnormality, has received surprisingly little attention. We refer here to the question: What do our available intelligence tests measure? From the previous chapter one could conclude that these tests to a marked degree measure educational opportunity and achievement. While it is encouraging to know that these tests are significantly correlated with these variables, the implications of such correlations are both far reaching and disturbing. Since the contents and goals of our school curricula are extremely narrow in terms of the skills and contents encompassed, we are faced with the possibility that our intelligence tests measure a very restricted range of problem-solving stimuli and intellectual activities. Let us put the problem in cross-cultural terms: if one were to observe daily learning activities of an urban American 10-year-old and his counterparts among the Navaho or the Alorese, one would be struck by the differences in the kinds of problem-solving stimuli and intellectual activities which would be observed. Although the differences on the stimulus side would probably be greater than on the response side (i.e., the kinds of thinking sequences required for problem solution), the important point is that any conclusion about the "intellectual performance and capacities of 10-year-olds" would be limited and even misleading if based on the observation of any one of these cultural groups. In this connection it should be recalled that in the previous chapter it was pointed out that for many children in our culture, particularly those that have been labelled mentally retarded or slow-learners, there is reason for raising the possibility that the kinds of intellectual stimuli and activities which one observes in a test or school situation may be of a different level and/or kind than one would observe outside of such a situation. In other words, there is no a priori basis for rejecting the possibility that the range of differences we observe cross-culturally may be found, to a lesser degree, between and within certain groups in our own culture if a representative sample of their problem-solving behavior was obtained. It should perhaps be made explicit that we are not equating problem-solving with all intellectual activity or thinking behavior. We stress the problem-solving situation, be it a standardized one as in a test or one observed in a free situation, not only because of what we learn about the adequacy, level, and varieties of problem-solving behavior but also because it allows us to make inferences about kinds and characteristics of thought processes. Equally important is the fact that the problem-solving situation, being a clear instance of goal-directed or motivated behavior, gives us the possibility of studying the relationships between intellectual and personality variables.

That intelligence tests may be excellent indicators of educational achievement and poor indicators of non-test or non-academic intellectual activity is something to which the practicing clinician, particularly the one who has worked in an institutional setting, will readily attest.

More recently, in 1980, I was asked to review Jensen's (1979) *Bias in Mental Testing*. That gave me another opportunity to restate the issue. That review (Sarason, 1980) is reprinted here:[2]

I have never regarded Arthur Jensen as a racist, and always felt the epithets hurled at him to be unwarranted. He is a very sophisticated psychologist who surveyed a vast literature and had the courage to state conclusions he knew would be unpopular and controversial. His earlier monograph created a storm that has not yet subsided. That blacks view him with disdain goes without saying, but his critics go far beyond the black community and include diverse kinds of scientists no less sophisticated than he. Unlike combatants in nature-nurture controversies of earlier times, Jensen's critics seem to accept the fact that there is overwhelming evidence that blacks score lower than whites on intelligence tests. They accept the "fact" but argue that its "truth" lies elsewhere than in the genetic framework where Jensen places it. He has been attacked on the grounds that he does not really understand genetics, that he simply does not comprehend the influence of an adverse environment (sustained over centuries) on its victims, and that not all of his "facts" are facts. For example, in his book *The Cult of the Fact*, with the subtitle *A Psychologist's Autobiographical Critique of His Discipline*, the British psychologist Liam Hudson spends somewhat less than ten percent of the book criticizing Jensen's use of a study of people with Turner's syndrome, a chromosomal anomaly in which there are forty-five chromosomes instead of the usual forty-six. According to Jensen, this is "a genetic observation, clearly identifiable under the microscope, which has quite specific consequences on cognitive processes. Such specific intellectual deficiencies are thus entirely possible without there being any specific environmental deprivations needed to account for them." Hudson demonstrates that Jensen's reporting of this study is both incomplete and misleading and that the "facts" hardly justify Jensen's conclusions. (Long before Cyril Burt's faking of data was exposed, Hudson asserted that Jensen was accepting that research too uncritically.) Although Hudson is extremely critical of Jensen, he ends the discussion with the following statement:

> If my interpretation is approximately correct, and if one may
> be forgiven a cheap pun, Professor Jensen's impulse is to call a

spade a spade. And, under the influence of this impulse, he has not
merely misinterpreted evidence but also confused the purposes to
which it can logically be put. One's initial reaction is that of high-
minded indignation—followed quickly by a wave of fear lest you
have blundered equally publicly yourself. But in the light of truths
about the nature of psychology now dawning, both responses seem
inadequate. Our perception of meaning in our own research is a
subtle affair, related only in a complex way to fact and logic. Trans-
gressions as blatant as those surrounding Turner's syndrome one
can still condemn in the conventional way: but more baffling are the
processes of selective attention that involve all of us, as soon as we
relate factual evidence to some more generally interpretative theme.
Jensen's article could be dismissed as lying—at least in part—outside the normal confines of scientific debate; he could be discred-
ited as someone who has fallen from the straight ways of Science.
But this, I am now convinced, would be to miss the exemplary point
he unwittingly affords us. Namely, that the search for meaning in
data is bound to involve all of us in distortion to a greater or lesser
degree. Psychology should be pictured not as a society of good men
and true, harbouring the occasional malefactor, but rather, as one in
which everyone is searching for sense; in which differences are
largely those of temperament, tradition, allegiance and style; and in
which transgression consists not so much in a clean break with
professional ethics, as in an unusually high-handed, extreme or
self-deceptive attempt to promote one particular view of reality at
the expense of all others. On this second view, Jensen is certainly
not alone, and his company may prove to be very numerous indeed.

Hudson is obviously a person who does not take himself and his field
(and the "facts") with deadly seriousness. Jensen does, or seems to, and
that characteristic, I suggest, is what has been most bothersome to his
critics. I do not offer this as an argumentum ad hominèm but as a way of
saying that it is puzzling how deadly serious Jensen can be about issues
and conclusions that at this time cannot be solved in the natural-science
sense of solution. It would be one thing for Jensen to raise a question and
suggest an answer. It is quite another thing to raise the question and insist on the answer. One could argue that if Jensen (or anyone else) were
so sure of the answer, it would have been worse than hypocritical not to
have said so. Besides, the argument could continue, Jensen's deadly seriousness and insistence will sharpen the issues through controversy
and research and, with the passage of time, the field may come around to
accepting the validity of his position. But that argument concedes the
point: at this time Jensen's interpretation of the facts has not been persuasive to many people and, therefore, cannot and should not be the
basis for any social action. It may turn out that Jensen was right; it may
turn out that he was wrong. We are not dealing with quantity and quality

of facts, and with clarifying explanations of those facts, to justify any public policy. Have we not learned anything from the arrogance and failures
of the field of economics?

The above is by way of prologue to comments about Jensen's *Bias in
Mental Testing*. It contains 786 pages, weighs about five pounds, and is
not bedside reading. It is, without question, the most serious and boring
book I have read since the days long ago when I tried (unsuccessfully) to
read Talcott Parsons. It is an unremittingly humorless book that in countless ways tries to convince one that there is a psychometric science, that
it is based on many discoveries about the nature of intelligence and its
measurements, and that those who oppose mental testing simply do not
know what they are talking about: they confuse fact with myth, wish with
reality. Jensen always presents two sides (sometimes more) to an issue:
his side and the wrong one. There is, however, a good deal in this book
that anyone with an interest in mental testing ought to know. If the critics
of mental testing understood much of that material, they could marshall
their arguments far better than they do. Similarly, some of the people
who are unreflective partisans of mental testing would become less certain of their position if they absorbed much that is in this work. This is
not a book one should ignore. One has to contend with it. Jensen, far
from being a fool, is a very astute person who tries to be fair. The problem
is that in reading this book, I get the feeling that when Jensen is stating
positions opposed to his own, he is trying to be fair but his heart is not in
it. When he states his own position, it is obvious where his heart is. But,
as Hudson indicated, that characteristic does not differentiate Jensen
from the rest of us.

I shall not attempt to review the contents of this book for reasons
that I hope will become clear. Suffice it to say that as soon as one takes on
Jensen on his grounds, one has accepted a very restricted view of the
concept of intelligence in terms of its nature and measurement, social
history, and societal uses. The Achilles heel in Jensen's position, as well
in those of his critics, is the significance they all attach to standardized
tests and testing conditions. The question I wish to discuss is: what is the
relation between problem solving in test situations and in non-contrived,
naturally occurring situations?

I came to ask myself that question shortly after I took my first professional job testing individuals in a new institution for the mentally retarded, a very innovative institution in the middle of nowhere. There was
a certain problem with runaways. Although people ran away infrequently,
there was always the fear when they did so that they would get lost in the
woods and get hurt. Although I do not know how many of these runaways succeeded in not getting caught at all or only being found days
later in their homes miles away, I did become aware that some of them
had exhibited a kind and quality of problem-solving behavior that was
simply not predictable from my testing of them. For example, I routinely

administered the Porteus Mazes, which are scaled in difficulty from simple to complex. Some of the runaways who had done poorly on these mazes had managed to plan and execute their flights successfully: i.e., they demonstrated a level of planning and foresight quite at variance with their test performance. Part of my job was to make recommendations, on the basis of tests, for job placement within the institution. I began to learn that in a fair number of instances there was little relationship between the problem-solving behavior of an individual in testing and non-testing situations. I do not want to exaggerate the number of these instances; but their occurrence was frequent enough, and the discrepancies often dramatic enough, to make me wary of predicting from testing situations. This wariness received further support from the literature on what happened to mentally retarded individuals after they left special classes in the schools. They became part of the community in ways and at levels of competence that were at variance with their problem-solving test behavior.

In 1953 Ginzberg and Bray wrote *The Uneducated*, an analysis of World War II soldiers who were illiterate and/or mentally retarded by a psychometric criterion. That book contains some extraordinary descriptions of discrepancies between problem-solving behavior in test and non-test situations, the latter occurring under conditions of battle stress. Here is one example from Ginzberg and Bray:

> E.H., a white soldier, born and still living in rural Kentucky when inducted, represents perhaps the clearest case of a man who should be classified as a very good soldier. He was inducted at the age of 19 in the summer of 1943 . . . Shortly after induction, he was sent to the Special Training Unit at Camp Atterbury, Indiana, where he spent two months. The date is not given, but when E.H. took the Army General Classification Test, probably prior to his assignment to the Special Training Unit, he received the very low score of 42. After completing the special training, he was sent to the Infantry Replacement Training Center at Camp Blanding, Florida. Although many men received ratings of excellent for character and efficiency during their basic training, E.H. was graded very good in character and only satisfactory in efficiency. He was trained as a rifleman. Immediately after "D Day" he was en route to the European Theater as a member of the 8th Infantry Division. He received the Combat Infantry Badge, which made him automatically eligible for the Bronze Star Medal. Moreover, he earned three Bronze Service Stars for the Campaigns in Northern France, the Rhineland, and Central Europe. But his most important achievement was the award of the Silver Star for gallantry in action, which carried the following citation:
>
> Sgt. H., a squad leader, exposed himself to enemy small arms, mortar and artillery fire to work his way within 25 yards of an en-

emy machine gun position which was holding up their advance. He
threw two hand grenades and then overran the position, killing one
of the enemy and wounding two others. Later, during the attack, his
squad accounted for more than 30 Germans. Sgt. H.'s great courage,
coolness under fire, and devotion to duty were an inspiration to his
men. (pp. 87, 122)

Although I do not know the kinds of intellectual activities or problem-solving behavior involved in being a squad leader, more particularly,
a successful squad leader under conditions of stress, it seems not unreasonable to conclude that this man's intellectual activity is not predictable
either from his meager educational achievements or very low test score.

Jensen is quite aware that one of the major criticisms of mental tests
is the restricted range of cognitive functions they sample. But in making
that criticism, the critic is saying that we need better, more encompass-
ing standardized tests. Neither Jensen nor his critics ever seem to consider the problems of the relation between problem solving in and outside of the test situation, although the importance of this problem is
implied in their writings. For example, when one finds that there are pervasive differences between social or ethnic or racial groupings, are there
similar differences when the everyday problem-solving behavior of these
groups is studied? Phrased alternatively, are the differences in level of
problem-solving behavior in the test situation observable in all problem-
solving behavior outside of the test situation? While it should be necessary in constructing a test to observe non-test behavior as a guide in selection of items, it should also be essential to demonstrate that the level
of problem solving elicited by these test items is highly correlated with
behavior toward these items when they are met with in everyday life. In
constructing a test to select certain machine operators, one selects items
which clearly reflect what these operators actually do or will be required
to do, and one endeavors to construct the test so that it will differentiate
between levels of performance. Similarly with our intelligence tests: im-
plicitly and explicitly they have been validated on the basis of scholastic
achievement and the content of these tests reflect such an aim. If one's
goal is to construct a test which will predict problem-solving behavior
outside of school-like situations, then it would seem necessary to study
and demonstrate the relationship between performance in such situations and in response to the test.

The question I am raising goes far beyond mental testing. Indeed, it
has been explicitly raised by a highly sophisticated group of experimental
cognitive psychologists led by Michael Cole at Rockefeller University. I refer specifically to their monograph bearing the delightful title: *Ecological,
Niche Picking: Ecological Invalidity as an Axiom of Experimental Cognitive
Psychology*. On the basis of their studies of test and non-test behavior,
these researchers are forced to the conclusion that at the present time,

"laboratory models preclude the operation of principles essential to the organization of behavior in non-laboratory environments (and that) theories and data derived from the laboratory cannot be used as a basis for predictions about the behavior of individuals once they leave the laboratory."

Cole's studies and conclusions should be alarming to both Jensen and his critics because they point to a severe limitation, and possibly semi-lethal defect, in the practice of validating performance in one standardized testing situation by another. I raised this issue a quarter of a century ago and Cole has raised it again in a more systematic, data-based way. Some day, perhaps, psychologists will start looking at performance in naturally occurring situations. That will be the day!

It has never been my position that formal psychologic tests are evil inventions that ought to be made illegal. I think of tests as somewhat like a body thermometer in that in the face of presenting symptoms, abnormal *and* normal "readings" are no basis for inaction but require one to look elsewhere to understand what the symptoms may reflect. But where does or should one look? In psychology the emphasis has been on other tests and trying to see a pattern among their different findings. That can be productive—or at least not misleading—in the case of problem-solving behavior, but only up to a point. That point is reached (and very quickly) when an extrapolation is made from what is observed in formal, contrived, standardized testing situations to what one infers would be observed in informal, nonstandardized, or naturally occurring situations. That kind of extrapolation is unwarranted—or should be made with more than lip service to the underlying assumption—in view of the fact that there is no existing body of literature to warn one of the cautions that should be observed. Cole's work is a real beginning to an examination of these kinds of extrapolations. What he reported is almost of the nature of pulling the rug from under a superstructure of assumption and practice.

Gladwin's *East Is a Big Bird*

Problem solving in naturally occurring stituations—how can I write about that without discussing my relationship with anthropologist Thomas Gladwin? I came to know Tom shortly after World War II when he was taking a course from me in projective testing as preparation for his doctoral thesis in the South Pacific. We became very close friends and later collaborators (Sarason and Gladwin, 1958). Although I had long had an interest in anthropology, it was not until I started to work with Tom that I began to see how important that field could be to anyone prone to make judgments about human nature. The diversity of cultures, past and present, was and is awesome and properly bewilders the person seeking generalizations about the sources and contexts of human behavior. With the passage of the years, I can see that there was one feature of the anthropologic literature that mightily fascinated and influenced me: the descriptions of how people in so-called "primitive cultures" solved problems confronting them in daily living. I say "so-called" because it never made sense to me to attach the label "primitive" to people who could do the things anthropologists described. The label effectively obscured the complexity of thinking of which they were capable. And the situation was made even worse when anthropologists, enamored with psychologic tests, began to employ them in field studies, unjustifiably concluding that poor test performance confirmed the appropriateness of the label "primitive." Like psychologists, the anthropologists attached far more significance to performance in contrived than in naturally occurring situations. This had the effect of placing personality/emotional concepts into the foreground and the cognitive/problem-solving processes farther into the background. In the paper "The Contents of Human Problem Solving" (Sarason, 1961), I put the problem this way:[3]

I have mentioned a number of problems which I assume to be universal, e.g., time, anatomical sex difference, birth theories, space, and number, but I have made and shall make no attempt to present a comprehensive listing of such problems. One of my aims in this paper is to indicate some of the consequences of the recognition that there are an undetermined number of problem-solving tasks which at one time or another are experienced by everyone. One such consequence which I have not mentioned concerns its cross-cultural implications.

In the past thirty years many psychologists and anthropologists have focused their attention on the culture-personality problem. Implicit in these studies is the assumption that any theory of human personality development must cope with the problem in the diversity of cultures in which man is found. Just as learning theories based on the white rat are viewed as at best incomplete when applied to humans, so theories of personality based on studies of Western man have been viewed skeptically as a result of their being applied to markedly different cultures. Put more correctly, perhaps, cross-cultural studies of the relationships between personality and culture do not permit us to conclude that our current theories of personality development encompass the major variables of development or state their interrelationships in a clear way.

In this connection it is interesting to note that in a recent discussion Gladwin points out, in a vein of surprise and chagrin, that anthropologists have rarely been interested in cognitive processes and development. In studying personality development their emphasis has been almost exclusively on emotional determinants rather than the cognitive aspects of personality. "It is truly ironic that of all the fields of inquiry into human behavior, anthropology, with its primary emphasis on the regularities of behavior as they are transmitted through culture from one generation to the next, is the one which most completely ignores the learning involved in this cultural transmission."

The importance of the cognitive aspects of personality and the explicit recognition of their neglect have in recent years become a matter of concern not only to psychologists but to the psychoanalyst as well. In light of Gladwin's surprised reaction to and criticism of the tendency of his fellow anthropologists to emphasize almost exclusively the "emotional determinants rather than the cognitive aspects of personality," I am emboldened to add my own surprise reaction which I shall put in the form of hyperbole for the purpose of emphasis.

In studies of diverse societies the emphasis has been in inter-society differences, with little or no attention to how such differences emerge despite universally experienced problem-solving tasks. If all individuals in all cultures experience and cope with certain problems involving a cognitive change or solution, is it not incumbent on a science of man to understand the ways in which different societies pose these problems for their members and how the experience of these problems affects (e.g., to restrict or to enlarge) the processes and contents of subsequent problem solving? I assume that the major variables necessary for understanding the learning processes and the development of cognitive structures do not, or will not be found to, differ as a result of cultural variations. How a society poses a problem, the ways in which it is experienced by the individual, and the ways in which different experiences with different content problems become interrelated—it is in relation to these factors that different cultures produce personalities who experience the world very differently. For example, all cultures have ways of denoting the passage of time. While it is of obvious importance to understand how a child in any one culture learns that culture's way of telling time, I am not sure that such an understanding leads (at least it has not led) one to a comprehension of the experience of the problem, i.e., an experience which reflects in an indivisible manner a perceptual, cognitive, and attitudinal gestalt. What is important in the fact that we tell time differently than the Trukese is that we experience time differently, and that it is this latter difference which insures that American and Trukese children will experience and solve the problem of time differently. The important fact is that in all cultures there are some central problems to which all people are exposed early in their life experience. Some of these, like anatomical sex differences, probably are universal in their primary importance, but others are not. If, for example, we approach Trukese culture from our frame of reference, we can make a case for the time dimension presenting problems to Trukese. Unquestionably it does, but it may be sufficiently peripheral and inconsequential so that it is not a core problem for the young child. In contrast, the relatively unique directional problem (land-sea, upwind-downwind) pervades the language to the extent that every verb implying motion must have a directional suffix. Therefore the child must become aware very early that he is operating within a strongly direction-oriented environment. The directional referents are not immediately self-evident (e.g., the upwind-downwind orientation is maintained in accordance with the trade winds even in those months when those winds do not prevail) so that the problem of learning to operate within this directional framework must be very nearly as puzzling as it is for an American child to learn to operate within a time-oriented framework.

When one considers that anthropologists have time and again demonstrated to the more parochial behavioral sciences that individuals in different cultures experience this world very differently, it would be ironical if in their new interest in cognitive aspects of personality development they overlooked the experienced contents of problem solving, contents which can only be incompletely gleaned from a description of the external stimulus.

If all children in all cultures are confronted with, cope with, and in one or another way solve certain problems, does it not follow that the differences which exist among cultures in problem-solving behavior must reflect to a large degree differences in how these childhood problems are posed for and experienced by the children? One of the favored ways in which the culture and personality problem has been studied is by putting the spotlight of inquiry on parent-child relationships, be it in our own or in a so-called primitive culture. What might one conclude if one reviewed the literature with these questions in mind: What do these studies tell us about the ways in which different cultures pose these problems (time, distance, number, anatomical sex differences, causality, birth theories) for children, and how are these problems experienced by the children? There are two conclusions which could be drawn from such a review: (a) There is a dearth of studies in which any of these problems has been systematically (or even near-systematically) studied, and (b) comprehending the development of a child primarily requires a knowledge of the pattern of affective relationships between parent and child and, in addition, a description of parental practice in regards to feeding, toilet training, discipline, etc. The first conclusion reflects an astonishing gap in our knowledge, while the second represents, as Gladwin indicated, an unjustified lack of attention to the nature and development of cognitive functions.

It is obvious that I was very much influenced by Gladwin's long-standing interest in *how* problems were cognitively experienced and solved. Although anthropologists had described these problems and solutions, most of them underestimated the level and complexity of thought required. The possibility that these "primitives" may be capable of a high level of abstraction was rarely seriously considered. It is, of course, not fortuitous that a major theme in the monograph *Psychological and Cultural Factors in Mental Subnormality* (Sarason and Gladwin, 1958) was on the importance of distinguishing between problem solving in contrived and standardized versus naturally occurring situations.

East Is a Big Bird is the title of a book and the name given to a celestial pattern of stars used by the Puluwatans in the South Pacific as a navigational guide. The book was recognized as a classic as soon as it was published in 1970. In it, Gladwin addressed this question: What are the cognitive processes and maps by which the Puluwatans traverse the trackless ocean for hundreds of miles and reach their destination? Gladwin, an engineer *and* an anthropologist, had long been interested in their celestial navigation, especially as it had bearing on assumptions about the native's presumed low level of abstract ability. So, knowing the language and the people, he arranged to apprentice himself to one of their navigators, spending several months "feeling" himself into their experience of the problems and modes of solution. I shall not attempt to go into any detail about what that book contains. I can only plead with any reader who is interested in the significance of problem-solving behavior in naturally occurring situations to study the book. Two of Gladwin's conclusions are particularly relevant here. First, the level of abstraction required of these natives for navigation is far beyond what is ordinarily connoted by the label "primitive." Second, there is a fantastic difference between their level of abstraction in navigating and their level on *our* kind of standardized tests. In Gladwin's (1970) words:

> Since we have already established that there is in Puluwat navigation a reliance on abstractions, we must now inquire about concrete thinking in the same context. Each observation a navigator makes of waves, stars, or birds is related directly without any logical reordering or interpretation to a conclusion about position, direction, or weather. Each such conclusion in turn permits of only one or at most two or three clearly defined alternative responses. Some of the observations are based on perceptions we (but not the Puluwatans) would consider extraordinarily acute, and some of the responses are complex, but once the initial observation has been made the steps which follow upon it are unequivocal. Is this concrete thinking? Few psychologists would argue otherwise. Not only is it concrete but direct pathways of this sort between observation and response comprise the principal operational mode of the entire navigation system. In other words, Puluwat navigation is a system which simultaneously employs fairly high orders of abstraction and yet is pervaded by concrete thinking.
>
> If these two kinds of cognitive operations, abstract and con-

crete, can so intimately coexist in the working mind of a Puluwat navigator, how can these same qualities of thinking in the United States provide a basis of contrast and comparison between classes of people? In the United States the abstract-concrete, middle-class lower-class distinctions have been elevated to particular prominence in the critically important context of remedial educational programs for poor children. Yet it is ironic to discover that the authors who originally defined the contrast never proposed that these qualities should be used at all to discriminate between people, especially normal people. In their classic monograph on the subject Goldstein and Scheerer on the first page, before they even define the two terms, insist that abstract and concrete "attitudes" (as they call them) are mutually interdependent within each total personality. They are levels of intellectual operation differentially utilized by every person for different tasks, not necessarily differentially utilized by different people. Nor did they propose these concepts in relation to social class-determined behaviors. Their concern was better to understand the thinking of persons whose brains were damaged or who were psychotic. Although they argue effectively that both abstract and concrete thinking occur as major modalities in the cognitive processes of all persons, it is doubtful that they would have selected this particular distinction for emphasis were it not especially germane to their interests in psychopathology. However, they did. Not only that but they devised a number of tests and tasks to be used to assess these thinking styles. In time the tests were tried out on different populations from those for which they were initially designed and applied to different problems. Then, as so often happens in psychology—intelligence tests are the classic case—results of the tests came to stand for the thing they were said to measure. Thereupon all manner of distinctions became possible, including that between lower- and middle-class thinking. (pp. 222–223)

This quotation explains one of Gladwin's purposes in doing what he did: Based on his knowledge of the literature in mental subnormality as well as of the controversies surrounding social class differences in test performance, he wanted to study problem-solving behavior in nontesting situations among people considered "primitive." If his book quickly became a classic in anthropology, its significance for the field of mental subnormality has not been recognized, a fate similar to that of Ginzberg and Bray's (1953) *The Uneducated*. In our society terms like "mental subnormality" and "mental retardation"—like the term "primitive"—have connotations and denotations that are so overlearned that it is practically impossible to entertain the possibility that they are egregiously misleading both for science and social action.

What Is Artistic Activity?

In some vague way we know that artistic activity involves problem solving. It's one thing to know this in some abstract way; it is another thing to observe the struggle of the artist as he or she seeks to achieve "peace" between internal visual conception and the expression that conception takes in external form. It is not that the internal determines the external but rather that the two are continuously in transaction with each other. The process more resembles two people dueling: Does it make sense to say that the motions of one cause the motions of the other? The analogy would not be lost on the artist who experiences the materials at his or her disposal as enemies that must be subdued if the internal visual conception is to be expressed externally in some appropriate and satisfactory way. The materials are also friends (they do make the expression of the internal visual conception possible), but of the kind that makes it appropriate to say "with friends like that you do not need enemies."

It may seem strange to include in this chapter a discussion of artistic activity. I ask the reader's patience and indulgence because I shall be talking about a man and his work that altered the substance and direction of my thinking. And not least of all that got altered through sustained observation were my preconceptions of problem solving in non-contrived, self-propelled situations.

The man is Henry Schaefer-Simmern, a political refugee from Nazi Germany. He had been a university professor in Frankfurt, with a background in art history and art education. To say "background" or even "training" is a distortion of galactic proportions. His fund of historical knowledge and memory for place and time were awesome. Nothing in his manner flaunted what he knew. For example, when he talked about Goethe travelling through Italy saying this about that painting in x month of y year, he was not trying to sound impressive. Rather, he was always organizing experience into densely and tightly organized contexts. A date was not a date, a name was not a name—both had meanings derived from interrelationship contained in contexts.

Schaefer-Simmern came to this country in 1939. The Russell Sage Foundation gave him a fellowship that allowed him both to acclimate himself to a new language and country and to continue his work in theory and demonstration of artistic development, of the stage-like characteristics through which the artistic form achieves increasing differentiation. In this country, as in Europe, Schaefer-Simmern worked with widely different groups (in terms of ethnicity, culture, age, social class, etc.) in order to show that the creation of the artistic form and its subsequent development are remarkably similar in their *formal* aspects despite differences among groups. So, when he came to this country, he immediately sought opportunities where he could demonstrate his theory and practices with groups ordinarily seen as devoid of or not interested in artistic activity. He chose Southbury for two reasons. First, he had never worked with retarded individuals. Second, Mr. Roselle, the superintendent, enthusiastically responded to the request that came from the Russell Sage Foundation. And that enthusiasm was reflected in tangible ways: Schaefer-Simmern would be given a "studio," materials, access to any of the "children" with whom he wished to work, and housing on those days when he was at the institution. (Schaefer-Simmern lived in New York City and planned on being in Southbury on two or three consecutive days.) He started his work there in 1943, soon after he had finished a similar project with incarcerated juveniles. Mr. Roselle asked me to be helpful to Schaefer-Simmern. Despite the fact that he was at least 20 years my senior (I was then 24), that his pronunciation of the English language was by no means perfect, and his bearing and expression of opinions were Prussian-like, and that he was a man passionately absorbed in *his* ideas and work, we hit it off extremely well. For one thing, I respected him precisely because he was a political, not a religious, refugee from Nazi Germany, i.e., he voluntarily gave up security because he could not abide what was happening there. Also, when he showed me the work of his widely varying "students," I was both skeptical and impressed because I found it difficult to believe that these were the works of individuals who would never have been suspected as capable of such impressive artistic works. (Like most everybody else, I divided the world into two kinds of people: those who had artistic talent and those who did not. Schaefer-Simmern had spent his life challenging—and demonstrating the invalidity of—precisely that belief.) Finally, once you got behind his somewhat forbidding manner (he never suffered fools gladly; he was in modern parlance a male chauvinist; and engaging in small talk was utterly impossible for him), he was a feeling and sensitive person. Whenever I was with him I felt I was in the presence of an intellectual, lonely giant struggling with a world that ignored or demeaned people's creative potentials. He needed me because my respect for him was obvious and deep; I was a good listener and sounding board; and I would try to be as helpful as possible in bringing him and his ideas to a wider audience. I needed him because he opened new worlds to me. Let me give but one example. The first time we went together to the Metropolitan Museum of Art, he stood me before a large pastoral scene by Poussin. I told him I did not like farm scenes. He replied firmly but without anger: "For now it makes no difference whether you like the content or not. It is insufficient to look at a painting in terms of personal likes or dislikes. Your job is to determine the artistic *problem* the artist was grappling with. I want you to study that painting and tell me what colors or forms in any part of the painting can be changed without affecting the painting as a whole or the colors and forms that surround that part." For the first time, I truly understood what a gestalt was because every effort of mine to change color or form in any part of the painting clearly upset the painting's unity of form and color. Once I understood that, I could understand another of Schaefer-Simmern's points: *That* unity was a feature of *all* stages in an *individual's* artistic development, regardless of whether that individual was at the earliest or most advanced stages of artistic activity. Schaefer-Simmern did not attach to the labels "primitive" or "folk art" the negative judgments typically associated with these art forms, because for him these artistic expressions shared with so-called great art this gestalt-like characteristic. In brief, here are (as I have understood them) the essential features of Schaefer-Simmern's "theory."

1. Artistic activity, understood as the external representation of an internal visual conception, is a human attribute found in all cultures, past or present. It is not a special talent that some have and others do not.
2. The earliest scribbles may be meaningless to us but not to the very young child (= "artist") experiencing the consequences of physical movement, perceiving alterations in the "out there" associated with those movements, and stimulating further artistic activity. It is not happenstance that those scribbles are antecedents to circular and oval-like forms which can become very complex (relative to the initial scribbles) but which always retain their gestalt-like quality. These oval-like forms take on horizontal-vertical features with which single horizontal-vertical lines become associated. Just as creeping precedes walking, so scribbles precede more complex expressions: Artistic activity and development are characterized by an "unfolding."
3. This unfolding *always* involves a *transaction* between the internal visual conception and its external representation. It is not an unfolding like a process programmed in genes, and it is not explainable only in terms of internal processes and visual conceptions. Rather, it is an unfolding in which the internal and the external are each both cause and effect; that is, it is a continuous transaction. It is an unfolding in the sense that if there is any arbitrary or alien intrusion into the activity, development ceases, is diverted, or loses its gestalt-like feature.
4. The young child never seeks to represent, let alone copy, the complexity of external reality. When the child puts horizontal and vertical lines in relationship with each other and calls it a tree, that representation is as real to the child as the tree on the street. That representation *is* a tree, a gestalt-like representation in conformity with the child's level both of visual conception and capacity of external representation. The transactional nature of the process (among other things) contributes to the child's perception of new problems and to a new visual conception that the child will seek to represent. Increased differentiation in and complexity of the artistic product are as much (if not more) functions of the child's reflection on what he or she has created "out there"

as of any increased conceptual knowledge about the content, e.g., a tree or a dog.

5. The unfolding of artistic activity, however much it reflects the biologic limitations as well as potentialities of the human organism, never takes place in a social vacuum. The availability of materials, the witting and unwitting instigations to artistic activity, and the ways by which—and the extent to which—such activity is supported are obviously crucial social-contextual features in the unfolding process. Any environmental pressure that seeks to impose on the child content and technique that are foreign to his or her visual conceptions far more often than not reduce the child's interest in and enjoyment of artistic activity. Indeed, if most people see themselves as lacking artistic "talent," this says far less about talent than it does about the arbitrary criteria schools employ for content and technique—criteria that judge copying an uncopyable reality more worthy than attempting to give configurated expression to a child's visual conceptions. It is one thing to copy or imitate external reality; it is another thing to *transform* that reality in a way that gives it a configurated shape. By their very nature, copying and imitating inhibit much of the individual's distinctiveness from entering the process.

How did Schaefer-Simmern select Southbury residents to work in his studio? He asked me to call individuals to my office. I cannot recall with clarity how I selected individuals, but it could not have been a rational process because at the time I was still at sea about what Schaefer-Simmern was after and had absolutely no knowledge about which individuals had an interest or a demonstrated "track record" in artistic activity. As it turned out, these things really made no difference. He first asked each individual to draw anything he or she wished, taking whatever time was needed. When the person was through, Schaefer-Simmern would study the product, and he might then ask any or all of the following questions: How do you like what you have done? Do you see what you wanted to see? Do you think you can do it better? Would you like to make another drawing?

Schaefer-Simmern's manner with these residents was different from his manner with other people. He immediately conveyed both interest and respect in what was for him an atypically soft, fatherly, caring voice. The more I observed him, the more I realized that he had a gift for conveying his desire to establish a relationship of mutuality in which he was a facilitator for and not an intruder into what the individual sought to do. In his interactions with his pupils the focus was always on the "out there"—asking the pupils to study and ponder what they had just done, inquiring about their dissatisfactions (if they were dissatisfied), and encouraging them to make another effort. Sometimes he would make a suggestion about this or that aspect of the work, especially if the aspect took away from the gestalt-like quality of the work. But he never said: "Do this or that. This is right, that is wrong." Whatever the suggestion, it was derived from what the individual had done and was intended to suggest that there was a problem "out there" that the person should ponder. For him and his pupils artistic activity was a cognitive process with cognitive products—not an indulgence of affect and expressiveness. Personality factors were of course always at work, but once the artistic process began, the problem was a cognitive one. And it was a *problem* that the individual had to solve, albeit temporarily, in a configurated way, integrating line and color. And solving one problem brought in its wake new problems. Problem creation through problem solution—there was a developmental sequence.

Schaefer-Simmern chose to work with those residents whose drawings were most simple or "primitive" in the sense that they reflected an early stage of visual conception and representation. From his perspective, the ones he chose were not yet "spoiled" by the belief that artistic activity meant copying external reality. (As he often noted, not even a da Vinci could, if he had tried, copy the details and complexities of a tree. Regardless of whether a person is a da Vinci or a very young child, he or she always transforms that reality, alters and simplifies it in some ways). In short, he chose those who had less to *unlearn*.

What follows is an article I wrote with Schaefer-Simmern about one of the Southbury residents (Sarason and Schaefer-Simmern, 1944).

Therapeutic Implications of Artistic Activity: A Case Study[4]

This report presents an experiment in creative therapy with a thirty-year-old feebleminded woman. The experiment is based upon the assumption that there is an unfolding and development of inherent "gestalt formation" in the field of visual arts which takes place according to definite laws. It is also supposed that this lawful growth will affect the personality of the individual. First, however, it will be necessary to throw light upon the theory underlying the experiment. Artistic activity is usually understood in a restricted sense—that is, as formative processes in the accomplishment of only highly developed works of art. However, it can also be found in simple beginnings, such as in the pictorial production of prehistoric man, primitive tribes, folk art, and in the spontaneous drawings of children.

Recent studies have revealed that drawings of children, not yet distorted by external methods of teaching or imitations of nature, possess a definite structural order of form which in essence is similar to that of more highly developed works of art. This organization of form not only

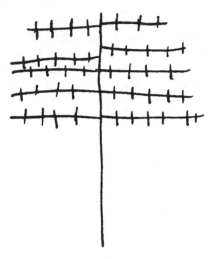

Number 1

reflects factors such as visual thinking, emotional expression, directed conceptual thinking, content, and even physical behavior, but also embodies them in an indissoluble whole. This totality of form, which is to be understood as the artistic form, is the criterion by means of which one can distinguish a work of art from any other work of non-artistic origin. In order to demonstrate this approach it is necessary to judge the following drawings according to their pictorial data only.

Observation of drawing Number I shows that the child, a seven-year-old boy, drew a vertical line, representing the trunk of a tree, and three horizontal lines crossing the trunk at right angles. Furthermore, attached to the horizontal lines, representing branches are smaller vertical lines which cross the branches also at right angles. All parts are related to one another by the greatest contrast of direction. *Not one line's direction can be changed without disturbing the structural order.* If a change is undertaken in one part, it demands also a change in the others in order to maintain the balance and harmony of the whole drawing. Only in their relation to the whole do the parts receive their meaning. In addition, each single line stands for itself without interfering with any other one. The light background of the paper sets off each part very clearly, as well as the whole figure. One can, therefore, speak of a definite relation between the figure of the tree and the background of the paper. One brings out the other and vice versa. The relationships of the greatest contrast of direction of lines and that of the figure and ground generate an indivisible unity of form—a gestalt formation.

Two other pictures of the same child, done shortly after the tree drawing and representing a man and a horse, show the same character-

Number 2

istic of form (Picture Number 2). All lines are again organized according to the same horizontal-vertical relationship. The same unity of form is obtained. A comparison of the pictorial production of this child with that of other children of similar age and mental level will substantiate a great similarity in their pictorial construction of form. The personality factors expressed in different lines and colors, content, etc., vary widely, but the structural organization is always closely related. It becomes clear that these drawings are not reproductions of special aspects of the objects represented. Nor can they be considered as being the pictorial realization of abstract concepts of objects. That a child knows a horse has four legs or that a human being possesses two arms and two legs does by no means explain the definite order of form within the structural building up of his drawings. What the child draws is something completely new. For the variety of shapes in nature he creates a unity of form by which he comprehends the world. His drawings must, therefore, be considered as independent entities. Their existence can only be explained as the result of a definite mental activity of conceiving relationships of form in the realm of perception, an activity which has been termed visual conception. The term visual conception is used in a literal sense; that which is conceived or begotten within the very domain of the human mind and which results in the birth of a visual gestalt. Mental activity which leads to grasping the multiplicity of visual impressions by way of self-created visual unities results in visual cognition. In the achievement of visual cognition lies the mental significance of the child's artistic activity.

A child who has for a certain period of time grasped objects by the unity of form built upon the greatest concept of direction will gradually be able to change direction of lines. Thus it can be understood why the same child a year later came to the pictorial conclusion seen in Picture Number 3. Now the lines of the branches are differently related to the vertical line of the trunk. All branches are attached to the trunk at sharper angles. The same occurred within other drawings of the child done at the same time (see Picture Number 4). The arms and the legs of the man as

Number 3

well as the legs of the dog show the same relationship of changing direction of lines as did the branches of the tree to the trunk. Through this
new stage of changing direction the whole drawing receives a greater vital-
ity. Now the action of walking becomes visible. This child of eight years of
age has seen people walking countless times, but he never drew them in
the way he does now. This new expression can only be explained by the
fact that he has reached a more differentiated stage of visual conceiving.

It is not the intent of this report to go into an extended analysis of
children's drawings. The two stages of visual conception noted indicate
that in the course of the child's entire development simple gestalt forma-
tions always precede more complicated ones. There are of course many
stages of transition. In summary, it can be stated that already in the simplest beginnings of the child's pictorial activity, order and organization
exist as a result of a definite mental activity to conceive relationships
of form.

In the education of most people the ability of visual conceiving has
not been developed beyond the early stages of childhood. But the ability
itself has not vanished. It is always latent and needs only to be awakened.
The beginning of such pictorial activity is usually depressing, because
the first steps are so primitive and in such a contrast to the conceptual
abilities of a grown-up person that he tends to give up after the first attempts. This is naturally very different in the case of a mentally defective
adult individual whose mentality is still on the level of a child. This dis-

Number 4

crepancy between the development of conceptual capacities of a normal adult and his undeveloped stage of visual conception does not exist for the defective individual. There is, therefore, the possibility of a natural unfolding of mental energies which can take place in full conformity with the mental level of such a person, assuming that the instructor is able to understand and evaluate his pictorial language of form.

The development of a central function like visual conceiving, which means the unfolding of visual cognition, can be of decisive importance for individuals whose total capacities are primarily of a concrete nature. The dominant role of visual conceiving is order and organization of visual experiences within the realm of perception. It is likely that the order and balance which govern visual conception must in turn be reflected in other parts of the psycho-biological organism. This assumption served as the basis for the experiment with the thirty-year-old retarded woman. The explanation of the two early stages of visual conception is sufficient for an understanding of her development and its therapeutic implications.

Selma has a mental age of six years and six months and an intelligence quotient of 43, which means that she is on the border line between imbecile and moron. She had never gone to regular school. At the time of her admission to an institution for mental defectives she had only attended special classes. While she was in a former institution, she showed little inclination to learn and was reported by the teachers to be "lazy and indifferent." Upon admission to the Southbury Training School, Selma was "unresponsive, inarticulate, and phlegmatic. She was sloppy, fat, and unattractive in appearance, and had a vague empty stare. Her responses to all questions consisted of a shake of her head or a groan. She would obey a direct command, never caused any trouble or disturbance, but showed absolutely no initiative in making friends or social contacts. She preferred to withdraw to the fringe of a crowd, and be a spectator and never a participant in cottage activities."

When one of the writers (H.S.-S.) met her for the first time, she gave the impression of being very shy. It was difficult to have a conversation with her because she answered reluctantly and in monosyllables. She seemed to be very restless and unhappy when unoccupied, at which time she walked through the work-shop talking to herself. In order to find the individual's stage of visual conception, he is generally asked to draw whatever he wishes. From a person of Selma's mental level any spontaneous creative activity could hardly be expected. For this reason she was not requested to draw something of her own choice. It would not only have been impossible for her to respond to a sudden request that demanded a quick decision, but might also have endangered her emotional equilibrium. In order to stimulate her, Selma was shown a drawing done by a seven-year-old child. According to her mental age it was thought that her stage of development of visual conception would correspond to that of a normal child of approximately the same mental age. It was reasonable to suppose that she could grasp only the pictures of others that were in conformity with the stage of visual conception which she had already reached. Obviously, she was able to react to the clear cut, outlined picture shown her, since she found it "very pretty" (Picture Number 5). After she had observed it for about ten minutes it was removed and she was asked to make something similar in her own way. She started to work immediately and finished her drawing in twenty minutes.

When she was requested to show her work her feelings of inferiority, her shyness, and even a certain anxiety gripped her. Turning her face away, she submitted her drawing with shaking hands. She obviously feared attention and criticism.

Her picture represents trees and flowers with air, sky, and sun above (see Picture Number 6). Compared with the drawing shown her it reveals a similar subject because trees and flowers are also the main content of that drawing. Further, the structural order is almost the same; each single object stands for itself and is determined in its vertical direction by a horizontal base-line. The forms of the tree are also visualized, as in the sample picture, by changing direction of lines. But in spite of all these similarities, Selma's drawing is by no means a copy of the picture shown. The similarity concerns the stage of development of visual conception. The peculiarity in the form of the trees, their parallel arrangement, the large extended horizontal base-line by which the whole attains a clear order, brings out the difference in the individual application of this stage of development. It is clear from this drawing that an independent way of visual conceiving, regardless of how crude and simple it appears, must be recognized.

Selma's first picture, and according to her own statement, the first she has ever done, already indicates that even a mentally deficient person of the low-moron type seems to be able to create, in a modest degree, an ordered pictorial whole.

Number 5

Number 6

Surprised by her unexpected ability to accomplish even such a simple pictorial result, she was praised. Apparently she needed a good word of encouragement because her reserved attitude immediately disappeared and a big smile spread over her face. Then she went to the desk, took some paper and started voluntarily on a new drawing. When she was requested to show her new work she again displayed a sudden shyness and anxiety. After receiving some praise she hesitatingly expressed a glad "thank you."

After a second drawing Selma selected some colored oil crayons out of a box which was at her disposal. Following the suggestion that she paint very slowly and distinctly, Selma went to work. She spent almost an hour for the execution of the third drawing (Picture No. 7). The picture again represents familiar content. Three trees are placed on a wavy baseline. The space between the lower edge of the sheet of paper and the base-line is filled in with green color. Obviously it carries the meaning of hills. The lower edge forms the horizontal base for the five large flowers colored in a darker green. As in the previous pictures the lower line marking the sky is drawn parallel to the base-line, and again the sun appears

Number 7

in the right side of the blue sky. *The clearness in the construction of the whole drawing and the more careful execution reveals that Selma, who usually works very fast and sloppily, is able to achieve accurate results when she acquires a personal interest in her subject, and when it can be performed in correspondence with the stage of her mental development; in other words, when the work can be fully grasped by her.* Under such conditions, her drive for visual cognition impels her to a clear pictorial realization which serves as an impetus for the development of new pictorial ideas. This occurred in the new formation of trees. While in the previous drawings the branches were differentiated by either simple dots or strokes, she now applies both in a rhythmic order representing blossoms and leaves. Within this rhythmic order the various colors find their best application. They become an essential factor in the pictorial structure. Different colors are employed to distinguish the trees from one another which indicates that, for Selma, color has primarily the function of ordering rather than a faithful reproduction.

Selma's creative ability may appear to many observers very insignificant. But these tiny signs of creativeness become of great importance if they concern individuals who are usually thought of as creatively sterile. Although such insignificant results when compared with those of normal persons will always remain modest, their effect on the creator may be of decisive consequence.

After one or two five-hour days weekly for several months Selma had already progressed so far that she was able to work independently. Usually, immediately after entering the studio, she took some drawing paper and colored crayons and started to work spontaneously. Her pictures still consisted of her trees, the smaller ones with dots and strokes, the larger ones with different kinds of blossoms; also still evident were flowers, dogs, bluebirds, fish, and waves for water and hills. *In the next two months Selma produced thirty complete designs, all entirely different. Not only did she display an extraordinary ability to apply the forms of her objects in great variety, but the forms of those objects in which she was most interested—such as trees—reveal a greater differentiation of her stage of visual conception. In the further course of her spontaneous activity she developed a mental attitude characterized by constant observation and an attempt to control the effects which each form has upon the following one.* This formative process of creating a lawfully constructed order emerged so intently that it gave the impression of her striving to master the entire design. Structural interrelationship of pictorial elements is characteristic of a real work of art—regardless of how simple it may appear—and distinguishes it from all other works of non-artistic origin. Analysis of these colored designs (of which only four examples are presented—Picture Numbers 8, 9, 10, and 11) shows that each one achieves a definite order by the structural inter-relationship of all pictorial elements. Thus each design receives its validity of form. First, all objects, such as trees, flowers, grass, fish, dogs, and hills, are represented as total forms. Their complete figures, as well as their parts, are organized so that each one stands for itself and is set off from its surrounding. Further, the structural upbuilding reveals the stage of changing direction; only the forms of the dogs are still represented on the stage of horizontal-vertical. The objects themselves as well as their colors are placed in a rhythmic balance, one bringing out the other. Finally, all pictures display individuality in their expression of lines. All of these factors together constitute an integral unity of form. It is obvious that an inner mental and emotional balance and order underlie the creation of the pictorial organization. And as there is an inter-relationship between the formative processes and the mental and emotional state of the individual who creates such order of forms, it can be said that he who forms something in turn forms himself.

Since she became more aware of her productive capacities, Selma has undergone a definite change, a change toward a more "formed personality." A few months ago she was indecisive and even insecure about what to do with herself. She wandered helplessly through the studio. Today she starts her work spontaneously. She has definite ideas about her pictorial themes; she is determined in the execution of her ideas as well as in the manipulation of her material. Her former nervous impulsiveness has been replaced by a controlled and quiet determination. If she makes mistakes, such as spoiling the order of form, she changes her color-drawing independently until she re-establishes the pictorial organization. All of these spontaneous actions indicate an increased self-assurance and inner security through which she has reached a greater amount of freedom. Months ago she was reserved, silent, and shy; she even avoided any kind of conversation. Now she frequently initiates conversations with her co-workers. She always looks impatiently forward to making a new design. During her work she sings her favorite song, "There'll Be Bluebirds over the White Cliffs of Dover." Step by step, with

Number 8

Number 9

each new work, she builds up her creative self—her self-realization. She attains results, she "masters" situations. For the first time, Selma feels her own worth. She seems to be finding her niche, and that discovery gives her security. Signs of a normal and healthy human being emerge from her.

From the psychological viewpoint several problems present themselves when considering Selma's development. *The first problem is concerned with the relation between intelligence test data and the artistic results which have just been presented and discussed.* It is obvious that the pictorial productions of this girl are not typical of an individual with a mental level of six years and six months (Terman-Merrill (L)). If psychometric results are to have meaning in this case beyond what is involved in merely reporting a mental age or an intelligence quotient, it is necessary that one analyze more finely the test performance itself. The necessity of such a procedure, not only in this but in all cases, is indicated since by its very nature any given mental age may be obtained from numerous combinations of successes and failures of the items which comprise the test. When one also keeps in mind the fact that the items in a

Number 10

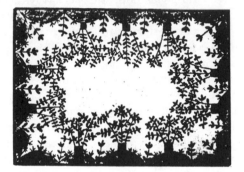

Number 11

test vary in the kind of function they are supposed to measure, the hazards of accepting a mental age as an accurate description of mental functioning become clear. *A tentative conclusion one is forced to draw from Selma's pictorial activity is that the concept of mental age is unilluminating in regard to creative activity. Since one could not defend the separation of creative activity from intelligence, regardless of level, it follows that the mental age does not, as indeed clinical experience indicates, adequately represent mental functioning.* The following analysis is made in order to see to what extent this girl's creative activity could be indicated from her psychometric performance.

A problem that is of much psychological importance is the relation between Selma's artistic activity and personality development. What is there about the background of this girl that might help explain the surprising quality of her pictures? Is the marked change in her behavior the result of her artistic activity alone? The answers to these questions cannot be fully answered in this report but an initial attempt is warranted.

The following is a brief abstract of this girl's case history:

At the time of admission in 1927 Selma was living with her aunt. The father had died when she was ten and the mother when Selma was twelve. At the age of three Selma had been burned over a large portion of her body and extensive scars have remained. According to informants the aunt frequently and severely maltreated the girl. She would hit her on the head, whip her unmercifully, and call her all kinds of names. The aunt frequently drank. At one time she dragged Selma by the hair and beat her. There is little known about Selma's parents except that both drank a good deal also. The aunt wanted to get rid of Selma and was responsible for her institutionalization. After admission Selma received only one visitor during the first five years and in 1943 there is a record of another. Her institutional behavior was rather poor and she was considered quiet, deceitful, peculiar, and possibly hallucinated because she talked to herself and grimaced and smiled in a strange fashion. She was always assigned the most routine and simple tasks which she would complete only under close supervision. In 1942 she was transferred to the Southbury Training School.

In view of such a background Selma's fearfulness, marked introversion, impulsiveness and inefficiency become more understandable. Attention, affection, and sympathetic understanding were rarely, if ever, extended to her. Considered severely retarded and peculiar it is not strange that she was given work which in no way served as an outlet for her ability or feelings. There was no realization that this girl could develop within her own limitations in any activity in an orderly and organized fashion.

This distorted personality development helps illuminate not only Selma's artistic activity but the significance of the educational and therapeutic procedure which brought it about. For the first time this girl was presented with a task which she could do in her own way. She was not told how to do it and did not have to conform with the preconceived ideas of others. Her initial work was rewarded with praise which served as the impetus for further attempts. Each new work, in itself an indestructible gestalt formation, was a source of satisfaction to Selma. She was able to see for herself the growth in her drawings. A critical awareness became evident in her striving to correct her mistakes and to do better the next time. Selma achieved stature and esteem not only in her own eyes but in the eyes of others as well. More and more of her attention and energies became focussed on her work. Selma was accepted and praised by people for something which came from herself and was truly "her own." Her impulsiveness decreased; she became fastidious in the execution of her drawings, she became bolder in the scope of her work. One might say that the artist had identified herself with her work.

Concomitant with the development in the realm of visual conceiving was a striking change in Selma's institutional behavior. The growth and totality of form evident in her drawings corresponds with Selma's development toward a more unified personality. She did not hide her head or run away when engaged in conversation. She would seek a person out and talk to him—something which she had never been observed to do.

Even when visitors in the institution tried to talk to her, Selma would not manifest the panic or fear she formerly did. The girl seemed happier and more secure than ever before.

It might be said that the change in Selma's behavior could be attributed to the fact that she was receiving praise and attention to an extent which had never before been given her. Such an interpretation disregards the fact that there is in her work an observable, orderly development of gestalt formation which cannot be considered as fortuitous or extraneous. That praise and attention played a role cannot be denied. However, what seems basic in this case is that this girl was given an opportunity to merge in one activity emotional satisfaction, full utilization of energies, planning and foresight, and configurated visual expression. It is the educational and therapeutic significance of the artistic process that it embodies in an indivisible manner so many different aspects of human functioning.

The significance of Selma's case is that it demonstrates the importance of basing educational and therapeutic procedures on the individual's natural potentialities for organized development. To ask a person to reproduce, either from a model or memory, a particular scene or object is to neglect the fact that such a task may be well beyond his particular level of visual conceiving. In such a case the discrepancy between intent and results does not allow the individual to identify himself with what he has done; no opportunity has been given "to grow into his work." One might generalize and say that unless work stems from the natural growth of abilities, it will have little effect on the personality. This approach helps explain, on the one hand, the desire of people for expression in the visual arts and, on the other hand, their feelings of inferiority and inadequacy toward their attempts.

In summary: A year ago Selma lived a barren existence filled only with daily routine kitchen work. The simple tasks she performed were the result of manipulations that had been drilled into her. They brought her neither interest nor stimulation. There seemed to be no place where she could fit into the life of the institution. The childhood had been exceedingly unfortunate, she made no friends among the other "children" in the school. Constantly indifferent, unable to establish any contact between her occupation and her needs and interests she developed a chronic apprehension and shyness that made her so restless and insecure that she avoided the smallest difficulties. A basic function of human mental existence to conceive and to grasp one's own world by images and even to realize them in a pictorially configurated fashion, has been awakened and developed lawfully within her in conformity with her natural capacity. Through these processes, her entire interest, her feeling and thinking, her physical behavior, even her personality as a whole, has been affected. She overcomes her instability arising from her clash with the world not by virtue "of anxiety, but through the joy of coming to terms with the world."

Words are inadequate for the purpose of describing a work of art, let alone describing an individual's artistic development. *The Unfolding of Artistic Activity* (Schaefer-Simmern, 1948), is a significant book that has been through numerous printings. Aside from containing Selma's development in great detail, the book contains the development of many individuals of diverse backgrounds. What is common to all is that their artistic development not only surprised (and transformed) them but it reflected a degree and quality of problem solving quite discrepant (in most instances) with their problem solving in other areas of their lives. And that is the point: In an activity in which they were interested, indeed challenged and engrossed, they showed a level and quality of cognitive functioning unpredictable from observation of them in contrived testing situations. Even today, mentally retarded individuals are seen, judged, and planned for on the basis of what is learned from formal test results. Schaefer-Simmern's approach and demonstrations expose the invalidity and unfairness of such thinking and practice. It is not happenstance that one of the last pieces John Dewey wrote in his long life was the preface to Schaefer-Simmern's remarkable book.

The first part of this chapter discussed Ginzberg and Bray, the second Tom Gladwin, and finally Henry Schaefer-Simmern. One of the things all of these people have in common (aside from their emphasis on problem-solving in naturally occurring, challenging situations) is that they have had no impact on the fields of mental subnormality and psychology. Ginzberg and Bray had impact elsewhere, and Tom clearly has been influential in anthropology. Schaefer-Simmern is the tragic one of the group because he has had no impact anywhere. No one has said it better than Kerwin Whitnah, a student and friend of Henry, in the following letter, a letter that brought me close to tears.[5] Henry deserves a better fate.

Dear Dr. Sarason:

I am delighted that you are going to do a chapter on Henry's work at Southbury. This would be most valuable for several reasons, chief of which is to give an intimate and well-documented look at Henry's actual pedagogical method and how that method found integration in the psychological sphere of mental retardation. Also valuable for the many who value *The Unfolding of Artistic Activity* would be your commentary as to the mise-en-scene, so to speak, which produced the book—the complex interactions of yourself, Henry, and the participating patients there. It would be interesting for people to know in more detail what psychological changes manifested (and how they manifested) in someone like Selma. Henry told me something about it years ago, but I have forgotten the details.

As I mentioned in my first letter, *The Unfolding* has been out for 36 years and it has not changed art education. Henry himself, in

his lifetime, became deeply discouraged over the failure of the art
education academy in this country to take serious note of his book.
He told me in 1971: "I have often the temptation to throw up the
whole thing (his art education work and the publishing of his great
book on *The Essence of the Art Form*). I could go to Europe by the
next plane. There I could look at exhibitions and enjoy art and live a
completely different kind of life. But I have, I might say, a kind of
guilty conscience in the face of such thought. I have a responsibility in full conscience to do this work." And I said: "And if you had
not published the *Unfolding of Artistic Activity*"—he broke in: "Yes,
but not more than ten people in the whole world understood that
book"—And I interrupted: ". . . then my life would have been inex-
pressibly poorer, and I would have been diminished if you had kept
the book a secret and written it, yet simply put it away." These are
exact quotes from a conversation I had with him on the subject of
exhibiting art. He had become so discouraged with the general art
scene at this point that he did not even wish to have his own students exhibit work!

You see, Dr. Sarason, Henry suffered a great deal of ignominy,
spite, misunderstanding, neglect and downright hostility from established academic art educators. He was extremely sensitive to
this, especially so, since he himself was a professional in education,
fully qualified, and a great teacher whose students produced work
of outstanding quality. He was good, and he knew it. He had something of utmost importance to offer to educators, psychologists, art-
ists, architects and laymen, to mention only a few categories.

But, with the advent of Abstract Expressionism in the 1950s
and the steady rise of a kind of graphic and pictorial work which
was profoundly anti-Gestalt, the temper of the times was against his
implementation of the hard-won conclusions which make up his
book, his work and his life. He had told me: "When I left Europe I
looked at the continent receding over the horizon and I took a sol-
emn oath that I would take this Idea to the United States and make
it a living Reality." He fulfilled this oath by publishing *The Unfolding*
and by the productive years which followed in the forties and the
fifties. But, as he got better, the general art scene got worse! He
would go to Europe in the summer and there be told by young art
students that the old Gothic painters like Grunewald and Durer (if
there *are* any like them!) were nothing but "old nonsense."

When Henry died I asked the responsible parties at St. Mary's
College to put on an event which would review and sum up his
achievement as a writer, thinker, and active art educator. Somehow,
this never got done, I don't know why, and it always bothered me
that such a man should thus slip, unnoticed and unacclaimed, out
of this world. Perhaps one of the reasons for the hostility and neglect which he suffered was the fact that excellence in a field is not

always admired, but often envied. Also the fact that he was never noted for his tact and had little of the small talk and social personality so useful in the educational field. He was passionately devoted to The Artistic Form and he was delighted when he found another who shared that passion. And he had little time for anything else.

The temper of the times has changed. People are beginning to understand that anti-gestalt pictorial products have nothing to do with art in its most fundamental, ancient and highest sense. Many professionals are beginning to see that *quality* is the hallmark of artistic excellence and indeed excellence in any field, whether it be psychology, artisanship or architecture. Recently, my wife and I had the good luck to meet a fine architect, world-renowned, currently engaged in building a university in Japan. He is also a professor at the University of California, but not too busy to take an interest in the project of building a house and studios for us here in Northern California. He lives in Berkeley, and when I met him I mentioned that Schaefer-Simmern used to live a few blocks away, and that his books had reminded me of the ideas in *The Unfolding*. Well, Dr. Sarason, this man caught on fire! He said when he was studying architecture at Harvard that he had read *The Unfolding* every day and had kept it by him as a source book. But he had no idea that Schaefer-Simmern had lived in Berkeley, or that his work had continued at all after the publication of the book. He has very kindly offered to sponsor a lecture for me at the University of California.

Now, then, the reason I suggested the lecture to you: I did so because I was reasonably certain that there are also many people at Yale, faculty and students in art, in education, in psychology and philosophy who would be deeply interested in the visual results of Henry's long career as well as the pedagogical means by which these came into being. When I lecture and show the slides, people are amazed. They can't believe that work of such outstanding quality, and such a radically simple approach to art can be such a well kept secret. They are also astonished to learn of the existence of *The Unfolding* and that it is still in print.

There is also the paradoxical factor of diminishing returns as time races onward. When Henry told me in 1971 that only ten people in the world understood his book, he was speaking correctly. Now, 12 years later, I am sorry to reckon that those numbers have shrunk. As far as I know there are no young people who have taken up this Idea with the vigor and conviction which will make it operable to future generations. There is, thus, a certain urgency, depending on our viewpoint. Quite possibly, the availability of *The Unfolding* may be lost for many generations and only rediscovered years hence by some group or individual. In this case they would have to reconstruct it from the external evidence inward—no easy task! But I think such a creative hiatus would be a pity since it is the living instruction that gets the message across, and there are still a few left who worked directly with Henry, having grasped the pedagogical method in their bones, so to speak, and thus can transmit it without distortion.

But my reason for writing you was simpler still: You were with Henry in the old days and you helped him get his book written, both by your active cooperation and your true understanding of what he was doing. Above all, he needed that understanding and in you he had it. You are one of the ten people who understand the book. He told me that. So, you see, when I heard that you were doing some writing about Henry I thought the least I could do would be to offer you a lecture. And though the materials I show are not specifically about mental retardation, they apply (as you well know) with equal force on the scale of measurable "intelligence" up or down. Selma was no genius, but look what she produced! I show slides of her work to my eight-year-olds and tell them about Selma and the discipline she brought to her art. My children can relate directly to her work and feel strong encouragement through her example.

Anyway, I wanted *you* to see the kind of achievements which have flowered since *The Unfolding of Artistic Activity* was published, both for specific application in your field of expertise and for the larger frame of reference where psychology relates directly to the human potential.

Again, thanks for your letter.

Sincere regards,

Kevin Whitnah

Notes

1. From *Psychological Problems in Mental Deficiency* (4th ed., pp. 103–121) by S. B. Sarason, 1969, New York: Harper and Row. (Out of print)
2. From "Review: Jensen's Bias in Mental Testing" by S. B. Sarason, 1980, *Society*, 18(1), pp. 86–88. Copyright 1980 by Transaction Publishers. Reprinted by permission.
3. From "The Content of Human Problem Solving" by S. B. Sarason, 1961, *Nebraska Symposium on Motivation*, pp. 85–92.
4. From "Therapeutic Implications of Artistic Activity: A Case Study" by S. B. Sarason and H. Schaefer-Simmern, 1944, *American Journal of Mental Deficiency*, 49(2), pp. 185–196. Copyright 1944 by American Association on Mental Deficiency. Reprinted by permission.
5. Letter published by permission.

CHAPTER 4

The Family

If anything is apparent from the previous chapters it is my developing sensitivity to the retarded individual as an integral part of a family. The importance of the family may seem obvious, but it is nevertheless the case that only infrequently do studies take the obvious seriously. In fact, it is my belief that one of the factors that powered the growth, militancy, and force of the parent movements was parents' angry reaction against professional and institutional attitudes and practices that were insensitive to the ways in which family organization and dynamics are affected by and in turn affect the retarded person. Researchers who have studied families with retarded individuals have documented the different ways that individuals, on the one hand, and parents and siblings, on the other hand, influence each other for good or for bad. (That the story of a family with a retarded child, far from being a horror story, may be an inspiring one would have been incomprehensible to the great bulk of professionals of two or more decades ago, when the prepotent recommendation to parents was: Institutionalize.) In practice, however, the focus was and still is almost always on the individual. The object of help is the individual, even though the helper knows, at some level of abstraction, that the person's development and behavior are not comprehensible outside of the

historical dynamics of that person in his or her family. When that abstraction takes on concreteness and enlarges your view of individuals and
their physical and social psychologic surroundings, it influences your
practice. When that kind of influence is absent, there is a drastic restric-
tion on the kind and degree of help that can be rendered. Although I understood this point early in my work at Southbury, I do not think I articulated it as succinctly and concretely as in the following excerpt from
Chapter 4 of *Educational Handicap, Public Policy, and Social History. A
Broadened Perspective on Mental Retardation* (Sarason and Doris, 1979).[1]

Ordinarily we think of clinical diagnosis as a process geared to making an assessment of an individual who has come for help. It has often
been said that the *sine qua non* of the clinician is that he does his best on
the basis of his knowledge and experience to help another person with
his or her problems, and the nature of the help derives from a searching
attempt to organize data and observation about the nature, significance,
and probable course of the individual's symptoms. Diagnosis is a serious
affair precisely because it is the basis for recommended action that will
influence the life of a human being. This characterization of diagnosis
holds regardless of whether the person comes on his own to the clinician
or is brought by others.

However, when a child is brought by others to the clinician the diagnostic process perforce has two parts: a first one during which the clinician focuses directly on "the patient" and a second part in which the
clinician seeks information from those who brought the individual. Because the information these people provide reflects more than "facts"
about the child—inevitably reflecting the personal-familial impact of the
child—the diagnostic process is a social one in that it involves more than
an *individual*. This is obvious enough but as we shall soon see the implications of the social context of diagnosis are rarely drawn and acted
upon. The entire diagnostic process tends to be carried out as if only *one*
individual required assessment and help, as if the locus of the problem
inhered "in" him or her; whatever the consequences of "his" problem,
they are of secondary significance, however upsetting or disruptive to
others.

Diagnosis is seen as a drama having a beginning and an end, with
several acts in between. Like all drama, however, it soon becomes obvious
that we are witnessing events, thoughts, and interactions related to the
past, present, and future. As a production a drama does have a beginning
and an end, but by the end the audience knows that there is no end just
as it learned that there really was no one beginning point. Similarly, by
the end of the diagnostic drama, the cast of characters is pointed to a
future shaped by knowledge about the near and distant past. The analogy
between the diagnostic process and a theatrical drama is that there is a
cast of characters whose lives are interrelated. There is more than one

character in the cast and it is the diagnostician's task to make sense of how the web of relationships has altered as a result of events. The question, of course, is what makes "sense"—what convinces us that we understand why things happened as they did to produce the dilemmas of choice in action.

Let us discuss the social context of diagnosis, of its "dramatic" qualities, with an example using a small cast of characters.

A Retarded Newborn

Alice and Harold have been married for five years. Alice has been a schoolteacher and her husband a graduate student in anthropology. When they married they knew they could not have a child for several years and that Alice would have to work until Harold finished his doctorate and had a job. Alice never saw herself as a full-time mother and housewife but she was prepared, depending on circumstances and economics, to be at home until their child was of nursery school age. Both of them came from modest-sized families with modest financial resources. The families lived in very different parts of the country quite far from the couple. Two years before their child was born Harold was nearing the end of his graduate work and had good reason to believe that he would receive a university position. The question in their minds was whether to have their first child before they moved or after they were settled in the city where Harold's position would be. Alice was then thirty-one years of age, and Harold, twenty-nine. Both, particularly Alice, were anxious about the effects of her age on childbearing and wished to try to have a child as soon as possible. Harold felt that the turmoil that was to be expected in moving with a very young child argued against Alice's understandable anxiety and desire. Besides, he argued, if the child were born during the crucial phases of dissertation writing, he could be helpful to Alice but perhaps at the expense of not finishing his dissertation on time. As it turned out, their decision to try to have the child early foundered on the fact that Alice did not conceive until five months before they were to move. Four months after they had settled into their new quarters they became the parents of a girl. The delivery was uneventful.

There was, however, a "problem" of which neither Harold nor Alice were aware. That is to say, this was not a problem the parents were bringing to the pediatrician but rather one that the latter discerned very soon after the child's birth. The infant's cries were weak, some expected reflexes were absent, and she had trouble sucking and taking nourishment. No one "symptom" was flagrant but in combination they made the pediatrician quite uneasy. He was convinced that something was radically wrong although the symptoms fell into no recognizable or established syndrome.

The pediatrician was quite upset. Why? That may seem like a silly question, but how one answers it has enormous consequences, not the least of which involves what we traditionally mean by diagnosis. Many things were bothering him about the infant: What caused the child's condition? Why did her listlessness and unresponsiveness persist? For how long should he keep the infant for observation in the hospital nursery? In his discussions with the parents he had no basis for assuming that something untoward had happened to the mother or that their genetic history should be suspect. If, as the pediatrician feared, this was a retarded infant, how serious would the retardation be? His guess was that the retardation was and would be of a serious degree.

In truth, the pediatrician was less bothered by these questions than by others: What should I tell the parents? When? How much? With what degree of certainty? How would the parents react? How do I handle the inevitable tears and despair? And all those questions about how to react to the child? What a shame and mess! Two nice people like that to have a retarded child! These questions and reactions are no less diagnostic in nature than those asked only about the infant. But they are not about neurological, developmental data. They are about a social-interpersonal situation that will obviously be changed drastically when knowledge about one of the cast is communicated to the others. What is bothering the pediatrician is that he feels far less secure and competent to handle *that* kind of diagnosis than when he focuses only on the infant. He can look at the infant, test her reflexes, get laboratory data on biological-chemical functioning, alert nurses to a special kind of record-keeping, try different types of stimulation, and bring in consultants to check his diagnostic formulation.

But how does one diagnose what kind of parents one is dealing with as a basis for action? Now, if we were to ask the pediatrician what he meant by diagnosis, he would describe for us what he did that led to his diagnosis of the infant. He would not label the questions he had about the parents as similarly reflecting a diagnostic process, one no less thorny and complex than "physical" diagnosis. He would see his task, albeit an unpleasant one, as communicating a diagnosis about the infant. The consequences of that communication, the basis on which it is justified, as well as its implicit connection with a picture of the future, are not conceptualized as a diagnostic process. We shall have more to say about this in later chapters. Suffice it to say here that physicians proudly proclaim that their expertise is in relation to a patient, or a part of the patient, not to the social-familial context in which patients play out their lives. We prize specialization highly, but it takes an instance such as we have described to realize that in restricting the conception of diagnosis to a process between a professional and a patient we pay a high price. Such a conception does not mirror the realities of social living, even though conventional practice does violence and injustice to those realities.

Let us now turn to some of the ways pediatricians, or any other types of professional, communicate the diagnosis of mental retardation to the infant's parents. Our interest here is to elucidate some of the characteristics and effects of their social diagnosis, such as their assessment of the past, present, and future of a social context, and how that assessment justifies their definition of help.

1. The "whole" truth. The physician feels obligated to tell the parents precisely what his diagnostic conclusions are and that in his judgment the child will always be retarded. Parents, he feels, should know the truth and begin the difficult process of coming to grips with it and choosing among alternatives for action. It is the physician's job to answer all questions about what to do and how to do it, but it is the parents who must make final decisions. The physician is never neutral; he knows what he would do if he were in the parent's place but he must refrain from influencing decisions. There are no data about how well these physicians maintain neutrality. There are physicians who deliberately eschew neutrality for two reasons: They assume they know what is best and they believe that in these crisis situations parents are unable to make decisions rationally. So, if the physician believes the child should go home with the parents, he will say so, even though the parents feel otherwise. Similarly, if he believes that for the good of the parents and future children, the child should be institutionalized, he will say so, usually cataloguing the obstacles to normal living in rearing a child. And, let us not forget, there are physicians who, in very severe cases of retardation, will suggest that no special efforts be made to keep the infant alive.

2. The "partial" truth. Here the physician tells the parents that the child does not seem to be normal but it is far too early to tell to what degree, if any, the infant's development will continue to be problematic. "Let's play it by ear and see what happens." The most frequent basis for this stance is that parents have to learn by direct experience the degree and consequences of the child's impairments. By learning the truth in this way they will make their own decisions, and in the long run that is far more healthy than following other people's recommendations or having to be persuaded to consider a particular course of action.

3. Conceal the truth. If by the time the mother and infant are ready to leave the hospital the family has not raised questions about the infant's developmental status, some physicians will say little or nothing and wait to see what is brought up at the first office or hospital check-up. Here too, the belief that it is best to deal with issues arising from parents' experience.

If the appropriate studies were available, we could undoubtedly come up with finer descriptions and categories, but our experience indicates that for our purposes in this chapter, little is lost. *Behind all the ways physicians view the retarded infant is the assumption that it creates a social-interpersonal disaster. This "diagnosis" says far more about the value systems of our society than it does about the retarded infant.* There are cultures that would not view this infant in such catastrophic terms, and even within our own culture families differ in how much of a catastrophe they would perceive. The fact that the physician's view does reflect a widely accepted set of values must not obscure its consequences: the turmoil it engenders in the physician, and the effects of this on his actions and definition of help. It is fair to say that the view of the model physician stems far more directly from *his* value system than it does from anything we would dignify as social-interpersonal diagnosis.

On their own, Alice and Harold surmised by the fifth day that something was wrong but, nevertheless, when the pediatrician told them of the diagnosis of severe retardation, it had predictably catastrophic effects. After all, here were two highly educated, professional people who had the usual plans and fantasies about what their child would be. Like so many of us in our society they set great store on educational achievement, professional status, and independent living. To be told that their child would be unable to go the "onward and upward" route was bitter news. They (Harold particularly) quickly came to see the possible implications for their daily lives and professional careers. Understandably, they were beginning to mourn the death of *their* plans and fantasies, and only secondarily were they concerned with their infant's fate.

This in no way should be construed as criticism of Alice and Harold but rather as a demonstration of how the diagnosis of individual retardation takes place and alters an ongoing set of relationships. From the very beginning, the diagnostic process is social and cultural in nature and consequence. If it is traditionally presented as an objective process uncontaminated by judgment and values, not suffused with feeling and cultural givens, it is not the first time that we have been led to confuse description with reality. As long as we restrict our conception of diagnosis to that which one individual "does" in regard to another, we cannot appreciate how from beginning to end everyone in the drama, especially the diagnostician, is sensitive to its social context. His sensitivity, however, rarely extends to the recognition that the criteria with which he is familiar for individual diagnosis should also hold for his inevitable but rarely formulated social-interpersonal diagnosis.

Conventional individual diagnosis involves more than observing, collecting facts, and making judgments according to standardized scales. In instances where serious pathology is suspected the diagnostician will seek ways to deliberately intervene (e.g., biologically, chemically, surgically) in order to better ascertain the stability and validity of the individual's symptoms. He will perform experiments, so to speak, to find out the conditions under which the individual's status can be desirably altered. His diagnosis does not rest on conditions as they are but also on what they might be through strategic efforts at manipulation. In the case of Alice and Harold's infant, the pediatrician tried numerous strategies aimed at altering the infant's sluggish behavior and he was able to bring about and sustain some improvement, albeit slight. One might characterize this diagnostic process as one which assesses the extent of the discrepancy between what is and should be and seeks to determine how influenceable that discrepancy is. The aim of diagnosis is not to append a label on someone but to formulate the nature of symptom relationship that can serve as a basis for helpful action. The boundaries between diagnosis and treatment are far more clear in our language than they are in the realities of practice and action.

The Diagnosis of a Social-Interpersonal Catastrophe

The pediatrician predicted rightly that Alice and Harold would react as though faced with a catastrophe. This prediction rested less on any knowledge about their personalities or their interpersonal relationships than it did on society's reaction to mentally retarded individuals, of which his own reaction was typical. Let us now try to address some of the questions which this type of diagnosis raises, bearing in mind that the aim is to obtain information that can serve as a basis for help—not stemming only from kindness or sympathy but from as intimate knowledge as can be gained about the parents and their social context. How will each of the parents react to and interpret the significance of the child's condition? How will each perceive the other's reaction, and what are the immediate consequences that they see themselves facing as a couple? Put in another way, how will their perceptions of themselves as individuals and as a couple change? A second set of issues concerns their sense of competence as parents: How should they react to the infant? What special precautions should they take? What special problems may arise and who may be available to help if something goes wrong? A third set of questions concerns the future: Will the child be able to walk and talk, go to school? Will special help be needed and be available? Will all our children be this way? Should we have other children? When? What will be the effect of this child on the others?

Parents who take their first child home from the hospital are apprehensive, but relieved and happy. When that child is retarded, however, anxiety and depression suffuse everything. The thrust of the diagnostic questions stated above (and there are many more) is how to understand *and* interrelate the answers so that helpful actions can be taken. *Just as the pediatrician and his hospital colleagues searchingly sought over a period of days to get answers to questions about the infant's status and behavior in order to alter her condition or to prevent it from deteriorating, precisely the same task and process is required to deal with the social-interpersonal context. Indeed, whatever implications the diagnosis of the infant has for her development will depend on how the diagnosis of the social-interpersonal context is conceived and handled.* This last point deserves emphasis: the diagnosis of the infant's condition has developmental consequences but the quality and quantity of those consequences will always be a function of the total social-interpersonal context of which the infant is a part.

If in practice the concept of diagnosis is seen as taking place only in regard to the infant, even though the developmental implications of the diagnosis will inevitably be shaped by a larger context, it says more about the weight of tradition than about requirements for helpful action. Unfortunately, this constricting view of diagnosis has profound and upsetting consequences. For example, consider the fact that the diagnosis of the infant did not take place at one point in time but rather evolved over a period of days in which data was collected and careful observations made.

When we say that diagnosis is a process, we mean that it is a series of actions and checks taking place over time and, not infrequently, involving interventions and treatments that give a more secure base to diagnosis. Similarly, diagnosis and treatment of the social-interpersonal context is an ongoing process that should not terminate when the mother and infant leave the hospital, to be resumed at the first office or hospital visit, or to be changed as a function of telephone calls from parents to physician. After all, from the moment the family leaves the hospital the quality and quantity of interactions within that social unit take on a fateful and changing character that is far from predictable. And what is at stake is no less than the direction of change in the lives of three interrelated human beings. The sad fact is that the diagnosis of the social-interpersonal context almost never is carried out in the sustained, painstaking, probing manner that characterized the diagnosis of the infant's condition. In point of fact we know amazingly little in these instances about what goes on, less because so much is going on and more because our conceptions and practices are inappropriately neglectful of the issues.

In the case of Alice and Harold the first few weeks were a nightmare. But as the father said: "You wake up from nightmares." A pediatrician once said with humor that the hardest job with parents of their first newborn was to convince them that their child would live. One function of humor is to allay anxiety, and pediatricians are not without anxiety but the strength of it is as nothing compared to that in parents. When that newborn is clearly retarded, the anxiety is usually exponentially more persistent and disabling. Harold came to one of the authors one week after the infant had been brought home, plying him with all sorts of questions which neither he nor his wife could ask the pediatrician because they were "personal" and not "medical" questions. One did not have to be all that sophisticated to conclude that these personal questions not only illustrated how the parents were being affected by the infant but, no less important, how the infant was probably being affected by the parents.

Interpretation of Mental Deficiency to Parents

The importance of family was reflected in *Psychological Problems in Mental Deficiency* (Sarason, 1949) in the chapter "Interpretation of Mental Deficiency to Parents." Parents and professionals reacted positively to that chapter, although among the professionals who responded there was not a single physician. That did not surprise me; in the same book I was very critical of the preparation of physicians for the very sensitive task of communicating the diagnosis to parents. By far, most of the letters I received were from parents. The chapter, which is reprinted below, was kept in the first three editions of that book but was dropped from later editions because I thought that the approach to interpreting the diagnosis to parents had become noticeably more sophisticated and sensitive. I *thought* that a dramatic change had occurred but that was more a reflection of my hopes than of an assessment based on clinical practice and realities. Over the years I had received such positive response to the chapter that I ignored the simple fact that those who wrote to me were a self-selected, biased sample. More on that after the following chapter from *Psychological Problems in Mental Deficiency.*[2]

The failure adequately to communicate to parents the nature and implications of a diagnosis of mental deficiency probably causes more unnecessary problems and suffering than any other factor, with the obvious exception of those factors which originally produced the mental deficiency. By the word "communicate" is meant not only the imparting of facts but, in addition, the attempt on the part of a qualified person to help parents recognize and adjust to the realities of their child's condition. The imparting of facts does not insure that parents either will recognize or adjust to the child's condition. Resistance, anxiety, despair, hostility, and frustration—these experiences and reactions are not quieted or eliminated by a recital of facts. One might even say that when the nature of the child's condition is explained to the parents, their tendencies to resist the explanation and to react in an emotional way are strengthened rather than decreased.

Before becoming specific about the handling of the interpretation of mental defect to parents, the following statements about the goals of such a situation should be made explicit:

1. The parents should be completely informed about the probable causes of the child's condition, the severity of the mental defect, and the probable course (educationally, vocationally, socially) of the child's development.
2. A specific program geared to the needs and capabilities of the child should be explained, discussed, and planned with the parents.
3. The personal problems of the parents, caused or exacerbated by the child's condition, should be dealt with in a manner so as to maximize the probability that parents and child will be able to function in a socially constructive and self-satisfying manner.
4. Provision should be made for periodic discussion with the parents and observation of the child in order to check on the nature of the child's and parents' adjustment and to re-evaluate the correctness of the initial program.

With these goals in mind, what follows is an attempt to describe in some detail the problems one frequently encounters and the ways in which one might handle them.

The Setting

In discussing here the interpretation of mental defect with parents it is impossible to take into account all the different settings in which a problem is encountered. The physician in his office, the teacher in the school, the psychologist or social worker in the clinic—these and other professional specialists are called upon to handle the parents of the defective child. In each case the setting is different in terms of various diagnostic services, availability of case-history material, previous experience with the problem, knowledge of community resources, and time available for any one case. For the purposes of the present discussion we shall assume that the parents have brought their child to a clinic where psychological, medical, and social work facilities are available. We shall further assume that the child has been comprehensively examined, background data secured, and a diagnosis of mental defect made. The problem now is to communicate the findings to the parents.

Some Preliminary Considerations

In arranging for the interviews it is extremely important to have *both* parents present. One must never assume that both parents have the same conception of the problem, the same attitudes toward the child, experience a similar degree of frustration, or possess a similar degree of stability and maturity. By working only with the mother, as is most frequent, one may never find out, for example, either that the parents quarrel violently about the handling of their child, or that the father rejects the child, or that he now rejects the mother. One simply cannot assume that the mother's report is a necessarily valid or complete one, *even though she may be motivated to give what she thinks is an objective presentation of the facts.* Since carrying out a recommended program successfully depends in large part on a harmonious relationship between the parents, it is imperative that at the outset one be in a position to evaluate the nature of that relationship. In more than a few cases the primary problem is not the defective child but unhappy, mutually aggressive parents who have become emotionally distant from each other. To focus on the defective child not only overlooks important influences on his behavior but increases the likelihood that a recommended program will fail completely or fall short of its mark.

Another difficulty in working with one parent, say the mother, is that she may not communicate to her husband the contents of the interview in an undistorted fashion. She may forget to relate certain aspects of the discussion, distort others, and attempt to answer questions posed by the husband which had not been discussed at all with the counselor. *The tendency to perceive and report in a selective manner is a human characteristic which appears to become increasingly operative when strongly felt, personal problems are aroused.* It is for this reason that so much emphasis has been and will be given here to the recognition and prevention (as far as possible) of selective perception and reporting by parents of mentally defective children.

Another advantage in having the father at the interview is that he is then more likely to share the responsibilities of caring for the child. In our culture the primary responsibility in child rearing falls on the mother. One can say with no hesitation that rearing a defective child is certainly one of the most difficult tasks which can confront a mother. In many cases, especially when the child is severely defective, it is too much to expect the mother to handle the problem by herself; it can be done but with the likelihood that the health of the mother sooner or later deteriorates. A sickly, irritable, frustrated mother is not likely to be a satisfactory wife. Where such a problem exists an attempt should be made to get the father to see the nature of the situation and *to want* to share the responsibilities.

One of the most obvious cautions to be observed in arranging for the interview is that the child should not be present. This caution is necessary not only to protect the child but to enable the parents to discuss the problem without the distracting presence of the child.

Structuring the Interview

In working with parents of defective children one must never lose sight of the fact that they have experienced keen frustration and hardship, have generally previously been given ambiguous or contradictory advice, and have been given little or no opportunity to unburden their anguish and disappointment. Unfortunately, there are too many professional specialists who give parents the feeling that they have little or limited time in which to discuss the problem with them, conduct the interview in the form of a monologue so that the parents are seldom given an opportunity to ask questions, communicate in a technical jargon which effectively confuses and overwhelms the parents, and in general manifest little or no interest in the personal problems or reactions of the parents. Unless one is able to identify with the problems and feelings of the parents one is likely to conduct the interview in an impersonal, superficial, routine fashion— a fashion which may be considered "successful" by the specialist but is frustrating and confusing to the parents. In working with the parents of defective children—in fact, in working with the parents of any problem child—one must not only be able to experience vicariously the nature and strength of their frustrations but also to structure the relationships so as to enable one to facilitate change in parental attitude and practice.

The following represents the writer's way of structuring the interview:

> Before we discuss in any detail the conclusions we have reached about your child there are a few things I would like to say by way of introduction. The first this is that I hope that you will feel free *at any time* to ask questions or express an opinion—or disagreement. If I should say something you do not understand, please ask me about it immediately. All of us, you know, do not always say things as clearly as we should, so that if something is not clear to you I hope you will not feel that it is your fault and be afraid to ask questions. Sometimes we have found that parents have had important things they wanted to say or ask but for some reason they thought we might think them silly. The more questions you ask and we discuss the more help we can be to you. If I should use a word or phrase which you do not understand please interrupt and tell me. Sometimes we forget that words which mean something to us do not mean anything to another person. So I will look upon it as a favor if you will tell me when you do not understand something. One more thing: in the hour or so we have at our disposal it may not be possible for us to go over every problem in great detail. We have found in the past that it is not always possible to discuss everything in one session. So at the end of our talk today I will be happy to

make another appointment when we can talk some more. You may find that when you go home questions will occur to you which you forgot to ask, or what seemed clear to you now may not seem so clear later, or you may find yourself disagreeing with our conclusions. Whatever it is, I hope you will not feel that today is the only time you will have to discuss your problems with us. We will be eager to see you as many times as you think we can be of help to you.

The significance of the above lies not in the words employed or the order in which the statements are made but rather in the attempt to engender in the parents the following set of attitudes:

1. It is not only "permissible" for them to talk and ask questions but *it is expected of them.*
2. They are talking to someone whose manner does not suggest he is impatient to get on to what is next on his appointment calendar.
3. Parents have something important to contribute to the discussion.

Needless to say, parroting words or phrases will not necessarily produce the desired effects. The words and phrases must reflect personal conviction and feeling—if they do not, the parents are likely to recognize the insincerity and react accordingly. The tone of one's voice, one's facial expression, and the manifestation of a genuine desire to understand and help—these are the media by which the words one utters gain their force.

Obtaining Parental Attitudes, Practices, and Goals

Having attempted to establish the kind of relationship described above, it has then been found helpful to determine parental attitudes about the etiology of their child's condition, how they have handled the problems he has presented, and goals they have set for him. *Without knowledge or consideration of these factors the extent to which the parent's personal problems and, consequently, the child's particular problems can be helped will be minimal.* It has been the failure to consider these factors which has caused so much ineffective planning, wasted effort, and continued disappointment and frustration. Advice about child rearing, schooling, institutionalization and similar problems must take into account parental behavior and attitudes if such advice is to have a reasonable chance of success.

At this point in the interview the writer has found the following statements helpful:

Although we have studied your child very carefully from many points of view—which we will discuss in a little while—I think you will understand when I say that our examinations do not always give us all the information we would like. In our experience we have found that at this point parents can be very helpful to us about certain questions. You have known your child longer than we have and you have observed him in a way that we have not. We have learned from many cases in the past that by sharing our experiences and conclusions we might see things somewhat differently than before. You might have talked some of these things over before but it would be very helpful to all of us if you could do it again. For example, I wonder if you might tell me what *you* have thought was the cause of your child's condition? From time to time several possible answers have probably occurred to you and I wonder if you could talk about them—even though you might have thought they were silly or, as sometimes happens, too unpleasant to think about. Whatever these were, it would be extremely helpful if we could talk about them.

It is clear that these statements are intended to get the parents to verbalize *their* conception of the etiology of the child's condition. The havoc which can be wrought by parental misconceptions about etiology has been nicely pointed out by Kanner and Tietze (p. 269):

Popular notions regarding heredity have provided a handy means of transferring the blame to some afflicted relative. If the hunt for a skeleton in the family closet did just that, it would serve a fairly useful function of absolving the parents from a feeling of personal guilt. But often enough a parent comes to believe, or is made to believe by hostile in-laws, that the present or past existence of such a relative is his or her own fault and contribution to the child's condition. The in-laws thus wash their hands of any complicity. The clan members of the accused spouse cannot remain idle. They usually manage, sometimes after considerable search worthy of a genealogist, to uncover some conjugal counterpart of the skeleton, and mutual recriminations are the order of the day. Psychotherapeutic consideration of the parents of retarded children cannot afford to disregard such bickering arising between and within families from the desire to put the stigma and odium of an ancestral culprit on either parent.

Misconceptions about heredity are not the only ones which parents may harbor. Some mothers have concluded that they were too active during pregnancy, or that they had experienced some frightening situation during pregnancy, or that they did not feed their child adequately in his early days, or that they did not obtain for him prompt or proper medical attention, or that the child had once slipped or fell from the mother's arms and had then cried most excessively. Parental explanations many and varied but they usually have three characteristics in common:

1. They sound plausible and may contain a germ of truth; in other words, it would be difficult for a professional specialist to say

that these factors have never been a possible factor in any case.

2. In the individual case the parental explanation usually cannot explain *their* child's condition. For example, an infant may receive a brain injury because of a fall, but when the neurological findings point unmistakably to early embryonic disfunction the parental explanation obviously loses its etiological relevance.

3. The parental explanation usually involves self-plaguings and feelings of guilt.

When one bears in mind to what extent parental misconception about etiology can adversely affect parental happiness and adjustment, the importance of determining the nature of such conceptions is clear. In order to disabuse parents of misconceptions and thereby give them a basis for relinquishing unrealistic and irrational attitudes it is first necessary for parents to verbalize their feelings.

The next area about which parents should be encouraged to talk might be indicated in the form of a question: "What are the main problems you have had to face as your child has developed and how have you coped with them?" Here one is interested in specific child rearing practices and problems: *When and how* did they try to teach their child to talk, walk, eat, and control toilet functions? When and how did they try to teach their child letters, words, and numbers? How did the parents handle the problem of their child's inability to play and compete with others? What are the attitudes of their siblings toward the child? Of neighbors? Have the social activities of the parents been in any way affected by the condition of their child? One of the main considerations giving rise to these questions is the importance of determining the degree of emotionality which the parents experience in responding to the problems which their child has presented. Have the parents accepted his limitations or have they pushed him? Do they feel that other children and neighbors are unfair in their response to the child? Have the parents restricted excessively their own activities in order to devote their energies to the child? Do the parents see eye-to-eye on the handling of these problems? Are there indications that the parents have been unable to take advice offered previously by other agencies?

The last area about which parents should be encouraged to talk concerns their expectations of or goals for their child. What have they hoped that this child will be able to do? What are their expectations or hopes about his schooling? About his social and vocational activities? *It is through parental report about their hopes and aspirations for their child that one can best determine how realistic an understanding of their child's abilities the parents have. At the same time one can also evaluate the extent of one's task in helping the parents to adopt a more realistic approach.* A parent who says that he does not expect his child to go to college but would like him to finish high school reveals not only an unrealistic conception of his child but very frequently also a need to avoid accepting the child's limitations. The parent who says that he is not interested in the child's academic schooling but only wants him to be able to learn a trade and to maintain himself independently is also revealing a lack of understanding. The difficulty parents experience in accepting their child's limitations has been well described by Kanner and Tietze (p. 269):

> During the past centuries our culture has put a special premium on good cognitive endowment, in an increasing degree. Our communal life is so constituted that to people with sufficiently high intelligence quotients go, of necessity, the functions of governing, the jobs with good incomes, the respect of contemporaries. They are the acknowledged inheritors of the earth. They are the cream of society. To have a child with a lower-than-average I.Q. means that his parents must from the beginning expect that he will be excluded from leadership, riches and esteem. Regardless of everything else, the low I.Q., as such, marks the child as socially inferior. Physical attractiveness, good manners, emotional stability and manual dexterity may create attenuating circumstances, but even though they are all combined in one person, if the I.Q. does not measure up to the existing requirements, they still fail to admit the bearer to a seat among the elite.
>
> It is, quite understandably, difficult for many parents, especially those who themselves have been blessed with a good I.Q., to accept their child's intellectual retardation as an Act of God, as something unpredictable, inevitable and unalterable. There comes often a search for the possibility of parental contribution to the child's inadequacy. The question, "Why do we have such a child?" soon assumes the form of "What have we done to have such a child?"
>
> Some parents do their best to escape the discomforts of trying to find an answer by flatly refusing to recognize the fact as such. The feeling, not ever verbalized, goes something like this: "If my child were really retarded, I should be forced to ascribe his condition somehow to some shortcoming or transgression of my own. But I simply refuse to admit that he is retarded." Then comes a hunt for excuses, usually looked for in the child's physical health. The child's admittedly poor performance must be based on unrecognized poor eyesight, glandular anomaly or something pressing on the brain. If the doctors could only find the somatic culprit, then the child will be all right and the parents will have reason to feel exculpated. If it is not an organ of the child's body, then it must be the teacher's lack of understanding, the crowded class, or the faulty school system. And if it isn't that, then the tester didn't know his business, or didn't know how to handle the child, or the child wasn't in the proper mood just then. It would be wrong to attribute this

attitude, as is often done, to parental stubbornness, wicked and dis-
respectful lack of cooperation, or mental dishonesty. Such parents
need the kind of guidance which makes it possible for them to express their feelings, frees them of any implied necessity of considering themselves personally responsible for the child's retardation,
and thereby helps them to lift their heads from below the ostrich
sand pile.

The point which deserves emphasis is that parental misunderstanding and overevaluation of their child's behavior and capabilities
stem not from stubbornness but from a need to avoid wounding their
own pride and facing self-devaluation. The conception which a parent
has of his child is a reflection of his conception of himself. To admit that
his child is "stupid" is very likely to arouse in the parent thoughts of his
own limitations.

The Interview up to this Point

Thus far we have endeavored to engender in the parents a set of attitudes
toward the counselor and the interview, and we have also attempted to
get the parents to talk about themselves in relation to their child. *In the
latter attempt the emphasis has been on what the parents have to report,
the counselor adopting a relatively passive role in which he expresses no
opinions but attempts in as nonleading a way as possible to get the parents
to clarify and elaborate upon their thoughts and feelings.* Without the parental report it is difficult to identify oneself with them: to understand
why they have reacted to their problem in the way they have and how
their reactions have influenced their child. In addition, *by obtaining the
parental report one is then in the position to utilize the diagnostic findings
to help the parents achieve a more realistic basis for their conceptions,
practices and goals.*

Communicating the Diagnostic Findings

At this point in the interview the writer has said the following to the
parents:

> I find that what you have told me is extremely interesting and
> has given me a better understanding of what you have been think-
> ing and experiencing. Now I would like to share with you the results
> of our studies. As you know we have studied your child from many
> points of view and we have come to certain conclusions. Before tell-
> ing you of our conclusions I would first like to tell you of some of
> our experiences with other parents. Sometimes parents are at first
> disappointed at what we have to say and sometimes do not want to
> accept our findings. *This is very understandable to us—no one likes*

to hear that his child will always have certain limitations which other children will not have. It is not easy to accept the fact that your child will never be able to do certain kinds of activities. But we feel that it is our obligation to speak with you as frankly as we can—as we feel you would want us to do. Again I would like to remind you to ask questions whenever they occur to you, and to disagree if that is how you feel. And please remember that we will be glad to talk with you further—we will always be glad to make an appointment to discuss any matter that you want.

These statements are intended to achieve the following:

1. To reward parents for their participation and to reinforce the feeling that they have something to contribute.
2. To prepare the parents, in those cases where it is indicated, for what will be conflict-arousing information.
3. To facilitate for the parents the experiencing and verbalizing of feeling. Anxiety, hostility, disappointment, and despair—these are the feelings one should enable parents to express rather than inhibit. While the inhibition of such feeling makes for a more "pleasant" interview, it also reduces the amount of help that one can be to parents.

It is not possible to describe in detail how the diagnostic findings are presented to the parents because the order in which they are presented and the degree of emphasis which they receive are determined by the problems arising from the parental report. As was said before, *the diagnostic findings are used as the bases for helping parents give up erroneous ideas and adopt a more realistic approach to their own and their child's problems.* For example, if the diagnostic findings offer no support for parental conceptions of etiology, then this point must be made explicit—and emphasized. It is not enough to tell parents that they are "wrong"; one must not give them the impression that their conceptions are silly. One must make parents feel that one understands why they arrived at their particular conceptions—but that the findings offer no support for their convictions. If parents have unrealistic anticipations about their child's future schooling, then this should be explicitly discussed. To parents who would like their child at least to finish public or high school it is not enough to say that this is not possible; one must state the basis for one's conclusion and give as explicitly as possible the probable lower and upper limits of the child's academic achievements.

In many cases parents have already indirectly revealed that many of the day-to-day problems which they experience in relation to their child stem from highly emotionally tinged attitudes which in turn adversely affect their child's behavior. It is difficult for these parents to see that such attitudes defeat, or at the least interfere with, the goals which they want to achieve. *In discussing this with parents one must be careful to avoid making them feel guilty. One must explicitly recognize and verbalize that what the parents had been doing, however ineffective, was based on "good intentions," as indeed it usually is.*

The Importance of a Specific Program

One of the most important functions of the interview is to offer to and discuss with parents a specific program for their child. A great deal of unnecessary unhappiness has resulted from the failure to give to the parents detailed advice about the handling of their child. Parents of defective children need guidance and emotional support. It is not enough to tell them that their child is defective and they should not expect much from him. The following is a list of questions which parents frequently ask— the questions, of course, varying with the age of the child, severity of defect, degree of physical handicap, etc.:

> Should I try to teach my child to walk now? Am I teaching him the right way?
>
> How can I get other children to refrain from teasing him?
>
> Is there any way I can train my child to stop being as destructive as he is?
>
> Should I punish him the way I do my other children?
>
> When should he start school? Is there a school for him?
>
> Should we institutionalize him? What are these institutions? Are they expensive?
>
> Should we have other children? Will my child be a bad influence on my other children? My other child who is normal resents him— what should I do about it?

One could list a great many more problems for which parents seek guidance. Some of the problems require a detailed knowledge and understanding of the child, parents, and family constellation. Other problems require, in addition, a knowledge of community resources: educational, recreational, and institutional. But in discussing any problem with parents one must wherever possible give specific advice and guidance. For example, if a mother is bothered because her child is frequently teased by neighborhood children, one must attempt to outline concrete steps which might be taken by the mother to cope with the problem. One should, of course, first determine how the mother has previously handled the problem: Has she "bawled out" the other children? Has she asked their parents to punish them? If the parent has reacted in this way then one must point out why such an approach is likely to be self-defeating. One might then suggest that the mother have a talk with the children and explain to them that her child cannot do some of the things that they can, that he needs a little more consideration and protection, that he is not as able to protect or defend himself as they are, and that she is discussing the matter with them because she knows that if they understood her child better they would not tease him. Another suggestion concerns discussing the matter in a similar vein with the parents of the neighborhood children.

One should not give the parent of the defective child the impression that one's suggestions are sure to work after one application. In addition, one must avoid giving suggestions which, while correct in general, cannot be properly acted upon by the parent because of their excessive emotionality:

If the problem concerns the future schooling of the child one should acquaint the parent with the nature of local facilities, the people who administer them, and the requirements for entrance. One should urge the parents to visit the facilities and, if possible, arrange for the visit and for a later discussion of parental reactions and questions. Too frequently parents have had to find out about local facilities in a trial-and-error kind of way, during which time their feelings of frustration and helplessness have mounted.

The Interview to this Point

Thus far we have attempted to do four things: (1) engender in the parents a particular attitude toward the interview, (2) identify the nature of the parents' problems, (3) utilize the diagnostic findings in order to help the parents adopt a realistic conception of their child's condition, and (4) formulate and discuss with the parents a specific attack on their child's and their own problems.

As was indicated before, it is not always possible or desirable to achieve all the goals of the interview with one session. The availability and advisability of another session or sessions should be again pointed out to the parents, the decision about returning being left to them. In terminating the interview one must convey to the parents that the need for further visits is not due to a present lack of interview time but to the need for the parents to digest what has been discussed, raise new questions or problems which usually occur to them after an initial visit, and to give the interviewer more time to mull over the discussion and the problems raised.

Some Cautions

The reader should not conclude that by following the contents of this chapter he will always be able smoothly and painlessly to achieve the goals outlined earlier. Parents do not always say or do what we would like or expect. The fact that one attempts to get parents to talk about their conceptions of the origins of their child's condition does not mean that they will do so. One may try to make parents feel free to talk and raise questions but the attempt does not mean that they will act accordingly. In some cases it is not until the second or third interview that a parent will really feel free to talk and raise questions. In working with parents one must be ready to change one's approach and, with unusually emotional or unstable parents, even to narrow one's goals. But in these cases extreme care must be taken to insure that a change in approach or narrowing of goals is not the result of one's own emotional reactions. For example, *some parents seem so hostile or resistant that one reacts similarly to them, reactions which then enable the parent to continue to be hostile and resistant. In working with parents (as in therapeutic work with anyone) it is self-defeating to respond emotionally to the deliberate or unwitting provocations of those whom one is trying to help.* The task is to recognize the hostility and to help the parents see its lack of justification in this situation.

The subjective reactions of the counselor can be an interfering factor in those instances when he fears the reaction of the parent to what will probably be highly disappointing news—the interviewer wants and yet does not want to state the truth. As a consequence he will sometimes relate the findings in an ambiguous manner so that the parents can interpret them in any manner that they choose—the interviewer unknowingly speaks out of both sides of his mouth. The writer has spoken to physicians who have frankly said that they did not "have the heart" to tell parents that their child was defective. Others have adopted the position that ignorance is bliss and "they (the parents) will find out for themselves later on." Both attitudes reveal a need to avoid an unpleasant situation, an avoidance which may make life more pleasant for the physician but creates undue hardship, now and in the future, for parents and child.

Interpreting mental defect to parents is not a simple or pleasant task and cannot be approached in a perfunctory way. In Chapter 13 the problem of who should handle such tasks and what the requisite training should be will be discussed.

The "Untreatable" Parents

There are always parents who are unable to face the problems brought up in the interview despite all of one's efforts. In such cases the counselor must neither lose patience nor take it as an affront. Terminating the relationship with such parents, however, should not necessarily be looked upon as a negative step. The following information should be conveyed to the parents:

1. That one understands that it is not easy to accept and to adjust to the problems and conclusions which have been discussed. Should the

parents at any time in the future desire to resume discussion, or feel that the agency can in any way be of help to them, they should not hesitate to call for an appointment.

2. Should the parents feel that they would like to take their child to another agency for evaluation, it might be helpful if they were given a list of agencies or professional specialists who are competent to make such an evaluation.

It is clear that the last statement represents an attempt to insure that parents, if they are "to shop around," go to reputable and competent specialists and agencies. In more than a few cases shopping around among recommended agencies has helped parents to accept conclusions which were discussed with them earlier. In other cases, of course, the shopping around never has any beneficial effects.

It is sometimes forgotten that although parents may achieve new insights during the interview and may give clear indications that their attitudes are beginning to change, the crucial test of the efficacy of one's efforts is if after the interview the parents can *act* on the basis of what they have learned. It is unusual if inter- and intrapersonal conflicts can be resolved either during or because of a single interview. What is perhaps more usual is that after the interview previous conflicts are experienced in their original or increased strength. One must remember that strongly held beliefs, unrealistic or not, are maintained because they are in one way or other satisfying to the believer. These beliefs serve the purpose of enabling the individual to defend himself against recognizing what for him would be an unpleasant or even impossible situation. It is because such beliefs serve this defensive purpose that they are not easily given up even when adherence to contrary beliefs is apparently being achieved. It is because of these considerations that emphasis has been given to the need for several interviews. In addition, these considerations contain the implication that in those cases where parents have achieved new insights the counselor should actively aid the parent wherever possible to follow through on their new insights. In some cases, for example, a visit to the home might not only reinforce more realistic parental behavior but might allow the counselor to be of more concrete help to the parents—a suggestion which Yepmen and Cianci have shown to possess marked therapeutic possibilities.

And now a note on "progress":

Consider the following two instances: minutes after a mother has delivered her child, and still groggy and dazed from the experience, she is told that her child has mongolism. The second instance is that of a mother who has come for the first time to a pediatric clinic a few weeks after delivery; in the hall she meets her doctor who in the process of saying hello and continuing down the hall tells her that her child is mentally retarded. Both instances took place in 1976 in a prestigious medical center. (Sarason and Doris, 1979, p. 108)

Recent work leaves no doubt that my hope that the interpretation of the diagnosis to parents had noticeably improved was a hope bearing little relationship to reality, at least the realities of the scandalous lack of preparation of physicians for talking *with* (not to) parents. I confess that I harbor the hope that other professionals do better than physicians, although that is like damning with the faintest of praise. In the case of the rare physician (regardless of specialty) who knows how to listen and how to be helpful to parents of a retarded child, it says little or nothing about that physician's training and a great deal about what he or she is and has been as a person.

How to *listen?* *Who* can listen? Those questions bring to mind a memorable experience. Back in the fifties John Carver, a parent of a retarded and institutionalized child and a professor of sociology at Southern Connecticut State College, came to ask me if I would support his application for a fellowship from the National Institute of Mental Health. He wanted (together with his wife) to interview parents of retarded children because he believed that professionals and the lay public did not comprehend the dilemmas of parents of retarded children. I knew John slightly, and what I knew did not suggest that he could do justice to what he proposed. For one thing, he was a very shy person who seemed to ooze insecurity and uncertainty. He was not a prepossessing person. When he spoke, it was in a faltering way, with long pauses between words and even longer ones between sentences. In fact, if you closed your eyes and listened to his speech, you might entertain the hypothesis that he was aphasic. Candor requires that I admit that John's manner of talking taxed my patience. That it did not exhaust my patience was due only to the obvious fact that John was as decent a person as I have ever known. He was one of those people for whom it was appropriate to say: "He could not harm a fly even if he tried." Given my view of John, I had to conclude that he could not do justice to what he proposed. How to tell him? What I said was that although his proposal addressed a crucial problem in the field, I felt that he ought to first conduct two or three trial runs. This would help him determine what the interviews were eliciting. Besides, his application would be stronger if he could say that he had done some preliminary interviews that demonstrated he was on the right track. Further, I told him, I would be in a better position to support his application. In short, I stalled. Several weeks later John returned with some of the most revealing, poignant, compelling interviews I had ever read. (One of the interviews started at 9 p.m. and did not end until one o'clock in the morning.) I wrote an enthusiastic letter of support. His request was not approved. That did not stop John. He and his wife did the interviews, which were not published in book form (*The Retarded Child in the Family*) until many years later (Carver and Carver, 1972). John wrote slowly! Unfortunately, he was killed in an auto accident not long after the book was published. John taught me a good deal, not the least of which was the fact that when parents sense that you really want to listen and to understand, it all comes pouring out. And to understand means that you understand them *as a family*.

The Family's View of the Future

The knowledge that their child is retarded causes parents to seek an explanation in the past, to confront problems in the immediate present, and to try to read and anticipate an ambiguous future. In my experience, parental concern for the future is the most persistent. As is frequently the case, the novelist helps us to understand reality better, and so in writing about time and the family I found it helpful to use Heller's (1975) *Something Happened*. The following excerpts are from Chapter 5 of *Educational Handicap, Public Policy, and Social History* (Sarason and Doris, 1979).[3]

When parents have a child their lives are forever changed and at the time of birth the changes they foresee are almost always positive. They can introduce stress in their lives. Economic, pyschological, sexual, physical and recreational areas of functioning may be adversely affected by having to care for the developing child. The point is that even when a child is developing according to norms, the balance between satisfactions and dissatisfactions, between personal freedom and frustration, changes for all members of the family.

Several decades ago, one would have said that the balance in the relationship between positive and negative factors was clearly in favor of the positive. Today, however, with the dramatic increase in the rate of divorce it is obvious that marriage and the family have become more fragile institutions. This, of course, in no way implies that this increase is due in the larger part to the stresses engendered by rearing children, but it does suggest that the attitudes and expectations people bring to marriage decrease their tolerance to frustration. And when we bear in mind that, increasingly, women as well as men are planning lifelong working careers, the problems surrounding child rearing can be expected to put added burdens on family stability. All of this is by way of saying that fantasy and reality, great expectations and the restrictions of marriage and family, are polarities that few families seem to balance satisfactorily.

If what we have said characterizes the family with "normal" children, we would expect that the vulnerability of a family would become greater when it confronts the task of rearing a retarded child. The fact is that this expectation cannot be demonstrated by data because the relevant studies have not been done. Grossman's study, which we discussed in the previous chapter, did indicate that many brothers and sisters seemed to have benefited by the fact that they had a retarded sib. But she cautioned that the number of those instances would probably be far less on a percentage basis if she had chosen her subjects in a way more representative of the population of families with retarded children. Also, Grossman studied only the normal sibs and it was from them that she obtained an indirect and admittedly incomplete picture of family dynamics. And, as she emphasizes, social-economic factors played an important role, a point we shall return to later. There is still another factor that should temper expectations, and that is the development in the past two decades of community programs that never existed before and have enabled families to cope better with their retarded children.

One would expect that the study done in the fifties by the Carvers (1972) of the dispiriting and disabling consequences for families with retarded children would be inapplicable to the current scene. Although this may be true, our experience suggests that it is less true than some people would like us to believe. There can be no doubt that the recent changes in society's verbal expressions about the needs and rights of retarded children and their families, accompanied as these have been by dramatic increases in public funds for a wide array of programs and services, have been helpful to families. But just as we should not uncritically accept the belief that the presence of a retarded child in a family has only catastrophic effects, we should not smugly assume that increased funding and programs have dramatically and positively altered the experience of families. The history of the field of mental retardation contains too many instances where progress was confused with increased expenditures or public resolves to give more than lip service to the idea of humane treatment. In 1843, Dorothea Dix gave her famous, searing address to the Massachusetts legislature, detailing the inhumane conditions of the state's "humane" institutions. We like to believe that in the century following that address the conditions she described were eliminated, and humaneness restored to its appropriate governing role in this sphere of human affairs. In 1967, Burton Blatt described similar conditions to the same legislature. There is a difference between change and progress!

Something Happened

Something Happened is a novel by Joseph Heller, published in 1974 to wide critical acclaim. The major themes of the book are by no means new: the driven, competitive, materialistic, married, Don Juanish American male whose personal and familial instability and disintegration increase as he climbs the ladder of "success." The book is an indictment of many aspects of our society and, although it describes a tragedy, it does contain, as one would expect from the author of *Catch-22*, zany and comical moments. By the end of the story the narrator and the central character, Slocum, is a prematurely aged, empty, lost soul bereft of any social intimacies or anchors. To those around him Slocum is still whole, but he is going to pieces. How this came about is beyond our purposes here. Suffice it to say that Heller, as a serious novelist, gives no simple cause and effect explanation. Indeed, novelists tend to take the transactional approach more seriously than other students of human behavior and, therefore, do not easily fall prey to simple cause and effect explanations. One way of describing a novel is that it is a diagnosis of social context based on the transactional principle.

What is relevant to our purpose is that Slocum is the father of three children one of whom is Derek, brain damaged and mentally retarded from birth. What picture is drawn about Derek's perceived effects on the family as a unit and on each of its members as individuals? Not surprisingly, the clearest picture we get is Slocum. To say that he is ambivalent toward the child is misleading because that would obscure the fact that his negative feelings are stronger than his positive ones. He is, of course, guilt-ridden because of his feelings; he admits his dislike for the child, only to himself. When he reviews the birth of the child; the dry, insensitive way in which Derek's diagnosis was communicated; the maddening unhelpfulness of the physicians; his early attempts to interact with the child and the lack of responsiveness Derek could give in return; the kind and quality of person the family hired to take care of Derek; Slocum's unwillingness to interact with families who also had a retarded child; his wife's complete unwillingness to consider institutionalizing the child; the worry about what would happen to Derek if something happened to Slocum and his wife—these ruminations exacerbate other keenly felt personal disappointments and inadequacies. Slocum would rather have Derek dead, not because Slocum is a hateful or sadistic person but because the child is such an obvious reminder of almost all of the father's vulnerabilities. Derek was not a "cause" but an addition to a social-familial context, to a web of interrelationships the strands of which varied considerably in strength, durability, and historical origins.

We are given less detail about the reactions of Slocum's wife to Derek. Her personal slide downhill, social withdrawal, and alcoholism are not attributed only to Derek, to whom she seems to have a religious, protective but aloof attitude. As for Derek's two siblings, the one thing we are told is that the sister worries that Derek's presence in the family may interfere with her social attractiveness to males. All in all, what comes through in the novel is a family where the members increasingly become strangers to each other. Derek is seen by them as an object who is "there"; empty, unresponsive, unconnected.

What about Derek? What kind of *person* is he? We are told next to nothing. It is as if no one inside or outside the family ever focused on Derek as a human being deserving special thought and attention. From the moment Derek's condition was "diagnosed," the world seemed to give up on him. Since money was no problem, Derek received "care"; there was always hired help to be with him. He had custodians, but there is not the faintest suggestion that anyone was devoted to him as a human being with some capability, however modest, for development. And so the author leaves the reader with the impression that Derek was what he was because of his "condition," as if he did not inevitably reflect how he was perceived and treated. The self-fulfilling prophecy claimed another victim.

Something Happened is fiction but it is faithful to what frequently occurs in reality in several important respects. First, the impact of the retarded child on the family has to be seen in terms of the existing strengths and weaknesses of the marital relationship. Second, the developmental fate of the retarded child has to be understood in light of the marital relationship. Third, no member of the family escapes the impact of the retarded individual, be it positive, negative, or, more likely, both. Fourth, the family tends to view proffered help as inadequate, ineffective, and even inappropriate. Fifth, there are forces in our society that engender and reinforce personal isolation and feelings of loneliness so that when a personal or family tragedy occurs it tends to aggravate these feelings.

When we talk about the retarded child we must never forget that that child is in a particular family in a particular society at a particular time. There are societies quite different from ours and it is not surprising, therefore, that in some of them a Derek would be perceived by the family and the social surroundings in a fashion opposite to that described in Heller's novel. To understand the significance of this point, the reader is urged to read Eaton and Weil's (1955) study of Hutterite society.

Aging and the Passage of Time

Near the end of *Something Happened*, immediately after another unsatisfying attempt by Slocum to establish rapport with his favorite child, Derek's male sib, Slocum says to himself:

> My memory's failing, my bladder is weak, my arches are falling, my tonsils and adenoids are gone, and my jawbone is rotting, and now my little boy wants to cast me away and leave me behind for reasons he won't give me. What else will I have? My job? When I am fifty-five, I will have nothing more to look forward to than Arthur Baron's job and reaching sixty-five. When I am sixty-five, I will have nothing more to look forward to than reaching seventy-five, or dying

before then. And when I am seventy-five, I will have nothing more to look forward to than dying before eighty-five, or geriatric care in a nursing home. I will have to take enemas. (Will I have to be dressed in double-layer waterproof undershorts designed especially for incontinent gentlemen?) I will be incontinent. I don't want to live longer than eighty-five, and I don't want to die sooner than a hundred and eighty-six.

Oh, my father—why have you done this to me?

I want him back. (pp. 523–524)

For Slocum the future, like the present, is oppressive and prolonged. Throughout the novel Slocum fears that tomorrow will be like today, and next year like this one. He does not, understandably, reach for the future. Instead, he longs for a past where he did not have to protect others, but others protected him. It is as if he feels that his life is over and the future will be mere existence, a kind of penance for past misdeeds. Slocum feels old, very old, and psychologically he is like some aged people who wait, sometimes eagerly, to meet death. It would, as we have emphasized, be mindless to attribute Slocum's view of the future to the fact and consequences of Derek's retardation. Derek is but one strand, albeit an important one, in the fabric of Slocum's social living that suffuses the future with anxiety, loneliness, and pathetic dependence. The point is that Heller is describing well how a person's sense of the passing of time is one of the core ingredients of the sense of aging. The sense of aging is *not* a function of chronological age (Becker 1973; Sarason 1977) but can be experienced because of events and experiences that make one feel that the best of life has passed and the future is a downhill slide. *This concern with the passage of time and a foreboding future—those obsessive thoughts about one's death and its consequences for one's kin—are almost never absent in parents of retarded children. Indeed, historically speaking, these parents as a group knew about the poignancy of the aging process long before it became a topic of public concern.*

This is what Heller's artistry has shown. When Slocum was told about Derek's retardation, it was like throwing a bomb in a smoldering volcano. Suddenly, his accustomed view of the future changed. It no longer was an endless upward and onward course but more like a mine field in which he was trapped. He was hemmed in and that was the way it was always going to be. And what if he died? Where would Derek go? Who would take care of him? And when Slocum fantasied about how nice it would be if they put Derek into an institution where they could visit him a couple of times a year, and then they could forget him, it indicated how dearly Slocum wanted to reexperience the old sense of the future, a future toward which one willingly goes. But these fantasies only emphasized the bitter reality.

We are not suggesting that what happened to Slocum and his family is a representative story. What our experience clearly suggests, however, is that what they thought and felt would be found in the internal dialogues of members of families with retarded children. Our society approves of expressions of love toward our children, not hate or ambivalence. We are expected to give priority to our children's needs over our own, to deny ourselves self-expression and self-fulfillment in order that our children's needs for untrammeled growth will be met.

Some parents can follow society's dictates and contain the negative side of their ambivalence at no great cost. The negative side is there but it does not become unduly disruptive to self or others. Other parents follow society's dictates but at the high cost of their sense of well-being and family integration, and the Slocums are only one of many types who fall into this group. And then there are those parents (like Cynthia and Harold, and Keith's parents) who reject society's dictates, with massive disruptions to existing relationships. What is common to all of these parents, because of how mental retardation is perceived in our society, is that they are confronted with the task of accommodating an altered future, with its consequences and quality, preceded by upset, mourning, grief, and the extension of the sense of isolation.

We have been concentrating on parental reaction for two reasons. First, these parents are coping with one of the most difficult experiences people in our society can have. That may sound obvious enough but the obvious is not always taken seriously, as we have been at pains to stress in earlier chapters. Second, focusing on them illuminates the enormous difference between the experience of the normal and retarded infant and young child. The gleeful, doting parents approach, touch, manipulate, hug the normal infant, concerned, perhaps, that they are too intrusive and may "spoil" the child, "spoil" meaning that the child may come to think that the world exists only to fulfill his or her needs. The parents seize, rightly or wrongly, on any action that suggests that their child may be precocious. They know he is normal, they would like him to be supernormal. Rarely is one human being so aware of, responsive, indulgent, and selfless to another human being as in the parent-infant relationship.

But what about the parents of a retarded infant? Preoccupied with their own altered needs, plagued with anxiety, guilt, and anger, searching the past for reasons and the present for hope, they cannot evade the knowledge that planning and hoping are frail needs on which to restructure lives. Experiencing those too frequent, piercing reminders that by virtue of someone coming into their lives a good deal has gone out of it and they must bury treasured hopes and fantasies—caught up in this swirl of personal despair, it is the rare parent who can respond unanxiously, spontaneously, and competently to the infant. When you are absorbed with yourself and your future, a limit is set to what you can be aware of and respond to in others. To give of yourself to someone else when you feel you need so much of it for yourself is extraordinarily difficult, if not impossible.

Matters are usually made worse by the professionals who communicate the fateful diagnosis to the parents. For one thing, they confuse communicating the diagnosis with being helpful. It does not follow that if diagnosticians were more sensitive and competent with social-familial diagnosis and, therefore, understood better the difference between communicating a diagnosis and being helpful, they would *always* be able to be helpful. That is not the issue, but rather the failure of diagnosticians to recognize and feel a responsibility for those who comprise the social-familial context. For another thing, they usually discuss the infant as if it were a thing rather than a human being, a damaged or incomplete object toward whom the usual parental response will not have productive consequences.

The infant can become an object of fear, a strange puzzle the parents cannot figure out. The parents have been given a diagnosis but no guidelines or specific directions about how to think and act in the course of days and nights. We stressed earlier the significance of parental coping with an altered *personal* future. The difficulty of that deeply personal and private task is increased by parental inability to imagine what the child will be like in the future. Will the child walk, talk, laugh, respond, play, go to school? Will the child look different? The questions are endless; in reality the number of questions are finite but they are asked and unanswered endlessly. Behind these questions is an assumption that professionals too often have instilled in parents: *The answers to questions about the child's future will be determined exclusively or largely by the nature of the child's condition, and minimally or far less by the transactions between parents and child.* That is to say, the condition will unravel itself, and parents and others who participate in the child's rearing are more like bystanders watching a predetermined developmental unfolding. This, of course, is conceptual nonsense and in flat contradiction to experience and research, but, unfortunately, that has not prevented the acceptance of this unwarranted assumption in clinical diagnosis and action. . . .

Community Services and the Psychological Sense of Community

Far more often than not, aloneness and isolation characterize the feelings of the family, especially the parents. The intervals between dispiriting thoughts about the retarded young child are not long. Sometimes, the scope of parental socialization is narrowed considerably but even when not, there is the piercing knowledge that they are alone with their problems. We are no longer a society in which one can count on extended families living near each other, or on having one's neighbors as friends, or on belonging to a church from which help is spontaneously forthcoming. Loneliness, anomie, alienation—these words have come to reflect what plagues people generally in our society (Nisbet, 1970; Sarason, 1974).

The family with a retarded young child knows these feelings only too well. But families begin to adapt to their problems, and the word adapt is used neutrally. They begin to cope in good or bad fashion depending on what criteria one employs. They continue to mourn the death of past hopes while at the same time trying to envision and shape a future. They want and need advice and help to prepare for that future. They ply themselves and their physicians with all sorts of questions about that future but the answers inevitably are vague because of reluctance to be too specific about what services the child may require or benefit from in the future. They may feel reassured when told that mental retardation has finally been accorded the attention it never had, and that diverse programs and services are now available. They may even join the local chapter of the National Association of Retarded Citizens. Our experience suggests, however, that they are not likely to join until the child is well beyond infancy. If they do join, they may experience that sense of community with others that may otherwise be absent. However, very few physicians urge parents to join for what psychological and social benefits they, the parents, may derive. Whether parents even hear about the parents' group appears to be a matter of chance.

It is not many months after the child's birth that certain questions can begin to take on an obsessional quality. Broadly speaking, they may be termed social-educational questions. Will the child be able to walk, talk, go to school, learn to read? Will he or she have playmates or is the child doomed to a life of isolation? Will the child require a special school or program? What about nursery school? Would the child be better off in a residential institution? Public or private? How does one determine quality? Where are these special schools and institutions? How do I determine what is best for the child, given the fact that I have conflicting feelings? Should we have another child? When, and what will that mean for us as a family? Will it be fair to this and the next child? Some of these questions seek clarification of alternatives involved in decision-making, and others are exquisitely and agonizingly personal-moral in nature, but they are all pointed to a cloudy, anxious, puzzling future. And, for the most part, they are questions that rarely have a satisfactory forum for discussion. They tend to remain private and festering.

Bruner (1972) pointed out that "there is no known human culture that is not marked by reciprocal help in times of danger and trouble, by food sharing, by communal nurturance for the young or disabled and by the sharing of knowledge and implements for expressing skill." Human cultures, however, differ markedly in the quantity and quality of the reciprocity, and in the case of our own culture, unfortunately, the troubled family with a young retarded child experiences little of the reciprocity that comes from the sense that one is an integral part of a larger community. On the contrary, many of these parents conclude that they live in a cold, uncaring world indifferent to the dangers and troubles of its inhabitants.

What happens when the child becomes somewhat older and the questions above take on an unavoidable urgency? What community services and programs are available and how does a "match" between them and the needs of the family come about? It used to be that this question was not a difficult one to answer because the options a family had to consider were relatively few: institutionalization or a special class *if* one were available and the criteria for acceptance could be met. Today, as a result of organized parent pressures, increased public funding, and court decisions, there are more services and programs available. In our large urban centers there may be scores of services and programs, public or private, although even the private depend on grants from public agencies. In a moderate-sized community and its environs there can be as many as twenty to thirty discrete programs and agencies providing some kind of service to mentally retarded individuals and families.

For example, in an area containing about a quarter of a million people, London (1977) found twenty agencies and programs providing some sort of explicit service. In each of these agencies she interviewed an administrator in relation to three questions: What services were they rendering; How well informed were they about other services and programs; What was the quality of agency relationships? The results were staggeringly discouraging. Here are some of the clearest findings:

1. Less than a handful of these agencies had any kind of meaningful relationship with the state department of mental retardation and its satellite offices, programs, and settings. They had surprisingly little knowledge of the nature and scope of the state's programs, resources, and responsibilities. One could look at that in another way: the state department did not seem to have taken the initiative to establish some kind of cooperative arrangement between it and the agencies.
2. Not one community agency had any real knowledge about more than three or four other community agencies, and some of that information was either obsolete or wrong. Some community agencies, amazingly, had no real knowledge of any other community agency or program.
3. Cooperation of any kind among agencies was, for all practical purposes, nonexistent. This was true for the relationship between school system programs and community agencies.
4. Agencies tended to be very critical of each other.
5. Every agency bemoaned the lack of cooperation.
6. Every agency uttered the universal complaint: They did not have the

resources either to meet the demands made of them or to give service according to the highest qualitative standards.

It would be illegitimate to come to any conclusions about the quality of services and the programs. That was not the point of London's study. The major significance of her findings is the picture we get of fragmentation, unrelatedness, and ignorance of existing community services. *If these are valid characterizations of community agencies under the leadership of highly trained, knowledgeable professionals, what can one predict about the experience of parents who are seeking community resources in order to make informed choices?*

Parental experiences are of two types. There are parents who never get a sense of the variety of programs and services that exists, and they seek out the one program that "somebody" told them about. There are parents who try to find out what exists, become frustrated at their inability to get the kind of information they want, and end up angry at themselves and the world. In short, many parents see themselves in relation to programs and services in much the same way as agencies do. In the case of parents, though, they feel far more alone as they try to manage the present in order to make a more desirable future likely. This does not distinguish parents of retarded individuals from those with normal young children.

Parents are future-oriented, but in the case of parents of retarded children they are always in the position of trying "to cut their losses," that is, keeping a difficult situation in the present from becoming more so in the future. It is by no means rare to hear these parents labeled as "anxious, demanding, and controlling." The use of these labels is sometimes, of course, justified but many times their use reflects an insensitivity to the degree to which the parental view of the present and future is suffused, and realistically so, with anxiety and the sense of aloneness.

When someone is ill and a physician is called, we make two assumptions: He will do his best to be helpful, and in the event he concludes that the services of other professionals are needed he will tell us and help us make appropriate arrangements. For example, he may call the hospital to find out if a bed is available, alert the admitting service and the laboratories, and secure the services of other colleagues he deems necessary. Put in another way: We count on the physician not only to know what facilities exist, and to tell us what he thinks needs to be done but, crucially, that he will assume supervisory responsibility for the entire process.

In the case of the retarded infant or young child, no one assumes that kind of role in relation to community programs and agencies. Generally speaking, physicians know little about existing programs and agencies, although they are by no means alone in this respect. However, given the relationship of physicians to the family, they are potentially in the best position to render the most help. Their inability to exploit that potentiality may be understandable in terms of the limitations of their training and the pressures of a medical practice, but that should not prevent us from recognizing the significance of missed opportunities.

Some Socioeconomic Differences

Grossman (1972) found that socioeconomic differences among families were related to how brothers and sisters seemed to have been affected by their retarded siblings. It obviously makes a difference if a family can afford to hire extra household help, possess ample living space, or as was true in a number of Grossman's cases, place the child in a private institution. Being relatively free from financial worry, however, does not guarantee family tranquility depending as that does on parental attitudes. As Heller demonstrated so well in *Something Happened*, the Slocum family had financial security and yet they were tragic figures. It could also be argued that because of the correlation between income and education, the more affluent families are better able to obtain whatever information and services they feel they need. One of the most significant differences between rich and poor people is in their ability to exploit "the system." And yet, the more highly educated the parents the greater the expectations for their children and, therefore, they may experience their retarded child as a greater disappointment. It may be more correct to say that the fact that families differ widely in economic resources does not permit us blithely to assume that the depth and consequences of the psychological wound are radically different.

Rich or poor, parents with young retarded children are anxious about the future and that anxiety can be put in the form of plaguing questions. Are we doing the *right* thing? Is our child getting the best available help, and how will we feel in the future if we learn that we did not make the best choices? What will happen to our child when we are gone? People do not like to contemplate their own death, and if we are forced to do so as the years go on, it is not because we like to. Parents with young retarded children feel compelled to confront the possible consequences of their own death; this is another way of saying that they are forced to confront the long-term future long before other people their age.

It was not too many decades ago that parents with severely retarded children had very few options about how to care for the child. One of these options was institutional placement. Affluent parents tended to place the child in a private setting. The financial costs were considerable so that if a family had moderate means it could place the child there only at a great sacrifice. Private placement was out of the question for the family of low income and even for many with above average incomes. The only placement available to them was the state institution.

People have always been inclined to believe that the quality of care in a private institution is better than that in the state institution. Private institutions were smaller; by virtue of being profit-making, they were disposed to be more sensitive to the needs and attitudes of parents, in contrast to the large, bureaucratized state institutions. In light of the class of parents to which they catered, the private institution was able to be more selective about the quality of its staff. And, almost always, the private institution appeared esthetically more pleasant than the usual, formidable and depressing buildings of the state institution. It was hard to tell some of these state institutions from one's mental picture of a prison.

Belief in the superiority of the private institution was probably justified, although in our experience the degree of superiority was always less than touted. This belief had upsetting consequences for those families who could not afford the private setting. After all, if one believes, rightly or wrongly, that one's child is getting second-rate care, it is not a thought that is easy to live with.

But for parents with a child in the state institution there was one considerable benefit: in the event of the parents' death the individual would continue to be taken care of. This was not necessarily the case for families with children in private settings, unless they happened to be that wealthy and willing to endow, so to speak, their child's care in perpetuity. Few were that wealthy or willing, especially if it meant drastically reducing what the other siblings would inherit. It could get very complicated, indeed, for parents and siblings each of whom in different ways was trying to secure a satisfactory future.

In the past two decades there have been two major changes in attitudes. One fact has been the rise and influence of parent groups seeking an increase in the variety of community programs and services enabling parents to keep their child at home. In earlier days institutionalization as often as not had been the reluctant choice of parents who saw no other option. A second, related factor has been the public recognition of the scandalous conditions in institutions. Inhumane conditions were more characteristic of the public than the private institution—and institutions for the mentally retarded were by no means unique in their conditions— but a generalized, deeply negative attitude toward all boarding institutions was aroused in people. These two factors converged to make it easier for parents of young retarded children to keep them in the community.

"Mentally retarded individuals can and should remain in their homes and community"—this new societal attitude became a matter of public policy. But this attitudinal change has added a new aspect to an old problem. If the child remains at home and is entered in one or more educational-community programs, the parents are again faced with an old question: Who *in the community* will care for our child when we are gone? And this question is given force as parents learn that satisfactory program options for the maturing retarded individuals hardly exist. In many communities they do not exist at all. Parents may be prepared to keep their child at home or in some community setting as long as they live but at the same time they know that living in the community is subject to risks and dangers. They also believe that these risks would be less than in a state institution.

The fact is that the risks and dangers are different; one set is not "better" than the other. The point, however, is that we rather grossly mislead ourselves, run the risk of being seen as dense, and dilute our effectiveness if·we underestimate the centrality of concern for the future in the lives of parents of retarded individuals.

In this and the previous chapters, our focus has been primarily though not exclusively psychological in emphasizing what happens to parents and families—their feelings, expectations, frustrations—when confronted with the knowledge that their child has been called retarded. We saw, however, that there are several major limitations to psychological oversimplification. One of these limitations is the tendency to think in cause and effect terms. For example, far more has been written about how parents have been affected by the child than about how children have been affected by parents, whereas in reality we are not dealing with separable processes. This limitation is not merely psychological but is in itself a reflection of certain characteristics of a society that has always demeaned the worth of the retarded child.

Psychology, neither in theory nor practice, operates in a social vacuum, but directly or indirectly reflects the larger society. And in our society the retarded child has always been a second-class human being for whom one should have pity, and toward whom one should be humane, but for whom society has no use. As a concept mental retardation will always reflect characteristics of a society at a particular time, and this means that we need more than psychology to understand the concept of mental retardation. So, to talk about mental retardation without comprehending how much of its history is in the living present is like talking about racial issues as if they are products of today or the recent past. To talk about mental retardation without confronting the fact that we are not homogeneous in social class, and that we are a very heterogeneous society in a cultural sense, is like talking about people as if they did not vary in age, size, gender, race, and religion. And, finally, to talk about mental retardation without comprehending why and how it has become embroiled in legislation, public policy, and the courts, is like trying to understand a school system independent of these same instrumentalities and their history.

In closing this chapter, mention must be made of a dramatic change in the field of mental retardation—a change that says a good deal both about our society and families. The change is in the efforts being made by social agencies to place retarded individuals in adoptive homes. As recently as 10 years ago, no social agency made serious and sustained efforts to locate such adoptive homes. Indeed, if an infant or young child was retarded, especially if seriously retarded and physically handicapped, he or she was considered unsuitable for adoption. Two assumptions underlay that practice. The first was that knowledgeable parents would not wish to adopt such a child. The second was that parents' willingness to adopt such a child said something negative about the stability of those parents; that is, stable and rational parents *ought* not to want to adopt such a child. These assumptions spoke volumes about how the larger society regarded people with mental handicap: their worth, loveability, and effect on the family. Why would any family *want* to adopt a retarded child? I confess that I shared this view, not because I derogated mentally retarded individuals but because I knew (or thought I knew) how inordinately difficult it was to rear a retarded child in a society that so overvalued a high IQ, that considered the high IQ person more worthy than the low IQ person.

Several changes in the society began to alter the conventional wisdom. Put in another way, there is nothing like necessity to force one to think the unthinkable. One change was the plunging birthrate and the consequent decrease in the number of normal children available for adoption. Another change was the pressure for deinstitutionalization and, therefore, the need for homes and other types of community placements. The third change was the necessity on the part of states to reduce budgets—to consider alternatives that would be less costly than maintaining individuals over their lifetime in different types of residential settings. (The bottom line is green!) In the early seventies I began to hear that social agencies were seeking families willing to adopt (to become "real" parents, not foster parents) mentally retarded individuals, even those with severe physical handicap. To their surprise, they found many families willing and eager for such adoptions. In the mid-1970s, there was a special presentation at Syracuse University where such adoptions were discussed and photographs of the children were shown. Those adoptions included blind, cerebral palsied, spina bifida (etc.) children. Everyone in the audience was amazed at the willingness of families to adopt such children and surprised at the high rate of success these adoptions seemed to be enjoying. A year or so after that meeting one of my graduate students, Elizabeth Scarf Stone, talked about doing her dissertation on families who had adopted seriously mentally retarded and/or seriously physically handicapped children. She had come to the problem independently of my own interests in it. Her dissertation (Stone, 1982) is one of the most engrossing that I and her thesis committee had ever read. She did intensive interviewing of the families in their homes. Her major findings were:

1. A fair number of the families (almost all of whom had one or more "biological" children) were motivated by religious considerations: They were on this earth to help others.
2. In most instances, the decision to adopt was a consequence of discussion among all members of the family.
3. There was no instance of an unsuccessful adoption or a blatant mismatch between family and the adoptee. Overall, the adopted child presents no particular problem and has become integrated into the family.

An earlier chapter pointed out that longitudinal studies of retarded infants and young children are remarkable for their absence in the literature. And by longitudinal studies I do not mean getting test scores once or twice a year, i.e., concentrating on the child, and then from a very narrow perspective. That kind of longitudinal approach studies people as individuals, not as persons. To study them as persons requires that you see them in the context of family, that you try to see how they affect family structure and dynamics and in turn how family structure and dynamics affect them. Studying people as persons requires you to focus on how they are shaped and given direction by complicated and relatively constant *social transactions* in the context of family. In short, you study them in precisely the same way you would want to be studied if someone wanted to understand what you are and why you are what you are.

This plea for longitudinal studies is no less appropriate in the case of adoptions. One can safely predict that over the next decade there will be studies of adoptions of mentally retarded and/or severely physically and neurologically impaired children. Unfortunately, one can also safely predict that these golden opportunities for deepening our understanding of the sources of variation in atypical development will not be seized. And in overlooking these opportunities, we are very likely to continue to explain development and its vicissitudes exclusively in terms of an individual and not a "person" psychology.

And what do I mean by an individual psychology? That is a question to which the book *Psychology Misdirected* (Sarason, 1981) was devoted. However, that book argues neither for a focus on the person-in-a-family or for longitudinal studies. Psychology had by that time come to respect such a focus and methodology. What I do argue against in that book is psychology's failure to see the person and family—and the ways by which the transmission of social practice and tradition occurs—in the wider context of the social order and social history. It is, so to speak, carrying the argument one step forward in order to demonstrate how misleading the emphasis on the individual organism can be. The family, the social order, and social history are all part of the conceptual configuration into which the person has to be seen in order to be understood.

1. From *Educational Handicap, Public Policy, and Social History* (pp. 40–47) by S. B. Sarason and J. Doris, 1979, New York: Free Press. Copyright 1979 by Free Press. Reprinted by permission.
2. From *Psychological Problems in Mental Deficiency* (1st ed., pp. 331–346) by S. B. Sarason, 1949, New York: Harper and Row. (Out of print)
3. From *Educational Handicap, Public Policy, and Social History* (pp. 59–77) by S. B. Sarason and J. Doris, 1979, New York: Free Press. Copyright 1979 by Free Press. Reprinted by permission.

CHAPTER 5

Infancy-Childhood: Cultural Factors and History

I came to the field of mental retardation after obtaining formal and traditional training and education in psychology. This meant that I was hardly exposed to the history of and problems in mental retardation. Partial or complete ignorance of a field is certainly a handicap when you are plunged into that field. But potentially that handicap can become an asset if the perspective you bring becomes a basis for raising new problems or new emphases. In my case, my background in psychology (child development, psychoanalytic theory, and social psychology) led me to see that the developmental orientation was hardly taken seriously in mental retardation. It was, of course, recognized that mental retardation was a developmental condition arising in the prenatal, postnatal, or early childhood periods that set limits to the individual's intellectual and social competencies. But, as I have stressed in earlier chapters of this volume, this orientation was hardly developmental in its conceptualization of the familial

183

and cultural context in which the condition was found. The emphasis was on the *individual*, not the family, local culture, and features of the larger society—a triad inevitably interrelated whether or not we are aware of it. There was one notable (and partial) exception—the diagnostic category, containing by far the largest number of individuals, that used to be called the familial, subcultural, garden-variety, or Kallikak-type of mental retardation. These labels clearly implied that the development of these individuals was adversely affected not only by inferior genes but also by an intellectually impoverished and a socially/morally debilitating family and neighborhood ambience. So-labelled individuals were frequently found in "geographical pockets" (rural or urban) that were culturally different from and inferior to (*sub*cultural) the rest of the community. These were the individuals around whom the cyclical nature-nurture controversies revolved. How much of their limitations were determined by inferior genes and how much by an environment lacking the kinds of stimulation that would maximize the realization of what developmental potential they had? There were two major reasons why I viewed the substance of nature-nurture controversies (past and present) as unproductive. The first was that my education in psychology had forced me to conclude that historically the ethnic and cultural groups around whom these controversies swirled—almost always one or another immigrant group—tended in later generations to be indistinguishable from other groups. The significance of the fact that *every* new immigrant group (e.g., Italians, Irish, Jews) was considered to be of intellectually inferior stock cannot be overestimated. The second reason was that I was not aware of a single study that dispassionately examined child rearing in these groups. It is one thing to say that a particular developmental social-family context does not stimulate the child the way that child would be stimulated in the dominant middle-class setting. It is quite another thing to say that the context is "unstimulating." Of course it is stimulating, but with goals and means that are remarkably different from what *we* value or desire. To say that the contexts are different is not arguable; to say that one is better is to say nothing about intelligence and a great deal about our particular worldview. If they are different, wherein do they differ in the child-environment transactions? No anthropologist, for example, would go from an analysis of the differences between the Sioux Indians and the Eskimos to an explanation in terms of genes. The Sioux and the Eskimos may in fact differ genetically, but the point is that the two cultures are so obviously different, leading to such vastly different experiences in the socialization process, that the leap to a genetic interpretation is, to be charitable, unjustified in the extreme. Even the most passionate advocate of the hereditarian position would not, when forced, so to speak, against the wall, argue that the genetic potential with which the infant comes into the world determines everything that follows. Of course, the hereditarian would argue that the socialization process plays a role, albeit secondary to that of the genes. But, I had concluded, our knowledge of that process was so pathetically meager that assigning weights to the role of nature and nurture was quite premature.

There is an irony here. My position was in large part based on the details and complexities of infancy and early childhood illuminated by Freud. Without necessarily subscribing to all of the major aspects of psychoanalytic theory, I was impressed with those aspects that attempted to understand motivational and cognitive development in the context of family dynamics. If psychoanalytic theory raised as many questions as it seemed to answer, it nevertheless was (or should have been) a caution against underestimating the significance of those early years. The irony is that the psychoanalytic theorists, dominated by Freud's emphases, made the same type of error that the extreme hereditarians were making. That is to say, the analytic theorist seemed to assume that lifetime development was an unfolding or continuation of the personality style forged in the earliest years. Genes were for the hereditarian what the earliest years were for the psychoanalyst. These were not only oversimplifications but egregious examples of reductionism.

During my early years in the field of mental retardation I became increasingly upset by the gulf between it and the broad field of child development, which stressed (in varying degrees) the importance of infancy and early childhood, the family context, and cultural factors (largely because of anthropologic investigations). One of the major aims of *Psychological Problems in Mental Deficiency* was to suggest that the gulf between the field of mental retardation and child development had to be bridged. The book was directed to the parochialism of both fields: What was then "mainstream child development" had little interest in mental retardation. If the situation is a little better in the 1980s, it is far from being a source of satisfaction. Few things have given me more satisfaction than the response I got from people who said that the cultural emphasis in that first book widened their horizons about the significances of mental retardation *in our culture*.

Although it has been a continuous source of despair to me, I have long recognized that there were very definite limits to my thinking and knowledge. From the first time I walked into a library I experienced two conflicting feelings: exhilaration at the endless delights that awaited me on those bookshelves and despair that I would never be able to read all of the books. I am a mixture of grandiosity and realistic modesty. Although I was satisfied with my first book as an initial step toward the recognition of the importance of the developmental approach and of cultural factors, I was quite aware that the boundaries of my knowledge did not allow me to do justice to the issues. So, when in the mid-fifties I was asked by Dr. Richard Masland (then Assistant Director of the National Institute of Neurological Diseases and Blindness) and the National Association of Retarded Children (later Citizens) to survey research in the psychologic and cultural aspects of mental retardation, I agreed provided that I could do it with anthropologist Tom Gladwin. Tom and I had become close friends; his understanding of culture and its transmission was far beyond mine, he had a special interest in developing problems, and he was an independent thinker. No anthropologist, good or bad, had ever seriously looked into the field of mental retardation. Anthropology, like the rest of the social sciences, had little or no interest in this field. If Tom could be enticed to collaborate with me, I knew that it would be very productive for the field of mental retardation. He had knowledge and skills that I wished I had but never would. I said yes, Tom said yes, and Dr. Masland was most helpful in making the collaboration possible. The result was the monograph *Psychological and Cultural Problems in Mental Subnormality: A Review of Research* (Sarason and Gladwin, 1958). Our emphasis and hopes can be seen in the following excerpt from the Introduction (pp. 145–77):

> The participation of an anthropologist in this undertaking reflects a conviction on the part of both authors that real understanding of the nature and implications of subnormality can only be approached by paying more than lip service to the fact that this is a social and cultural as well as a biological and psychological problem. In our society the problem looms large, statistically, financially, and emotionally; in most non-European societies it is inconsequential, confined to cases of severe pathological defect who are cared for, as long as they live, with a minimum of distress or dislocation. The difference lies in culturally determined attitudes, behaviors, and criteria of social acceptability, as we shall endeavor to make clear. Therefore, although we shall be concerned primarily with the sources of retardation rooted in the individual and his environment, we must pay equal attention to the way in which society defines, perceives, reacts to, and attempts to cope with mental subnormality regardless of its origin. Even a child with severe mental defect must be viewed as deficient *relative* to cultural standards of acceptability; the cause of his deficiency may be organic, but its magnitude is dependent upon social criteria.
>
> Viewed in a different light, the study of mental subnormality can make important theoretical and substantive contributions to our understanding of the nature and development of normal intellectual functioning, in much the same way that we have enriched our understanding of normal biological and psychological processes through the study of pathologies in those spheres of functioning. In this way, for example, we can relate deficits in childhood learning to failures and successes in later adjustment and thus obtain a clearer picture of those aspects of learning (the acquisition of culture) most essential for social living, and at the same time isolate

cognitive or intellectual components from the totality of demands a society makes on its members. One of our primary objectives in writing this report is to present the problem in terms which we hope will encourage social scientists, who have thus far been almost totally uninterested, to view mental subnormality as an important research area. We also hope to lure more psychologists, psychiatrists, and others whose disciplines are already somewhat represented in the field, to join our ranks, and perhaps provide them with a few fresh perspectives. There are undoubtedly many reasons for the lack of interest by competent researchers in subnormal mental ability, but we believe few if any of these reasons have a realistic basis. We are convinced that the result of this disinterest has been a serious loss in the development of the science of human behavior as well as a failure by our society to come to grips with a problem it has itself largely created.

Our primary concern is necessarily with etiology. The fact that subnormality can only be meaningful with reference to some external criterion of normality is important, but from a practical point of view it would be unrealistic to hope for a change in the cultural standards of mental normality sufficient to resolve the problems with which we are here concerned. We must therefore take as our point of departure the realization that only a minority of the population falls into that end of the distribution we label "subnormal." In seeking the causes of the misfortunes of this minority we immediately discover the multiplicity of factors operative within individuals and within groups which culminates in a diagnosis of subnormality, and we find that this diagnosis itself is highly variable and dependent upon shifting criteria. Under these conditions it is not surprising that the field at present has some of the attributes of chaos, particularly from the research point of view. No matter how determined our intentions we cannot hope to bring all the issues into orderly focus, and will be satisfied if we can clarify the range of questions which must be answered before such order can be achieved.

Section VII in that monograph illustrates well how fertile the cross-cultural-developmental thrust can be. Unfortunately, if Tom and I were writing the monograph today (30 years later), we would still have to express the hope that this interdisciplinary conceptual approach will be taken seriously. Over the years, scores of people have told me that they were very much influenced by this monograph. That may well be true but the fact remains that the conceptual thrust of that monograph was hardly reflected in the subsequent research literature on mental retardation. Why that is so I shall discuss later.

Intelligence and Culture [1]

Problem Solving Ability in Subcultural Groups

In the preceding chapter we have considered at some length the cultural implications of performance on intelligence tests for persons at both normal and subnormal levels of mental functioning. Intelligence tests, however, are but one of several criteria usually employed in assessing the capabilities and prospects of both normal and subnormal persons in our own Western society, and are of minimal or no consequence in this regard in many other cultures. So in this chapter we will look at intellectual processes in a broader cultural framework, seeking to determine what factors influence the development of various modes of attacking problems, and what kinds of levels of problem-solving ability are acceptable and approved in different sorts of cultures. For this purpose we have to pay attention not merely to the mechanics of the thinking process and how it is learned, but also motivations and attitudes toward intellectual achievement as these affect both children and adults. With respect to problem-solving, we will be concerned with the levels of ability (both high and low) the culture can accept, and in addition with the question of what kinds of problems are considered worth solving at all, and in what ways it is allowable to seek solutions. In other words, whereas in the preceding section our focus on tests forced us to remain largely within the limits accepted in our middle-class culture for definitions of intelligence, here we may take a broader view of what intelligence and normality mean to people living in other cultures and within subcultural groups in our own society. In attempting to apply the results of existing cross-cultural research—or of that which we might suggest should be done—to the problem of subnormality in our society, we must bear in mind that the solutions found in other cultures are not necessarily applicable to our own. The fact that in another society physical ability is more highly valued than mental, and that all but the most severely mentally deficient persons are therefore not particularly penalized or even noticeable, will not help us to find a place for similarly handicapped persons within the framework of rigid intellectual demands characteristic of our social environment. Nevertheless cross-cultural research can provide us with valuable insights and perspectives on our own problems, can illuminate the causes and perhaps some solutions for retardation within subcultural groups in our society, and can make an important contribution to our understanding of the etiology of identifiable pathological conditions the occurrence of which follows different patterns in other cultural settings.

Unfortunately there are practically no systematic studies of subnormal functioning in non-European cultures, so this chapter necessarily must offer more hunches and hypotheses than facts. This meager prospect is relieved by one outstanding exception, the study of the Hutterites by Eaton and Weil (1955). Because it is virtually unique in its field and because it will provide a setting against which a number of problems may be raised in the remainder of this chapter, a fairly extensive review of those aspects of Eaton and Weil's study which bear on mental subnormality will provide an appropriate starting point:

> Hutterites believe in the communal ownership and control of all property. Like the Catholic orders, they live under economic communism in the classical and nonpolitical sense. Christ and the Bible are their ideological guides. Hutterites expect the community to assume a great deal of responsibility for each member. It is the community which buys clothing, doles out pocket money to each person, and pays a traffic ticket. No wages are paid. Each person is expected to work to the best of his ability. He eats his meals in the community dining room; the meals prepared by different women in rotation. If he is sick, the colony pays for all necessary care. In case of male death, widows and dependents have no financial worries; the loss of a breadwinner never means the loss of bread. The Hutterite way of life provides social security from the womb to the tomb. The religious creed of the group gives the members a further guarantee of security beyond the tomb. It promises absolute salvation to all who follow its precepts.

> The average Hutterite baby is delivered at home with a midwife in attendance and by "natural childbirth." Ultimately he will have between ten and eleven siblings. Children are generally wanted. Birth control practices are considered sinful; violations of this taboo are extremely rare. There is much communal cooperation in the care and education of the children. Infants are looked after by the mother for the first two months after birth. Then the mother must work part of each day in the community kitchen or garden, and an older girl, not necessarily a relative, helps out. After the age of two-and-a-half, all healthy youngsters attend a communal kindergarten, where they stay most of the day. When they reach school age, they continue to spend many of their waking hours as a group, often under the supervision of a Hutterite religious teacher. He is responsible for much of the discipline outside of the hours when the children attend public school. Since both mother and father work for the colony at least part of the day, older siblings assume much of the care of their younger brothers and sisters.

> In general, young people do a great deal of their growing up within a stable and closely-knit group of peers. The process of socialization and development depends greatly on "horizontal" iden-

tification with their peer group. Imagination and expectations are influenced considerably by other children of similar physical and mental development. The Hutterite nuclear family performs fewer functions than is general in American society, but there is strong emphasis on kinship ties in all social relations. The cultural pattern of growing up to become a Hutterite adult varies little from colony to colony, but as in every human group, there are important variations in the emotional relationships between parents and children. Two mothers may be equally determined to teach an eight-year-old daughter to be an efficient caretaker of the baby and resist the temptation to run off in the yard to play with boys of her age (who have no such similar work expectations to live up to); but where one mother may teach and discipline with patience, humor, and love, another may be vindictive and infantile, almost forgetful of the fact that an eight-year-old girl is still a child.

Virtually all Hutterites leave school on their fifteenth birthday, the day which marks their assignment to an adult job. Full membership status is acquired after baptism, between the ages of 18 and 25. Very few people remain single. Several decades ago parents and community leaders exerted some influence on the choice of marriage partners; at present, however, this is rare. After marriage men tend to acquire more prestige and are given more responsible work assignments. They are put in charge of the carpentry, welding shop, horses, pigs, or some other department of the large-scale community farm enterprise. Women begin to raise a family. They also acquire more prestige in the informal discussions which precede all formal community decisions. Women can retire from regular community chores at the age of 45; retirement for men takes place later. No one is pushed to exert himself much beyond what he himself regards to be his capacity. "Do the best you can" rather than a competitive slogan, is characteristic of the entire life cycle.

All Hutterites live in small and nearly self-sufficient settlements in which social relationships are generally informal or primary. They have an average of 92 members, with 16 family units. There is virtually no movement from one to another, except for women at marriage when, with few exceptions, they move to the husband's community. Most members of the sect spend their entire life within the same group. When a community grows too large through natural increase, new land is purchased and another village is built. Half the membership, chosen by lot, "swarm" to form a new "hive," as Hutterites like to refer to this process of binary fission. In each of the 93 settlements there are individual differences in prestige, which are largely a function of age, sex, and work. However, this society comes as close to being classless as any we know. (pp. 27–30)

In the study the fields of sociology, anthropology, psychology, and psychiatry were represented. What is unusual in this study is that a serious attempt was made to screen the entire Hutterite population. "There was no sample; the entire population of 8,542 persons living in a large geographical area, including parts of South Dakota, North Dakota, Manitoba, Alberta, and Montana, was screened for cases of mental disorders. The staff visited 84 of the 93 colonies in existence at the time the field work was completed; the remaining nine colonies were screened through a variety of informants" (p. 230). Before presenting the findings of this study it should be pointed out that Hutterites are "quick to recognize severe or moderate forms of mental deficiency" (p. 149).

Of the 51 cases diagnosed as mental defective, 15 were severely defective, being unable to talk or walk normally and frequently unable to feed themselves. Four of these were mongoloid, two of basal ganglion disease, two of Little's disease, two of hydrocephalus, one of dwarfism, and four of epilepsy (cases of epilepsy not associated with mental deficiency were considered separately).[2]

Twenty of the 51 cases diagnosed as mentally defective were considered as moderately defective. "They could dress themselves . . . and could do simple work under supervision. . . . They could all qualify for admission to an institution for mental defectives" (p. 151). The remaining 16 patients were diagnosed as mildly defective. "They generally had some schooling and knew of rudiments of reading and writing. They participated in the work of their colony and as adults had a regular work assignment which required little initiative or skill" (p. 151).

Although Eaton and Weil felt they had located virtually all the moderate and severe cases, they recognized that they had probably failed to enumerate many cases which should have been diagnosed as mildly defective. There were several lines of evidence pointing in this direction. In the first place, in those settlements personally visited by the staff in which all members were examined the rates were 10 percent higher than in the population as a whole. Secondly, on a rating sheet filled out by the Hutterite religious teachers and also by the non-Hutterite public school teachers, the public school teachers rated more children as "dull" than did the Hutterite teachers—a finding which did not become known until the field work was over so that these children could not be diagnosed by the research staff. Finally, 70 percent of all cases diagnosed were of severe and moderate degree—i.e., presumably reflecting pathology rather than learning deficits—whereas other populations studied have shown a much higher proportion of mild degree. We may therefore conclude that if intelligence tests or other diagnostic criteria utilized within our culture were applied to the Hutterite population more cases of mild deficit would probably be found, although we cannot predict with confidence what the prevalence rates would be. The explanation for this discrepancy is almost certain to be found in the observation by Eaton and

Weil discussed below that the Hutterites show a high level of social acceptance of mentally deficient persons, and thus might be able to absorb into the normal population without special attention persons who could not meet the sharply drawn levels of tolerance characteristic of our culture. This point deserves some emphasis, not because we wish to raise doubts as to the prevalence rates cited by the authors of this study, although these have been criticized, but because it makes clear the hazards involved in attempting to determine epidemiological statistics in other cultures with regard to mental subnormality. A diagnosis of mental deficiency or retardation is compounded in our culture of medical, psychological, social, and cultural considerations (implicit or explicit), and a setting in which the relevance of any one of these is different will produce a different distribution of individuals identified as subnormal by the members of the society under study.

There is an unusual amount of in-group marrying among the Hutterites, a fact which led Eaton and Weil to ask: "Is there evidence to support the widely held assumption that inbreeding in a population necessarily leads to deterioration in the germ plasm of a population, which shows up in a high frequency of mental deficiency?" (p. 152). The apparently moderate rate of mental deficiency among the Hutterites is sufficient basis for answering this question in the negative. However, Eaton and Weil did not report geneologies for the diagnosed cases of mental deficiency. In addition, we do not have clinical descriptions which would allow for a possible etiological classification. Consequently, we cannot evaluate the specific role of genetic factors in those cases which are reported. Neither can we ascertain whether certain types of mental deficiency (e.g., phenylketonuria) occur at all among the Hutterites. At one point Eaton and Weil (p. 152) state: "None of the defective adult women could find a husband, but four men married and had families. They had a total of 22 children in 1951, two of whom were moderately defective." Since we do not know the clinical picture either of the fathers or the two offspring, we cannot evaluate whether two defective offspring (which could only be from one or two of the four fathers) is an inordinately low or an expected number. In a community that can be as comprehensively studied as the Hutterites much valuable data on genetic factors in mental deficiency could be obtained—perhaps obtained more quickly than through similar studies in our own culture.

An important finding of the study is that none of the defectives has ever been institutionalized, although the Hutterites are not opposed to commitment. Even in the case of the psychoses institutionalization among the Hutterites is rare.

There is considerable social acceptance of mentally defective persons among the Hutterites. Once a child's retardation is recognized, he is usually taken to a doctor to determine if there is any medical remedy for the condition. If there is none, the child and his limitations are accepted fatalistically. The community provides the family with additional help, if needed, to give optimum physical care to the youngster. In some families the mother will turn the child over to a sister or her mother, who may have more time and patience. Feelings of rejection by the parents exist, but they are usually well repressed. Other children are punished if they ridicule or take advantage of the afflicted child. Defectives who reach adult life are encouraged to work.

Defectives are not thought to be morally responsible for what they do. Those who engage in antisocial activities are punished only if they show sufficient insight to be affected by punishment. The community keeps them in line by watching them carefully. In two cases where mildly defective individuals violated a number of religious rules, the community "cancelled their baptism" rather than excommunicate them. By cancellation of their baptism they were reduced to the status of children, who are thought to be incapable of sinning and therefore can attain salvation automatically. (p. 157)

One cannot find a greater contrast between Hutterite and American culture than in regard to institutionalization: in our own culture available institutional facilities are overtaxed, more facilities are in the planning stage, and the end is not in sight. More important than the staggering financial burden of the situation is the unhappy fact that institutionalization frequently raises as many psychological problems as it resolves (p. 225). These are problems which the Hutterites, as well as people of many other cultures, do not have to resolve.

Granting that Eaton and Weil, focusing primarily on the neuroses and psychoses rather than on mental deficiency, did not provide us with clinical descriptions, genealogical charts, or other appurtenances of an ideal study of subnormality, yet they have documented some of the most important of the cultural implications of mental retardation. Particularly, it is clear that among the Hutterites—however they may appear to outsiders—the intellectual preparation provided within the culture is adequate to meet the needs of adult life within that setting. Furthermore, the standards of adequacy set by the culture appear to be wide enough to embrace most people who function at anything but a pathologically deficient level, a fact strikingly reflected in the very small proportion (compared to our culture) of the population identified as subnormal which falls in the "slight deficiency" category. Finally, the Hutterite society is so organized that it can take care of *all* persons, whatever their level of functioning, within itself without resort to special institutional or other devices. In all these respects the Hutterites conform much more closely to the patterns characteristic of the non-European cultures of the world than they do to the standards of our own society which surrounds them.

A more concrete comparison is perhaps in order. On the one hand we may cite the Trukese, studied by the present authors (Gladwin and Sarason, 1953). In this island society in the Pacific inadequacy in intellectual functioning is simply not viewed as a problem except for a scattering of obvious pathological cases; people of both sexes appear to fall readily into productive activities they are fully competent to perform. Younger men, however, often seek employment at the American administrative center, sometimes at the garage where trucks and other vehicles are maintained under the supervision of Americans.

> These jobs were eagerly sought after, under the impression that one could thus quickly learn the facility in working with machinery which the Trukese greatly admire in Americans. These youths were anxious to learn and within the limits of their understanding of English followed carefully the instructions they were given. But if what they had been taught did not work they were helpless. An American boy interested in mechanics is soon inculcated with the idea that every new piece of equipment is a challenge; if he does not know how it works, much less what may be wrong with it, he should take it apart, find out how it works, and then fix it. This approach was incomprehensible to the Trukese; even when given an old engine to practice on, their only solution to a problem was to ask someone who knew. (p. 142)

Compare this with the following description:

> She is cheerful, inclined to be quarrelsome, very active and restless, very affectionate, willing, and tries; is quick and excitable, fairly good-tempered. Learns a new occupation quickly, but requires a half-hour or twenty-four repetitions to learn four lines. Retains well what she has once learned. Needs close supervision. Is bold towards strangers, kind towards animals. Can run an electric sewing machine, cook, and do practically everything about the house. Has no noticeable defect. She is quick and observing, has a good memory, writes fairly well, does excellent work in wood-carving and kindergarten, is excellent in imitation. Is a poor reader and poor at numbers. Does fine basketry and gardening. Spelling is poor; music is excellent; sewing excellent; excellent in entertainment work. Very fond of children and good in helping care for them. Has a good sense of order and cleanliness. Is sometimes very stubborn and obstinate. Is not always truthful and has been known to steal, although does not have a reputation for this. Is proud of her clothes. Likes pretty dresses and likes to help in other cottages, even to temporarily taking charge of a group. (pp. 7–8)

This is Goddard's (1912) description of Deborah Kallikak, a girl of 22 who had spent the last 14 years of her life in an institution, presented by him as a classical example of mental deficiency. It is clear that the Trukese, completely adequate intellectually when operating within their own culture, perform no better than Deborah when faced with a problem from our culture which calls for rational thinking and logical induction. It should also be borne in mind that a garage mechanic in our society is viewed as a laborer—albeit skilled—and not an intellectual or professional.

Why do the Trukese develop such a concrete and limited approach to problem-solving? The answer must, as in our own society, be sought in childhood, the period when a person learns from the preceding generation the multiple facets of the cultural heritage to which he is born. Childhood for a Trukese is a period of freedom with almost complete lack of supervision by adults except for occasional, and inconsistent, reprimands and punishments. Children play in groups together and are given practically no systematic positive instruction. "They are viewed by adults as irresponsible and, not being able to do responsible and useful work, not worth instructing. The word for "child" in the Trukese language in fact means "does not comprehend."

This freedom and lack of supervision or direction, although it might be looked upon as utopian by a middle-class American child, provides a very poor climate in which to learn effectively and efficiently to cope with problems or to profit from the wisdom of past experience contained in the culturally defined solutions to such problems. In this connection we can recall the differences in the amount of freedom noted by Davis and Havighurst (1946) between lower- and middle-class children, with associated differences in intelligence test scores. This freedom can also leave an individual drifting, uncertain, and without emotional support, a thesis developed at length for our own European society by Erich Fromm (1941). The Trukese child suffers under these handicaps until he is close to adolescence, when he begins to be perceived as having a potential for usefulness and receives practically his first positive and systematic instruction of any kind.

> Having at first been told practically nothing, and later what not do to, now, finally, he is told what he should do. At long last he is given a guide by his parents for behavior, at least of certain kinds, and a more positive status in the household. He begins to learn that there are "right" ways as well as wrong ways of doing things for his parents. Set against the background of ambiguity which has surrounded his attempts to determine what his parents expected of him thus far in his life, these rather specific instructions take on more importance than one would otherwise anticipate. They are, in effect, likely to be overevaluated, not in the sense that the child would throw himself with overenthusiasm into his work, but rather that he would tend to take very literally and concretely his instructions, attempting to perform his tasks exactly as he had been told. Concreteness in following directions and a tendency to accept situ-

ations in their most literal sense is a characteristic of children even in our own society, and appears to be a means of responding to new situations for which past experience and immediate guidance is barely adequate. It is the "safest" way to react when one is unsure of the full significance of the total situation. If children in our society who are given consistent positive as well as negative guidance and instruction practically from the time they say their first words tend to respond concretely, it is small wonder that the Trukese child takes literally these directions which he finally receives for the first time in the latter part of his childhood. He has been left largely incapable of dealing with new situations both by the generalized anxiety he has learned to feel toward any interpersonal situation as a result of his unpredictable childhood relationships and by his failure to distill out of his inadequate attempts to identify with his parents any overall guide for behavior which would permit him to respond to his problems in any more generalized sort of way. Just as his relations with people are inherently superficial, so he looks in a new situation for the most superficial and obvious aspect which bears any resemblance to what he has encountered in his past experience, and interprets the situation in these terms.

Unlike Americans, however, the Trukese in general never lose this concreteness of response. It is a by-word among Americans that the spirit of the law is more important than the letter, and the ability to recognize this distinction in dealing with his problems is a measure of an American child's growing maturity. The Trukese, on the other hand, tend always to see the letter of the law and even as adults are seldom able to approach a situation with the more abstract view implied in seeing the spirit of it. Thinking in abstract terms involves a measure of ambiguity, a weighing of alternatives in terms of personal value judgments, which is an inherently more hazardous approach than simply to be literal and concrete, taking the situation at its face value and using its most obvious external signs as cues for behavior and response. By hazardous we mean that there is implicit in the abstract approach the possibility that one's opinions and reactions will not coincide with the interpretation of the situation made by one's fellows. If all situations are interpreted in the simplest and most literal terms the possibility of disagreement is reduced to a minimum, although the flexibility and creativity of the individual who habitually responds in this fashion is of course reduced. We see, then, why any child will tend to approach his problems literally and concretely: Being faced by a constant succession of new problems with which he is more or less inadequately prepared to deal, he plays it safe and responds in a minimum fashion to all of them. The Trukese, however, lives out many of his formative years without really beginning to acquire the knowledge or experience which will equip him to approach his life situations in a well-rounded sort of way. When he finally does begin to learn, he responds in a fashion which American children at a corresponding age are beginning to grow out of, and for the rest of his life is seldom able to improve upon this type of performance.

This does not mean that because after all these years the Trukese finally receives in late childhood some actual positive instructions, he takes them literally and adopts this approach to problems for the rest of his life out of sheer relief. Undoubtedly there is a measure of truth in this statement, for the security he feels in finding a mode of behavior which is indubitably "right" after a childhood spent in doubt and confusion is not likely soon to be forgotten. More important than the relief he now feels, however, are the years which have gone by, years during which he might have been learning how to deal with his parents and other people in a confident and effective manner, and how to express his opinions freely without fear of making some small misstatement and with it bringing down about him what little security he has been able to find in a generally hostile and unpredictable social environment. By the time the Trukese child has, at an age of perhaps nine or ten, begun to learn how he really should behave he has acquired a fundamental mistrust of his fellows and a lack of confidence in the adequacy of his own resources as a means of coping with his social problems; as we have discussed in some detail in the preceding pages, his response to this sense of social inadequacy is to attempt not to offend anyone, particularly his relatives. It is for this reason that he seeks the "safest," the least provocative, and therefore the most conventional and literal response he can find to every problem he faces. This conservatism and concreteness, rooted in the uncertainty and inconsistency of his childhood, he carries with him throughout his life. As long as he can structure a situation so there is but one correct solution he feels secure; but if the situation demands of him initiative, responsibility, or assuming a position of eminence and authority, he feels anxious and withdraws. (pp. 269–271)

Hogbin (1946), in one of the very few available descriptions of children's learning experiences in non-European cultures, describes a similar outcome of intellectual concreteness and rigidity resulting from a very different kind of learning process among the Wogeo of New Guinea. They are a people geographically in the same corner of the world as Truk, but culturally quite different. The Wogeo believe that everything valuable in their culture was handed down from mythical hero-ancestors and, being a traditionally oriented people, they are conservative and opposed to latter-day innovation and initiative. In keeping with this they provide children, much earlier in their lives than do the Trukese, with instructions and explanations "so detailed that the need for seeking additional information seldom arises, and 'why' questions, the everlasting bane of parents in our community, are rarely heard" (p. 285). The implications of these two very different sorts of learning process for the development of adult personality and for individual and cultural adjustment in the face of changing conditions are of major consequence, but the important aspect of both for our present discussion is that they each produce by different means an intellectual set toward the solution of problems characterized by concreteness and a severe limitation in the ability to contemplate an array of alternatives before reaching a solution. It would be safe to predict that a normal and adequate native of Truk or Wogeo, even though equipped with the necessary knowledge of language and formal cultural content, would do very badly indeed on the Stanford-Binet or in the fourth grade of school.

Cultural Learning and Intellect

The fact that so similar and—by our standards—meager intellectual development can be produced in such divergent ways in two cultures immediately raises the question whether the consistent intellectual inadequacies found in children of our lower-class groups, ethnic minorities, etc., may not actually have very different origins in one group as against another. This is a question for which we do not have an answer, and even a guess would probably not be justified. We have been aware of subcultural mental retardation ever since regional differences in intelligence test scores were established on the basis of World War I data; yet the 30-odd years which have intervened have been devoted almost entirely to determining the nature and extent of subcultural differences, not to seeking their causes, outside perhaps of identifying broad differences in the quality of school systems. We know, especially through the work of the Chicago group discussed in Section VI, some of the ways in which lower-class children, for example, fare in school and the handicaps under which they suffer, but we do not know what it is in their preschool and extracurricular experience which has equipped them so poorly for this task. This is a—perhaps *the*—most crucial question to answer with respect to retarded children of all sorts who do not show pathologies, but we have scarcely scratched the surface of exploring the group characteristics which must provide the background and basis for comparison in individual cases.

Cross-cultural studies can be helpful in suggesting the range of variables which should be examined, but much needs to be done within our own society right now. Studies of non-European societies have the disadvantage that often their members perceive no need for superior intellectual skills and can therefore afford to inhibit, as the Trukese and Wogeo do, the development of mental ability even in those individuals who for some reason tend in this direction. In our society, however, the rewards for intelligence combine with opportunities for mobility to assure that most persons can capitalize at least in some degree upon those intellectual tendencies which their inherent nature and their experience bring forth. Furthermore, few people in our society will deny the advantages of being intelligent and resourceful, even though they may vary widely in the amount of effort they are willing to devote to developing these qualities in themselves or in their children. In other words, the kinds of intellectual development valued in our society as a whole (the lack of which comprises mental retardation) can be assumed to be viewed as at least somewhat worthwhile by members of any subcultural group within it, something we cannot assume for many non-European peoples, and the values of his own subculture will not be likely severely to penalize an individual whose development is above average, thus assuring a full range of mental ability within the limits set by the opportunities offered within the given group. There will be exceptions, of course, such as adolescents who consider any boy who does well in school to be a teacher's pet (Margolin, Roman, and Harari, 1955), but limitations are far less likely to stifle possibly superior children when they know or believe that society at large will offer rewards for their efforts. There is a truly urgent need for this kind of research. We have a surfeit of testing and the derivation of ethnic and social class IQ's. What is needed now is a more exploratory anthropological type of approach to the values and processes governing the learning situation for children.

In view of the long-standing concern of anthropologists with culture and cultural transmission, it is difficult to explain the small amount of attention they have paid to the mechanics of this transmission. How early, and particularly how consistent, is instruction? Who assumes responsibility for instruction, not merely of formal skills, but also in the subtler aspects of values and social relationships? Who is available and recommended for emulation? Of great importance, what happens when a child asks, "Why?"—is he rewarded or punished, answered or not, answered in terms of logic or of tradition or is he told he is too young, is he encouraged or discouraged to think about himself, etc.? What kinds of skills are presented as valuable? If these include mental skills, are they rational, memory, or what? What means are used to foster their acquisition? These, and a host of others, are the questions which must be answered if we are to understand how learning takes place, and how the intellectual tools for further learning are acquired. Persons studying non-European peoples should seek answers to them, and they are equally at the core of the problem of mental retardation in our own society.

In the absence of any detectable pathology there is at present available no valid explanation of a child's retardation except a deficit in learning. Furthermore, since all or most children in a given group are exposed at least formally to the same classroom environment, yet some do well and some do not, we must assume that the deficit results from the foundation of skills, attitudes, emotional sets, and social and intellectual habits the child brings to that environment. This foundation is built in the cultural and individual milieu of his home and peer group. Until we can identify those factors which are relevant to the building of a foundation for learning, and establish some norms with respect to these, we have nothing against which to evaluate individual experience and opportunity. For this purpose we have available in our society not only the "average" middle-class children of old American ancestry, but a variety of subcultural groups in which we know the children are less well-prepared to learn the intellectual skills demanded by the larger culture and within which research should be able to isolate significant and important differences in the process of learning and preparation for further learning. Once some of these are identified and assessed more systematic means of observing and perhaps measuring them can be devised, and individual studies as well as surveys can have more meaning. We know that neither present intelligence scales nor any other single instrument can be expected reliably to predict subsequent failures when administered to preschool children, and therefore certainly cannot be used to identify those aspects of a child's experience which are helping or hindering his learning at the time. The study of learning in children from subcultural groups, whose later performance our present knowledge permits us to predict will in many cases be below average, can reveal at least some of the factors necessary to fill this large gap in our knowledge of mental retardation.

As we suggested in the preceding section, we may find that lower class Italian children—who consistently average low in IQ and often do poorly in school—are expected to do many tasks around the home strictly in the manner they are told, without inquiring as to the reason for doing these tasks in a certain way or as to why the tasks need be done at all. This might be expected to produce some rigidity in their approach to problem-solving, and hence a low intelligence test score. If this is so, are German children—who usually score higher and do better in school—assigned their tasks differently, and if so, in what way is the process different? Or if not, both being treated inflexibly in this regard, what makes the later difference? We may then find that the Italians tend more toward the common non-European thesis that manual skills are more important than mental, thus lowering the motivation of children toward school. Or perhaps Italian children during school years are expected to do some of their household jobs in the morning, and thus arrive at school (where most testing is also done) tired whereas German children do not—not a profound difference, but if it exists, important to know. These examples are speculative, but suggest the kinds of avenues which need exploring. They also reflect variations which can be expected to appear on an individual basis in middle-class families; the findings of such research would by no means be applicable only to the particular groups studied.

Some beginnings have been made in exploring the subcultural differences in learning experience of the sort discussed here. The work of

Davis and Havighurst (1946) and of Sears, Maccoby, and Levin (1957) on social class differences in child rearing discussed in Section VI is of course highly relevant, although the primary focus of both studies is on emotional development and any conclusions we may reach about the effect of the differences found on intellectual development are largely inferential. The exploratory nature of their approach, guided by theory in the kinds of questions asked but otherwise taking little for granted, is however precisely what is needed at this stage in the study of learning processes.

McClelland and his associates have done considerable work in the study of motivation, using as a starting point an achievement score derived from stories told by the people tested (McClelland, Atkinson, Clark, and Lowell, 1953); the procedure is similar to that used in the Thematic Apperception Test except that the stimulus material is verbal rather than pictorial and the test situation is structured to be variously relaxed, neutral, and achievement-oriented. The stories are then scored for achievement motivation in accordance with a special set of criteria. Winterbottom, in connection with this study, established a series of 13 aspects of independence training of children, determining that those mothers who sought to have their children reach these goals of independence at an early age were those who also had high achievement scores. In other words, the mothers appeared to project their own achievement motivation, be it high or low, upon their children in terms of seeking early or later independence training. McClelland, Rindlisbacher, and deCharms (1955) administered questionnaires regarding the desired age of independence training to a series of parents aged 30 to 50 who had at least one child, utilizing those items found by Winterbottom to correlate highly with achievement score in mothers only. Dividing the parents on a religious basis, the means for all items and both parents were as follows, each figure representing the age at which they hoped their children would become independent in the 13 types of activity: Protestant, 6.64; Jewish, 6.59; Irish Catholic, 8.42. On the basis of these findings the Catholics could be expected to push their children's development less hard than the others; at the same time the difference between Italian and Irish Catholics makes it clear that religious affiliation is but one aspect of broader subcultural differences which are at work. With respect to education of the parents, parents who did not graduate from high school hoped for an average independence age of 7.81, those graduated from high school but not college, 7.43, and college graduates 6.75. We cannot of course tell here whether educational level itself creates a desire to push the children along, or whether both reflect social class or perhaps ethnic differences. Finally, they found that mothers were more eager than fathers, the means being 6.88 and 7.77 respectively. We do not know what this means, but the plausible explanation comes to mind that independent children give more independence to their mothers than to their

fathers. This ingeniously contrived series of studies can provide, in themselves and in the further exploration of this method, many fruitful hypotheses. Unfortunately, for our purposes, however, they fail to examine
the crucial variable: the intellectual and motivational development of the
young children of these parents, and how it is affected by the aspirations
of their parents for them.

Other studies in intellectual motivation, although dealing with the
children themselves, do not focus on the preschool years. However, insofar as motivation during school is subculturally determined it is affecting
the performance of children in these groups at the time when differences
between subcultural groups become more apparent. A number of studies
have demonstrated that motivation for academic achievement is less in
lower social classes (Hollingshead, 1949; Girard, 1953). Rosen (1957) found
this reflected in the projective achievement score described in the preceding paragraph. He established scores for 427 boys, aged 8–14, in New
England, identified by ethnicity, religion, and social class. Although the
ranking of motivation (from high to low) in the total sample followed
the expected order—Greek Orthodox, Jews, white Protestants, Catholics
(French-Canadian and Italian), and Negroes—when middle-class groups
only were compared the white Protestants were highest and the Negroes
not significantly different from them, higher than any other group. An
analysis of variance indicated that social class was a stronger overall determinant of motivation than ethnicity. A questionnaire survey of the
mothers of these boys ranked them on their vocational and educational
aspirations for their sons in slightly different order, the Jews being highest, closely followed by the Greeks, and the French-Canadians lowest.

There is some agreement that the social class impact on intellectual
motivation results at least in part from the lesser rewards, tangible and
intangible, received by lower-class boys from middle-class teachers who
find children of their own class more acceptable (Davis, 1941; Abrahamson, 1952). This probably provides some realistic basis for the already
noted opinion of some lower-class boys, particularly with behavior problems, who attribute school success of their companions to currying favor
with the teacher (Margolin, Roman, and Harari, 1955; Glueck and Glueck,
1950). We do not know to what degree these attitudes are derived from
parents, and how much they are based on the perceptions and resent-
ments generated within the peer group of children themselves. Some indication of this is, however, found in a study by Stendler (1951) in which
she interviewed 250 mothers of first-graders. She found that whereas the
mothers' aspirations for (and preparation of) their children increased
with higher social class, criticism of the school's handling of their children showed no relationship to class position. If these findings were
found to be generally true they would suggest that the level of aspiration
is determined at least partially by parental attitude, but that the resent-
ments or satisfactions are derived from the children's own experience.

Another aspect of motivation emerges from studies of the disparity between level of aspiration and level of performance. A greater disparity between aspiration for occupational and social achievement on the one hand and test or academic performance on the other seems to be characteristic of minority groups. Beckham (1944) and Boyd (1952) found this to be true in testing Negroes as compared to whites. We do not know to what degree these findings are affected by the social class differences in Negro motivation noted by Rosen. Gould (1941) concluded from a study of Columbia College students that those in which the discrepancy between present and expected future achievement was greatest belonged in more cases to minority groups: lower class, foreign parentage, and/or minority religions. All three of these studies, however, applied to urban populations who were presumably maximally exposed to the philosophy of personal success which permeates our culture. In contrast to this Lewis (1946) found white children in the Cumberland Mountains of Tennessee attending poor schools with no encouragement from their parents and with no personal aspirations, in most cases, other than to remain as they were and where they were.

It is clear from this brief review of the motivational aspects of learning that important differences in both parents and children exist within the subcultural groups of our society, and that the origins of these differences are complex and probably often multiple. The examples of Truk and Wogeo, as well as other cultures for which intellectual motivation is more sketchily described, suggest that the differences are even greater when we look at non-European peoples. Undoubtedly motivational factors, subcultural and individual, play a major role in precipitating mental retardation and deserve careful attention in assessing individual cases. Outside of fairly crude value judgments, however, we do not have any basis for determining how much and what kinds of motivation are really beneficial for learning. Low motivation will undoubtedly in most cases lower achievement, but it may also lower frustration if a discrepancy between aspiration and attainment might otherwise exist, and through better emotional balance lead ultimately to more effective social and even occupational performance. Too much pressure from parents may lead to withdrawal, and, as Kanner (1949) suggests, even to autism. At present we really know very little of the manner in which motivation is dynamically related to learning, or which aspects of motivation deserve most attention. Yet motivation is the one factor in the learning process on which we have any information which is at all adequate regarding subcultural or cultural differences.

If we turn from research in the motivation for learning to seek subcultural differences in the intellectual processes of learning—ways of thinking and attacking problems—we find virtually no studies available. We do know from the many studies referred to in the preceding section and in Section II that highly significant and consistent differences do exist between the school and test performance of children in various sub-cultural groups. But we cannot tell where the determinants of these differences lie. The effects of social class, ethnic subcultures, language, etc., are confounded together. We do not even know as a starting point how much should be attributed to different ways of thinking as against different motivations for thinking. The data cited from non-European cultures suggest that we should look for differences between groups in our own society in the mode of attacking problems, a conclusion supported by the very few studies of American children in which subcultural differences in subtest profiles have been analyzed. Haggard's (1954) analysis of test results of high and low social status Midwestern schoolchildren pointed in this direction. Brown (1944) reported a study of second generation Jewish and Scandinavian kindergarten children in Minneapolis which suggests that even identical overall IQ averages may mask differences in problem-solving approach; this study is of particular interest due to the young, essentially preschool, age of the subjects. There were 324 Jewish children and 323 of Scandinavian extraction. Although the IQ varied in both groups with social class, ethnicity alone created no significant difference in average total scores. However, when performance on subtests (of the Stanford-Binet) was compared for both sexes the Scandinavian children excelled on tests involving motor coordination (draw a square, copying diamond, and ball-and-field) and patience, whereas the Jewish children excelled in counting pennies, distinguishing right from left, comprehension, naming coins, giving the date, and repeating four digits backwards. These findings are reminiscent of the rural-urban differences discussed in the last chapter, in which rural boys somewhat older than Brown's subjects do better on mechanical assembly tests and urban boys better on intelligence tests.

Paradoxically, although we have been pressing our contention that research should be devoted to cultural and subcultural differences in intellectual development in order to shed light on the causes of mental retardation, studies of the intellectual environment of severely retarded children, regardless of cultural affiliation, provide our most graphic picture of the importance of differences in the context of and stimulus for learning—in these cases characterized by extreme impoverishment. One of the present writers has already reviewed this subject (Sarason, 1953, Chapter 6) so it will be necessary here only to cite material illustrative of the kinds of factors involved. Skeels, Updegraff, Wellman, and Williams (1938) have provided us with a striking description of the effects of an orphanage environment (coupled with generally bleak earlier experiences) on the intellectual functioning of a group of 21 children, aged 18 months to five-and-a-half years, who were enrolled in a special preschool training project in an otherwise typically understaffed and poorly equipped orphanage in Iowa:

Language and speech were greatly retarded. Not only was the vocabulary meager and based upon very limited experience but the sentence structure was far below that ordinarily expected. Coupled to these two serious handicaps were such faulty enunciation and poor speech habits that the language of the children was in the great majority of cases either entirely or practically unintelligible. Although children who were already acquainted were able to make each other understand some few simple interchanges, any constructive conversation seemed out of the question. Voices were unpleasantly monotonous, mumbling was common. With little provocation, talking voices would become loudly demanding. Finally, and of great significance in the teaching situation, was the fact that these children were not accustomed to listening to the words of adults or of other children in order to acquire ideas. Words as a medium of communication were poor commodities in this environment. In fact, the urgency for communication seemed to confine itself to situations of extreme discomfort (anything looked upon as discomfort by the child seemed to him extreme) and in such situations a loud crying was the favorite resort. On the other hand, there was a considerable amount of what might be called "verbalization," which consisted of imitation of the sounds of words of others, more with the idea of filling space than with definite communicative purpose. A phrase or word said by one child would be repeated by several not as a game, not in hilarity, but more as an activity arising from nothing and resulting in nothing.

The attitude toward adults was a strange mixture of defiance, wish for affection, and desire for attention. It was rather startling to find that there was little desire for the teachers' approval; the children seemed to crave attention but whether that attention was due to disapproval or approval mattered little. There seemed to exist what might be termed a feeling of the individual against the world, expecting no quarter and giving none. That a promise or consequence would follow simply because its prospect was stated seemed not so much to be disbelieved as to be ignored. There were few reactions which indicated a recognition of individual differences in adults. Strangers and visitors were objects of curiosity and overwhelming attention but the children's reaction would probably have been the same to wax figures. In other words, interest in clothing and appearances were uppermost and conversations were limited to a few stereotyped questions such as "What's that?" and "Who are you?" with little attention to or understanding of replies. (pp. 23–24)

It might be added that the efforts of the staff to communicate with and help these children were heroic, and in many cases notably successful, as was a different experiment reported by Skeels and Dye (1939) in which one- and two-year-olds from the same orphanage were placed under the supervised care of adolescent retarded girls in a training school. In both cases, of course, the children were suffering from severe emotional deprivation as well as from a lack of educational opportunity, but they provide us with some understanding of the nature of at least one kind of intellectual deficit as such, and the means whereby it can be remedied once a child has become emotionally accessible.

The unsatisfactory characteristics of the institutional environment will not necessarily be improved upon if a child is left at home with a mother who is herself retarded. Town (1939) has forcefully described the environmental factors which can readily produce generations of Kallikaks.

> Without any assumption concerning why certain families are apparently foci for feeblemindedness, the simple, unelaborated fact that they are has far-reaching social implications. It means that in these families there are "blind leaders of the blind"; it means that feeble-minded mothers, mere children in common sense, are rearing and caring for children, many of whom present problems that might well daunt the wisest of mothers; it means that children sicken and starve because their mothers are incapable of preparing their food and serving it at regular intervals; it means that babies die because their feebleminded mothers see not that they are ill; it means suffering, squalor and starvation of body and spirit. (p. 1)

There can be little question as to the validity of this characterization; it would be seconded by any caseworker who has visited severely retarded mothers with children in their homes. It is even confirmed in a series of descriptions by Goddard (1912, pp. 70–100) of visits to the homes of Kallikaks although he failed to perceive that he was thereby describing an environment in itself sufficient to explain the deficiencies of the Kallikaks without recourse to the hereditary deficit whose existence he believed he was documenting.

But if the effects of being reared by a retarded mother are so devastating, how can we account for the outcome of the Skeels and Dye experiment mentioned above? Here we have the example of 13 retarded orphanage children who were placed on the wards of a home for feebleminded girls, usually one to a ward, where their IQ's increased an average of 27.5 points over a two-year period while their companions left in the orphanage were dropping an average of 26.2 points. Granted that the physical needs of the experimental children were better met than in the homes Town describes (although this was also true of the orphanage control group) and that the institutional girls were perhaps not quite as severely handicapped as Town's (or Goddard's) mothers, but these factors alone would not account adequately for the completely opposite outcomes. Skeels and Dye concluded that their substitute parents, although performing well below the norms for their ages, were nevertheless sufficiently ahead of their young charges to be able to provide them with an apparently rich (for babies) dose of intellectual stimulation. It is only reasonable to assume a similar capability is also present in the mother who keeps her child at home. Aside from matters of physical care, the important difference appears to lie in the fact that the institutional girls were living a life devoid of excitement or any particular focus of emotional interest; they were able and delighted to shower upon the babies in their care endless affection and attention along with the minimal but adequate intellectual stimulation which created the increase in IQ. At home on her own, however, the feebleminded mother is already overwhelmed by problems and activities with which she cannot cope and has nothing left over to give her child. What we are saying in effect is that whereas subcultural differences which result in higher rates of slight retardation are compounded of motivation and of patterned differences in approaches to problem-solving, in severely retarded families motivational deficits appear to be primary and result in reduced *amounts* of problem-solving activity rather than necessarily in different *ways* of solving problems.

Nevertheless if we take as our objective the determination of the full range of relationships between kinds of learning situation and kinds of thinking and problem-solving which result from this learning, the plight of the child of severely retarded parents or in an institution can be illuminating and is worthy of more research. At present this is the only group, distinctively different in intellectual development from the "typical" middle-class child, on which we have any real information with regard to thinking processes as distinct from motivation for thinking. Furthermore, in the severely retarded group we know about both intellect and motivation and can see the relationship between them. The only systematic studies of subcultural differences in intellectual motivation—those discussed above based on McClelland's work—do not have corresponding data from their subjects on intellectual achievement, so that we cannot asses the effects of one on the other. This seriously limits the applicability of this body of research to the problems with which we are here concerned.

We do of course know a good deal about the adverse effects of some sorts of emotional maladjustment which block intellectual development. This, however, is a different problem from that of motivation for learning; its resolution is to be sought in personality theory and in psychotherapy and counseling. We recognize that it may often be difficult in the individual case to determine immediately whether we are dealing with a child who has never developed any real motivation to learn or whether his motivation has been blocked by other factors. This difficulty probably has played a large part in the failure of all the behavior sciences to give adequate attention to the positive aspects of intellectual motivation and their effect on cultural learning. If, however, we are concerned as we are here in determining the bases for research in the etiology of mental retardation we must make such a distinction very clearly in our research thinking. Differences in intellectual motivation and in intellectual process appear to affect large groups of people fairly uniformly, although they are at present little understood; emotional blocks, on the other hand, are more idiosyncratic in origin and have been and are being fairly extensively studied. Both contribute heavily to our population of retarded children and both equally deserve extended study. Intelligence is an integral aspect of personality, and there is no reason why, for example, anthropologists studying the relationship between personality and culture should not devote as much attention to the learning process as they do to weaning. In fact, since as we have already pointed out learning is the mechanism of cultural transmission, perhaps they should place learning near the head of their list of research priorities.

Before leaving the problem of learning to turn to the life situations for which this learning is the preparation it may be well to summarize what little we do know about subcultural aspects of the learning process. Because our data are thus far very fragmentary, we can express only impressions rather than conclusions. We can at least be fairly sure that the learning process, both in mechanics and in motivation, differs between subcultural groups whether these are defined on the basis of a social class, ethnic origin, rural urban, or other criteria. Of these various groupings we will hazard the opinion that, taking Western Europe and North America as a whole, social class probably exerts the most decisive effect— in other words that a lower-class Frenchman is more like a lower-class American along the dimensions with which we have been concerned than he is like a middle-class Frenchman. There are of course differences, even if of a lesser order, between the two lower-class groups also, with the result that when lower-class Europeans emigrate to the United States they are doubly disadvantaged and thus contribute more than their share to the retarded population.

As to the nature of the differences we are still quite uncertain. We hope that this problem will become more manageable when research employing factor analysis and related approaches tells us more about the organization of intellect, and these findings have been applied to diverse segments of the population. It is here that we feel particularly acutely the interruption in the work of Jastak on the verge of his analysis of data from the state of Delaware, for his theoretical position is very close to that which we urge repeatedly in our report, and his is the first study of subnormality in our society to be based on a probability sample which can be expected to yield true prevalence data rather than merely rates of referral. The work of Guilford (1956) and of Hebb (1949) is promising, but has yet to be applied to subcultural differences. Meanwhile, we do know that there are some subcultural differences with respect to the motivation for intellectual achievement, although we cannot define the effects of these differences other than inferentially, and we also know that level of motivation correlates generally with higher social class.

With respect to kinds of thinking process, the continuum from concreteness to abstraction in thinking appears the most fruitful to explore until our tools become more refined. We know this dimension is important with respect to school and test performance, and it seems reasonable to assume that it is relevant also to total life experience. However, the fact that many school failures do not lead to lifelong failures requires that this projection be made with caution. Again, there is evidence that concreteness is particularly limiting to the intellectual ability of lower-class children and probably adults, and perhaps also rural residents, but we cannot locate any ethnic differences along this continuum unless we wish to do so entirely by inference from IQ's. This about sums up the extent of our knowledge. Yet every time we refer to a limitation we are speaking also of a disproportionate contribution to the population of retarded children; viewed in this light it becomes urgent that we add to the very meager store of knowledge on subcultural intellectual differences we have summarized here.

Intelligence and Social Functioning

We have repeatedly stressed the fact that mental retardation or mental deficiency (in other than severe cases), regardless of cause becomes a problem only insofar as it interferes with the ability of an individual to function as a member of his society. We have had in Section II the example of our society rejecting as unfit vast numbers of its "uneducated" members, and in contrast to this we saw the Hutterites finding no difficulty in utilizing fully the energies of people often referred to by non-Hutterite teachers as "dull." The contrast becomes even more dramatic when we turn to non-European cultures, of which Wogeo and Truk have already been cited as examples. These comprise total populations all of whose members would probably be classified by our standards as markedly subnormal in intellectual functioning and, if we may accept the findings of cross-cultural intelligence testing reviewed in Section VI as a valid indicator, this outcome would probably be true also for many other non-European peoples.

One should not conclude from this that all these "primitive" cultures are characterized by extreme simplicity and a rather vegetative sort of existence. The Trukese, for example, have a complex social organization and an often intricate technology. To cite but one aspect of the latter, they build sailing canoes which are as notable for their hydrodynamic efficiency as they are for craftsmanship, and possess skills in open-ocean dead-reckoning navigation without the use of either compass or chronometer greater than any other people in the world. The Australian aborigines, who lack clothing and use only the crudest of tools, are all able to regulate their social relationships within a system of kinship so complex that it required the efforts of two generations of anthropologists to unravel its subtleties. These people have intelligence and use it very well; it is simply that they do not use it in the same ways we do, or perhaps we should say more properly that they do not define intelligence in our terms—if indeed they treat it as a separate conceptual entity at all. It is for this reason that we remarked earlier that knowledge concerning the intellectual requirements for functioning in cultures other than our own can be of little practical utility in the solution of our problems. It is the demands of our own society which are critical in determining who shall be rejected from our midst, and we must therefore have knowledge primarily of our own culture in order properly to define our task.

Cross-cultural comparisons do, however, provide us with some perspective for this task. We have noted in the non-European societies mentioned thus far that mental retardation appears generally to be no serious problem, and even the comparatively few mentally defective persons who may be found have to be fairly severe in degree or defect before they require special attention; these observations could be extended to most of the other cultures upon which we have any information at all. Yet we have also noted that the members of these societies have to possess considerable mental ability, even if this does not coincide with our definition of intelligence, in order to fulfill their culturally defined roles. Furthermore, such societies seldom offer anything approaching the bewildering array of occupational and social choices we find in our own highly diversified culture, which means that within limits a person in a non-European society has to fit a certain set of requirements or else be unable to function—a plight an American college graduate would undoubtedly find himself in for a long time if he tried to become a member of Australian aboriginal society. Why, then, are there so few intellectual misfits, and most of these a result of organic disorders? The answer appears to be that practically all non-European children learn ways of thinking and behaving which are consistently appropriate to the requirements which will be placed upon them by their culture as adults. The conclusion is then inescapable that this is true in far fewer cases in our own culture.

We have already considered the first half of the equation, the learning of intellectual skills, and were forced to conclude that we are at present able to isolate for study only a very few of the doubtless many variables in the learning situation which affect a child's preparation for later life, and that we know very little about the effects of even those few factors we have identified as relevant, particularly as these factors affect groups rather than just individuals. If we look at the other side of the equation, the functional intellectual requirements of our society, the harvest is equally sparse.

One fact does stand out prominently, however, and that is that the criteria customarily used to define mental retardation are not adequate to predict social and occupational success or failure except at the extremes. We are fairly safe in predicting that even a borderline case will never reach the higher categories of professional-intellectual status, and we can be reasonably certain that a severely retarded individual will never be able to function fully independently in society.

One of these is the age-specific prevalence of referred mental retardation, best and most recently exemplified in the Onondaga County survey mentioned in earlier sections. At each age level we see the reported prevalence of retardation rising steadily, until at the age at which compulsory school attendance is no longer required an abrupt decrease is evident to a reported rate lower than for any of the school-age years. This means that children who have actually been considered retarded and intellectually inadequate in almost two out of three cases cease to be so identified as soon as their school obligations are outgrown, and can therefore be presumed to have made some sort of satisfactory adjustment.

The nature of this adjustment is suggested by a number of follow-up studies which have been done in various parts of the United States on persons who some years before had been judged as children, largely on the basis of IQ, to be morons, subnormal, defective, or the like. With relatively few exceptions, the individuals in all of these studies were found to have made a social adjustment which would have to be considered at least adequate, .the great majority of them being self-supporting, and when retested showed a consistent rise an IQ, often to dull normal levels or higher. Compared to individuals earlier judged "normal" who were used as controls, the formerly retarded persons have slightly higher divorce and minor civil offense rates and somewhat lower grades of occupations with lower standards of living. They are therefore not spectacularly successful, but can scarcely be called failures, inadequate to cope with the requirements of social living.

Further support comes from studies of occupational placement with respect to IQ. Hegge (1944) examined the employment records of 117 boys who were paroled from the Wayne County Training School to meet war manpower shortages in 1941–42; they averaged 17 years of age with a mean IQ of 71.8. Eighty percent of these obtained jobs, but the striking finding is that although these jobs covered a wide range of activities, including many in skilled categories, there was no significant correlation between the IQ at time of parole and the wage level obtained. A more extensive study by Himmelweit and Whitfield (1944) points in the same direction. They related the scores of 10,000 British army recruits on a 10-minute paper-and-pencil test which gave a rough approximation of IQ to placement of these recruits in 39 selected occupations. Although there was tendency for persons of higher intelligence to enter into the higher grade positions, in all but the highest grades of work the full range of intellectual scores was found. In other words, persons of the lowest intelligence levels were able to perform successfully in all but the highest level jobs. Also in England, O'Connor (1953) examined the ability of a group of 47 "feebleminded" (IQ mean 70, range 65–79) adolescents to obtain employment in the two years preceding Army service and found it no different than that of a control group who had normal IQ's (mean 99.5, range 94–106) although the normal group generally obtained more skilled jobs.

The most systematic research on this problem has been undertaken by Jastak. Although, as previously noted, the analysis of his data has unfortunately been interrupted, he has published with Whiteman . . . some preliminary findings on the social adjustment of the individuals in his sample who were classified as retarded. They comprised approximately five percent of a random probability sample which included slightly over one percent of the population of the State of Delaware. The criteria used for a definition of retardation were as follows: (a) an IQ, based on the combined results of 15 different tests, (b) an attitude score, representing the highest standard score attained on any of the subtests, (c) a schooling achievement index (number of grades achieved divided by the average number of grades achieved by his age group); and (d) an occupational achievement index based on the intercorrelated variables of skill level, salary, increase in salary from preceding job, whether or not he supervised others, mobility from his father's occupation, and mobility from his own first job. A person was considered retarded if he fell into the lowest 25 percent of the distribution for each of the four criteria—in other words, although 25 percent of the sample was for example considered low in IQ, only about one in five of these was also low enough on all of the other three criteria to be classified retarded. After examining the social and occupational adjustment of this retarded group Jastak and Whiteman (1957) concluded:

> One cannot help but be struck by the many similarities between the retarded and non-retarded in many areas of adjustment. The lower degree of intelligence of the retarded group does not prevent a sizable number of them from working gainfully, with a good deal of stability and satisfaction. Marital adjustment reveals no gross signs of disharmony. The retarded do not impose a disproportionate load upon community resources either in the form of legal infractions or excessive demands for social service. They are distinguishable from the non-retarded mainly by their dissatisfaction with educational experiences, by their absence from formal social participation, and by their dependence in choosing leisure-time activities.
>
> Mental subnormality, it appears, need not connote an inability to fill an acceptable social role. (pp. 66–67)

If one does not have to be mentally "normal" in order to fill an acceptable social role, what significance does the line dividing "subnormality" from "normality" really have? Certainly we would reject the suggestion that the jobs requiring lesser skills which these people (along with many "normals") fill are somehow fit only for outcasts of our society. It is in fact clear from the evidence presented that there is no criterion of culturally acceptable performance which most retarded individuals cannot meet, even if minimally, with one glaring exception. Were it not for this exception our society would probably have a problem of retardation little greater than that of the Hutterites or the Trukese. The exception is of course school performance, and the IQ concept which is a part of the same complex of standards and values.

Because of the hurdle of school, when we think of retardation we think of retarded *children*, and rightly so because it is only at school age that prevalence rates reach alarming proportions. We have already discussed in sufficient detail in this and the preceding section the various experiences and handicaps which a retarded child encounters in school under the screening of middle-class criteria of behavior and performance. We do not need to repeat the discussion, and for our purposes here will only draw attention again to the emotional impact upon a child in his formative years of being segregated because of mental subnormality. Although we know very little about the nature and magnitude of this impact, it must be substantial, particularly in the areas of motivation for initiative and ambition which are so vital to occupational and social success in our society. No amount of intelligent dedication on the part of teachers of special classes can erase the fact that their pupils have been declared unfit to participate with their peers in an activity which society inflexibly demands of all its members of a certain age.

Worse off than those who are merely emotionally damaged by school failure are those who are institutionalized needlessly as a result of this failure. Happily the proportion of subcultural or "garden-variety" retarded children in institutions is constantly decreasing, for the great majority of these can be expected on the basis of our present knowledge to be able with some help to make an acceptable social adjustment if they are not kept too long in the institutional environment described earlier in this section. Quite probably some of the children with milder degrees of organic defect who now go to institutions could also make an acceptable adjustment if they were pointed in this direction throughout their developmental years without regard to school standards. This is of course the objective of many special classes, but it is often implemented only after the child has tried and failed to cope with a normal curriculum, with all the damaged hopes and disillusionment of parents and child which this implies.

What is needed is a battery of scales which will predict to some degree at least the ability to develop social and occupational skills adequate for social living, scales which will be divorced as far as possible from the IQ concept. There are of course available tests of motor coordination, mechanical aptitude, social maturity, and the like which can be used with fairly young children, but their relationship to adult adjustment has been little explored, so we do not really know whether they will predict this or not. Here again we must return to Jastak's research. His data include the results of administering a large number and variety of tests and scales to persons of a wide range of ages and levels of social and occupational achievement. Although he cannot perforce supply longitudinal information leading from childhood tests to adult performance in a single individual, his research otherwise comes closer than anything undertaken thus far to determining the relationships between test variables of all sorts and the intellectual functioning required by our culture for adult nonschool social adequacy in a broad range of activities. If we had the results of this study, and of others which it would undoubtedly stimulate, we would be much better prepared to advise parents on courses of action they should take, to help teachers of special classes for retarded children in establishing curricula, and to evaluate the importance of subcultural differences in learning with respect to social living as a whole rather than just school performance. We might even be able to make some suggestions to school administrators—who are after all trying to do the best job they can—as to what the elements of a realistic curriculum might be instead of just criticizing them for being unrealistic. Although it is quite correct to say that teachers belong to the middle class and therefore teach in terms of the values and standards they have learned, it is scarcely just to hurl the middle class label at them as an epithet without even being able validly to propose other ways of teaching which might be more valuable for certain purposes and certain pupils.

In speaking of social adequacy we must not assume that this is an absolute standard or level of performance, common to all situations, or we will fall into many of the same fallacies which plague us when we try to interpret the meaning of the IQ. At the same time we must not particularize the concept so that we fail to take into account the variety of day-to-day activities in all of which an "adequate" individual must be competent within a given social setting. What we are referring to rather is the presumption that the different intellectual habits which we know are learned in different subcultural environments must reflect in some degree the criteria of normal mental ability demanded in these various settings. This is comparable to saying that the thinking patterns learned by the Trukese, although different from our own, are appropriate, adequate, and normal for functioning in Trukese society. The lower IQ's characteristic of the rural South doubtless reflect different ways of thinking and levels of adequacy for those who live in that part of the country, as compared to the Northeast for example. It is important that we should know what these differences are. But at the same time we should not assume that these standards are permanent, or even adequate for all the individuals who are members of a given group at one time. Both individual mobility and overall social change can alter requirements. People move up and down the social scale between classes, children of immigrants move out of their ethnic enclaves, people move from the rural South to the urban North, and even the South itself is becoming industrialized and more like the North. A person who is adequate at one time and place may later prove inadequate, or the reverse, but we can neither predict nor advise in these matters until we know much more than we now do about the intellectual requirements for social adequacy. This is another area in which we know much more about emotional factors, and particularly emotional impediments, than we do about the equally crucial cognitive factors.

Cultural Stereotypes of Retardation

We should mention briefly the usually negative reactions conjured up in many people in our society by the idea of mental retardation and particularly mental deficiency. These range perhaps from the gamut of "happy moron" jokes to real anxiety over the kind of social blight envisioned in Goddard's Kallikak study. The Kallikaks had their share of criminals, and they are often linked with the Jukes, who had even more. The presence of such unfounded stereotypes greatly aggravates the entire problem. It can be very damaging to the self-perceptions of retarded children and of their parents, and is likely to launch the child into any new social situation with two strikes against him. It generates unwarranted pressures within our society to get rid of the problem through the self-defeating device of institutionalization (in remote places) and through sterilization. And it undoubtedly has much to do with the lack we have so repeatedly noted of interest on the part of competent researchers to work in the field.

As we have already noted, many non-European peoples are, like the Hutterites, very accepting of even severely defective persons, caring for them patiently, often affectionately, and even sometimes striving to discover even one skill or attribute they can admire (cf. Bogaras, 1904, p. 43; Hawes, 1903, p. 250; Joseph and Murray, 1951, p. 285; League of Nations, 1937, p. 126). This information does not, however, help us to deal with the problem in our own society. It is essentially an educational problem, and there is little doubt that the virulent stereotypes are already gradually weakening. But a systematic social psychological study of the origins and strengths and distributions of these attitudes in our culture could provide a valuable educational tool for accelerating the present scattered progress in growth of understanding. The techniques and personnel for this kind of study are readily available and the price would be small compared to living longer in a climate of damaging public stereotypes.

Cross-Cultural Research in Organic Disorders

Although we have concluded that there are serious limitations to the practical application of cross-cultural research on either learning processes or criteria of social inadequacy, just the reverse is true of the possibilities for research into the etiology of organic disorders resulting in mental deficiency. We know that diet, blood chemistry, heredity, and a variety of environmental factors play a part in at least some of these entities. Yet in our society we find extreme genetic heterogeneity coupled with usually very inadequate genealogical information, diets which vary widely between individuals and places and even from day to day and extensive artificial manipulation of the environment from drinking water to air temperature.

Many of these factors are far more constant and determinate in non-European cultures, even those which have been subject to considerable foreign impact. Many of these peoples pay much more attention to preserving genealogies than do we; although in many cases the system of reckoning kinship may leave some of the geneticist's questions unanswered, the available data are still far superior to those provided by our sloppy practices. At the same time breeding populations are likely to be more stable, even though never completely isolated; this is particularly true of islands widely separated from each other. The research currently being conducted on Guam in amyotropic lateral sclerosis (ALS) is an example of the possibilities offered by such a population showing comparative genetic homogeneity.

Dietary patterns are often nearly uniform throughout large areas, particularly if regular supplies of imported foods are not available, and variation occurs predictably with the seasons. This applies not only to the kinds and quantities of food eaten, but to methods of preparation. At the same time adjacent tribes may often be found who eat the same kinds of foods but prepare them differently, thus permitting controlled comparisons.

Although all cultures have means for controlling the external environment, this control is usually much less complete than it is in ours. The introduction of foreign clothing and housing, of public health services, and a variety of other factors are closing the gap slowly, but it remains wide, leaving non-Europeans more directly exposed to environmental effects. It should be remembered that the major theoretical frontier established by the study of sickle-cell anemia had its beginning in observations in the malarial regions of Africa, among non-European peoples.

If for example societies could be discovered in which mongolism did not occur and others in which it did, and it is our impression that both exist, hypotheses which involved blood chemistry or diet or environmental factors could readily be tested by a study of conditions obtaining in these societies and their members. There is also the possibility that a genetic hypothesis, if one were developed along some new line with respect to mongolism, could receive a more definitive test in a non-European culture where the disorder occurs. Furthermore, if it is possible to survey the entire population as Eaton and Weil attempted with the Hutterites we need not confine ourselves merely to presence or absence of a disorder, but can perhaps determine changes in incidence under measurable changes in external conditions.

The opportunities of cross-cultural research into the etiology and epidemiology of a variety of metabolic and other disorders, not merely those affecting mental capacity, are almost limitless and have been little utilized. Yet we know enough about a sufficient number of cultures to provide a basis for planning carefully controlled studies. Furthermore, anthropologists and other scientists often go out to study other cultures and conditions; with a little additional training they might well be prepared to undertake exploratory investigations before a major investment was made. This is one research area in which we feel cross-cultural research, as against studies of the cultural variations within our own society, can pay off handsomely.

We are captives of the way in which the present structure of the university evolved. We are used to hearing that the university is a community of scholars. That is true in the sense that the faculty shares common values in regard to the obligations of inquiry, to the criteria of quality and excellence, and to the sharing of findings and ideas. But it is not true, except to a surprisingly small degree, in regard to breaking down or making more porous the obstacles to interdisciplinary efforts. The university is multidisciplinary, not interdisciplinary; it is a conglomerate of disciplines the members of each of which identify with their own particular discipline. Indeed, within many disciplines there is such a degree of specialization that, for example, one type of psychologist may be ignorant of what another type of psychologist does (and why). The university is not set up to facilitate meaningful interconnections among disciplines, even when there is obvious conceptual overlap among them, for example, psychology, sociology, and anthropology. Only in small part, however, does this feature of the university account for the lack of interdisciplinary approaches to mental retardation. It does not, for example, account for the lack of interest in mental retardation in the social sciences. We must look elsewhere. Staying within the university one must look at the medical fields where there is interest in mental retardation, more specifically, in the biologic-etiologic factors that give rise to this or that particular type of condition of which mental retardation is but one consequence. The medical researcher cannot be expected to concentrate on psychologic and cultural factors. However, the fact that mental retardation is represented in medical research is an indication of a belief widely held in our society (and in the social sciences) that mental retardation is *primarily* a biologic condition. It is one thing to believe that biologic factors are always in the picture; it is quite another thing to give them such a reductionistic emphasis as to blot out the ever-present role of psychologic and cultural factors. So, no one would doubt that in the cases Eaton and Weil located among the Hutterites, biologic factors have to be taken into account, but, as Eaton and Weil demonstrated, it is myopic in the extreme to overlook the fact that mental retardation is conceived differently and accommodated differently in Hutterite society than in our own. In any event, the attitude that mental retardation is a biologic condition has made it all too easy for the social sciences to ignore it, except for the oddball social scientist who is then viewed as out of the mainstream of his or her discipline.

There is one more related factor: the belief that mentally retarded people are uninteresting as objects of study and service. When I came to Southbury some of my friends were puzzled by my decision to work with "that kind," or "feebs." (Moron jokes were then in vogue.) In subsequent years I was *always* involved in varying ways and degrees with the field, even though I was also developing interest in other problem areas. Friends and colleagues would always show surprise when they learned that I was still very much interested in mental retardation. Tom Gladwin (and later John Doris) was a striking exception. If my collaboration with Tom did not start a trend, it certainly contributed to my education!

If Tom Gladwin broadened my understanding of cultural factors, John Doris reinforced and deepened my respect for history, i.e., the ways in which the past is in our present, even though we manage to ignore and deny it. *Educational Handicap, Public Policy and Social History: A Broadened Perspective on Mental Retardation* (Sarason and Doris, 1979), represents our effort to bring together the developmental, cultural, and historical approaches. If sales are any barometer, this book has had little or no influence, largely, I think, because there is so much history in it. And if Henry Ford, Sr. was stupidly wrong (you can be intelligently wrong) when he said "history is bunk," it is not wrong to say that if a publication is called history, it conjures up images of dates, battles, and persons from bygone decades and centuries. And why read about a dead world? The last chapter of that book, reprinted below, summarizes our answer not only in regard to history but also to the developmental-transactional processes between child and family:

Mental Retardation and Society: Four Themes[3]

Someone recently said that it is no longer possible to write a text on mental retardation that does justice to all of the major substantive issues of the field. If we had any doubts about that, they were dispelled in the course of writing this book. As we look back over the ground we have covered, being sensitive to what we did not cover, we are more impressed than ever before with how intimidating a venture it is to try to see the "whole field." However, we have discerned several major themes that deserve summary, if only in the hope that they will stimulate others to go beyond us.

The first of these themes is as fascinating as it is obvious: mental retardation, be it in its etiological, definitional, diagnostic, or treatment-educational aspects, is not comprehensible apart from American society, culture, and history. When one takes into account how intertwined our history has been with European history, with Africa in connection with slavery, and with the repercussions of Africa's emergence from colonial domination, the social history of mental retardation has staggering dimensions. Immigration, slavery, religious conflict, and urbanization have been dominant factors influencing how we conceive of the nature of retardation, in how we think we understand and deal with it, and how our views have changed as these forces have changed.

There are many perspectives from which one can view our society and history. There is no one valid way, especially if we believe that our knowledge of ourselves, as individuals or a society, inevitably changes with time and we find ourselves perceiving and coping with new worlds. Mental retardation is one of those perspectives, and an illuminating one for at least two reasons. First, it enables us to see our past differently, even though in the distant past mental retardation was not the "issue" it is today; yet we see how the stage was being set for it to become a matter of public policy and discussion. Be it in our individual or collective lives, we know that our actions have consequences, and one of the unintended consequences of universal compulsory education was the need to develop special education. It is fair to say that only in recent years have we begun to confront how the composition of these classes was correlated with immigration, urbanization, and poverty. Like other features of our schools, these classes historically reflected enduring features of our society.

Why has it taken so long for these correlations to gain general recognition? In our opinion, a large part of the answer has been the tendency to conceptualize mental retardation in an ahistorical manner; the failure to conceptualize it as possessing a social historical influence. This theme, however, should not be interpreted as advocating a respect for the past but rather as a plea to become more sensitive to the fact that within the boundaries of the present are the influences of the past.

We like to think that our values, ideas and practices are "modern" and sharply differentiated from those that came before. We are also prone to believe that today's problems are basically different than those of previous generations. There is, of course, a kernel of truth to this, but in the case of mental retardation the history we have traced suggests that we, as individuals and a society, have much in common with those of earlier times.

But, it could be argued, look at all the legislative and judicial actions taken in the past decade to treat mentally retarded individuals as *citizens* entitled to all constitutional rights. Haven't we *finally* recognized how we used to segregate them in dehumanizing institutions, to separate them from the educational "mainstream," and to stigmatize them with pejorative labels? From a social-historical perspective, the answer has to be that we must be wary of confusing change with progress; at the same time, there are grounds for satisfaction in the recent trends. But that satisfaction must be tempered by the knowledge that institutions, prejudice, and tradition do not quickly change. They adjust to impacts, changing their overt stance but prepared to reassert themselves. This will be as true for the changing scene in mental retardation as it was for racial discrimination, even with the 1954 Supreme Court decision.

A second major theme has to do with the changing role of public policy. Up until the end of the last century one could say there was no public policy in regard to mental retardation, except on a local and state level for the purpose of institutional segregation. If a federal role were nonexistent, that should not be taken to mean that there were not other federal policies that mightily influenced people's reactions to "intellectual inferiority." The most fateful of these policies, and one that became more focused and discriminatory as the decades went on, had the aim of keeping out "poor stock." It was a policy that had general support and reflected the tendency to devalue people who appeared intellectually inferior. It was a policy that was influenced by and in turn influenced the different versions of the nature-nurture controversy. There can be no doubt that what prevented the emergence of a clear federal public policy in regard to mental retardation was the shared distrust of federal intervention and power. That view of a federal role changed as a result of the Great Depression. It was not until World War II that a federal policy truly began to develop, but even then it was directed to education generally, not mental retardation.

We would like to believe that public policy reflects a rational process in which facts, experience, and research were three factors that influenced the formation of a public policy. The first was the amazingly swift and effective fashion with which parents of retarded individuals became a potent lobbying force in the national scene. The second was that at the height of the parents' movement, President Kennedy had taken office. Given his family's interests in mental retardation, it was only a matter of time before a policy would emerge.

The stage had already been set by federal policy to change and support public education. Just as universal compulsory education set the stage for the emergence of special education, so the post-World War II development of a federal policy for education set the stage for one specifically directed to mental retardation. One could not have predicted when this would happen, or what the scope of the policy would be.

A decade ago, few people would have thought that the mainstreaming legislation, Public Law 94-142, would be enacted. As we look back over the past ten years, we can see that what was being underestimated was the strength of the diverse forces seeking equality before the law— racial and ethnic minorities, women, homosexuals, older people, mental patients, the physically handicapped. Rarely is public policy in regard to one problem or group independent of policies being forged for other problems or groups. The term public policy is a kind of shorthand for societal forces and movements pervading the society at a particular time, and they get reflected in public policies in different ways. That is why the 1954 desegregation decision and the mainstreaming legislation of 1975 have to be seen as related reflections in a public policy of changing moods and opinions.

It was not by chance that the mainstreaming legislation was not specifically directed to the needs of mentally retarded individuals but to those of *all* handicapped students, a recognition of the fact that we are living at a time when there is a heightened sensitivity to the implications and consequences of past denials of constitutional rights of diverse "minorities." From the standpoint of mentally retarded people, it is a distinctive and momentous change to be given recognition in public policy.

But there is one aspect to the emergence of public policies that requires special emphasis, for what it may portend for the future. We refer here to the seemingly inexorable momentum for public policies to be initiated, implemented, and require funding support from the federal government. Up until the end of World War II, public policy in regard to education generally, and mental retardation in particular, was "local." Indeed, the idea that the federal government should play other than the most minor of roles in this area was considered anathema. "That government is best that governs least" was a widely shared belief.

Times have changed, and there are people who feel that the federal government should get even more involved in shaping a differentiated, standardized national education system. Such a suggestion may sound today no less strange than the idea of universal compulsory education did to people in the early nineteenth century. Without trying to forecast the future, one has to note that the increased federal role has not been without its problems and critics. The fact is that even supporters of an increased federal role are aware of the dangers of dependence upon the control by centralized authority. The dangers do not inhere in the motivations and personality of individuals but in a fantastically intricate and often ambiguous system of federal-state-local interrelationships in which the shape of actions takes precedence over the substance and spirit of actions. We must not forget that where we are today is in large measure a response to the perception that local authority was unwilling or unable to cope with pressing educational problems, some of them of a constitutional nature that the federal government could not ignore. Professor Murray Levine's maxim "problem creation through problem solution" characterizes the fate of all public policies.

What we have said about policy brings us to a third theme: the changing views and policies about institutions for the mentally retarded. The idea that most mentally retarded individuals can and *should* live in their natural community has only recently taken root in our society, and only in the past few years become part of public policy. But, as in the case of mainstreaming, it is one thing to proclaim a policy, and quite another thing to implement it appropriately.

The fact is that the continued existence of the residential institution receives support not only from ingrained views and perceptions of what mental retardation "is" but from two other sources. The first of these is the economic stake that states have invested in these institutions, i.e., buildings, staff, and state administrative bureaus and departments. The second is diverse, and often subtle, resistances from local communities. Here again it would be a mistake to interpret this in individual terms as if those in opposition are morally perverse.

Rather it has to be seen as a principled and opening battle in a long war, the social-historical background of which goes back a long way. What is involved in deinstitutionalization is a social change that will have reverberations in our major social institutions, and change always encounters obstacles. The strength of the obstacles is proportionate to the number of people and institutions that will be affected. It is precisely because deinstitutionalization requires community change that it will continue to be opposed by many people.

Religious bigotry and racial and ethnic discrimination are less potent today than during the nineteenth century when our society was riddled with hot and cold wars: Catholics versus Protestants, German Catholics versus Irish Catholics, ethnic group versus ethnic group, South versus North, and "natives" versus immigrants. But who will say that these wars are over? How can one argue that the wars were avoidable? When people are arrayed in opposition to each other because they see the world differently, because their definitions of themselves stem from differing perceptions of what is right and wrong, truth and heresy, a social change is begun in the form of social conflict.

In the case of institutionalization the conflict has begun among state departments, community groups, and the courts. We must not forget that the move to deinstitutionalization, as was the case with so many of the conflicts around education, came from court decisions and not from a ground swell of outraged public opinion.

In the middle of the last century, Dorothea Dix described for the Massachusetts legislature the inhumane conditions in that state's "humane" institutions. A century later, to the same legislature, Dr. Burton Blatt gave a similar description with pictures. And a decade later, in his presidential address to the American Association on Mental Deficiency, he demonstrated again with the pictures that relatively little had changed except in a superficially esthetic way.

If we have emphasized the institutional issue, it is because it has a long seamy history explainable only by the fact that mental retardation has never been a "thing" but a conceptual invention bearing the imprint of society's structure, traditions, values, and prejudices. If today that imprint does not seem to give priority to institutionalization, to the tendency to segregate, we will only be deluding ourselves if we believe that an opposing tendency supported by near-and long-term social history has been extinguished. We say this not to dampen the spirit of those who have led the deinstitutionalization movement, but to remind them that modes of thinking reinforced over the centuries are not easily changed. The change has begun and it will take future Dorothea Dixes and Burton Blatts to consolidate past accomplishments and accelerate the pace of change. The time to be discouraged is when there is no Dorothea Dix, Burton Blatt, or Thomas Szasz on the scene.

The final theme is one with which this book began: mental retardation is never a thing or a characteristic of an individual but rather a social invention stemming from time-bound societal values and ideology that make diagnosis and management seem both necessary and socially desirable. The shifting definitions and management of mental retardation are not understandable in terms of the "essence" of the "condition" but rather in terms of changing social values and conditions.

We are beginning to comprehend that in the case of the mentally retarded individual, regardless of etiological considerations, development is *always* transactional; the individual affects and is affected by the family setting into which he or she is born. We are not dealing with simple cause-and-effect relationships but dynamic transactions in a complicated familial web. This may be obvious but it is another instance where the obvious has not penetrated into clinical practice.

When one looks at diagnostic and treatment-management programs, one finds a concentration on the *individual* rather than on those who comprise the family network. The result is that one drastically reduces the understanding one can gain and the help one can provide to all who are part of the network. How much we are unwitting prisoners of conceptual tunnel vision is most clearly illustrated by the custom of only seeing the mentally retarded individual in our offices and clinics, robbing us of valuable information and opportunities to alter what needs to be altered in the natural setting.

Criticism of customary practice has received substantial empirical support from research on home-based observations and the use of parents as "therapists." As in the case of institutionalization, the obstacles to change are rooted in habits of thinking, professional training, and the economic-political structure of human services. To translate the transactional approach appropriately into practice is no less than to encounter the relationships among culture, social history, organizational structure, and the constraints of existing ideologies. So we see again that in pursuing the societal context in which mental retardation becomes defined and managed, we are provided a perspective from which to look at the nature of our society. When we study mental retardation we are studying our society, and the failure to understand that goes a long way to explaining the seamy history of mental retardation in our society.

The above, as mentioned, was a summary of our "answer." It was a summary of a far more detailed, formal, scholarly account. But on the occasion of receiving an award in 1973 from the American Association on Mental Deficiency, I gave a personal answer, the most personal paper I have ever published. The title is *Jewishness, Blackishness, and the Nature-Nurture Controversy*. It was written at a time when the cyclical nature-nurture controversy was taking on new life. I did not want to discuss the controversy in the context of theories, research studies, and other impersonal ways of making points. Besides, as indicated earlier, I thought these ways had managed to obscure the failure to take early childhood, history, and cultural transmission seriously. Could I illustrate the significance of this failure by using my own religious and cultural heritage? Could I convincingly demonstrate that I am at my personal core a product of the millenia, of a long, long past that, far from being dead, is stirringly alive, of a family and a cultural tradition that respected learning at that same time that it made me feel a stranger in the land? Could I, by using myself, demonstrate how we had to begin to understand blacks other than in terms of tests and the ahistorical stance? Could I make clear the colossal nonsense involved in discussing black intelligence independent of their history in Africa *and* our society? Would blacks be affronted by what I had to say about what their past meant for the next century or more? I gave my answer. It may not be the most original piece I have written but I like to believe it is the wisest.

Jewishness, Blackishness, and the Nature-Nurture Controversy[4]

Those who have participated in the recent version of the nature-nurture controversy have, for the most part, neglected to confront the derivation of their time perspective in relation to social change in general and historically rooted group attitudes and performance in particular. As in past versions of the controversy, the issues have centered around personal and social values, methodology, the content of the measuring instruments, sampling problems, and genetic theories and laws, and the consequences of these issues for programs of social action. There seems to be recognition by all that inequity and prejudice have been and are rampant, and that it is probably impossible at the present time to discuss the controversy in a dispassionate way. Within scientific circles it is an explosive issue, just as it is in the society at large. I assume that if a study were done asking people if they thought that future versions of controversy (say 20 or 40 years from now) would be conducted in a less explosive climate, almost all would reply in the negative. Indeed, many would probably predict a more explosive climate. If a similar study had been done 50 years ago when, after World War I, the nature-nurture controversy was once again peaking, far fewer people would have correctly predicted the present climate of social explosiveness in which the controversy is taking place. (At that time, though, blacks were not central to the controversy. The inferiority of blacks was not then a burning issue, presumably because it was uncritically accepted by most people [white and black] as a fact which did not need to be labored. It was the flood of immigrant groups from Europe and Asia that brought together questions of national policy and the status of knowledge about the determinants of intellectual performance.) Today, sides have been taken and with a degree of partisanship that the passage of time will not easily change—a variant of my thesis that changes in attitude and performance of historically rooted groups are relatively immune to change except when viewed from a time perspective in which the basic measuring unit may be a century. When I say a century I do not mean it in a precise or literal way, but rather as a means to emphasize a time perspective far longer than that which we ordinarily adopt.

For a statement and description of my position convincingly to reflect my thinking requires that I be unusually personal and relatively unhindered by considerations of modesty, politeness, and that undefined criterion of "good taste." I shall talk about aspects of myself and my family not only because they are the "data" I know best, but because I assume (phenomenologically I *know*) that I am quite representative of Jews, possessed of all the ingredients that comprise Jewishness. What I have to say has been said, and far better, by other Jews. I justify going over old ground because, as the title of this article suggests, I wish to relate it to an important and fateful social and scientific issue. Here, too, I make no claim to originality, although I believe that I provide an emphasis that has been lacking in the scientific literature.

Jewishness

I begin with my father, a simple, unassuming, relatively inarticulate man who spent a long working life as a cutter of children's dresses. He was not an impressive person. He did not read books, but he went to the synagogue and obviously knew the Old Testament (in Hebrew) backward and forward. As he prayed, he kept the books open and turned the pages, but rarely did more than glance at them. He recited the prayers in a most undeviating, ritualistic manner. Beginning at age 8 or 9, having enrolled me in Hebrew school, he expected me to sit and pray with him. Of course, I did not understand what I was reading (or even why), and when from time to time my boredom and anger forced me to ask why the book could not be put into English, he never deemed the question worthy of a response.

He loved children and had a gentleness with them to which they responded, but my memory contains nothing that would support the notion that he had other than a primitive notion of children and learning. The early sources of my anger toward my father were many, but two are particularly relevant here. One concerns a leather-covered Oxford dictionary which I had not the strength to pick up until I was six or seven. I still have the dictionary, and when it comes to its weight I know whereof I speak. I never saw my father use that dictionary, and to me its presence was symbolic of his selfishness: Why did we have *that* around the house when we (I) needed other things? Why didn't we hide it, sell it, or throw it out? Occasionally I would peruse its pages, but the book was so large and heavy that even when I did not have to hold it, I could not comfortably use it. Related to this was our battle about the *New York Times*, which he bought and read every day. Why buy a newspaper that did not have funnies? How more selfish could a father be than to deprive his children of newspaper funnies, particularly on Sundays when all other newspapers contained loads of them? I hated the *New York Times*, which, I need not tell you, I now read every day. I also have an aversion to funnies and truly cannot comprehend why my wife and daughter read them first when the local paper arrives—and sometimes even argue about who will read them first.

And then there were my older male cousins who, when I was in elementary school, were preparing to go to college. At that time I knew as much about college as I did about astronomy. There was a place called college and there were stars in the sky, and that exhausted my knowledge of both. But in the numerous meetings of the extended family that word *college* kept coming up in reverent and awesome tones. Cousin Leo was not going to any college, he was going to a place called Cornell and that showed (not to me) that Leo was smart because not many Jewish boys were *allowed* there. And if Leo did well there, as *of course* he would, he was then going to go to still another kind of college and become a doctor. Cousin Moey was a very smart fellow, too, and wasn't it too bad that he had to work during the day and go to college at night. Go to college at night! What kind of craziness was that? To me that meant he couldn't listen to the radio at night, those being the days when having a radio was still a novelty. It was during these early years that I kept hearing the phrase "He will make something of himself" applied to some of my relatives.

There was Leo's brother, Oscar, who was special. If I had available to me then the words I have now I would have described Oscar to my friends as smart-smart. That's the way the family regarded him. But Oscar posed a real problem because he played football, and extremely well. He was as good in football as he was in the classroom. That Oscar was on the small side was only one reason for family opposition to playing football. It was important because he might get "good and hurt," not be able to go to school, and maybe not even go to college. The more important point was that nice Jewish boys, particularly if they were smart-smart, didn't play football. That was for the gentiles (goys), who were by nature not smart; they were, instead, and again by nature, crudely physical and aggressive. Football was quintessentially goyish, and it was stupid for Jewish boys to compete in that arena. David may have slain Goliath, thanks to God, but that was in another world. Let's respect David, but let us not go so far as to identify with his actions! One Saturday morning I walked into my cousin's apartment—we lived upstairs, those being the days of extended families in restricted areas, and I use the word "restricted" in its geographical and discriminatory senses—and I heard my aunt yelling and screaming in Oscar's room. There was Oscar curled up womblike being pounded by my aunt at the same time that she was telling him and the world what she thought of a Jewish boy who was going to play football for his high school *on Saturday*. What had she done to deserve such punishment? What would *they* think? "They" referred to all her Jewish friends and neighbors who, she was sure, would blame and sympathize with her on one of the worst fates a Jewish mother could experience. How could a mother stand by and watch her child, with such a "good head," go straight to hell? It was an awesome display of physical energy and verbal imagery—my Aunt Jennie was regarded by all as having no equal when it came to using and inventing the Yiddish equivalents of longshoreman language. When her physical energy was spent (the verbal flow never ceased), Oscar got up from bed, collected his football suit, calmly but sweetly said good-bye, and went off to join the goyim in defense of the glory of Newark's Barringer High School. Needless to say, when he went to Brown, where he was quite a football player during the years when that college had its best teams, my aunt attended a number of games (*on Saturday*) because, I assume, she wanted to be on hand when her little boy would be near-fatally injured. He was no more than five feet nine inches tall and probably weighed no more than 170 pounds. Leonard Carmichael, who was then chairman of the Department of Psychology at Brown, once got Oscar aside and expressed concern that he could be injured and was, perhaps, wasting his time playing football when he could start making a career in psychology, in which Professor Carmichael had concluded Oscar had shown considerable aptitude.

Oscar was directly important in my life. Toward the end of the first semester of my first year in junior high school, Oscar, home from college for a few days, visited our family. He interrogated my mother about the courses I was taking and was horrified to learn that I was enrolled in the commercial curriculum, taking such courses as typing, junior business training, etc. He told my mother that if I stayed in the commercial curriculum I would not be admitted to college. My mother was aghast and took action. A few weeks later, at the beginning of the next semester, I found myself taking Latin, ancient history, and algebra.

I do not have to relate more anecdotes to make the point that being Jewish was inextricably interwoven with attitudes toward intellectual accomplishment. To separate the one from the other was impossible. This did not mean that being Jewish meant that one was smart or capable of intellectual accomplishments, but it meant that one had respect for such strivings. Respect is too weak a word to convey the force and role of these attitudes. It is like saying that we have respect for breathing. We did not have to learn these attitudes in any consciously deliberate way. We had no choice in the matter, just as we had no choice in choosing our parents. As children, we did not have to verbalize these attitudes to ourselves, we would not have known how. The word *attitudes* is a poor one to describe what and how we absorbed what we did. We learned those attitudes in as "natural" a way as learning to like lox and bagels, gefilte fish, or knishes.

How do we account for the strength and frequency of these aspects of Jewishness? Please note that I am not asking how to account for individuals like myself or my mother and father or my cousins, but rather why these aspects are characteristics of Jews as a group. This is, initially, at least, a cultural, not a psychological, question. It is a question which directs us, among other things, to history and tradition and requires the adoption of a time perspective quite different from what we ordinarily use when our focus is on a single individual or generation. Obviously if these aspects of Jewishness have been manifested for generations and centuries, the outlines of an answer to my question become clear—and I do not confuse clarity of outlines with complexity of the substantive answer. These aspects, when looked upon in the context of the sweep of social-cultural history, have always characterized Jewish life. Indeed, when one looks at my question from this time perspective, one ends up by asking another question: So what else is new? Or, one becomes intrigued by individual Jews who do not possess these characteristics, whose mental breathing apparatus inexplicably did not take in ingredients ever-present in his social-cultural atmosphere.

The aspects of Jewishness I have thus far discussed are not understandable by looking only at the present or near past. That is an obvious point which needed to be said in order to make a second one: *These aspects have been and will continue to be immune to change in any short period of time, by which I mean a minimum of a century.* Leaving aside Hitler's "final solution" as well as other types of world catastrophes, I can think of no set of circumstances in which these aspects of Jewishness would disappear or be noticeably diluted in less than several or scores of generations. These circumstances could not be casual or indirect, they would have to be extremely potent and persistent. More of this later when I question the rationale behind the expectation that certain consequences of some aspects of blackishness can be changed noticeably in a decade or so, or that if blacks and whites differ on tests, one can ignore the relation of these differences to differences in the psychological core of blackishness and whiteishness, or that when you have equated a group of blacks and whites on an intelligence test or on a measure of academic achievement you have controlled for the most influential psychological determinants of intellectual performance in real life. (It's like saying that everybody is equal before the law, the person on welfare as well as the millionaire. There *is* a difference between facts and the truth.)

Now to another aspect of Jewishness to which I have alluded: the knowledge (it is not a feeling, it is phenomenologically a fact) that one is in a hostile world. This was crystal clear in my parents' and grandparents' generations. Their thinking went like this: Built into the mental core of every non-Jew is a dislike of and an enmity toward Jews. Yes, there were some nice Gentiles and up to a point you could trust and work with them, but let any conflict or dissension enter into the relationship and you would find that core of hatred asserting itself. It might not be verbalized, but, nonetheless, you could count on it. In the end, and there is always an end, you would get it in the neck—no ifs, ands, or buts. I have long felt that their resistance to mixed marriages—and the word *resistance* does not begin to convey the bitterness and strength of their feelings—was less a consequence of religion or clannishness than it was of the fear of physical injury to or destruction of one's child. To say they mistrusted the non-Jewish world is to reveal a genius for understatement. And if you tried to reason with them it was no contest because they could overwhelm you with history. They could marshall evidence from past centuries, as well as events in their own lives, with a rapidity, force, and cogency that doctoral students in history must fantasize about when they approach their orals. If you get a kick out of unproductive arguments, I suggest you specialize in combating history with logic and good will— the kicks are endless. (If orthodox Jews are unavailable, try it with blacks, who have more kinship to Jews in this respect than they know.) If an aspect of you is poignantly and consciously rooted in history, you are not a candidate for attitude change. We would have had a more solid and realistic foundation for our efforts at social change if American social psychology had dealt with historically rooted, conscious attitudes of historically rooted groups. At the very least, it might have provided a more realistic time perspective about the attainment of the goals of these efforts.

What about me and my generation who, unlike our parents and

grandparents, were born in this country with its traditions of opportunity and freedom? Did we possess the aspect of Jewishness that says this is a hostile world, even though "objectively" we grew up in a social environment radically different from that of previous generations? The very fact that our family had been created in this country and not in a European one meant that it would be different from what went before. You could write for years about the differences and when you were all through and began to list the similarities you would soon be listing the aspect "This is a hostile world for Jews." Some anecdotes from my adult life: When in 1938 I applied for admission to graduate school the knotty question was whether or not I would lie about being Jewish. Those were the days when you were asked for your religion and a photograph. They also wanted to know your father's occupation. So if I told them my father was a cutter of children's dresses, that I was Jewish, plus the fact that I would be graduated from an unrecognized college (Dana College, renamed the University of Newark, housed then in the former Feigenspan Brewery) what would be my chances? The point is not what was objectively true but the strength of my feelings that my application would be read by people hostile to Jews. The strength of my feeling and its automatic and indiscriminate application were not justified, but it is the hallmark of historically rooted attitudes of historically rooted groups that there is a discrepancy between external conditions and subjective impressions. (This is true for blacks in regard to whites, as it is for the Irish in regard to the English, etc.) The fact that these attitudes receive periodic reinforcement is sufficient to maintain their strength and indiscriminateness. For example, why does a colleague of mine still have in his possession a letter written to him in 1939 by a most eminent person who was then chairman of the department of psychology of a prestigious university? I have seen the letter. It is a remarkable but not surprising document because it says that although my colleague had all the paper credentials to be admitted to the doctoral program, he should think hard about coming because, as a Jew, he would not be able to be placed in a teaching job. A list of names is given of Jewish students who finished their doctorates in that department but who could not get jobs. Come, the letter says, but only if you regard it as an "intellectual adventure" and not as preparation for a career. How complicated a theory do we need to understand why my colleague, like myself, generalized our expectation of discrimination indiscriminately?

I lived in a radically different world than my parents and grandparents. I differed from them in countless important ways, but I differed not at all from them in the possession of this aspect of Jewishness. When I was finishing graduate school in 1942, there were two other students, and good friends (Jorma Niven, Harry Older), who were also going into the job market. To avoid competition among us, we did not apply for jobs at the same colleges or universities. Jorma and Harry were not Jewish, but they understood what was at stake when I wondered whether on my vita I should note that I was Jewish and so avoid interviews at places that did not look kindly on Jews. The point of these anecdotes is not to say something about the external world or even my perception of it but rather the pervasiveness and strength of my psychological radar about Jewishness, a constantly tuned instrument that was always at work and always sighting "objects" about which I had to decide whether they were friend or foe. But why do I say *was*? It is as true of me today as it was then, and with far less justification. My external world has changed dramatically within my lifetime, it has changed even more in relation to my parents' world, and yet that radar continues to work as if the external world has not changed.

A year ago when I was at a social gathering at Yale's Hillel, the Rabbi told me, in confidence and with that all too familiar mixture of pride and fear, that approximately one-third of all students at Yale were Jewish. He did not have to put into words (or even bother to look at me to see if I understood his message) that this information should not be bandied about because it might arouse the envy and enmity of non-Jews. You might expect such an attitude in a rabbi but not in me, but such an expectation simply ignores what fine-tuned, efficient processes and mechanisms cultural transmission consists of, insuring that the most central aspects of our sense of identity are independent of choice and changes in our external world.

I have known scores of Jews of my generation who have visited Israel. They were heterogeneous in many respects so that if you administered to them every psychological test that has ever been standardized, I predict you would find that, intelligence tests and political attitudes aside, the scores would be distributed in a fairly normal fashion. With no exception, every one of them spontaneously described the feeling—compounded of surprise, disbelief, relief, and security—they had in response to the fact that "everyone there is Jewish." As one of them said in deep puzzlement: "Even though I knew everyone was Jewish, I found that I continued to ask myself whether this or that person was Jewish. It was very unsettling at times." There are some attitudinal radars that cannot be turned off, because they have no off-on switch. These visitors shared another reaction, this one compounded of respect, envy, and pride and put by one of them in this way: "They have no fear. They don't care what the rest of the world thinks and does. They are prepared to fight and they have no doubt who will win in the end." To the non-Israeli Jew, "in the end" meant and still means getting it in the neck; to the Israeli it means quite the reverse. It took several generations of Israeli sabras, with an assist from Hitler, to effect a change in attitude. Put more correctly: It took all of that for a millenia-old identification to reassert itself. It was all right now to identify with David because one had to, and like David, but unlike those at Masada, the Goliath would be defeated. How strange this is to the American Jew. How strange it would be to the Israeli to learn about my reaction to an item in last week's *Yale Daily* that 50% of this year's Phi Beta Kappas were Jewish. He would have difficulty understanding my un-reflective fear that this would not sit well in the minds of many non-Jews.

What about the younger generations of Jews in our society? Is this aspect of Jewishness in them or has it been eroded? As best as I can determine, this core of Jewishness is in them despite the obvious changes in our society. When I asked a group of Jewish students about this, they looked me as only smart-smart teenagers can look at dumb-dumb professors, and one of them said: "In high school I read *The Wall*. There *was* the 1967 six-day war. And when I apply to medical school I know the chances of Jews have been decreased because they will take more minority people. How are we supposed to feel when we read that an African leader is sorry that Hitler did not win and that some black groups in our country seem to talk in the same way?" Toward the end of the discussion a young woman said, somewhat hostilely: "Because my parents were like you. What did *you* tell your daughter about going with or marrying a non-Jew?" A bull's-eye! Her comments recalled to me the time our family of three was about to leave our house to begin our first trip abroad. Just as we were ready to leave, my daughter (who then was 10) said she had forgotten something and went upstairs to get it. The "it" turned out to be a chain to which was attached a gold star of David. No, my wife and I had not given it to her because we are not religious.[5] It had been given to her by a Catholic nun who was head of an agency to which I had been a consultant, but that is another story, albeit a quite relevant one.

Before continuing, let me summarize what I have tried to say:

1. There are certain attitudinal characteristics which are part of the core of Jewishness. What is notable is their frequency and strength.
2. These characteristics are a kind of "second nature," learned, absorbed, and inculcated with all the force, subtleness, and efficiency of the processes of cultural transmission.
3. To understand the frequency and strength of these characteristics requires a time and perspective of centuries.
4. Similarly, these characteristics could not be extinguished or diluted in strength except over very long periods of time. What centuries have produced will not quickly change even under external pressures.
5. It is impossible to understand and evaluate intellectual performance of groups without taking account of each group's attitudes toward such activity. This is an obvious point to anyone who has engaged in clinical work, and it has received substantial support in the research literature, for example, the test anxiety literature. It is no less valid a point when one deals with the intellectual performance of historically rooted groups and their historically rooted attitudes. (Women's liberation groups, now and in the distant past, understood this point quite

well. The original title of this article was "Jewishness, Blackishness, Femaleness, and the Nature-Nurture Controversy.")

I have no difficulty accepting the notion that intelligence has its genetic components, nor do I have difficulty with the idea that different groups may possess different patterns of abilities. It would require mental derangement of a most serious sort to deny that different groups get different scores on various tests of intelligence. But I have the greatest difficulty understanding how anyone can come to a definitive conclusion in these matters based on studies which assume that what culture and history have created can be changed in a matter of years or decades. What combination of ignorance and presumption, what kind of understanding of human history does one have to possess to accept the hypothesis that the central psychological core of *historically* rooted groups can markedly change in a lifetime? It is a fact that Jews as a group score high on intelligence tests, do well on achievement tests, and are disproportionately represented in the professions and academia. It may be true that this is in part a consequence of selected survival and breeding over the centuries. But if one invokes the law of parsimony (not for the purposes of denying a hypothesis or preventing anyone from pursuing a particular line of research) for the purpose of assigning weights to variables on the basis of what we know about culture, one must conclude that the transmission of Jewishness from generation to generation has been fantastically successful—a view of "success" understood but probably not shared by those approaching their deaths in the Nazi holocaust, the Spanish inquisition, and countless other Jew-murdering periods in history. My genes have a long history, an indisputable fact. My Jewishness also has a long history, another indisputable fact. At this point in time we know far more about my Jewishness than about my genes. When as a society we mount programs of social amelioration, I would prefer to act on the basis of the known, recognizing that I will not be alive to know the ultimate outcome.

Blackishness

What I have to say about "blackishness" has been foreshadowed by my description of certain aspects of Jewishness.[6] Jews and blacks share the characteristic "this is a hostile world." Some would argue that the sensitivity of blacks to anticipated hostility is stronger than it is in Jews. I am not sure this is the case, although some blacks and Jews would consider it self-evidently true. The more I talk to Jews about this, the more I am impressed by two things: how strong this aspect is and how much they want to believe that it isn't strong. Their self-report about its workings is discrepant with its strength. I stick with this point because it is instructive about what happens when two historically rooted attitudes contradict each other: "This is a hostile world" and "this is a society free of prejudice." In any event, this aspect of blackishness (in white society) is historically rooted and will be immune to change except over a long, long period of time. Blacks, of course, are absolutely correct when they say that an equally long period of time will be required for whites to overcome *their* historically rooted attitudes toward blacks.

In our society, at least, blackishness has not had at its core unbounded respect for book learning and the acquisition of academically soaked, cognitive skills. Just as when the Jews in Egypt were slaves, did manual labor, and could only hope for survival and dream of freedom, so in black culture, intellectuality or bookishness (call it what you will) has been far from the top of the priority list. As groups, Jews and blacks could not be more far apart than on the degree to which their cultures are suffused with "intellectuality." On intelligence tests Jews get higher scores than blacks.[7] *From my perspective, the important question is not how to explain the difference but why the difference is not greater.* This reminds me of Goddard's description of the Kallikak culture and his use of it as proof of Kallikak mental inferiority passed on from generation to generation. From his description of that encapsulated culture, one might conclude that the Kallikaks were a biologically superior group, that is, anyone who could grow up and survive in that culture must have been extremely well endowed constitutionally.

Over the past century, more and more blacks have "made it" in the intellectual arena, but they have represented a very small percentage of all blacks. It is my impression that compared even to three decades ago, more black children experience something akin to what I described of my childhood, but there is no basis at all for concluding that this has become a characteristic experience. What warrant is there in psychological theory and research that would lead to the expectation that the attitudinal core of blackishness could, under the most favorable conditions, be changed in less than scores of generations? And is there a psychologist who would argue that we have even remotely approximated "the most favorable conditions?"

For me, the central question is how theories determine time perspective, that is, how one's conception of what man and society are determines one's time perspective about changing either? I have discussed this in connection with the problem of changing schools and creating new settings (Sarason, 1971, 1972). Two examples of what I mean: What if someone came to us and asked why we cannot teach children to read in 24 hours? Assuming that we knew the person to be sane and we could control the tendency to throw him out of our office, what would we say? It would probably take us 24 hours of uninterrupted talk to explain how children develop physically, mentally, and socially; the inevitable social and interpersonal context in which learning takes place; the complexity of motivation and its vicissitudes; the knowledge and cognitive skills that are necessary for the productive assimilation and use of symbols; and the problems that can be created when external pressures do not take developmental stages readiness into account. Besides, we might ask this irritating ignoramus, "Do you mean why can't we teach a child to read in 24 hours or do you mean a *group* of children in a classroom?"

A second example: What if we went to a psychoanalyst friend and asked him really to level with us and explain how he justifies seeing a patient for one hour a day, four or five days a week, perhaps for two, three, four, or more years. "Why does it take that long? Do you really believe," we ask him, "that it takes that long to be helpful to someone? Aren't there quicker ways of giving help?" "Friend (?)," he replies, "there is much you do not understand." He then proceeds to summarize for us what the human organism is at birth, how its cognitive and affective equipment is organized and develops, the ways in which it becomes increasingly psychologically and physically differentiated, how it develops and utilizes a variety of coping mechanisms, the sources of inevitable internal and external conflict, the nature and strength of resistances to change, the relationship of all of this to the interpersonal dynamics of the nuclear family, and on and on depending on whether our psychoanalyst friend is summarizing Freud's *Introductory Lectures* or multivolumed collected works. (If he happens to be a true believer, we would also hear about parricide and the primal horde in the dawning history of mankind.) "Now," he would say, "you can begin to understand why psychoanalytic treatment takes so long. It is not that we desire to prolong it, but rather that our understanding of man requires it if we are to be able meaningfully to help somebody radically change accustomed ways of thinking and acting. Of course," he would admit, "you can help troubled people in a shorter period of time by focusing only on the elimination of symptoms, but that is not our goal, which is to illuminate for our patients their psychological core and its dynamics, and we are not always successful."

I do not have to labor the point that one's conception of a problem or process determines one's time perspective about how to influence or change it. The relationship may be grossly invalid either because one's conception is faulty, or one's time perspective poorly deduced, or both, but the fact remains that there is always a relationship. In my opinion, the failure or inability to confront this relationship in a systematic and realistic way is one of the most frequent sources of personal disillusionment and conflict, as it is also one of the central defects in most social science theorizing. Is it not amazing how many social scientists reacted to the Supreme Court desegregation in 1954 as if it were really meant that desegregation was ended, or would be ended in a matter of a decade or so? Is it not equally amazing how many people really believed that if disadvantaged groups, like the blacks, were provided new and enriched educational experiences they would as a group blossom quickly in terms

of conventional educational and intellectual criteria? Is it not pathetic
how eager we were to believe that we possessed the knowledge to justify
these expectations? What combination of ignorance and arrogance permitted people to proclaim that if we delivered the right kinds of programs and spent the appropriate sums of money we could quickly undo
what centuries had built up? When the expectations that powered these
efforts were obviously not being fulfilled, what permitted some people to
conclude that perhaps the victim was in some ways different from (less
endowed than) those in the dominant society? Why were they so ready to
"blame the victim" instead of the thinking from which derived such an
unrealistic time perspective? And again I must ask: What is there in man's
history and in the corpus of social science knowledge which contradicts
the statements that few things are as immune to quick changes as the
historically rooted, psychological core of ethnic and racial groups? Jewishness and blackishness are products, among other things (and I assume there *are* other things), of social and cultural history, and their
psychological cores will successfully resist short-term efforts aimed at
changing them.

In one of his syndicated columns, William F. Buckley, Jr. (*New Haven
Journal Courier* March 20, 1969) has provided support of my thesis: needless to say, he does this unknowingly. Buckley quoted approvingly from
an article by Ernest van den Haag:

> The heart of Mr. van den Haag's analysis, so critically useful at
> the present moment, should be committed to memory before the
> ideologists of racism take the Jensen findings and mount a cam-
> paign of I-told-you-soism with truly ugly implications. Van den
> Haag asked himself:
> Q. Suppose the average native intelligence of Negroes is in-
> ferior to that of whites. Would that mean that Negroes are inferior to
> whites?
> A. One may regard others as inferior to oneself, or to one's
> group, on the basis of any criterion, such as mating, eating, drinking
> or language habits, religious practices, or competence in sports,
> business, politics, art or finally, by preferring one's own type, quality
> or degree of intelligence, skin or hair color and so forth.
> By selecting appropriate criteria each group can establish the
> inferiority of others, and its own superiority. . . . The selection of
> criteria for superiority or inferiority is arbitrary, of course . . . I do
> not believe that intelligence is any more relevant to the judgments
> of inferiority than, say, skin color is.
> If Negroes on the average turn out to have a genetically lower
> learning ability than whites in some respects, e.g., the manipulation
> of abstract symbols, and if one chooses this ability as the ranking
> criterion, it would make Negroes on the average inferior to some

whites and superior to others. Suppose four-fifths of Negroes fall into the lower half of intelligence distribution. Chances are that, say, one-third of the whites will too. Hence, if intelligence is the criterion, the four-fifths of the Negro group would be no more "inferior" than the one-third of the white group. Judgments of inferiority among whites are rarely based solely on intelligence. There certainly are many people who do not rank high on intelligence tests but are, nonetheless, preferable, and preferred, to others who do. I know of no one who selects his associates—let alone friends— purely in terms of intelligence. God knows, we certainly do not elect to political office those who are most intelligent. I would conclude that whatever we may find out about Negro intelligence would not entail any judgment about general inferiority.

Buckley concluded the column with these words aimed at those who "by their dogmatic insistence on 'equality' at every level succeeded in persuading typical Americans to put far too great an emphasis on 'intelligence'":

Add to these observations the Christian point: namely that all men are equal in the truest sense of the word, and the findings of Dr. Jensen are placed in perspective. But it will take time to undo the damage brought by the ideologization of science during the reign of American liberalism.

It will take time to undo the damage! Mr. Buckley seems to have grasped the principle that historically rooted attitudes do not change quickly with time or evidence. He knows this to be true for political attitudes, that is, the liberal or conservative ideology. He knows this to be true of himself as a historically minded Catholic. If he cannot apply the principle to the nature and consequences of blackishness in our society, we should not be harsh, because it is a principle that, unless rooted firmly in self-knowledge *as well as* knowledge of the force and processes of cultural transmission, cannot be applied as a general principle.

Mr. Buckley's column was his answer to a study sponsored by the Anti-Defamation League of the B'nai Brith. It is understandable that he paid attention to the study and not to its sponsor. If he had asked why this Jewish group sponsored such a study, he would have gotten the conventional response: For obvious historical reasons, Jews are not indifferent to any form of religious, racial, or ethnic discrimination; if they do not defend *any* victim of discrimination, their own vulnerability to discrimination is increased; discrimination is a wound-producing act, the effects of which never heal in the lifetime of the victim. Mr. Buckley knows all this and knows it well. But what Mr. Buckley does not know, and what many Jews sense but would have difficulty conceptualizing and articulating, is that historically rooted discrimination (its causes and consequences) is immune to change by efforts based on our accustomed short-time perspective. I suspect that the guilt of whites in relation to blacks has less to do with acts of the past than with the intuitive feeling that black freedom is a long, long way off. I also suspect that the anger of blacks toward whites has the same source. The future is determining the present.

Why say all of this? The answer, which goes back 30 years to when I started work at the Southbury Training School, is suggested in two statements. First, if a neighbor's child had an IQ of 180 and strangled a dog to death, we would not say he did it *because* he had an IQ of 180. Second, if that neighbor's child had an IQ of 60, our prepotent response, *our act of discrimination*, would be to point to the IQ of 60 as the etiological agent without which the strangling would not have taken place.[8] This pernicious double-standard way of thinking, the essence of discrimination, is so ingrained in us that when we recognize our logical error we feel helpless about how we should proceed to think and act. Life is so much easier when we, the experts, like most other people, can "blame the victim" for what he is and "is" means that he has a low IQ, and what more do we need to know to understand him? Why complicate our thinking by confronting the fact that the act of constructing and using tests is both a reflection and determinant of cultural attitudes and deeply rooted ways of thinking which, as long as they go unrecognized, guarantee that facts will be confused with truth? Why get into these messy issues when you can talk about genetics? Of course, we should study the genetics of intelligence (high, low, black, white) but, unless I misread the history of genetics, productive theorizing about genotypes follows upon clearly described, stable phenotypes. In regard to the genetics of intelligence, we are far from the point at which we can say that we have a well-described, stable phenotype. The one thing we can say with assurance is that our concepts of intelligence are value-laden, culture- and timebound, and deficient in cross-cultural validity. *It has not even been demonstrated that the level of problem-solving behavior in nontest situations is highly correlated with the level of similar types of problem-solving processes in the standardized test situations* (Sarason and Doris, 1969). And, as I have tried to demonstrate in this article, relatively little attention has been paid either to the different ways in which attitudes toward intellectual activity are absorbed by and inculcated in us, or to how the presence or absence of these group attitudes has behind it the force of decades or centuries.

I began with a story about my father and I shall end with one. He was in the hospital recovering from an operation. I visited him on one day, and my brother visited him on the next. The nurse asked my father what work his sons did. When he told her that they were both professors of psychology, she semifacetiously asked him: "Mr. Sarason, how come *you* have two sons like *that*?" My sister reported that my father, without a moment's hesitation and with the most profound seriousness, replied: "Don't you know that smartness sometimes skips generations?" The nature and force of cultural transmission never skip generations, particularly when their ways have been finely honed over the centuries. They will not be quickly blunted. I excuse my father for not knowing this (although he may have known it). I cannot excuse this in the participants of the recent nature-nurture controversy. There is a point when one must regard the consequences of ignorance as sinful, and that point was reached for the advocates of nurture when they expected that the core of blackishness would quickly change; and it was reached by the advocates of nature when they concluded that the overall failure of compensatory programs demonstrated the significance of genetic factors on which new programs should be based. With friends like that, the blacks need not waste time worrying about enemies, a lesson Jews learned well over the centuries.

I confess to the fantasy that a century or so from now, when I and my writings had long been deposited in the ashcan of history, some strange scholar will recover this paper and ask: "He was right. Where are all of those genetically inferior blacks?"

Notes

1. From "Psychological and Cultural Factors in Mental Subnormality" by S. B. Sarason and T. Gladwin, 1958, *Genetic Psychology Monographs*, 57, pp. 145–177.
2. The data on mongolism presented by Eaton and Weil raise some intriguing questions. Although these were not explored by the authors, they illustrate the kinds of opportunities cross-cultural research in mental deficiency—i.e., in organic disorders which result in mental subnormality—can provide. The cases of mongolism reported for the Hutterites yield a prevalence rate not notably different from that found in our own culture, but the mothers of these children averaged 29 years of age at the time of delivery whereas in our culture the average age is 41. Investigators of this disorder have frequently emphasized both the advanced age of mothers and so-called reproductive exhaustion; in the case of the Hutterites the first of these explanations does not appear applicable. Should we then conclude that reproductive exhaustion is the more crucial etiological factor? Or are there perhaps differences in diet, care of mothers during pregnancy, protection against heat or cold, or any one of a multitude of other possible cultural factors we should investigate? We would not venture an answer. The point rather is that we have here a population similar (as far as we know) to ourselves in a biological sense yet differing with respect to a frequently cited aspect of mongolism and at the same time experiencing—much more uniformly than we—significantly different culturally determined relationships with their environment. The investigator with a hunch or hypothesis

regarding external factors in the etiology of mongolism would do well to inquire whether it fits the situation of the Hutterites—or any one of the hundreds of non-European cultures available for study—before accepting a proof or disproof based only on evidence from our own society.

3. From *Educational Handicap, Public Policy, and Social History* (pp. 413–418) by S. B. Sarason and J. Doris, 1979, New York: Free Press. Copyright 1979 by Free Press. Reprinted by permission.

4. From "Jewishness, Blackishness, and the Nature-Nurture Controversy" by S. B. Sarason, 1973, *American Psychologist*, 28(11), pp. 962–971. Copyright 1973 by American Psychological Association. Reprinted by permission.

5. Jewishness, at least for many Jews in our society, is independent of religiousness, a fact which many rabbis keep complaining about, because they believe that when the two are experienced as independent, it will, over time, result in the disappearance of both. That they are experienced as independent was seen during the Israeli-Arab six-day war in 1967, as thousands of American Jews who had no interest in or commitment to Judaism spontaneously gave money for the support of Israel. The generosity of support is perhaps less relevant than the anxiety they felt about the threat to the continuation of Jewishness, not to the religion of their ancestors.

6. Obviously, I cannot talk about blackishness with the affective nuance and depth of knowledge and experience that I can talk about Jewishness, nor is it necessary that I try or important that I cannot do justice to an equally complex cultural-psychological core. Sufficient for my purpose is that I pinpoint certain commonalities and differences and their significance for the nature-nurture controversy.

7. There was a time decades ago when Jews, like blacks today, were viewed as being mentally inferior because of inferior genetic endowment. I am indebted to my colleague, Edward Zigler (personal communication, 1973) for pointing out to me the anti-Jewish attitudes of the early eugenicists, particularly Galton and Pearson. In a manuscript he is preparing, Zigler states:

> Pearson continually employed genetic arguments in his efforts to stem the immigration of Polish and Russian Jews into England, arguing that they were genetically inferior to the earlier settlers of the English nation. He concluded 'Taken on the average, and regarding both sexes, this alien Jewish population is somewhat inferior physically and mentally to the native population . . .'

> The anti-Jewish attitude of the early eugenicists finally culminated in the complete bastardization of the eugenics movement in Nazi Germany, where the "final solution" of dealing with "races" of inferior genetic stock was to murder them in gas ovens. It is interesting to note that less than 50 years after Pearson's assertion of the genetic inferiority of the Jews, another distinguished Englishman, C. P. Snow, argued that in light of the large number of Jewish Nobel laureates, the Jews must be a superior people. We thus see how tenuous indeed are those assertions that a particular group is inferior or superior.

8. We blame "bad" things on a low IQ, and we explain "good" ones by a high IQ, differences in language which are the hallmark of cultural influence. It is such a part of our thinking, it all appears so self-evident, that we cannot recognize the diverse ways in which these cultural influences work, for example, their

self-fulfilling tendencies. For example, 25 years ago, Catherine Cox Miles, a long-time colleague of Lewis Terman, told me that nowhere in his write-up of his studies of "gifted" California boys and girls did Terman indicate the amount of time he spent helping his subjects get into college and graduate school, and obtain jobs. There was absolutely no chicanery involved. It was so self-evident to him that a high IQ was the cause of superior accomplishment that he could not recognize that he was an intervening variable, that is, that he, Lewis Terman, was a reflection and guardian of certain cultural values.

CHAPTER 6

Resources, Values, and Schools

The process whereby a public policy is forged and articulated is terribly complex, involving as it does diverse individuals and groups with competing ideas and values who seek to influence the substance and modes of implementation of the policy. Public policy always represents compromises, insuring that very few of the participants will be completely satisfied. It is a process that engenders passion and controversy if only because a policy identifies problems that need remediation. As often as not, it is a morality play in that the participants have very different conceptions of what is good or bad for society. In the course of my career I engaged numerous times in these dramas, always finding them both stimulating and enervating, a source of hope and disappointment. It took me decades and a lot of reflection to recognize that there was one feature to these dramas that was as fateful for the success or failure of a policy as it was unnoticed. More correctly, it was a feature that went a long way to explain why in the area of human services so many public policies either were outright failures or fell dishearteningly short of their mark. That feature was what I came to call the "myth of unlimited resources": the unreflectively accepted belief that, as a society, we had the resources to do whatever we decided needed to be done, e.g., fight a war on poverty, carry out a "real" war in Vietnam, and pursue explorations in outer space. But if the strength of that myth was apparent on the level of national policy, it was no less apparent in those thousands of instances where people were creating new settings. And when I say thousands, I am not indulging in hyperbole. In the sixties, for example, more new settings were created than ever before in history. I define a new setting as any instance in which two or more people get together in a new and sustained relationship to achieve stated goals. As I put it in my book *The Creation of Settings and the Future Societies* (Sarason, 1972):

> I have labelled this set of problems the creation of settings that provisionally may be defined as any instance in which two or more people come together in new relationships over a sustained period of time in order to achieve new goals. The most frequent instance, of course, is when two people enter into marriage. The most ambitious instance would be when people band together for the express purpose of creating a new society, and this could be a setting (such as a commune) encapsulated within a society or an effort to "destroy" the larger society and to create a new one. In between marriage and the creation of a new society there is, on the surface at least, a bewildering array of attempts to create new settings. For example, when legislation was passed to set up the Peace Corps, it literally meant that scores of new settings would have to be created: the central setting in Washington and scores of others in countries around the world. In each of these instances people would be brought together in what were for them new relationships over a sustained period of time to achieve new objectives. The Head Start Program is an example of a single piece of legislation authorizing the creation of hundreds (if not thousands) of discrete settings each one of which required that people be brought together in new relationships in order to achieve over time the objectives of the program.
>
> The creation of a new university, hospital, clinic, school, or community agency is another example of the creation of a setting. For example, when a hospital decides to set up a new intensive-care unit, or when a university launches a new department, or when a community initiates a new program for the inner city we are again dealing with the creation of a setting. And then there is the business and industrial sector, where one can safely assume that new settings are developed with a very high frequency. It may be a new company, factory, restaurant, or store—the labels, overt forms, purposes, and size may vary in the extreme but almost always they possess the defining provisional characteristics of the creation of a setting.
>
> In the past decade or so, more new settings (leaving marriage

aside) have been created than in the entire previous history of the human race. It has never been very clear to me what people mean when they say that the world is changing at an ever accelerating rate. When pressed to elaborate, most people point to many technological advances, or discoveries, or events (such as the moon walk) which have had little or no effect on their lives but which they assume someday will result in a society markedly different from the one they know. Some people point to the plethora of social problems which seem to be overwhelming in their numbers and difficulty, although on reflection they realize that these problems are far from new in our society. Certainly there seems to be a sharpened awareness of what is happening in the world, but this is no warrant for the assumption that things are changing at an ever accelerating rate. It is likely that heightened awareness of problems feeds the hope that things are changing very quickly and that the problems will soon (that is, in the foreseeable future) disappear.

I would suggest that a major factor contributing to the belief that things are changing very swiftly is the perception that one cannot keep up with the new settings created daily to cope with one or another type of problem. (pp. 1–3)

My conceptualization of the creation of settings and my emphasis on the myth of unlimited resources stemmed in the most direct sense from three experiences in mental retardation. The first was my experience at the Southbury Training School: I came there a few months after it opened, and by the time I left (four years later), the hopes and glories of that beautiful setting were already fading, and in subsequent years no trace of its revolutionary origins were left. The second experience was in my active participation in the planning and creating of the New Haven Regional Center and affiliating the Yale Psycho-Educational Clinic with it during its early years. Indeed, the creation of that clinic (Sarason et al., 1966) was in part influenced by the fact that there would be a regional center in New Haven. The third experience in time, and in many ways the most intensive and intellectually productive, was in the planning, creating, and operation of the Central Connecticut Regional Center in Meriden (Sarason et al., 1972). Why these settings fell far short of their mark is a very long and complicated story and far beyond the scope of this book. But one fragment of that story may help explain why I came to see the myth of unlimited resources as one of the basic factors almost guaranteeing that human services will find themselves on a treadmill effectively limiting accomplishment of their goals.

The year before the New Haven Regional Center was to open, its core administrative staff was housed at our clinic. Facing us was the fact that there was already an "emergency waiting list," i.e., individuals who, so to speak, should have been admitted yesterday. Could we be of any help to these families in the meantime? If we established contact with them now could we plan better for their future admission and planning? So, we husbanded our limited resources and began to visit these families. What we quickly found out was that in almost every case the family needed help that would discernibly lighten its burden and, in a number of instances, make institutionalization unnecessary. In fact, there were many instances where the family would have preferred to keep the retarded individual if services to the family in its home were provided. And we attempted to do just that by "collecting" a heterogeneous assortment of people: firemen, policemen, clergy, Yale students, senior citizens, etc. What we found out was an instance of reinventing the wheel because, as Yepsen and Cianci (1946) had found earlier, a number of families no longer wanted to institutionalize their retarded members. These experiences explain why, at a meeting a week before the New Haven Regional Center opened, everyone agreed that not only had we seen our best days but that we did not need the center! We already saw clearly that once the center opened its door, it would not have the resources to maintain its beds and to work with families to prevent the need for residential care. Our resources were and would continue to be limited, and we would not be able to fulfill the major goal of the regional center concept: to help families and community agencies keep the retarded individual in his or her natural setting. The proponents of the concept (including myself) never really examined their hopes in relation to the fact that resources would inevitably be limited, that that inescapable fact meant that choices had to be made. There would not be sufficient resources to do A, B, C, and D equally well, i.e., to do justice to each. The fact of limited resources also required the examination of how resources were being defined. Who is a resource for what or for whom? The experience I am describing confirmed something that for years I was dimly aware of and did not want to face: the disease of professionalism. Very briefly put: Professionals define a problem in a way so as to require more professionals, thus rendering the problem utterly unsolvable, further aggravating the consequences of limited resources. In the flush of planning for and creating a new setting—accompanied as that is by visions of a rosy future, missionary zeal, a controllable world, and of obstacles that will crumble before good ideas and personal resolve—the brute fact of limited resources and its consequences is never confronted and the necessity for redefining resources is never recognized. But, as the process of creating a setting proceeds, especially as that setting becomes operational, the myth of unlimited resources is exposed for what it is, leading to what I call "organizational craziness." *The ending of this fragment is that when the opportunity to plan for and create the Central Connecticut Regional Center arose, we (the clinic and the newly appointed superintendent) petitioned that the center not be built.* We could use its building fund and its proposed operating budget in more productive ways than to put up buildings and support the usual administrative-professional-aide pattern of staffing. Put in another way, we could use our limited resources to garner additional and diverse resources in the community, unimprisoning ourselves from the traditional way of defining resources. We were not suggesting that we had a way of overcoming the consequences of limited resources, but rather that by redefining people as resources in regard to the problems of families, we could render more practical help to more individuals and families than would otherwise be the case. We were not anti-professional but rather we were pleading for the opportunity to deal with the fact of limited resources in new ways. Our petition was denied. The center was built, the staffing pattern predetermined (elsewhere, i.e., in the state capital) along familiar lines, and a lot of people ended up frustrated and disillusioned.

I regard *The Creation of Settings and the Future Societies* as the most distinctive book I have written. That the ideas in that book emerged largely from my involvement in the field of mental retardation is not the reason I reprint below Chapters 5 and 6 from that book. The major reason is that the substance of that book deals with assumptions and consequences that anyone in any human services setting must come to recognize. In the past two decades, the rate of creation of new settings for the mentally retarded—and the rate with which old settings are the objects of change—have dramatically increased. Quantity, of course, tells nothing about quality, a truism that is no more or less true in the field of mental retardation than it is in other areas of human service. Too frequently, however, the advocates for the mentally retarded emphasize how the needs of the mentally retarded differ from those of other handicapped groups. Of course there are differences, but I would argue that there have been and are certain assumptions common to the process whereby any helping service is created. For too long the field of mental retardation has viewed itself, and has been viewed by the society at large, as "special." The two chapters that follow attempt to alter (not negate) that view.

Myth of Unlimited Resources [1]

The myth of unlimited (or even adequate) resources has its general and specific aspects. The general aspect is seen in the belief that our society is capable of training enough professional people to render the quantity and quality of service that people are considered to require. For example, during World War II planning began for the development of mental health services which were going to be needed by returning veterans. Never before had the government been faced with the planning of personal services on such a vast scale. All kinds of hospitals and clinics would have to be built. It was obvious that mental health professionals would have to be trained in very large numbers and that in order to do so the government would have to underwrite financially the relevant university departments. Several guiding assumptions were basic to the planning. First, psychotherapeutic techniques of various sorts were the most effective means for dealing with the problems of individuals—psychotherapy, so to speak, was the mental aspirin to be dispensed en masse. Second, the chief dispenser of the mental aspirin was the psychiatrist, with the clinical psychologist and social worker performing primarily other, related functions peculiar to their traditions and training. Third, mental health professionals could be trained in numbers sufficient to make a discernible and effective dent in the size of the problem. (I would emphasize that all of this planning was only in relation to the veteran population which, although staggering enough, was insignificant in comparison to the demand which could be anticipated in the general population.) So we had the situation of national resolve and billions of dollars to do justice to the veterans. As important as what did happen is that it was all quite predictable that personnel could not be trained in numbers necessary to meet objectives. Even early on when it became quite clear that viewing psychotherapy as in the medical domain was an inexcusable indulgence of professional preciousness, and clinical psychologists and psychiatric social workers were thrown into the breach, the disparity between defined need and available service was in no way lessened—particularly as the demand for mental health services by nonveterans mushroomed. Other branches of the government got into the well heeled act in order to ensure that the mental aspirin would become generally available. Crash programs to train psychotherapists sprang up almost monthly. But the programs began to crash in unexpected ways, in part hastened in the late fifties by the reports of the Joint Commission on Mental Health, particularly the work of George Albee (1959, 1968a, 1968b). As he then and since has pointed out (among other things), our resources were far too limited to do the job in the ways the problem was conceived. Disillusionment set in both in the government and in the field. Disillusionment turned into chagrin and guilt when events in the larger society made it quite clear that blacks and poor people were not getting and could not purchase the aspirin. (It was no balm to the blacks and the poor to be told that purchasing a therapist's time was by no means easy even if one were rich and white.)

Let us take another example. One of the most frequent fantasies in which teachers indulge—and it is by no means restricted to teachers—is how enjoyable life in a classroom could be if class size were discernibly decreased. Like the heavens of religions, reduced class size is a teacher's ultimate reward in comparison to which inadequate salaries pale in significance. The reason I label this a fantasy is not only because it is incapable of fulfillment but because those who hold it tend to be unaware that it is unrealistic. Let us put it this way: if Congress in its infinite wisdom were to pass legislation making it financially possible to cut class size in half, the legislation could not be implemented. It is conceivable that over a period of a decade the necessary physical plant could be built—our society has rarely failed in crash programs of a technological nature. What would be impossible would be to train teachers and other educational specialists in the numbers necessary to implement the legislation. Our centers of training simply cannot train discernibly more people than they are now doing. In fact, our centers of training are quite aware that they are not now doing the quality job that is required in terms of selection of students and quality level of faculty. These centers cannot, nor will they, discernibly increase the numbers being trained. In short, the goal of dramatically reducing class size is far from a financial problem.

Essentially, the general belief—general because of the number of people who hold it and because of the number of social problems which give rise to it—is that by an act of national will or resolve, accompanied of course by appropriately sized expenditures we can train as many people as are necessary to meet a particular problem, if not all problems. Those who assume that there are really no justifiable bars to quantitative expansion also assume that qualitative improvement of existing and future personnel can be accomplished at the same time. The belief characterizes the thinking of many individuals who are starting new settings, particularly when seemingly large sums of money are available. The belief is that by virtue of money one will be able to hire enough people to provide services to eligible people in the best way those services should be rendered. (Another part of this belief is that one will be able to hire people all of whom will be equally competent or effective.) I have never known a setting, old or relatively new, which did not complain that it had inadequate numbers to do the job in the way it was conceived best to do. I have known many individuals who never entertained the idea that they would not be able to provide services to the number of people eligible for them. The complaint about inadequate number of staff is practically never seen as a possible function of how the setting was conceived but rather as (and only as) the indifference of society. As we shall see later, it is only in very recent years that there is evidence that the issue is at least being raised, and with the consequence of sharp controversy centering on heretofore implicit values and beliefs.

The extent of the discrepancy between intent and accomplishment is in large part a function of how one defines the service and the criteria of its quality. In practice, the higher the criteria of quality, the fewer people who meet them, and the longer the period of their training—a set of correlated factors which automatically limits resources even more. Defining the service in terms of highly specialized training and knowledge is usually viewed as an obvious professional virtue at the same time that its unavailability to most people who need it is viewed as a social sin. The sense of virtue and sin can exist side by side in the same individual because the virtue is seen as a characteristic of the individual while the sin is a reflection of society; that is, society must change by making it possible for many more people to obtain the specialized training, if society will only do so! There is little or no willingness to question how the service is being defined, the validity of the assumed degree of relationship between training and competence, and the justification of a situation which makes a service unavailable to many people. To ask these questions is to ask how one justifies the service (and the setting), and that involves explicating values and confronting the possibility of changing them. The reason that for decades there was little questioning of the adequacy of settings dealing with the poverty and other minority groups was that the values on which these settings rested were accepted and unscrutinized. It was not until the events in the larger society forced the question of values into the open that people began to think differently about resources, services, and settings (Sarason, Levine, Goldenberg, Cherlin, and Bennett, 1966; Levine and Levine, 1970; Goldenberg, 1971).

Most of us are aware that there is a limit to natural resources. "Scarcity of nature" is a fact and concept without which the field of economics would not exist.

> Man, not nature is the source of most of our economic problems, at least above the level of subsistence. To be sure, the economic problem itself—that is, the need to struggle for existence—derives ultimately from the scarcity of nature. If there were no scarcity, goods would be as free as air, and economics—at least in one sense of the word—would cease to exist as a social preoccupation.
>
> And yet if the scarcity of nature sets the stage for the economic problem, it does not impose the only strictures against which men must struggle. For scarcity, as a felt condition, is not solely the fault of nature. If Americans today, for instance, were content to live at the level of Mexican peasants, all of our material wants could be fully satisfied with but an hour or two of daily labor. We would experience little or no scarcity, and our economic problems would virtually disappear. Instead, we find in America—and indeed in all industrial societies—that as the ability to increase nature's yield has risen, so has the reach of human wants. In fact, in societies such as ours, where relative social status is importantly connected with the possession of material goods, we often find that "scarcity" as a psychological experience and goad becomes more pronounced as we grow wealthier: our desires to possess the fruits of nature race out ahead of our mounting ability to produce goods.
>
> Thus the "wants" that nature must satisfy are by no means fixed. But for that matter, nature's yield itself is not a constant. It varies over a wide range, depending on the social application of hu-

man energy and skill. Scarcity is therefore not attributable to nature alone but to "human nature" as well; and economics is ultimately concerned not merely with the stinginess of the physical environment, but equally with the appetite of the human being and the productive capability of the community. (Heilbroner, 1968, p. 5)

There is no reason to believe that scarcity of human resources is less a fact and problem than that of the scarcity of nature. And yet when one observes the creation of settings devoted to direct human service (schools, hospitals, clinics, colleges, universities, institutions for the so-called mentally ill or the mentally retarded, the aged, and delinquents, new societies, and the plethora of programs for poverty groups) the myth of unlimited or even adequate resources rather than the realities of scarcity dominates thinking. One should not expect it to be otherwise because to face the reality of scarcity forces one to examine alternatives which conflict with cherished values.

Origins

The origins of the myth are no less complex than its contents. The reader will recall that the decision to create a setting usually reflects dissatisfaction with an existing state of affairs which, at times, may best be characterized as scandalous. Hardly a year goes by without the appearance of books, congressional reports, and newspaper articles exposing the horrors of ghetto schools, homes for the aged, institutions for the retarded, reformatories, prisons, state hospitals, city hospitals, and sundry other types of "humane" institutions. The result is indignation and frustration and, not infrequently, a sincere resolve not only to change what exists but to create new settings which will not be contaminated or constricted by a sorry history. The new setting is a response to an inadequacy as well as to a felt need, and it is powered by money, resolve and hope. Something "bad" exists, sin has been uncovered, everyone wallows in virtue, and something "good" will be created. It is a context of movement and social pressure in which having some, or more, or even a lot of resources (such as money and people) is subtly transformed into the myth that one has enough resources. It is not a context conducive to questioning the assumption that money can purchase the *quantity* of the types of people the setting is deemed to require, or the assumption that what was wrong with the old setting was largely due to too few of the right kind of personnel. Both assumptions are usually grossly invalid. To question these assumptions is to confront the possibility that the task at hand is not solvable in the conventional way—a possibility as upsetting as the conditions giving rise to the new setting.

Some of the clearest examples of the adverse effects of the myth can be seen in those instances where those who were creating something new had something close to unlimited power. I refer again to the Russian and Cuban revolutions and to Lenin's and Castro's explicit descriptions of their mistake in assuming that political power can develop and harness human resources adequate to perform the services they wanted their citizens to have. It is too simple to attribute the admitted mistake to revolutionary fervor and enthusiasm, although there is no doubt that as these revolutionary movements picked up momentum, and as enthusiasm and hope escalated with the achievement of political power, the realities of scarcity (material and human) had no way of coming to the fore. The fact is that when one examines the publications of these and other revolutionaries written long before achieving power was a realistic possibility, the problem of scarcity is hardly discussed.

For our present purposes it is really not necessary that the reader agree with what I have said about the myth of unlimited or even adequate resources. I am fully aware how strong the belief is in all of us that where there is a will there is a way, and I am not advocating that this cliché be completely abandoned or denying that it is without validity. But there is a vast difference between viewing it as a saying and as a law having inevitable consequences. What the skeptical reader must confront and explain, however, are the following observations which I shall put in the form of questions. Why is it that in the earliest phases of the creation of a setting there tends to be little or no concern with the possibility that known available resources will not be adequate to rendering the quantity or quality of service to those who are eligible for it? Why is it that shortly after the setting is functional, concern with the problem markedly increases and becomes one of its major complaints? Why is competition for available resources one of the major sources of division among the core group in the setting? Why does each core member proceed as if there is no doubt that resources are indeed unlimited? These questions require explanation even if one does not assume that there are always limited resources.

Implicit Factors

The strength and perpetuation of the myth are only partly comprehensible in terms of the clamor and enthusiasm surrounding the sense of mission, the desire to right wrongs, and the sense of superiority stemming in part from the belief that what was wrong in the past inhered in adequate numbers and quality of personnel. Precisely because these factors are pretty much out in the open and accompany or lead to actions deemed socially desirable, they effectively distract attention away from other factors, implicit but no less part of the picture.

I can illustrate this point by describing what happened a decade or so ago when it became clear that the discrepancy between the numbers who seemed to need psychotherapeutic help and the number of professionals who could render such a service was growing increasingly large and was essentially unsolvable. Within the mental health professions there had been a growing number of individuals urging change, and from without there was even stronger pressure to change the pattern of traditional services so that they were not solely obtainable by the affluent segments of society. Up to this point the federal government had been pouring large sums of money into centers of training, with no discernible effect on the size of the discrepancy that the funding was supposed to reduce. When the federal government changed its emphasis, it was accompanied by a good deal of fanfare and (some thought) by a good deal of money. Let us listen to what President Kennedy said (what some mental health professionals wrote for him) in his special message in 1963 announcing the new comprehensive community mental health center program which meant that many new settings would be created. I present his message in some detail, as well as the enabling legislation, in order to provide the reader a basis independently to judge the extent of the variety of new services the new settings would provide and the increased number of people who would receive them. It also should help the reader judge my opinion that rarely in a situation of recognized scarcity was so much promised to so many.

> I propose a national mental health program to assist in the inauguration of a wholly new emphasis and approach to care for the mentally ill. This approach relies primarily upon the new knowledge and new drugs acquired and developed in recent years which make it possible for most of the mentally ill to be successfully and quickly treated in their own communities and returned to a useful place in society.

> These breakthroughs have rendered obsolete the traditional methods of treatment which imposed upon the mentally ill a social quarantine, a prolonged or permanent confinement in huge, unhappy mental hospitals where they were out of sight and forgotten. I am not unappreciative of the efforts undertaken by many states to improve conditions in these hospitals, or the dedicated work of many hospital staff members. But their task has been staggering and the results too often dismal, as the comprehensive study by the Joint Commission on Mental Illness and Health pointed out in 1961.

> ***Comprehensive Community Mental Health Centers***   Central to the new mental health program is comprehensive community care. Merely pouring federal funds into a continuation of the outmoded type of institutional care which now prevails would make little difference. We need a new type of health facility, one which

will return mental health care to the mainstream of American medicine, and at the same time upgrade mental health services. I recommend, therefore, that the Congress (1) authorize grants to the states for the construction of comprehensive community mental health centers, beginning in fiscal year 1965, with the federal government providing 45 to 75 percent of the project cost; (2) authorize short-term project grants for the initial staffing costs of comprehensive community mental health centers, with the federal government providing up to 75 percent of the cost in the early months, on a gradually declining basis, terminating such support for a project within slightly over four years; and (3) to facilitate the preparation of community plans for these new facilities as a necessary preliminary to any construction or staffing assistance, appropriate $4.2 million for planning grants under the National Institute of Mental Health. These planning funds, which would be in addition to a similar amount appropriated for fiscal year 1963, have been included in my proposed 1964 budget.

While the essential concept of the comprehensive community mental health center is new, the separate elements which would be combined in it are presently found in many communities: diagnostic and evaluation services, emergency psychiatric units, outpatient services, inpatient services, day and night care, foster home care, rehabilitation, consultative services to other community agencies, and mental health information and education.

These centers will focus on community resources and provide better community facilities for all aspects of mental health care. Prevention as well as treatment will be a major activity. Located in the patient's own environment and community, the center would make possible a better understanding of his needs, a more cordial atmosphere for his recovery, and a continuum of treatment. As his needs change, the patient could move without delay or difficulty to different services—from diagnosis, to cure, to rehabilitation—without need to transfer to different institutions located in different communities.

A comprehensive community mental health center in receipt of federal aid may be sponsored through a variety of local organizational arrangements. Construction can follow the successful Hill-Burton pattern, under which the federal government matches public or voluntary non-profit funds. Ideally, the center could be located at an appropriate community general hospital, many of which already have psychiatric units. In such instances, additional services and facilities could be added—either all at once or in several stages—to fill out the comprehensive program. In some instances, an existing outpatient psychiatric clinic might form the nucleus of such a center, its work expanded and integrated with other services in the community. Centers could also function effectively under a variety of other auspices: as affiliates of state mental hospitals, under state or local governments, or under voluntary nonprofit sponsorship.

Private physicians, including general practitioners, psychiatrists, and other medical specialists, would all be able to participate directly and cooperatively in the work of the center. For the first time, a large proportion of our private practitioners will have the opportunity to treat their patients in a mental health facility served by an auxiliary professional staff that is directly and quickly available for outpatient and inpatient care.

Research and Manpower Although we embark on a major national action program for mental health, there is still much more we need to know. We must not relax our effort to push back the frontiers of knowledge in basic and applied research into the mental processes, in therapy, and in other phases of research with a bearing upon mental illness. More needs to be done also to translate research findings into improved practices. I recommend an explanation of clinical, laboratory, and field research in mental illness and mental health.

Availability of trained manpower is a major factor in the determination of how fast we can expand our research and expand our new action program in the mental health field. At present manpower shortages exist in virtually all of the key professional and auxiliary personnel categories—psychiatrists, clinical psychologists, social workers, and psychiatric nurses. To achieve success, the current supply of professional manpower in these fields must be sharply increased—from about 45,000 in 1960 to approximately 85,000 by 1970. To help move toward this goal I recommend the appropriation of $66 million for training of personnel, an increase of $17 million over the current fiscal year.

I have, in addition, directed that the Manpower Development and Training Act be used to assist in the training of psychiatric aides and other auxiliary personnel for employment in mental institutions and community centers.

Success of these specialized training programs, however, requires that they be undergirded by basic training programs. It is essential to the success of our new national mental health program that Congress enact legislation authorizing aid to train more physicians and related health personnel. I will discuss this measure at greater length in the message on health which I will send to Congress shortly.

And now let us read how the Community Mental Health Centers Act of 1963 (Title II, Public Law, 88-164) defined adequate services:

(a) Adequate services. The state plan shall provide for the following elements of service which are necessary to provide adequate mental health services for persons residing in the state, which shall constitute the elements of comprehensive mental health services: (1) inpatient services; (2) outpatient services; (3) partial hospitalization services, such as day care, night care, and weekend care; (4) emergency services twenty-four hours per day must be available within at least one of the first three services listed above; (5) consultation and education services available to community agencies and professional personnel; (6) diagnostic services; (7) rehabilitative services, including vocational and educational programs; (8) precare and aftercare services in the community, including foster home placement, home visiting and half-way houses; (9) training; (10) research and evaluation.

(b) Adequate facilities. (1) Provision of services. Based on comprehensive mental health planning, the state plan shall provide for adequate community mental health facilities for the provision of programs of comprehensive mental health services to all persons residing in the state and for furnishing such services to persons unable to pay therefor, taking into account the population necessary to maintain and operate efficient facilities and the financial resources available therefor. (2) Accessibility of services. The state plan shall provide that every community mental health facility shall: (i) serve a population of not less than 75,000 and not more than 200,000 persons, except that the Surgeon General may, in particular cases, permit modifications of this population range if he finds that such modifications will not impair the effectiveness of the services to be provided; (ii) be so located as to be near and readily accessible to the community and population to be served, taking into account both political and geographical boundaries; (iii) provide a community service; and (iv) provide needed services for persons unable to pay therefor.

(c) Personnel administration. A system of personnel administration on a merit basis shall be established and maintained with respect to the personnel employed in the administration of the state plan. Such a system shall include provision for: (1) impartial administration of the merit system; (2) operation on the basis of published rules or regulations; (3) classification of all positions on the basis of duties and responsibilities and establishment of qualifications necessary for the satisfactory performance of such duties and responsibilities; (4) establishment of compensation schedules adjusted to the responsibility and difficulty of work; (5) selection of permanent appointees on the basis of examinations and so conducted as to afford all qualified applicants opportunity to compete; (6) advancement on the basis of capacity and meritorious service; and (7) tenure of permanent employees.

I am not concerned here that the law is the equivalent of making sure that there is a chicken in every pot and at least one car in every garage. Nor will I elaborate on the fervor, enthusiasm, and excitement which were experienced in certain segments of the mental health professions or on their sense of victory over traditional thinking and patterns of service. And I shall not attempt to describe how these new centers, created as most of them were out of an existing organization of settings (such as departments of psychiatry, hospitals), in every respect confirm what I have already discussed about the creation of settings. The significance of the quotation is in three assumptions. First, the solution of the problem requires certain kinds of personnel. Second, these personnel are specialists. Third, these personnel, already in fantastic short supply, can be trained in numbers adequate to a fantastic increase in range of services. (After all, what seemed to be a lot of money was going to be available). Yes, new knowledge would be necessary and research was not going to be left out of the picture. But when all is said and done the fact remains that what was most clear was that the problem was being defined in a way which dictated a solution requiring certain kinds and quantity of personnel. It could not be otherwise because the problem and the solution were formulated by these kinds of personnel. It would have been a distinctive page in human history if these professions had formulated the problem and solution in a way which would not have given them the central role.

Some readers will be troubled and will be asking the question: Do not people with "mental health problems" require help from those with very special knowledge and training? Are you suggesting that anyone (such as a surgeon, barber, taxi driver) can render help? These questions effectively obscure the problem of values because they rest on the assumption that adequate specialized resources exist or can be developed. If this assumption is invalid, as has been perfectly clear for a long time, one is confronted with the should and ought kind of question: How should one decide who gets the service? How do we justify providing nothing to those who are deemed to need it? Do we have an obligation to say that the problem is unsolvable as defined? Should we reformulate the problem (are there ways of reformulating it) so that more people will get more help? Does the value we attach to specialization conflict with the value (if one holds it) that health service is a right and not a privilege?

The reader who believes that adequate resources exist or can be developed should consult Albee (1959, 1968a, 1968b) and Matarazzo who, in 1971, summed it up: "The unfolding of this drama for the field of psychology is representative. First there was Albee's 1959 tradition-shattering analysis of the current and projected manpower problem for psychology as well as for psychiatry, social work, and nursing. His perceptive university resources revealed for the United States Congress, the core professions, and our educational institutions of higher learning that demand would continue to outdistance supply at an accelerated rate. Today, over a decade later, more current analyses of the same problem for psychology and, in some instances, the other three professions by Albee, Arnhoff, Boneau, and others have shown that the worst of Albee's 1959 projections are coming to pass."

As soon as one accepts the limitation of resources two things tend to happen: one confronts the contexts of one's values, and the formulation of the problem and its solutions take on different forms.

> Albee eloquently has affirmed and reaffirmed the fact that a shocking number of this country's state mental hospitals and psychiatric clinics did not have even a single psychiatrist on their full-time staff. I feel certain that most readers, much as I did, momentarily recoiled at this startling revelation by Albee but soon left it to pursue other issues. From hindsight now, it is clear that some of the professional and allied professional persons who worked in these hospitals and clinics, and select individuals in many local communities, did not merely recoil. Rather, impressive evidence is now at hand that although uncoordinated and at first largely unrecognized outside their own community, refreshing, innovative, and highly effective solutions were being employed in a large number of state hospitals, clinics, and other mental health facilities. These local solutions utilized no single manpower group but rather, as available in its own community, took advantage of a surprisingly heterogeneous set of heretofore neglected segments of the manpower pool making up its own local citizenry. . . . It is now becoming clear that beginning a decade ago, the occasional single physician, nurse, psychologist, or social worker practitioner in an isolated state hospital, finding himself solely responsible for a whole hospital, or two or three wards, was freed to a burst of innovative creativity by the concept of the therapeutic community with its key concept that each employee of the mental hospital was potentially a therapeutic agent. Almost overnight, and merely by a change in role definition and assigned responsibilities, such an administrator could transform his hospital from one-physician or no-physician statistic in Albee's actuarially factual table, to a hospital with dozens of professionally trained, actively working subprofessionals requiring only modest supervision and the barest numbers of hours of additional training. (Matarazzo, 1971, p. 365)

Necessity is sometimes the mother of invention and sometimes the spur to a different set of values. Unfortunately, the federal legislation of 1963 defined necessity in a way which reinvented failure.

Consequences

In choosing education or mental health as illustrative problems it was not my aim to convince the reader that it is axiomatic that human resources are always limited. My aims were more modest and they were to suggest (a) that for the most important problems of society for the solution of which new settings are being created at an ever-accelerating rate, there is a serious limitation of human resources; (b) that the seriousness of the limitation is in part a function of how the problem is defined; (c) that confronting the limitation of resources involves one in the problem of priorities and distribution, that is, the values by which they will be established; and (d) that in the context of creating a new setting the limitation of resources tends not only to be denied but to be replaced by the myth of unlimited or adequate resources.

The consequences of avoiding or denying the problem of resources depend in part on when and how the problem is confronted—and reality ensures that they will be confronted. It makes a difference whether early on the leader sees the problem, or it is forced on him by the demands of the core group for resources, or, as is increasingly the case, outside groups militantly expose the inadequacies of the setting's resources for the task at hand. In the instance where the leader begins truly to comprehend the nature and extent of the problem he is faced with a number of questions among which are whether or not to inform his core group, how much to inform, how to adapt to the reality, and how much the relevant outside world should be told, and when and how. It is precisely because comprehension of the problem brings in its wake the perception of the possibility of failure (in varying degrees) that the leader has difficulty making the problem public. The phenomenology of the leader will be taken up later in this book, but what needs to be said here is that the usual way in which the problem is experienced and handled by the leader tends to affect negatively his relations with his core group, to exacerbate the competition for resources among the core group, to set the stage for other settings and groups to raise the issue of competence and honesty, and to reinforce the leader's sense of aloneness.

Independent of the leader, the core group members at some point perceive the problem, and the consequences are fairly predictable: each becomes more concerned with the growth of his piece of the action; conflicts stemming from other sources (such as personality) are heightened or created; and not only do members begin to question the purposes of the setting but they become aware of sharp differences in the realm of values—the bases for justifying what is or is not important and how things should be done.

Another consequence of the recognition of the problem is as significant as it is subtle, and that is an increasing emphasis on production or results. The greater the perceived discrepancy between resources and

goals, the more the goals of the setting subtly become transformed or re-
formulated in ways productive of data proving that the setting is a success. The clearest examples of this I have seen over the years have been in
newly created direct service settings (public and private schools, clinics,
health centers) a major aim of which initially was to individualize service
or to create an atmosphere in which the quality of social relationships
and social learning were more important than the number of individuals
provided service. In the case of schools this took the form of criticizing
the value and relevance of measuring children's progress by standardized
achievement tests and valuing instead how children learned to live and
learn with each other without the pressures of meeting criteria predetermined by others. It all sounded refreshingly different. But then in almost
every instance a subtle transformation in the criteria of success began to
occur so that what had been criticized became a cherished standard of
performance. The word *subtle* has to be qualified because to some people
in the settings the transformation was blatant and they left. I am not contending that the transformation of goals was due to the failure to face the
problem of limited resources. I am contending that the failure to face
the problem realistically was an important ingredient contributing to
heightening pressures and conflicts stemming from other sources. What
is noteworthy and discouraging about the usual explanation of how
these transformations came about is that it does not address itself to how
the failure initially to deal with the problem of limited resources inter-
acted with other problems. One of the most important arguments of the
usual explanation, formulated after failure (partial or complete), is that
forces outside the setting denied it the resources it needed. The implication is that these forces had available unlimited or adequate resources,
and so we are back where we started.

Some colleagues and I had the opportunity to witness the creation
of what most people considered the most innovative community-action
program in this country, a program antedating in certain respects the
federal one. We have described in detail the context in which this setting
was born, emphasizing its explicit goal of delivering new services in new
and controversial ways (Sarason et al., 1966; Goldenberg, 1971). The program had bold and imaginative leadership, strong political support, and
several millions of dollars of foundation support. Once federal money became available, this program was, by virtue of experience and ideas, in a
position to get a good deal of it, proportionately more than any other
such program. Enthusiasm, sense of mission and superiority, and a vision of uninterrupted progress were among its more obvious characteristics. More subtle, however, was the impression its reports and news re-
leases created that this truly exciting setting was adequate to meet its
goals. Although in one part of their heads the leaders knew otherwise,
this was never reflected in any central way in their messages to the community. In our description and evaluation of the setting, published in

1966 but written in 1964–1965, two years after its beginnings, we emphasized the possible adverse consequences of the failure to deal realistically
with the obvious fact that it did not, nor would it have, the resources to
achieve its goals. At that time our concern was less for the sensibilities of
the community than for what was beginning to happen in the setting itself. What was happening was no less than an emphasis on numbers as
a criterion of success. How many clients were entered into new job-
training programs began to be more important than whether or not the
programs were adequate or appropriate. How many young people were
returned to high school was given more play than the number who sub-
sequently dropped out or the number who never should have been returned. The multiplication of new programs (and in those days they mul-
tiplied) took on far greater significance than concern for the inadequacies
of existing ones. Whereas the ethos initially was to avoid the mistakes and
dilemmas of the traditional social agency—its emphasis on professionalism and "psychologizing," as well as its timidity in relation to social action—in subtle ways it began to resemble what it wanted to avoid. Many
within the setting were quite aware of what was happening and the departure of the leaders accelerated the transformation.

I repeat: I am not saying that what happened was caused by the
failure to confront the realities of limited resources. It was far more complicated than that. But there is no doubt that as the leaders became
aware of the problem the pressure to do and get more mounted, the *basis*
for justifying doing and getting more resulted increasingly in a game of
numbers, morale plummeted, and competition within the setting for
available resources skyrocketed. It was only as the war on poverty de-
escalated into a skirmish that the leaders of the setting could state publicly in the most unequivocal way that the resources originally available
to them had been woefully inadequate and that even if funding had been
maintained on the previous level its goals could not have been reached.
And this brings us to still another myth which interacts with and is related to the myth of unlimited or adequate resources and that is that one
can count on the future as both untroubled and predictable—just like in
the literary utopias. Avoiding the problem of unlimited resources and
holding to the belief in a predictable future are among the most potent
factors influencing the creation and development of a setting, and their
potency is increased in proportion to the extent that they are implicit or
unverbalized.

The choice and use of human resources always partially rest on
value judgments which, for the most part, are confused with the dictates
of reality. It usually requires some drastic social events and changes for
us to become aware that the usual ways in which human resources have
been viewed and allocated were based on "shoulds" and "oughts" not
contained in nature or given by divine revelation. The great economic depression of the thirties is a particularly clear example of how a social ca-

tastrophe brought into question the nature and appropriateness of values heretofore viewed as natural and good. Before the Depression it was unthinkable to most people that an employed person *should* be provided with some means of support, or that a person *should* be protected against dependence in old age, or that the government *should* in any formal way assume any responsibility for resolving conflicts between labor and management. Obviously, these were not unthinkable ideas; rather it was that they were seen as socially and morally *wrong*. "Separate but equal" schools were accepted for a long time, as were child labor and discrimination on religious, ethnic, and sexual grounds. The conflicts surrounding changes in these practices had several sources, and deeply held values were certainly not the least of them. When with Ciceronian regularity the American Medical Association would sanctify the concept of the unregulated, private practitioner, it was a mistake to view it only as a reflection of economic self-interest and to fail to see that beyond economics was a set of values about what was good or bad in medical care. Professional imperialism, like the national variety, has economic underpinnings but its rallying points are almost always sincerely held statements of unalloyed virtue. The disbeliever may see connections between the economic and value structures, but that is no secure basis for assuming that the believer does.

Choosing and allocating human resources are some of the earliest and most important tasks in the creation of a setting. How these tasks inevitably reflect certain values, how the definition of the purposes of a setting illuminates these values, and how bypassing these issues helps defeat the purposes of a setting will become more clear in the next chapter where case material will be presented.

Resources and Values[2]

In this chapter I shall describe and discuss several settings in order to clarify further the relationships among the setting's definition of its task, its view of resources, and underlying values. The recognition that there is a need and the decision to create a setting to meet that need usually assume that the shape of the solution is known and in a way so that issues of values and resources need not be posed and clarified. That is why settings serving the same kinds of populations are amazingly similar. Their underlying values and view of resources are so similar that despite differences in rhetoric and architecture their atmosphere and practices are as predictable as those of a supermarket. From one era to another one can see marked changes in some types of settings and this is due as much to the obvious fact that the values of the society have changed as it is to new knowledge, and the latter generally is a function of the former. In one state the statute giving force to its juvenile court says, "As far as practicable, they (children seven to seventeen) shall be treated, not as criminals, but as children in need of aid, encouragement and guidance. Proceedings against children . . . shall not be deemed criminal proceedings." These children were not always viewed in this way. In earlier times their actions were judged by a different scale of values that dictated a different kind of solution. Whereas in earlier times it was considered "good and right" to hold these children responsible for their actions and to utilize punishment as the chief ingredient of the solution, these same actions today are viewed quite differently, with the result that the solution (aid, encouragement, and guidance) is of a different order and requires different kinds of human resources (such as psychiatrists, social workers, psychologists). Different theories of human behavior are involved but, as Levine and Levine (1970) so beautifully describe, these different theories are not unrelated to changing forces and values in the larger society. The current definition of the problem requires types and quantities of resources that were, and will be in shortest supply, which goes a long way to explaining why juvenile courts have been failures.

In describing those settings I shall be emphasizing how the process of defining a setting's task or goals is related to one's view of resources and at the same time that all of this reflects some basic values. This emphasis inevitably distorts the picture one gains of these settings but in each instance much fuller descriptions are available elsewhere.

Maximum Use of Resources

The reasons for starting the Yale Psycho-Educational Clinic were no less varied and complex than any other instance of motivation and action, but several things were quite clear and they are contained in the following propositions: (1) The mental health professions were oriented primarily to dealing with individuals who presented themselves (or in the case of children were presented by others) as having personal problems. (2) These problems were conceptualized in ways that required "treatment" by highly trained specialists. (3) The disparity between the number rendering and needing service was of a magnitude that was unresolvable. (4) Those who obtained service were almost exclusively white and middle class, and they represented a small fraction of white, middle-class people who wanted the service. (5) The most notable exception to all of this was our public "mental hospitals," where treatment as an individual human being was notable by its absence.

Today, it is hard for anyone to read these statements without spontaneously and unreflectively passing judgment: the situation is bad, sad, and wrong. Although these statements are and have always been true (in modern times), they did not always elicit strong negative feelings, within or without the professions. That the reaction is different today is due to the fact that both within and without the professions there has been growing awareness of the inequities in the distribution of services, an awareness that is explainable only on the basis of the value that color and money should not determine eligibility for service. In the previous chapter I described the actions and programs that were spurred by considerations of equity. Simply put: the problem continued to be defined in a way that required dependence on certain kinds of human resources which, given the increased scope of the proposed services, could only increase the disparity between the numbers rendering and needing service—and all of this was taking place before the dimensions of the drug problem were recognized.

What conclusions did we draw and how did they influence the shape of the clinic? There were six conclusions:

1. The clinic should not define its task in terms of service to individuals because if it did it would in short order have a waiting list. Although working with individuals was our area of training and expertise, and it was expected of us to capitalize on our strengths, we felt it was our obligation to explore new ways of thinking and acting. Our primary responsibility was to ourselves in the sense that we had to learn new things. We were going to judge ourselves only secondarily by how helpful we were to others. Conceivably we would not be very helpful, and conceivably we could even be harmful and yet be successful in terms of our personal learning and growth.

2. Anyone who spent his life helping individuals with their personal problems did not have to justify his existence, to us at least. However, if such a professional person was not acutely sensitive to the fact that many people could not obtain his kind of service, and if he did not support and justify some radically different ways of thinking about service, we considered him socially irresponsible. In the face of overwhelming need one should feel a responsibility to give as much service to as many people as possible without unduly diluting the quality of the service. To define a service according to the highest standards puts one on the side of the angels, but when this means that some will get all and most will get none of it one is making decisions that seem to lack divine guidance or inspiration. What is "unduly diluting" is a question of fact *and* value.

3. The clinic's focus would be on any kind of setting devoted to children and young adults—schools, reformatories, neighborhood centers, and a variety of other institutions. The goal would be to understand each setting so that we would have a basis for helping the setting better to cope with its problems, regardless of whether the problem stems from within or without the setting. Defining a setting as our object of understanding and change would have one immediate consequence: no one

would be clamoring for our service because each of them would see its problems as primarily those of individuals and not as reflections, in part at least, of the culture of the setting.

4. If we were ever faced with the problem of choosing between working with an ongoing setting or putting our energies into creating a new service setting, we would choose the latter and for two reasons. First, we placed a higher value on prevention than on repair, and second, *we* would learn more. Of course, in the best of all possible worlds one should not have to decide or make these kinds of choices but this is not the best of all possible worlds. The creation of the clinic was facilitated and shaped by our willingness to help create a state institution. We were quite aware that in creating our own setting and in helping to create another (and more complicated) one we were novices secure only in the belief that what we were doing needed to be done. We did it *for ourselves* and not because we were convinced that we were going to be all that helpful. If we were not helpful, it would be *our* fault and our primary responsibility would be to understand wherein we made our errors.

5. Being a member of the clinic would not be decided on the basis of professional title, paper credentials, or amount of education. The correlation between education and wisdom, or between training and competence, was sufficiently far from perfect to justify choosing personnel on other grounds. One of our major tasks was to locate people who, for whatever reasons of background and experience, seemed to have the talent which, under appropriate conditions, could be developed to a productive level of service. We had to be a talent-seeking setting, and this would make available to us a far larger pool of human resources than if we proceeded by more conventional criteria of selection. The problems we would be dealing with were not conceived or defined in ways that required personnel with certain titles and formal experiences. Of course, we were not antiprofessional. And we were not glorifying the untrained and the nonprofessional as possessing a special kind of superior folk wisdom, a sentiment no less shortsighted or stupid than that which makes for professional preciousness.

6. To an undetermined extent every member of the clinic would be doing what every other member was doing. There would be no departments or specialized functions. Obviously, people would have or develop special interests, but that could not be a basis for compartmentalization. To the extent that we would become a hierarchically organized setting, and members could be readily differentiated from each other in terms of what they did, we would have failed; the clinic would have become another item in the supermarket of professional settings.

These statements, formulated between 1961 and 1963 and implemented with the opening of the clinic in 1963, did not (locally) meet with a mixed reception. From all sides the reaction was at best skeptical and at worst damning, and it all centered on how we were organized (there seemed to be no organization) and who was performing services. It was incomprehensible to some that we did not have social workers or psychiatrists and that we had personnel who had no relevant professional training. We had people who had been classroom teachers but they were not teaching. We had recent college graduates who had important service responsibilities. We were all doing things we had never done before. What each of us had done before was respectable and definable; what we were now doing was ambiguous and held suspect. I point this out because these reactions clearly suggested that we were successful in that we were perceived as being different in a way consistent with our ideas and values. If we were perceived like other helping settings, we would have had good reason to be skeptical about any judgment of success based on our own perceptions and opinions.

If the clinic were to be created today, a decade after it was, the reaction would be rather different and far more positive, and therein lies the point of this chapter. In almost all spheres of human service there has been, *even* within the professional communities, a recognition of and reorientation to the fact of limited resources, with the result that many settings now contain individuals undreamed of a decade ago and give them responsibilities heretofore considered performable only by highly trained professionals. This has not happened because of choice or theory but because of the developments in the larger society which literally forced these settings to confront the disparity in numbers between those who received and those who needed service. For example, in the *New York Times* of May 12, 1971, there appeared the following news item:

> A bill creating the state-regulated positions of physician's and specialist's assistants was passed overwhelmingly by the Senate here today.
>
> The bill, which passed by a vote of 46 to 8 after almost three hours of debate, provides that persons with limited medical training, such as medical corpsmen, could assist doctors in aiding sick people and could relieve doctors from some of the more arduous routine tasks which did not require extensive training.
>
> Opponents of the paramedical bill argued that it was creating second-class medical services for the people of the state and would allow untrained persons to "practice medicine." They argued that the bill did not spell out what the qualifications or educational requirements were for the positions but left them up to the commissioners of education and health.
>
> Proponents of the measure argued that there was a severe shortage of medical personnel in the state and that some counties had virtually no doctors available to treat the sick. They said the bill

would allow persons licensed by the state and under the supervision of a doctor to relieve some of the problems in providing at least some medical care.

Ralph J. Marino, Nassau Republican and a former army medical corpsman, opposed the bill and said it would be "encouraging doctors to turn over the patients to assistants who are not qualified."

"We're going to pad the wallets of the doctors," he said. "We're approving legal mayhem on an unsuspecting public."

Senator Paul P. E. Bookson, Democrat of Manhattan, said the use of medical corpsmen was an acknowledgement that health care was a "battlefield." He said the bill would create "two classes of medicine," with the poor having the paramedics foisted on them, while those people with money wold continue to receive first-rate care.

Senator Seymour R. Thaler, Democrat-Liberal of Queens, a sponsor of the measure, said that he had visited hospitals in New York City—including Bellevue—where there were only licensed practical nurses to handle large numbers of patients.

He said that in Bedford-Stuyvesant there were only four doctors to treat the thousands of poor in the area and that the bill would allow medical corpsmen to help relieve the doctors so they could treat more patients.

Senator Waldaba H. Stewart, Democrat of Brooklyn, whose district includes Bedford-Stuyvesant, voted for the bill and said that the area did not have four doctors on weekends and that one of the doctors had stated that he would be unable to continue to treat Medicare patients.

Senator Robert Garcia, Democrat-Liberal of the Bronx, termed the bill "one of the most important pieces of legislation before us this year." He said that his experience in the army with medical corpsmen showed that many of them were highly qualified and that their help in battle conditions was greatly appreciated.

"The same situation prevails in my area," he said. "People are in desperate need of medical care."

The comparison between the view and utilization of resources in war and peace is instructive indeed because it demonstrates so clearly how in one situation the fact of limited resources was realistically faced, only to be ignored when the stress of that situation was over. Whereas in the war situation, attention was given to an individual's formal education, training experience, and paper credentials, his placement was by no means automatically decided on such grounds. Thousands of professionals found themselves doing things they would never have dreamed of doing, or would never have been allowed to do, in civilian life. Similarly, many nonprofessionals were performing tasks which in civilian life could only be done after a good deal of formal training and only with the sanction of the law. It is no exaggeration to say that in the war the problem of human services was so faced and defined that its solution obviously and automatically ruled out any solution based on the civilian traditions of prolonged training and specialization. And yet, irony of ironies, during the war when governmental groups were already planning for the care of veterans after the war and it was obvious that over the years the discrepancy between the numbers needing and receiving service was alarmingly great, the problem was defined so that the solution required people with prolonged training and ever-increasing specialization. It is not my purpose here to delve into the different factors which brought this about. Certainly economic considerations, the weight of tradition, and professional imperialism played their roles. Equally important, and paradoxically so, was a view based on what should be and not what could be, and therefore the problem was defined so as to be incapable of solution.

In creating the clinic we placed a good deal of significance on the different ways in which human resources were used in peace and war because the difference had helped us answer three related questions long troubling us: Why did service settings remain much the same over long periods of time? Why was it not troubling them that so many people were not getting the services they were considered to need? Why did they not see that the time would or might come when they would be forced to define the problem and its solutions differently? One part of the answer was in the overlearned tendency to think of solutions exclusively in terms of professionalism and specialization; the other part was the lack of a historical perspective or knowledge of social history which would not allow bypassing the fact that the major stimulus of changes in settings and professions have come from outside forces. In war these changes are made far more willingly and graciously than in peace.

The view of human resources which influenced the creation and organization of the clinic in no way reflected a penchant for a democratic ethos, or a belief in the universal equality in ability, or a view of organization tantamount to anarchy. It was rather that we defined our task in a way which discernibly increased the pool of human·resources available to us—in much the same way and for the same reasons as was done in war times. That settings devoted to human services are created and developed differently in times of war and peace says far less about differences in need than it does about the self-defeating aspects of narrow professionalism. It also underlines the obvious fact that one's view of resources is very much a function of time and social forces. But when other factors becloud the obvious—when one proceeds as if past and future history are not variables to be reckoned with—one of the necessary conditions is met for continuing to do what one has done because that is only what one knows to do, however socially irresponsible this may be.

The necessity of integrating history into the matrix of one's thoughts and practices is not a new theme in this book. The reader will recall that in earlier chapters when I was discussing the before-the-beginning and the beginning phases of the creation of a setting I placed great emphasis on confronting the past. In those discussions I was, of course, talking about "local" history, whereas in the present chapter I am talking about a broader social history. At best, professional training may alert the student to the history of certain aspects of his field, usually a token gesture to scholarliness. As to the history of the intimate and changing relationships between a field (not only a piece of it) and the larger society, the student gets nothing. It is not surprising, therefore, that professionals think that their ideas, theories, and practices are the descendants of the thinking of those who came before them—a lineage unrelated to social forces and changes. It is no wonder that when professionals have the opportunity to create a setting a historical perspective, local or otherwise, is almost always absent. Of the numerous times I have observed the creation of a setting and have heard the phrase *tooling up*—that phrase meant to give the impression of an engineering efficiency—it never reflected a historical stance.

The negative reaction to the clinic's view of resources and organization contained the implication that it was most unlikely that such a setting could render valuable service. Again and again we would be asked the question: How do you know you are being helpful? This was a troubling and, of course, a legitimate question. It was a troubling question not because we had no ways to answer it but because the question assumed agreement on a *primary* value: justifying one's existence in terms of what one does for others. The true answer to the question was: "You are asking a legitimate question, but if we answer only that question we would be misleading you into believing that help to others is the primary basis upon which we want to be judged. The fact is that our primary value concerns our need to help ourselves change and learn, for us to feel that we are growing in our understanding of where we have been, where we are, and what we are about, and that we are enjoying what we are doing. We are not here because we have solutions, and we do not believe that there is *a* solution." By accepting this value we are not likely to blame failure on others (*we* know the score but *they* don't even know the game) but instead would view it as a stimulus to change. To help others to change without this being preceded *and* accompanied by an exquisite awareness of the process in ourselves is "delivering a product or service" which truly has little or no significance for our personal and intellectual growth. If in the coming years we are thinking and doing the same things—that is, acting as if we have discovered the truth and know how to deliver it— we will have failed even though others might say we were helpful. When toward the end of his life Freud recommended that psychoanalysts should be reanalyzed every five years, it was not because he thought analysts were not being helpful but because he did not like what he saw happening to analysts in the role of helpers: *They* had stopped growing and that was fatal for them, for psychoanalysis in general, and ultimately for those who would be seeking help.

On those occasions when we gave this answer, the reactions varied, not surprisingly, from staring disbelief, to implicit accusations of narcissism and callousness, to a benevolence which seemed to view the answer as a kind of pious idealism which would not stand up in the real world. (There is, I know, a fine line between selfishness and a concern for one's self-development.) These reactions really reflect the heart of the matter because they reflect values and a way of thinking implicit in the creation of almost all settings. I use the word *implicit* advisedly because they are rarely verbalized. That is the way it *should* be, and what is there to say and think about? There is a good deal to say and think about, and I will use our schools as a case in point. Nobody would disagree with the statement that schools are primarily for the education of children. (This becomes quite clear when one has had the opportunity to observe or participate in the creation of a new school.) What children should be taught, what experiences children should have, how much progress children should make—these questions reveal who is center stage. I have spent thousands of hours in schools and one of the first things I sensed was that the longer the person had been a teacher the less excited, or alive, or stimulated he seemed to be about his role. It was not that they were uninterested, or felt that what they were doing was unimportant, or that they were not being helpful to their students, but simply that being a teacher was on the boring side. Generally speaking, these teachers were not as helpful to children as they might have been or as frequently as the teachers themselves would have liked to have been. It took me a long time to realize that what would be inexplicable would be if things turned out otherwise, because schools are not created to foster the intellectual and professional growth of teachers. The assumption that teachers can create and maintain those conditions which make school learning and school living stimulating for children, without those same conditions existing for teachers, has no warrant in the history of man. That the different efforts to improve the education of children have been remarkably short of their mark is in part a consequence of the implicit value that schools are primarily for children, a value which gives rise to ways of thinking, to a view of technology, to ways of training, and to modes of organization which make for one grand error of misplaced emphasis.

Dewey knew all of this well, as the book by Mayhew and Edwards (1966) demonstrates. Dewey created the conditions for his teachers which he wanted them to create for their students. When Dewey recommended that an elementary school teacher should receive the same salary as a university professor, it was because he expected of the teacher what he expected of the professor: to investigate, to learn, and to change, and to continue to do so. The error that Dewey made in trying to influence the public schools, the same error made by those eager to implement his ideas, was the failure to recognize that the public schools and those responsible for them were operating on the basis of a value that schools exist primarily for children. As a colleague once remarked: "It is hard to help people find their way when you have lost you own way."

The question about the success of the clinic breaks down into two questions. Did *we* feel we were successful according to our primary value? Did those we sought to help feel they were helped? To the first question I can only talk for myself, although I have no reason to believe that others who helped create and maintain that setting would answer the question differently. I had an intellectual and interpersonal ball, such as I had never had before or am likely to have again in another setting. As for the second question (and in part the first) I must refer the reader to other publications (Sarason, Levine, Goldenberg, Cherlin, and Bennett, 1966; Sarason and Kaplan, 1969); Levine and Levine, 1970; Goldenberg, 1971; and Grossman, 1972).

I must remind the reader that in this chapter it is my purpose to discuss certain settings in order to clarify the relationships among a setting's definition of its task, its view of resources, and underlying values. Although these relationships are the most important about which people must be aware in creating a setting, they receive the least amount of critical scrutiny, and sometimes they receive no scrutiny at all. The consequences are many and usually adverse: rigidity in function, insularity from changes in the larger society, increased competitiveness for resources within and among settings, decreasing satisfaction in work with a concomitant increase in the need for professional status and money, and the steady loss of the sense of community within the setting. The story, as later chapters will suggest, is more complicated than this but enough has been given the reader for him to begin to understand that creating a setting involves problems of values and resources which, although almost always viewed in individual, or local, or professional terms, turn out to be in large part a function of a particular society at a particular time. The failure to understand this, a direct consequence of an ahistorical stance and theories which pay no attention to social history, is what gives undue weight to tradition and makes it likely that changes in values and view of resources will come about more as a result, so to speak, of being hit on the head than as a consequence of using what is inside of it. To the extent that these problems are bypassed or, in the case of resources, are based on a myth, creating a setting is akin to engineering a building, and like so many of these products some settings are seen as obsolete or inappropriate soon after they are operational.

In the next section the issues of values and resources will be further discussed in terms of the creation of a setting quite different from the clinic. It is, perhaps, the best description we have of a setting from the standpoint of why and how it was created. The fact that the leader of that setting was a member of our clinic is noteworthy only because it may help explain how self-conscious he was of the process he engaged in and the need to describe it. Goldenberg's book (1971) was of inestimable value in clarifying for me the significance of the prehistory and beginning phases of the creation of a setting, and I urge the reader skeptical of the fateful dynamics of the before-the-beginning context to consult his detailed account. I must again remind the reader that in the next section I shall not (cannot) attempt to describe and discuss the creation of the setting except in terms of how its character and organization reflected certain values and views of resources. That even this is possible is a consequence of the fact that these issues were explicitly confronted. That is to say, from the earliest point these were seen as problems and not, as is usually the case, implicit "givens."

Residential Youth Center

The Residential Youth Center (RYC) in New Haven is a house in which twenty or so inner-city male youths (ages sixteen to twenty-one) live while they are learning about or adjusting or readjusting to the world of work and social living. The bulk of the residents are black, have disorganized or disorganizing homes, are school drop-outs, and have prison records or many skirmishes with the law. The label *hard core* is quite appropriate. For the first six months of its existence the staff members with one exception (Goldenberg) were nonprofessionals, some of whom had histories not much different from those of the residents. After the first six months all of the staff were indigenous nonprofessionals.

The RYC was created within the context of an existing organization of settings: Community Progress Incorporated (CPI), the local community action agency. As I indicated in earlier chapters, and as Goldenberg makes abundantly clear in his book, a setting created within the context of an existing organization of settings sets processes going (for example, for resources, direction, and control) which can change the character of the setting and usually in ways that transform innovative into traditional goals. This, however, was not something of which Goldenberg was much aware, as he forthrightly states:

> It was clearly understood by all those concerned (e.g., CPI, the Department of Labor, and the Psycho-Educational Clinic) that the RYC's first director, a member of the Yale faculty, would return to his academic responsibility on January 1, 1967, after having spent six months with the program on a full-time basis. After January 1, 1967, he was to be involved in the RYC program as a consultant. The reason for this type of arrangement was that one of the goals of the program was to prove that you did not need a "professional" to run a program—clinically oriented though it was—like the RYC. An-

other consequence of this arrangement—a consequence we only became aware of with the passage of time—was that the very fact that the first director of the RYC was not a full-time employee of CPI and, hence, was relatively immune to the social and political pressures of the "mother" organization, was an asset in the development and implementation of the program. It provided the director with the kind of leverage (i.e., that he did not "need" the job of directing the RYC) that enabled the RYC to function with a degree of latitude and freedom that might not have been possible were the director totally dependent upon CPI for his livelihood. (p. 131)

Goldenberg learned, and very fast, that the process of creating a setting within the context of an existing organization of setting makes naivete a gross liability. I cannot resist quoting him on this same point but this time in relation to an existing organization of settings in Washington:

There is also the situation in which the decision to create a new institution carries with it little or no pretense that the new institution will even try to coordinate the efforts of other agencies involved in similar areas of concern. This does not mean, however, that the new institution will not seek or need the help of agencies that already exist. All it means is that the new institution will function independently of, and will not try to coordinate in any formal sense, the efforts of existing agencies that are, and have been for a long time, trying to meet certain human needs in the same area. What is usually overlooked in this decision, however, is that the rise of the new organization is in many ways an indictment of the ways in which the more traditional agencies have been meeting (or, in reality, not meeting) the needs they were originally intended to serve. What often results, regardless of public protestations to the contrary, is that the new institution is perceived both as a condemnation of previous attempts to render service and as a distinct threat to the future existence of the more established agencies. Under these conditions, cooperation of any sort, formal or informal, is highly unlikely. More important, the overlapping and duplication of functions that inevitably result once the new agency begins operations guarantee the development and perpetuation of greater conflicts—the kind of interagency conflicts that are, in the long run, not only harmful to all the agencies involved but cruelly detrimental to the clients who hope to receive service. It is, in the final analysis, a situation in which "cooperation" becomes little more than a slogan to be used for purposes of public consumption, and political maneuvering and undermining become the accepted order of the day.
There is little doubt (at least now and in our own minds) that the creation of the Office of Economic Opportunity (OEO) was as much a reaction against the ways in which existing agencies were

waging their "undeclared" War on Poverty as it was a response to the newly grasped needs of the poor. The implied indictment was a simple and clear one: had the existing agencies (e.g., the Office of Education, the Department of Health, Education and Welfare, the Department of Labor) met their responsibilities and obligations to the poor in an appropriate and relevant manner, there would have been much less need for the launching of the War on Poverty in general, and for the creation of a new super poverty agency (OEO) in particular. From the very beginning, then, one might say that the War on Poverty, at least in terms of those already engaged in efforts to provide services to the poor, could have been perceived as a criticism of existing programs and agencies. Again, this may seem to be a glimpse of the obvious, but what is less apparent are the ways in which these perceptions can influence the development of new programs and the motivations behind them.

The reader will recall that . . . we described as "decidedly cool" our reception at Job Corps headquarters (OEO) in Washington when, in the process of developing the initial proposal for the Residential Youth Center, we visited them seeking information and assistance. In actuality, we now feel we were being rather gracious in describing our reception as "decidedly cool." In point of fact we were treated more as interlopers, meddlers, even spies, rather than as people who were genuinely interested in the problem and wanted to be of some help. But this reception was almost "warm" compared to the one we received some two months later when we returned to OEO to ask them to fund the RYC, which was now in proposal form. This time we received no reception at all. We were told in no uncertain terms that our proposal would not be considered, that the idea for the RYC was at variance with Job Corps philosophy, and that we should "go elsewhere to peddle the project." Somewhat shaken, we did just that. We walked two blocks to the Department of Labor (Office of Manpower, Policy, Evaluation and Research), where we recounted our experiences and presented our proposal. Within twenty minutes we found, to our utter amazement, that our proposal not only was being listened to with much enthusiasm and delight but also was almost guaranteed its funds. We left the Department of Labor feeling, quite naively we now believe, that at least someone understood our program, shared our belief in its values, and was willing to support it all the way. Only later were we to realize that there may have been many other reasons for the speed with which we were funded by the Department of Labor, reasons having at least as much to do with the relationship and conflicts between OEO and the Department of Labor as with the particular merits of the RYC proposal. On the basis of this kind of experience, as well as a variety of others to be described in later portions of this book, one wonders—or at least has a right to speculate—about the motivations that lie behind the funding of a variety of antipoverty programs. (pp. 47–49)

The immediate stimulus to the concept of a RYC was the failure of the Job Corps program, a failure Goldenberg and his colleagues in the community action program recognized within a few weeks after the first Job Corps camp was opened. They had sent some New Haven inner-city youths to one of these camps, they started to receive from them some disquieting letters, they went down to the camp, and the idiocy of it all became clear.

Creating the RYC was a direct consequence of some critical observations of and conclusions about resources, professionalism, history, and how labels and the definition of problems subtly undermine efforts at change. "A second aspect of the problem has to do with the ways in which nonprofessionals are perceived. Here, too, the situation is a somewhat curious one, for no sooner did the nonprofessional, via the Community Action Program, get into the "business" of delivering what for all intents and purposes were mental health services—and begin to show that he could do the job—than great pains began to be taken to indicate that he was, indeed, ill-equipped to perform that function with any high degree of competence" (p. 68).

Goldenberg's conclusions are not those of someone who is antiprofessional or a glorifier of the virtues of human ignorance or a partisan of the view that sheer experience in mystical ways produces skill and wisdom. They are not the comments of someone who views and defines problems in ways that make it seem "natural" that his training, special theories, and techniques contain the appropriate and best solution. They are the comments of one who believes that whatever the virtues of professionalism may be (and there are many), they cannot obscure the defect of the tendency to transform unfamiliar into familiar problems at the expense of relevance. This is like the job of the patient who after being examined by his physician was told to go home, open up a window, stand in front of it and breathe deeply, several times a day. Said the patient: "But, doctor, it is midwinter and if I do that I will get pneumonia." Replied the doctor: "But for that I know what to do."

Goldenberg goes on to point out that the traditional ways of thinking about service lead directly to the pyramidal type of organization. The RYC was organized horizontally and not pyramidally.

> The horizontal structure came to mean many things. On a clinical or service level it meant that each staff member, regardless of his position in the organization for formal "job description," would carry a case load. Carrying a case load was defined as assuming the total responsibility for all decisions and interventions involving a resident and his family. No staff member, regardless of his status in or out of the organization, would presume to make

clinical decisions involving another staff member's cases. Staff meetings were clearly to be utilized for purposes of trying to influence the decisions people made, but it was left completely up to the individual staff member to make the final determination in his case.

The rationale behind the "horizontal" sharing of clinical responsibilities was a simple one: that no one be spared the experience of dealing with a client and his family. This was undertaken in the hope that under such conditions, people would begin to participate in one another's problems, could share and work through the anxiety that such responsibilities inevitably create, and would eventually come to view one another as sources of knowledge, help, and support. We wanted to make it as difficult as possible for people inhabiting positions of differential status and power to look at one another and say: "You don't understand my problems. You sit up there and tell me what to do but you don't know what I'm feeling. You haven't been through it yourself." Clinical "horizontality" was designed to put everyone "on the line" in the hope that it would enable people of different backgrounds and experiences to learn from one another in an atmosphere of mutual trust and respect. (p. 128)

It is truly beside the point that these words were put into deeds and with a remarkable degree of success, despite anticipated and unanticipated problems. The RYC could have been early on a dismal failure without disproving the validity of its conception and the utilization and organization of resources. Similarly, the fact that it was successful does not permit one to claim that it was because of its basic views. The individual case can be seminal but not conclusive. The fact that this RYC gave rise to another in New Haven and many more around the country, fathered by those who started the first RYC, is suggestive, but we will have to await on each the kind of detailed report Goldenberg has given us. In the quest for validity we should not overlook that the rationale which Goldenberg has so clearly spelled out, and which shaped the organizational character of this setting, is not new and was present in almost all of the viable communes created in this country in the nineteenth century. Its similarity to the Israeli kibbutz is also noteworthy. The principle of interchangeability of roles, external need as the major determinant of the utilization and organization of human resources, and the importance of interchangeability as a way of preventing barriers against mutual understanding—these similarities emerge when one cuts through the differences in language in which these rationales are couched. Here, for example, are two statements from the *Circular*, the regular publication of the Oneida Community. The first is from the issue of October 8, 1853, and the second from August 29, 1854 (Robertson, 1970):

We feel roused to new earnestness to favor the mingling of the sexes in labor. We find that the spirit of the world is deadly opposed to this innovation, and would make it very easy to slip back into the old routine of separate employments for men and women. But the leaven of heavenly principles about labor, resists, from time to time, this backward tendency, and brings forth a new endorsement of the truths contained in the Bible argument on this subject. We believe that the great secret of securing enthusiasm in labor and producing a free, healthy, social equilibrium, is contained in the proposition "loving companionship and labor, and especially the mingling of the sexes, makes labor attractive. . . ."

Certainly we could not wish for better surroundings for a child, to make him—not indeed a distorted professional, or a hard-faced speculator—but to make him a gentle, thoughtful man of use and improvement. I hope he will be ever kept from the mercenary idea of doing things for pay, or making riches for himself. I am not afraid of its leading him to poverty. On the other hand, let him remain free from the absurd notion that one kind of employment is more honorable than another, which causes so much mischief in the world. He will be taught in the Community that it is not the kind of work that dignifies a man but that by good spirit and good manners the man dignifies every kind of work; and that he is the truest gentleman who is capable of doing the most useful things. (pp. 58–60)

The RYC, its rationale and rhetoric bearing the stamp of the 1960s, the war on poverty, and race, is in distinguished company. The Oneida Community later had as one of its outstanding, indeed amazing, characteristics that which we also find in the RYC as an explicit value: the purpose of the setting was quite self-consciously the development and growth of its members.

One would expect that when those who are creating a setting have never engaged in such venture before, they would assign primary value to their own development. This is far from the case, although I have seen numerous instances where this was recognized on a verbal level. Sometimes this has meant that individuals in the new setting will seek further knowledge and training. Rarely, if ever, will this be viewed as the collective responsibility of all who are creating the setting because in the pyramidal type of organization not everyone is seen as equally important or necessary. What I have seen with increasing frequency is the attempt to build in from the start "openness in communication," and this is done by bringing in an expert in group dynamics who employs procedures (usually over a very few days) intended to accomplish three things: for each member of the core group to see how he "comes across" to others, to make clear how the avoidance of "straight talk" leads to problems of communication, and to instill in the setting a tradition of candidness. In no instance that I observed, or I have been told about, were the desired effects lasting; in at least three instances the results were disastrous; and in one instance it began a tradition of group decision-making that effectively prevented most people from ever doing anything. It could hardly be otherwise because even where straight talk culminates in understanding and even agreement about how to live with each other, it may never reach or question the basic values and purposes of the setting. Straight talk about *feelings* is no substitute for clarity about values. More important yet, the very fact that an outsider is brought in already suggests a failure to take responsibility for one's collective growth and development, that is, to assign primacy to the value of the development of those in the setting. In no instance, either before or after the group procedures, was the possible primacy of this value raised, let alone its possible consequences explored. In all the instances I have observed or known about, all of them in the area of direct human service, there was never any question that the justification for the setting was only in terms of what one did for others. It is ironical that all of these settings wanted "to do good," although in regard to lay or nonprofessional people who would want "to do good," those same people would be the first to point out the real dangers involved in justifying action on that basis. They would rightly point out that to do good for others requires knowledge and experience by means of which one becomes changed or becomes a different kind of thinker. The point is well taken, of course, but what is not well taken is the implicit suggestion that learning and changing are not a continuous obligation and, therefore, always the primary value especially in the case of a new setting which almost never intends merely to replicate already existing settings. Most professionals stop learning and changing fairly early in their careers. I am raising the question of the nature of work, but more of this later.

Goldenberg has stated the primary value and its significances in a lucid and compelling way:

> It would be highly demoralizing, to say the least, for an institution to view itself as a potential candidate for the kinds of services it wishes to offer to others. From almost the very moment of conception, most institutions accept as fact the assumption that they are, and will continue to be, "healthier" than the clients whose needs they were created to serve. . . .
>
> By far the most important consequence of the assumption that the institution need not overly concern itself with its own mental health is that the institution rarely attempts to develop or build into itself any viable mechanisms for preventing or dealing with its own problems. By "viable mechanisms" we mean any processes that would enable the institution systematically and regularly to take a long, hard look at its functioning, its growth, and its conflicts. The fact that few institutions or institution-builders ever develop

such vehicles for self-scrutiny should not be taken as evidence of bad faith, poor judgment, or questionable motives. It is the inevitable result of a situation in which an organization does not view itself, its staff, and its problems as legitimate and important areas of concern. Once the assumption has been made that there is something inherently different between its own life and the lives of its clients (between its own needs and the needs of those it wishes to serve), a pattern of thinking is born which inhibits or stamps as irrelevant the development of vehicles for self-study and self-correction. In short, once the institution accepts as fact the alleged dichotomy between its own existence and those of its clients—a dichotomy which then allows the institution to rationalize and justify its being solely in terms of "helping others"—the institution need no longer "trouble" itself with questions of internal self-actualization or problems of self-confrontation. . . .

The tendency of an institution to avoid looking at itself and to refrain from the often agonizing search to develop internal mechanisms for dealing with its own problems does not bring with it any guarantee that serious problems will not occur. All it does is guarantee that when such problems arise they will be dealt with haphazardly, instinctively, and reflexively; in short, they will be dealt with in precisely the kinds of ways that the institution would never condone or allow to happen were it dealing with a problem of any of its clients. (pp. 97–99)

From the beginning this value was explicit at the RYC and one can say that it was part of its "constitution." It determined the development of its horizontal organizational structure and it also was the basis for allowing and encouraging each staff member to "pursue and develop these work-related areas of his life in which he, and he alone, had an abiding and personal interest. We assumed that such personal fulfillment would result in activities that would be exciting and helpful to our clients." What this meant, for example, was that each member was responsible for an evening program, growing out of his own interests, training, and experiences, that was available to all RYC residents and their families. But what was a most distinctive consequence of its primary value were the procedures that were explicitly developed and regularly employed to cope with two facts: the RYC would *always* have problems—and how people dealt with them would be a function of how they defined the problems—and it was imperative for an individual to understand how others are seeing the problems; these facts were a kind of preamble to its constitution which no one was allowed to forget. The staff gave a good deal of thought to how to deal with this issue but there was never any doubt that it was *their* issue and not one for which any outsider could be given responsibility.

Goldenberg's book contains verbatim transcripts of the different types of meetings and the reader is urged to consult them in order to judge for himself the degree to which they reflect the primacy given to the personal, interpersonal, and conceptual development of participants. It is not the practice of settings to transcribe their meetings in order to use them as a basis for reflection and change. Meetings are for the purpose of understanding and making decisions about "others" and only secondarily, if at all, as a means of self-scrutiny. For a setting to take self-scrutiny seriously, in the sense that its vehicles for discussion regularly have this as an explicit goal, requires, at the very least, agreement on the value that that is what the setting is for. The failure to confront this issue and the seductive and "self-evident" quality of do-goodism go a long way to explaining why over time most settings change little or not at all and why those who create and populate them only rarely experience the sense of change, growth, and accomplishment. On the level of settings we have yet to take seriously what Freud and Dewey knew so well: it is nonsense to think and act as if helper and helped, teacher and pupil, are different kinds of people and that the one can change or help the other in desired ways without experiencing change in himself.

What about the boys at the RYC? Were they helped? Did it pay off for *them*? By the requirements of its funding the RYC had to study and answer these questions. Needless to say, the source of funding was not interested in discussions of values and horizontality. They were interested in two questions. Did the boys at the center (the experimental group) do better after they left than a control group of boys who by random selection happened not to be chosen? Could the RYC remain viable after the first six months when Goldenberg left and no professionals were running the center? Goldenberg gives impressive evidence that the answers to both questions were affirmative.

Goldenberg leaves no doubt in his readers' minds that for those who created and maintained the RYC the experience was one that wrought great changes in them. They learned, developed, and changed. Such words, however, are far from clear as to their meaning and the values they are intended to reflect. When I use these words (as would Goldenberg, I am sure) they are meant to convey a complicated process during which an individual willingly accepts a challenge requiring him to think and act in unaccustomed ways and roles that, if the challenge is successfully met, change his perception of his capabilities and increase the range of new challenges—all of this being accompanied by a sense of satisfaction and an obligation to help others to have similar experiences. Those who created and maintained the RYC approximated this ideal to an extent I rarely have seen. For an individual or group to approximate this ideal requires certain internal conditions in the setting, coping with external factors stemming from these conditions, and overcoming in oneself the weight of tradition and previous training. The last characteristic is well illustrated in the next section where I shall discuss a different type of setting distinguished by its values and nontraditional view of human resources.

What happened to the staff and boys at the RYC is not "explained" by any combination of a particular value and a view of resources, because far more was involved than I have discussed here—for example, leadership. But certainly among the mix of ingredients present the two factors I have been stressing were alone and in combination distinctive.

Ward H

The book *Ward H* (Colarelli and Siegel, 1966) was discussed in an earlier chapter in connection with the various aspects of the prehistory, before-the-beginning, and beginning phases in the creation of a setting, and our focus was on the implications of the fact that this new setting in a state hospital lasted four years. Ward H is another good example of the dynamics set in motion when a new setting is created out of, or within the context of, an existing organization of settings.

The authors describe well the usual living arrangements on the ward for these kinds of patients, the absence of anything that might be dignified as "treatment," and the rarity of professional attention. They also point out how the needs of the patient were secondary to those of the hospital's professional training program.

> One consequence of the residency training program is a regularly scheduled change of residents on a ward every six, nine, or twelve months. As in every hospital, above all the psychiatric hospital, changes in assignment are essential for a well-rounded training program. Many patients, expecially the acute and newly admitted ones, benefit from these changes in personnel, where new ideas and personalities are constantly focused on problems and the ever-changing environment generated makes lapsing into a chronic role difficult. One negative aspect of this changing environment, however, is the frequent disruption of the therapeutic relationships built up between the patient and the resident, often resulting in a set-back or regression in the patient's recovery. A patient suffering a regression every six months as a result of the rotation of the ward physician may learn to resist therapy, by avoiding deep personal relationships with the physician. . . . Life on such a ward takes on a terrifying anonymity. (pp. 3, 12)

Ward H was created to implement a set of consequences about etiological factors in schizophrenia, the ways in which the usual hospital setting maintains and even exacerbates the condition, and the kind of social setting which would have more rehabilitative effects on the hospitalized, chronic schizophrenic patient. These conceptions were based on values and a view of human resources quite different from those of the usual ward. (See especially the authors' prefatory statement.) Three principles are enunciated, and their underlying similarity to those of the RYC and the Yale Psycho-Educational Clinic will be apparent:

> The first principle developed from the inconsistency evident in the fact that chronic schizophrenics are seen as non-responsible; they are brought to the hospital to become responsible, but there is no one near them behaving in a responsible way whom they can use as a model. The aides, though present, are the end point of a hierarchy; they receive and carry out orders but are not intended to make responsible decisions. The project altered the structure so that the aides might become models for the patients. It was believed that if these patients could be directly cared for by persons who are in the position of formulating policy and making decisions, then the possibility of the patients developing responsibility themselves would be greatly enhanced.
>
> The second principle guiding this project was the overwhelming importance of commitment, devotion, and above all, spontaneity in the care and treatment of these patients; the nature of their illness made these three qualities absolutely essential. Under the usual system many opportunities for treatment were missed because of the inevitable delay involved in several personnel observing, reporting, and studying a patient's bizarre behavior pattern; when the prescribed response was finally relayed back to the patient the opportune moment for a therapeutic intervention was past. The reaction to these patients must be immediate and spontaneous. But spontaneity and devotion cannot be expected of treatment personnel who in themselves do not feel the responsibility for the treatment of patients nor in any real sense have it. You cannot prescribe devotion and spontaneity, you can only provide the opportunity for its development. In giving the aides the responsibility for treatment, the project permitted them to be spontaneous as well as committed to these patients.
>
> A third guiding principle cannot really be separated from the above but does have other implications. This principle is the belief that one of the greatest resources we have to offer patients is ourselves. There is not sufficient difference between any two people, regardless of the amount of education, the degrees they have, the formal trappings of their status and prestige in society, to differentiate them basically in terms of their capacity to help one another. The inference of this principle is that with a certain amount of guidance and support there is no reason why a psychiatric aide who is on the lowest salary and prestige level of the institution cannot be given the opportunity and does not have the resources to do as

much as the person at the other extreme of the status and financial hierarchy of the institution. The potential for development and growth in the aide is as great as that of any other human being and merely requires an optimal structure in order to develop. The project was structured to provide opportunities for development and growth in the psychiatric aide group which would then make new abilities available for the treatment of the patient. (pp. 19–20)

This way of defining the problem does not lead to impossible solutions. On the contrary, it discernibly expands the pool of human resources that are available at the same time that it exposes the inhumanity of the armor protecting professional preciousness. Reading between the lines (and sometimes on them) it is no wonder that Ward H encountered the obstacles it did in its four years of existence.

The authors were quite aware that at least two processes had to be initiated and successfully carried out if Ward H stood a chance of meeting its objectives. The first was that the professional staff connected with the ward would have to undergo changes in their ways of thinking and in their attitudes toward their roles. The second was that the aides would have to change their accustomed ways of thinking and conception of their roles. The second could not occur without the first and neither could occur with ease, expectations that were amply confirmed. What makes *Ward H* such a moving and dramatic document is the way in which these struggles are described. It is easy (but not all that easy) for professionals to say that they will regard aides, patients, and themselves differently. When the game begins and the cards are on the table the realities one confronts can be quite upsetting, particularly when the game is being played before a variety of hostile kibbitzers. The rest of the hospital was not exactly a cheering section for their colleagues on Ward H. However eager the aides were to participate in this "adventure in innovation" they did not (could not) anticipate what they would confront and experience when they accepted new roles and responsibilities. The stakes were higher, the game far more significant, but shades of Pygmalion are discernible. In Shaw's play we *know* how Eliza Doolittle changed; at the end we are intrigued and tantalized by how much Professor Higgins has changed. On Ward H the struggle was neverending and always uphill but the increments of desired change in the actors were marked and gratifying.

But what happened to the chronic, schizophrenic patients? Colarelli and Siegel present a variety of comparative data demonstrating that their patients did significantly better than other comparable groups in the hospital.

The comparative data appear to confirm the observational data on the Ward H patients. Ward H, as a whole, had a discharge rate equivalent to that of the whole hospital for chronic schizophrenic patients from the same cohort. For patients who were institutionalized less than five years, this rate was somewhat higher than for the rest of the hospital, and the readmission rate to date has been dramatically lower. These results were especially remarkable in view of the fact that the Ward H population was generally assumed not to be amenable to treatment. At the same time, the personnel cost of the Ward H program was equivalent to that of the least expensive ward in the hospital. (pp. 168–169)

It would be, of course, nonsensical to say that the Yale Psycho-Educational Clinic, the RYC, and Ward H were not absorbed with the importance of helping others. It would be equally nonsensical to say that these settings were created for the sole purpose of the personal and intellectual development of their members. What these settings were based on was the conception that a setting that wished to help others to learn and change had to learn and change itself. Indeed, these changes had to be reflected in all phases of the creation of the setting and this was a continuous process; that is, it was not a problem which was ever "solved." The task of these settings was not "out there" (in schools, the ghetto, the minds of people) but "in here" *and* "out there." Creating a setting based on this conception makes an enormous difference in the character of the setting and is in dramatic contrast to the creation of other help-oriented settings. Most settings are created as if they know what needs to be done and their members are what they need to be. There is usually, of course, some basis for these assumptions. I do not wish to create the impression that knowledge is meager and that those engaged in the task of helping others are generally incompetent or personally inadequate. But I do maintain that most settings early on lose whatever innovative spirit they had, spontaneously change their services and thinking little or not at all, get caught up in internal struggles for status and resources, reflexively resist new ideas or practices, begin to change only when external conditions force them to question their basic values or obligations, and in the process of attempting to change transform the substance of the new challenge into the familiar rhetoric of an outworn tradition. Settings, like an individual, have an almost infinite capacity to treasure their "symptoms" at the same time they proclaim their desire to change. All of this is in part a consequence of justifying a setting's existence and purpose primarily in terms of what one does for others, a value which makes a productive self-consciousness either a luxury or a burden but never a necessity.

What significance can be attached to the fact that the three settings (and undoubtedly others) were created around the same time? There can be no doubt that the stress that each of the settings placed on the inequities of the distribution of services, and the obvious and scandalous consequences of the limitations of professional resources, reflected what the larger society was beginning to realize and to be disturbed about. The problems of race and poverty were catalysts for bringing out into the open what had long been true but obscured by unrealistic attitudes toward professionalism and resources. It is no exaggeration to say that the past two decades have witnessed an increasing antiprofessionalism, and among the most articulate critics have been professional people. Educators, physicians, social workers, mental health personnel, and others are on the defensive, and although the substance of the attack is not always clear, or rational, or justified, it in one way or another implicates the values and attitudes underneath the limitations of resources. The three settings reflected changes in the larger society. However, in contrast to many new and old settings which have attempted to reflect change in society, the three settings did not fall into the trap of defining their task in terms of solving problems "out there" but rather in terms of drastic changes in their thinking that had to precede and accompany whatever they did for others. It is a difference that makes an enormous difference.

Although these settings were created on the bases they were, a fact which eliminated many wearying and disillusioning issues confronting a setting, one should not underestimate the difficulty of their task. One set of problems was substituted for another. Leaving aside the skeptical, hostile (and even subverting) reactions which they encountered from external sources, these settings were faced with four critical issues, any one of which could have effectively killed the setting if not handled well. The first was in selecting nonprofessionals who could learn to do what only professionals heretofore were considered capable of doing. None of these settings considered the lack of professional knowledge and training a good indicator of courage, wisdom, and the capacity to learn. Just as possessing professional credentials is not, ipso facto, a defect, being a nonprofessional was not, ipso facto, a virtue. The second issue, confined to the professionals in the setting, was the degree to which they could really share responsibilities with the nonprofessionals consistent with the basic conception and not with noblesse oblige. The third issue was the degree to which the setting could support the nonprofessional in his difficulty with and anxiety about his new role. And the fourth was how to keep the enterprise "honest." A major factor which worked against succumbing to the challenge, and this is best poignantly described in the accounts of the RYC and Ward H, was the early recognition that these issues are never solved, that they will come up again and again in varying strengths and guises, and that the temptation to prevent their occurrence or to obscure them by administrative changes is the beginning of the end.

Review: Creation and Self-Development

Before going on with the life of a setting, it is appropriate to review the highlights of its earliest phases, literally the most creative aspects in that they concern the evolving of planned structure and form reflecting the thinking, attitudes, and energies of people confronted with a problem they willingly attempt to solve. As in all creative endeavors the structure and form may be rather different from the original conception but there is always a relationship between the two, and the inevitable discrepancy between original intent and actual result gives rise to varying degrees of discontent and frustration. Unlike the creative artist who, for example, can throw away his canvas and try again to solve his artistic problem, those who create human settings rarely have this option. The most notable exception is marriage. The more complicated settings are rarely dissolved even when they are obvious failures, but, as we shall see later in this chapter, the equivalent of divorce is quite frequent within the setting and for much the same reasons.

The creation of a setting is rooted in local and social history, and, as a consequence, it almost always reflects more or less conventional values and styles of thinking. Although the setting is always intended to be different from or better than existing ones, there are several factors which drastically limit the success of this intent. First is a lack of the sense of importance of local history which could allow for knowledge of and confrontation with the conflicting and often contradictory ideas and forces at work in the prehistory of the setting. The second factor is a dulled sensitivity to the historical relationships between settings and social forces, as a consequence of which there is a *belated* recognition of social changes, a tendency frantically to react, and an uncritical emphasis on quantity and numbers as the basis for solving the problem. The third factor (related to the second) is the tendency to define the problem in a way so as to contain a solution requiring those kinds of professional groups which heretofore had been inadequate in meeting the problem and which exist (and will exist) in numbers too small to meet the problem as defined. The final factor has to do with the consequences of a value which is almost always implicit because it is seen as so obviously "true": the primary justification of a new setting is what it does to help others. The failure to view as a coequal value what it must do for itself results over time in rigidity in thought and action, resistance to ideas requiring change, and a parochialism which insulates it from the changing needs of the society it purports to serve.

From a purely internal standpoint the major problems of creating a setting center on two related tasks: growth and differentiation, on the one hand, and the forging of a "constitution" by which the setting will be governed. The usual way in which the leader organizes his core group—the arrangements he makes with each, and the relationships of each with the others—usually reflects several assumptions held by the leader and each of the core group members. The first is that the appropriate kind and degree of motivation will overcome any and all obstacles, including those encountered by the leader and the core group in their precious settings. The second is that there is agreement on values and goals, perhaps the first assumption which in point of time is invalidated. The third assumption is that there are sufficient resources, or the promise of them, which will allow each of the core group members to realize his goals. The ambiguities inherent in the usual way of selecting and organizing the core group, ambiguities only later realized as such, are a consequence of the failure to view the creation of a setting as a constitutional problem among the most important aspects of which are the anticipation of problems and the ways they will be handled and the surfacing of differences in values among the participants. The failure to think in constitutional terms maximizes ambiguities which usually lead to informal, unambiguous, and individual kinds of resolutions, such as heightened competitiveness and individual empires. The process tends to be repeated as each core member organizes and develops his core group. What I have just summarized has less to do with the fact and problem of growth (and even size) than it does with the lack of a set of conceptions which would mirror the realities and complexities of the creation of a setting, and not, as is presently the case, the wish-fulfilling propensities of the human mind.

Much that I have summarized is not readily apparent to an observer viewing the creation of a setting. It is somewhat more apparent to the participants that there are powerful forces which prevent them from early recognition for what has happened and why. For one thing, in its earliest phases the setting is suffused with hope, enthusiasm, a sense of mission, and unity which maximizes selective perception. The dynamics of love have never been noted for their positive effects on the assessment of reality. Marriage, the smallest but most frequent instance of the creation of a setting, illustrates those dynamics best. Courtship, marriage, honeymoon, and the next year or so are times when the heart is dominant over the head. I do not say this with cynicism but, if anything, with despair because the feelings and fantasies experienced in the early phases of the creation of a setting are part of what is best in man; that they have the defects of their virtues is a fact which says a good deal about the dialectical character of man and his works. Another factor which prevents a realistic assessment of what is happening and why, and this is especially true of settings devoted to human service, is that they usually do help others. They do perform functions which others need and value. This result alone has tremendous "reward value," particularly because such a result is the basis for justifying the setting's existence. But there is a more subtle factor: in the early stages of the setting's existence the process of helping others is usually accompanied by a personal sense of growth. The service is not experienced as a routine without personal challenge and intellectual excitement. In other words, in these early phases it is *as if* the value of self-development were operative. However, precisely because this value is not viewed as equal to, or more important than, the value of help to others, over time the sense of challenge and change diminishes and routinization of thinking and action takes place—a process taking place in, and mutually interacting with, the other negative features of the setting's development I described earlier. With the passage of time the members of the setting feel locked in to their particular function and increasingly experience the disruptive discrepancy between a desire to learn and change (a need for novelty and stimulation) and the perception that this may not be satisfied. The exclusive focus on doing for others has been maintained at a very high personal price.

Earlier I used the preparation of a dramatic production for the commercial theatre to illustrate some aspects of the creation of a setting. It has additional relevance for the present discussion. Not unlike the discussion in this chapter, there has been a long-standing argument about the type and degree of formal training and knowledge an individual must have to become an actor. There are those who are partisans of certain schools of acting and those who claim that formal training is vastly overrated. There is agreement, however, on several factors. The first is that there must not be conveyed to the audience any distinction between the actor as a person and the actor in his particular role; he must not remain himself but he must change himself so that he is the role. He must become other than what he ordinarily is and feels; he must transform himself. Laurence Olivier (Cole and Chinoy, 1970, p. 410) says: "If somebody asked me to put in one sentence what acting was, I should say that acting was the art of persuasion. The actor persuades himself, first, and through himself, the audience." John Gielgud (p. 398) put it in this way:

> Of course, all acting should be character-acting, but in those days I did not realize this. When I played a part of my own age I was acutely aware of my own graces and defects. I could not imagine a young man unless he was like myself. My own personality kept interfering, and I began to consider how I was looking, whether my walk was bad, how I was standing; my attention was continually distracted and I could not keep inside the character I was trying to represent. In Trofimov for the first time I looked in the glass and thought, "I know how this man would speak and move and behave"; and to my great surprise I found I was able to keep that picture in my mind throughout the action, without my imagination deserting me for a moment, and to lose myself completely as my appearance and the circumstances of the play seemed to demand. I suppose the truth of the matter was that I was relaxed for the first time. The finest producers I have worked with since have told me that this relaxation is the secret of all good acting. But we were never taught it at the dramatic schools. One's instinct in trying to work oneself into an emotional state is to tighten up. When one is young and nervous one tightens the moment one attempts to act at all, and this violent nervous tension, if it is passionately sincere, can sometimes be effective on the stage. But it is utterly exhausting to the actor and only impresses the audience for a very short space of time.

What Olivier and Gielgud are saying the individual actor needs to do in principle is precisely what I have said a setting needs to value and do—to look at itself and to create the conditions whereby it changes. The actor who cannot do this is seen as an unconvincing routinizer. There are actors who despite different times and roles never change their style or get outside of themselves. They are the hacks who never experience change—like many settings. To carry the analogy one step further: there are actors who will change only when they are forced to change, and the account of the first English production of *Pygmalion* is a case in point. A second point of agreement is that over time the actor's performance in a particular role should deepen and even change. Even when his first performance has been greeted with critical acclaim, the actor's obligation is self-consciously to pursue his role, to continue to study the character. The third point, related to the second, is that performing the role several times a week over a period of months runs the risk of routinization and mechanical acting which may still satisfy the audience at the same time that the actor has lost interest and is bored. It is not unusual for an actor to be unaware that his performance has deteriorated and that he has lost his audience. To avoid this is the actor's primary responsibility. Some actors limit the time they will stay with the production. Another control is the director or his designate who regularly observes performances in order to detect the symptoms of the passionless performance.

Regarding the obligation of a setting to itself as co-equal with, and even more important than, its obligations to others has the sound of virtue but it has only the faintest echo in the creation of settings.

Notes

1. From *The Creation of Settings and the Future Societies* (pp. 97–113) by S. B. Sarason, 1972, San Francisco: Jossey-Bass. Copyright 1972 by Jossey-Bass. Reprinted by permission.
2. From *The Creation of Settings and the Future Societies* (pp. 114–144) by S. B. Sarason, 1972, San Francisco: Jossey-Bass. Copyright 1972 by Jossey-Bass. Reprinted by permission.

CHAPTER 7

Epilogue

The future is essentially unknowable and the past is a puzzle the answers to which keep changing as we as individuals and as a society change. What does that mean for the present which, in the flow of time, so quickly becomes the past and confronts us with a new future? That is a question that annoyingly kept coming up as I was preparing this volume. I say "annoyingly" because intuitively I felt that my answer to that question would reveal a lot about myself as a person and as a professional. And an answer was not forthcoming. We are organisms that plan for the future and reflect on our past; if we do both "naturally" this obviously does not mean we do them well. One source of error is our tendency to imagine a future that is in its broad outline a carbon copy of the present, a derivative of the belief that the future is knowable other than in the most global fashion. Another source of error is our tendency to interpret the past as if it had a single dynamic justifying our present and our plans for the future. I say "source of error" not because I think these tendencies are avoidable (to regard them as avoidable would be as effective as commanding the ocean waves to cease) but because we are so frequently unaware that our need for certainty or predictability infiltrates these tendencies and misleads us. Put in another way: At the same time that we must order our lives so that past, present, and future stand in what to us is a meaningful integration, it is inordinately difficult to bear in mind how inevitably narrow our view of past and future is. In short, this attribute of the human organism can be a mixed blessing. The narrowness of our view has the virtue of rendering experience meaningful and justifying our actions (no small virtue!), and it has the vice (no small vice!) of making humbleness and respect for complexity conspicuous by their absence. The need to believe that our view is the true one maximizes, among other things, polarizations, controversies, and even wars.

These are the thoughts that kept recurring as I was preparing this volume. At any one time in my career I thought I understood how past, present, and future would interconnect. But at any one time those interconnections differed in many respects from past points. Those differences are not explainable by such global concepts as maturation or development, if only because those concepts are value-laden and convey an onward and upward progression. You can be as much of a damned fool at 60 as at 25! I would like to believe that what I think I have learned represents more comprehensively and productively the social realities of past and present and the outlines of the future. And I live my days as if that were the case; i.e., it is the basis for what I advocate, and I do advocate as if I possessed at least part of the truth. I am not paralyzed by my doubts and I do not hem and haw when I write or teach. But I do have my doubts! On a purely actuarial basis I have probably been wrong more often than not in the ways I have interconnected past, present, and future. Indeed, as I look back over the years I see myself as coming out of one fog after another, although I did not realize that I had been in a fog until the intellectual weather cleared only to be followed by another fog. When I came to the Southbury Training School in 1942 to take my first professional position I was aware that I was in a fog, the thickness of which I did not appreciate until I left Southbury to come to Yale. It was no different at Yale. Phenomenologically, I have not been on a straight course over which logic and rationality reigned. This volume may well convey the impression that I have been on such a course, but that has less to do with the facts than with artistic license and sympathy for the reader. There is, I believe, a pattern (call it threads, themes, or concerns) in what I have written over the years, but it is a pattern with many ambiguities and everchanging boundaries. In the earliest pages of this volume I said that I would include those writings that concerned issues that both in the past and present have gotten insufficient attention. Although I believe that to be "true," a part of me knows that I may be wrong. That possibility really does not bother me, or it bothers me far less than it once did, but it certainly has instilled in me a tolerance for opposing views. Someone once said that it is extraordinarily difficult to be completely wrong. I shall take comfort from the fact that if this is true of views different from my own, it is also true of my own. In any event, I take my views very seriously but with more than a few grains of salt.

The recognition of one indisputable fact should prevent us from conceiving of our version of the truth as *the* truth, the *whole* truth, so help you God and Science: The concept of mental retardation is literally an invention of the human mind. A concept is something to which we give birth, a process of "conceiving." It is intended to say something illuminating about relationships "out there," but a concept does not have the status of a thing (e.g., a rock or a stick). And a concept, like mental retardation, does not spring from the human mind like Athena from the head of Zeus. The concept of mental retardation did not always exist. Its birth was not virginal but in every respect was a function of a society at a certain era in its social-economic-historical-ideologic development. It was conceived by individuals who were products of that era in the society. And as representative of that era, the invention carried with it unarticulated assumptions and values about what was needed, what was good and bad, and what were desirable actions: the purposes the invention should serve. But the uses to which an invention is put, copyright and patents to the contrary notwithstanding, cannot be controlled by the inventor. Alfred Binet, as his biographer Theta Wolf (1973) pointed out, would have been aghast at the uses society has made of his invention. Just as the concept of mental retardation is a cultural artifact, so have its uses been culturally determined. Familiarity with the different ways, today and in the past, that the connotative and denotative meanings of the concept have changed dispel any doubts on this score. Indeed in the post-World War II era, the concept of mental retardation (like the concepts of neurosis, adjustment, and freedom) has "officially" changed, and dramatically so, several times. These changes were not independent of sea swell changes in the society. Yet, when the term "mental retardation" is used, we tend to be unaware of the perceptions and attitudes toward the people we have put in this category as reflections of our culture rather than inherent or objective characteristics of these people. This is an obvious point, but it is surprising and disturbing how the label "mental retardation" is pinned on people as if the process has been solely concerned with data free from the effects of culture, tradition, habit, and morality.

Witness the tendency to describe mentally retarded people as "children." This designation was rooted not only in society's conceptions of social and intellectual behavior but also served to justify society's actions in protecting and segregating these people. When the extent to which the concept of mental retardation was tied to uncritically accepted value judgments began to be recognized, the idea that mental retardation was a purely scientific concept was exposed as fiction. When the National Association for Retarded *Children* changed its name to the National Association for Retarded *Citizens*, it signaled the societal change that was taking place.

We like to believe that when we apply the concept of mental retardation, we are uninfluenced by time, place, and society. The fact that this is an untenable belief is suggested by several considerations. First, over the centuries, description and explanation of people who were called mentally retarded have varied as a function of time, place, and society. This, of course, does not mean that the present must dictate the future. But, at the very least, knowledge of the past should give pause to those eager to believe that the concept of mental retardation they are using is coldly impersonal and scientific. Second, as a concept, mental retardation implies a decision about action, and this always reflects the society's view at a particular time about what is right and wrong, appropriate or inappropriate. Over time, a society does change its views toward those it regards as special or different—homosexuals, the elderly, children, women, alcoholics, or any individuals representing minority groups within that society. Third, within scientific and scholarly traditions, the one belief that seems not to change is that the more you know, the more you need to know. This belief should make one suspicious of a stance that says that our present concepts and actions will require no revision. As a social or scientific concept, mental retardation has undergone dramatic change, and there is every reason to believe that this process will continue. The concept and field of mental retardation is a window on our world, if only because our world built the house into which the concept and field were placed and shaped.

References

Abrahamson, S. (1952). School rewards and social class status. *Educational Research Bulletin, 31,* 8–15.

Albee, G. W. (1959). *Mental health manpower trends.* New York: Basic Books.

Albee, G. W. (1968a). Models, myths, and manpower. *Mental Hygiene, 52,* 168–180.

Albee, G. W. (1968b). Conceptual models and manpower requirements in psychology. *American Psychologist, 23,* 317–320.

Allen, F. H. (1942). *Psychotherapy with children.* New York: W. W. Norton.

Beckham, A. A. (1944). A study of the intelligence of colored adolescents of different social-economic status in typical metropolitan areas. *Journal of Social Psychology, 4,* 70–91.

Blom, G. (1979–1980). Heather's story: A handicapped person's rights to as normal a life as possible. *American Examiner, 8*(1), 35–56.

Bogaras, W. (1904). *The Chukchee: Memoirs of the American Museum of Natural History, 11,* 43.

Boyd, G. F. (1952). The levels of aspiration of white and negro children in a nonsegregated elementary school. *Journal of Social Psychology, 36,* 191–196.

Brown, F. (1944). A comparative study of the intelligence of Jewish and Scandinavian kindergarten children. *Journal of Genetic Psychology, 64,* 67–92.

Buckley, W. F., Jr. (1969, March 20). *New Haven Journal Courier.*

Carver, J., & Carver, M. (1972). *The retarded child in the family.* Syracuse: Syracuse University Press.

Chidester, L., & Menninger, K. (1936). The application of psychoanalytic methods to the study of mental retardation. *American Journal of Orthopsychiatry, 6,* 616–625.

Cole, T., & Chinoy, H. T. (Eds.). (1970). *Actors on acting.* New York: Crown.

Collarelli, N. O., & Siegel, S. M. (1966). *Ward H: An adventure in innovation.* New York: Van Nostrand.

Cooley, J. M. (1945–1946). The relative amenability of dull and bright children to child guidance. *Smith College Studies in Social Work, 16,* 26–43.

Davis, A. (1941). American status systems and the socialization of the child. *Sociology Review, 6*, 345–354.

Davis, A., & Havighurst, R. J. (1946). Social class and color differences in childrearing. *American Sociology Review, 11*, 698–710.

Eaton, J. W., & Weil, R. J. (1955). *Culture and mental disorders: A comparative study of the Hutterites and other populations.* Glenoe, IL: Free Press.

Freud, S. (1925). Analysis of a phobia in a five-year-old boy. *Collected Papers, Vol. 3.* London: Hogarth Press.

Freud, S. (1943). *A general introduction to psychoanalysis* (rev. ed.). Garden City, NY: Garden City Publishing.

Fromm, E. (1941). *Escape from freedom.* New York: Holt, Rinehart & Winston.

Gaudet, F. J., & Gaudet, H. (1940, May/June). The problem of the feebleminded patient in the mental hygiene clinic. *The Training School Bulletin*, 1–20.

Ginzberg, E., & Bray, D. (1953). *The uneducated.* New York: Columbia University Press.

Gladwin, T. (1970). *East is a big bird.* Cambridge, MA: Harvard University Press.

Gladwin, T., & Sarason, S. B. (1953). *Truk: Man in paradise.* Viking Fund Publications in Anthropology, No. 2, New York.

Glassman, L. (1945). Is dull normal intelligence a contraindication for psychotherapy? *Smith College Studies in Social Work, 13*, 274–298.

Glueck, S., & Glueck, E. (1950). *Unraveling juvenile delinquency.* New York: Commonwealth Fund.

Goddard, H. H. (1912). *The Kallikak family. A study in the heredity of feeblemindedness.* New York: Macmillan.

Goldenberg, I. I. (1971). *Build me a mountain: Youth, poverty, and the creation of a new setting.* Cambridge, MA: MIT Press.

Gould, R. (1941). Some sociological determinants of goal striving. *Journal of Social Psychology, 13*, 461–473.

Grossman, F. K. (1972). *Brother and sisters of retarded children.* Syracuse: Syracuse University Press.

Guilford, J. P. (1956). The structure of intellect. *Psychological Bulletin, 53*, 267–293.

Haggard, E. A. (1954). Social status and intelligence: An experimental study of certain cultural determinants of measured intelligence. *Genetic Psychology Monographs, 49*, 141–186.

Harrower-Erickson, M. R. (1941). Psychological studies of patients with epileptic seizures. In W. Penfield & T. C. Erickson (Eds.), *Epilepsy and cerebral localization.* Springfield, IL: Charles C. Thomas.

Hartwell, S. W. (1940). *Fifty-five "bad" boys.* New York: Alfred A. Knopf.

Hawes, C. H. (1903). *In the uttermost east.* New York: Harper & Row.

Healy, W., & Bronner, A. F. (1939). *Treatment and what happened afterward.* Boston: Judge Baker Guidance Center.

Hebb, D. O. (1949). *The organization of behavior.* New York: Wiley.

Hegge, T. G. (1944). The occupational status of higher-grade mental defectives in the present emergency: A study of parolees from the Wayne County Training School at Northville, Michigan. *American Journal of Mental Deficiency, 49*, 86–98.

Heilbroner, R. L. (1968). *The making of economic society* (2nd ed.). Englewood Cliffs, NJ: Prentice-Hall.

Heller, J. (1975). *Something happened.* New York: Ballantine Books.

Himmelweit, H. T., & Whitfield, J. W. (1944). Mean intelligence scores of a random sample of occupations. *British Journal of Industrial Medicine, 1*, 224–226.

Hogbin, H. I. (1946). A New Guinea childhood: From weaning till the eighth year in Wogeo. *Oceania, 16*, 275–296.

Hollingshead, A. B. (1949). *Elmtown's youth.* New York: Wiley.

Humphreys, E. J., & Howe, S. (1942). Range of psychiatric material within the state school. *American Journal of Psychiatry, 98*, 482–488.

Hutton, L. (1945). Length of treatment in child guidance clinics. *Journal of Mental Science, 91*, 511–517.

Jastak, J., & Whiteman, M. (1957). The prevalence of mental retardation in Delaware: Preliminary report on a state-wide survey. *The Nature and transmission of the genetic and cultural characteristics of human populations; Papers presented at the 1956 annual conference of the Milbank Memorial Fund* (pp. 51–67) New York: Milbank Memorial Fund.

Jensen, A. R. (1979). *Bias in mental testing.* New York: Free Press.

Joseph, A., & Murray, V. F. (1951). *Chammorros and Carolinians of Saipan.* Cambridge, MA: Harvard University Press.

Kanner, L. (1943). Autistic disturbances of affective contact. *The Nervous Child, 2*, 217–250.

Kanner, L. (1949). Problems of nosology and psychodynamics of early infantile autism. *American Journal of Orthopsychiatry, 19*, 416–426.

Kennedy, R. J. R. (1948). *The social adjustment of morons in a Connecticut city.* Hartford, CT: State Office Building, Social Services Department, Mansfield-Southbury Training Schools.

Lane, H. (1976). *The wild boy of Aveyron.* Cambridge, MA: Harvard University Press.

League of Nations, Health Organization. (1937). *Report of French Indo-China* (Conference on Rural Hygiene, p. 126). Geneva: Author.

Levine, M., & Levine, A. (1970). *A social history of helping services: Clinic, court, school and community.* New York: Appleton-Century-Crofts.

Lewis, C. (1946). *Children of the Cumberland.* New York: Columbia University Press.

Lurie, L. A., Levy, S., & Rosenthal, F. M. (1944). The defective delinquent. *American Journal of Orthopsychiatry, 14*, 95–103.

Margolin, J. B., Roman, M., & Harari, C. (1955). Reading disability in the delinquent child: A microcosm of psychosocial pathology. *American Journal of Orthopsychiatry, 25*, 25–35.

Matarazzo, J. D. (1971). Some national developments in the utilization of nontraditional mental health manpower. *American Psychologist, 26*(4), 363–365.

Mayhew, K. C., & Edwards, A. C. (1966). *The Dewey School.* New York: Atherton Press.

McClelland, D. C., Atkinson, J. W., Clark, R. A., & Lowell, E. I. (1953). *The achievement motive.* New York: Appleton-Century-Crofts.

McClelland, D. C., Rindlisbacher, A., & DeCharms, R. (1955). Religious and other sources of parental attitudes toward independence training. In D. C. McClelland (Ed.), *Studies in motivation* (pp. 60–85). New York: Appleton-Century-Crofts.

Muench, G. A. (1944). A follow-up of mental defectives after 18 years. *Journal of Abnormal and Social Psychology, 39*, 407–418.

Murray, H. (1938). *Explorations in personality: A clinical and experimental study of fifty men of college age*. New York: Oxford University Press.

Nisbet, R. (1970). *The quest for community*. New York: Oxford University Press.

O'Conner, N. (1953). The occupational success of feebleminded adolescents. *Occupational Psychology, 27*, 157–163.

Robertson, C. N. (1970). *Oneida community: An autobiography 1851–1876*. Syracuse: Syracuse University Press.

Rogers, C. R. (1937). Three surveys of treatment measures used with children. *American Journal of Orthopsychiatry, 7*, 48–57.

Rogers, C. R. (1942). *Counseling and psychotherapy*. New York: Houghton Mifflin.

Rosen, B. C. (1957, August 27). *The achievement motive and value systems of selected ethnic groups*. Paper presented at the meeting of the American Sociological Society, Washington, DC.

Sanford, N. (1982). Social psychology: Its place in personology. *American Psychologist, 37*(8), 903.

Sarason, S. B. (1943a). The use of the Thematic Apperception Test with mentally deficient children. *American Journal of Mental Deficiency, 47*(4), 414–421.

Sarason, S. B. (1943b). The use of the Thematic Apperception Test with mentally deficient children. *American Journal of Mental Deficiency, 48*(2), 169–173.

Sarason, S. B. (1944). Dreams and Thematic Apperception Test stories. *The Journal of Abnormal and Social Psychology, 39*(4), 121–126.

Sarason, S. B. (1945). Projective techniques in mental deficiency. *Journal of Personality, 13*(3), 237–245.

Sarason, S. B. (1949). *Psychological problems in mental deficiency* (1st ed.). New York: Harper & Row.

Sarason, S. B. (1953). Psychological problems in mental deficiency (2nd ed.). New York: Harper & Row.

Sarason, S. B. (1961). The contents of human problem solving. In *Nebraska Symposium on Motivation* (pp. 85–92). Lincoln.

Sarason, S. B. (1969). *Psychological problems in mental deficiency* (4th ed.). New York: Harper & Row.

Sarason, S. B. (1971). *The culture of the school and the problem of change* (1st ed.). Boston: Allyn & Bacon.

Sarason, S. B. (1972). *The creation of settings and the future societies*. San Francisco: Jossey-Bass.

Sarason, S. B. (1973). Jewishness, blackishness, and the nature-nurture controversy. *American Psychologist, 28*(11), 962–971.

Sarason, S. B. (1974). *The psychological sense of community: Prospects for a community psychology*. San Francisco: Jossey-Bass.

Sarason, S. B. (1980). Review: Jensen's bias in mental testing. *Society, 18*(1), 93–98.

Sarason, S. B. (1981). *Psychology misdirected*. New York: Free Press.

Sarason, S. B. (1982). *The culture of the school and the problem of change* (2nd ed.). Boston: Allyn & Bacon.

Sarason, S. B., & Doris, J. (1969). *Psychological problems in mental deficiency* (4th ed.). New York: Harper & Row.

Sarason, S. B., & Doris, J. (1979). *Educational handicap, public policy, and social history. A broadened perspective on mental retardation*. New York: Free Press.

Sarason, S. B., & Gladwin, T. (1958, February). Psychological and cultural factors in mental subnormality: A review in research. *Genetic Psychology Monographs, 57,* 3–289.

Sarason, S. B., Grossman, F. K., & Zitnay, G. (1972). *The creation of a community setting.* Syracuse: Syracuse University Press.

Sarason, S. B., & Kaplan, F. (1969). The creation of settings. In *The psychoeducational clinic: Papers and research studies.* Boston: Massachusetts State Department of Mental Health Monograph Series.

Sarason, S. B., Levine, M., Goldenberg, I. I., Cherlin, D., & Bennett, E. (1966). *Psychology in community settings: Clinical, education, vocational, social aspects.* New York: Wiley.

Sarason, S. B., & Schaefer-Simmern, H. (1944). Therapeutic implications of artistic activity: A case study. *American Journal of Mental Deficiency, 49*(2), 185–196.

Schaefer-Simmern, H. (1938). *The unfolding of artistic activity.* Berkeley: University of California Press.

Sears, R. R., Maccoby, E. E., & Levin, H. (1957). *Patterns of child rearing.* Evanston, IL: Row, Peterson.

Skeels, H. M., & Dye, H. B. (1939). A study of the effects of the differential stimulation on mentally retarded children. *Proceedings and Addresses of the American Association on Mental Deficiency, 44,* 114–136.

Skeels, H. M., Updegraff, R., Wellman, B. L., & Williams, H. M. (1938). A study of environmental stimulation, an orphanage preschool project. *University of Iowa Studies in Child Welfare, 15*(4).

Stendler, C. B. (1951). Social class differences in parental attitudes toward school at grade 1 level. *Child Development, 22,* 36–46.

Stone, E. (1982). *The adoption of handicapped children. An exploratory study.* Unpublished doctoral dissertation, Yale University, New Haven.

Thorne, F. C. (1948). Counseling and psychotherapy with mental defectives. *American Journal of Mental Deficiency, 52,* 263–271.

Town, C. H. (1939). *Familial feeblemindedness, a study of one hundred and forty-one families.* Buffalo: Foster & Stewart.

Wegman, B. S. (1943). Intelligence as a factor in the treatment of problem children. *Smith College Studies in Social Work, 14,* 244–245.

Witmer, H. L. (1946). *Psychiatric interviews with children.* New York: Commonwealth Fund.

Wolf, T. (1973). *Alfred Binet.* Chicago: University of Chicago Press.

Yepsen, L. N., & Cianci, V. (1946). Home training for mentally deficient children in New Jersey. *The Training School Bulletin, 43*: 21–26.

Index